For Our Students
3rd Edition

Laura Hammons, Senior Editor
Hinds Community College
Raymond, Mississippi

Beverly Fatherree, Editor Emerita
Hinds Community College
Raymond, Mississippi

TYCAM

Two-Year College
English Association
of Mississippi

hayden-mcneil
Macmillan Learning

macmillan learning
curriculum solutions

Sustainability
Hayden-McNeil's standard paper stock uses a minimum of 30% post-consumer waste. We offer higher % options by request, including a 100% recycled stock. Additionally, Hayden-McNeil Custom Digital provides authors with the opportunity to convert print products to a digital format. Hayden-McNeil is part of a larger sustainability initiative through Macmillan Learning. Visit http://sustainability.macmillan.com to learn more.

bedford/st. martin's • hayden-mcneil
w.h. freeman • worth publishers

Contents

13 Additional Rhetorical Modes 125

Description, Exemplification, Definition, Problem and Solution, Division and Classification, and Process

14 Grammar and Language Review 147

15 The Library Speaks Volumes 177

16 Reading for Research 185

Dedication

For my students.—LH

For Our Students, 3rd Edition

EDITORS

Laura Hammons, Senior Editor
Beverly Fatherree, Editor Emerita

STUDENT EDITOR

Victoria Mulqueen

ASSISTANTS TO THE EDITORS

Navdeep Kaur
William Stribling

Contributors

Mary Beth Applin
Stephanie Avery
Caleb Aultman
Clara Bailey
Sherita Bailey
Susan Bailey
Abigail Baker
Suhail Basalama
Dustin Bass
Tyler Bass
Hannah Beavers
Margaret Bell
Ken Bishop
Thomas Boone III
Jessica Booth
Susan Bosarge
Taylor Boswell
Chris Boudreaux
Joshua Boyce
Ryan Braswell
Anna Britt-Begnaud
April Bronis
Abbey Broome
Cynthia Broome
Suzi Brown
Charlotte Buckley
Melissa Buie

Vanita Bunce
Phillip Burkes
William Burks
Naylet Bustos
Charles Cannon
Lisa Chiang
Kristen Clark
Darby Cook
Jeanne Cook
Cara Cothern
Amanda Coward
Stacey Coulter
Susanne Cox
Sandra Currier
Morgan Cutturini
Oanh Dao
Dale Davis
Will Dawkins
James Dockery
Glynda Duncan
Lydia Edwards
Beverly Fatherree
Krysta Ferguson
Khalil Finch
Sarah Fitzgerald
Carrie Fleming
Angela Frazier

Charles Freeman
Tara Garriga
Sharon Gerald
Brooke Goff
Jeremy Graham
Vera Griffin
Kassie Grusz
James Gunn
Theresa Hamilton
Laura Hammons
Kim Hestle
Mary Holley
Raquel Hollingsworth
Kelly Hollis
Nathaniel House
Hayden Hunter
Ashley Johnson
Gregory Johnson
Joshua Johnson
Quincy Jones
Navdeep Kaur
Amber King
Levi King
Wilson Knight
Ashley Lancaster
Barbara Lawson
Beth Leishman

Mary Lipscomb
Robin Lowe
Tristan Lowry
Ford Maddox
Sandra Maggard
James Magnum
Donald Mangum
Hannah Marshall
Sara Mayor
Debbie McCollum
Nikki McCord
John McInnis
Orondé C. Milledge
Elvira Mitchell
Ryan Mitchell
Patricia Modenbach
Dustin Moore
Justin Moore
Judy Morris
Sheridan Morris
Xander Mosley
Victoria Mulqueen
Clyde Muse
Lauren Nabors
Marsha Newman
Cati Nunagen
Zach Odom
John Ouille
Victoria Pagan
Tommy Paige

Sydnie Palmer
Terry Parrish
Megha Patel
Stephanie Payne
Julia Peoples
Martha (Maj) Perkins
Cindy Pierce
Bethany Poppelreiter
Shuncey Pounds
Bejamin Rea
Kyle Reeder
Emanuella Reyes
Daniel Roach
Jerrold Robinson
Robert Rockett
Devin Rose
Samantha Ryan
Josh Sande
Kacey Sciple
Charles Shearer
Glenda Silverii
Anne Smith
Jane Smith
Rhonda Snell
Leah Spencer
Merrie Spencer
Haley Stanford
Katie Stone
William Stribling

Ashleigh
   Sumrall-Ferguson
John Sutherland
Setory Taylor
Nancy Tenhet
Madison Thornton
Linda Tombaga
Curtis Uihlein
Joshua Wahl
Clarissa Walker
Lauren Walker
Larkin Walker
Breanna Walton
J. Matthew Ward
Janet Wasson
Leslie Wasson
Blaine Watson
Brian Watson
Kim Watson
Evelyn Webb
Holly Wells
Teresa Wells
James White
Richard White
Deborah Wilbourn
Chris Williams
Gaye Winter
Duncan Wright
Holly Wright

Note from the Senior Editor

Using the singular noun "editor" in the above title seems completely foreign. This textbook has been influenced by so many colleagues, friends, and students, that to use the singular form of any noun in relation to *For Our Students* seems selfish. However, for this third edition, I have traveled a strange road, one mostly without my invaluable friend, Beverly Fatherree, who co-wrote and co-edited the prior two texts—along with the other dozens of folks who helped. Bev retired from teaching at Hinds a few years ago but has served ably as editor emerita on this edition.

I had an amazing assistant, Victoria Mulqueen, a student at Hinds. This young woman has mad skills as a writer and editor, and I am proud to say that they have gotten even sharper while working on this book. She volunteered to work on this book in January of 2016 and has never looked back. She never had a chance.

To acknowledge and reward her work, Victoria Mulqueen earned the title "Student Editor." I am happy to have a student on the cover of a textbook entitled *For Our Students*. I am also grateful that she has stuck with me as her English teacher.

But I will take that lonely phrase, "Senior Editor," and own it because of the afternoons spent trying to get air to circulate into my office. I have an elaborate system of wooden door props and a series of strategically located fans so that I don't dissolve into my keyboard.

I will certainly own the the phrase, "Senior Editor," because this book has taken over a decade of my life from the first vision that I had in my carport while unloading book bags. The dream was and is to provide a quality, affordable textbook and to support TYCAM, the Two-Year College English Association of Mississippi, through the sale of these textbooks. I don't regret a second of the journey and cherish my friends who've made it with me.

The third edition contains quite a few changes. Many of them were made at the behest of the instructors who use this text:

- It's longer. The chapters have been expanded. For example, the grammar and language chapter is triple the size in the second edition of the text.
- More student essays are contained in this edition. Many people have asked for extra examples. While we could not add hundreds of essay examples, we did add dozens.
- MLA and APA have been updated by the folks at Hayden-McNeil, an offshoot of Bedford/Macmillan, our longtime publisher.
- The Net-Savvy chapters have been refreshed and updated. These popular chapters, the brainchild of Sharon Gerald, were thoroughly re-examined by the great women of Itawamba.

- We have a new format and look. The publisher took over the type-setting, so I did not have to type and retype and format and reformat every single word. It was a blessing.

Many thanks to all those who have used this textbook in their classrooms. Some of the instructors who use this book have been subjected to kangaroo courts and inquisitions just to be able to have a quality textbook that saves the students money. Other publishers have also offered so many perks and incentives that many departments cannot even consider this text because of lost revenue for their colleges.

Though the process has been incredibly political and discouraging much of the time, I've still loved it. No petty smear campaign or gossip has stopped any of us from moving forward. Besides, the person who really matters to me, Hinds' president—Dr. Clyde Muse, has been a rock to me and a great supporter of TYCAM and TYCA-SE.

The production of this text now moves away from Hinds Community College to Itawamba Community College. They have consistently contributed to and worked on this text and are worthy successors. They are wonderful and will do a great job.

I cannot say how much I appreciate all the help I have gotten from students and colleagues. This labor of love has been a joy. —LH

Chapter 1

Expectations:
Ours and Yours

When you enrolled in college, you probably had certain expectations of the life you would find here—both social and educational. Those expectations might have come from friends, from high school teachers, from parents or siblings, or from watching movies set on college campuses. Some of your sources might have warned you that college is really hard, that you will have no time for anything but studying, and that your teachers will not care if you pass or fail.

Others might have said that college is just one party after another, that schoolwork and studying are secondary, and that you never have to attend class if you don't want to.

Still others might have presented a more balanced view, stressing the importance of class attendance and good study skills, at the same time that they encouraged extracurricular activities and student involvement.

The fact is, *some* truth exists in each of the scenarios, depending on what you want your college experience to be. So let's look at some of those expectations, at what you might have been accustomed to previously, and at where you are going.

Teachers' Expectations

College teachers expect students in college-level classes to do college-level work. It's that simple.

Information taught in college-level classes should be basically the same in any college setting—community college, online, university, four-year college, or dual enrollment.

That does not mean that all English instructors walk in lockstep, following an identical syllabus and turning to exactly the same textbook page on exactly the same day. Nothing could be further from the truth, actually.

However, what it does mean is that each college English department has defined a core skill set for each level of composition and literature, derived from the requirements of the Institutions of Higher Learning for upper-level institutions and from the Mississippi State Board for Community and Junior Colleges for two-year colleges, and a responsible teacher follows those department guidelines.

Not doing so might have repercussions beyond job security; it might mean that a student wasn't prepared adequately to move from one level of composition to the next or from composition to literature classes.

Because English teachers are individuals—all unique in their own ways—

- they have different ways of presenting material
- they have different preferences for formatting essays
- they have different "pet peeves" about everything from how a thesis is written to whether to put a comma after a short introductory prepositional phrase.

Pay attention to what *this* teacher says in *this* class. Your high school teacher, your mom, your last college instructor might have done things differently; there's nothing wrong with that. However, if you fail to listen to what your current teacher instructs you to do, you could find yourself on the bleeding end of a red pen.

Your last teacher might have required you to write a research paper using APA (American Psychological Association) style. APA style is a specialized style that is used when the date of publication is an integral part of the value of the cited source. *This* teacher that you have now will probably—but not always—require MLA (Modern Language Association) style for your research essays. Follow the style that *this* teacher requires if you want to receive a passing grade on the research essay.

If your last teacher thought only brainstorming or clustering was fine and didn't require a formal outline but *this* teacher wants a sentence outline with the main parts of your essay identified, do what *this* one wants. If your last teacher required you to compose all of your thesis statements with a three-part blueprint but *this* one says not to do that, do what *this* one says. Your last teacher might have allowed you to write informally, using contractions and colloquialisms and the second person pronoun "you." Those stylistic informalities are not accepted by every teacher. Again, follow your current teacher's requirements.

Aha, you might say! But this book is written informally, with contractions and colloquialisms and second person pronoun *you*. Indeed, it is. The editors' and authors' purpose in choosing an informal style is to speak directly to you, the reader/student/recipient of the knowledge contained within these pages. Rather than speak to an anonymous, random student, we are speaking directly to you—*our* students. We want the conversation to be friendly and casual at the same time that it is also very serious. Mostly, we want you to listen.

We have gone to college, taken this course, completed dozens of other English courses (with many research papers), gotten our four-year degrees, been accepted into graduate schools, written dozens more papers in additional classes, and written long Master's theses. We have been in your shoes. We are trained and have chosen to be teachers.

Part of maturing as a student is realizing that every teacher is different; one is not more right than the other—or more wrong. If you can accept that fact this early in your education, you'll be able to adjust as you go through the rest of your college career and into the work world.

Your Expectations

Most college students expect to do well in college or they wouldn't be here. You are probably no different. If you are in a Comp I class, you have been deemed competent to be here, with all of the skills necessary for your success in a college-level class. Should that not be the case, you may find yourself struggling to complete the course with a satisfactory grade.

What should you expect to have to do if you are struggling? You should get help, either through your campus Writing Center, peer tutors, or the instructor. Because Comp I and Comp II are college-level courses, grammar is generally not taught as part of the curriculum. If you need a grammar review or remediation, you can expect to have to take responsibility to do that review or get that remediation.

Another expectation that you should have is that your teacher will be fair and impartial in grading your essays, regardless of whether he or she agrees with the opinion you have presented in your thesis and proven in your body paragraphs. Your instructor's job is not to brainwash you; your instructor's job is to teach you to express and support your opinions in the best way possible. You should expect that to be done.

When you leave Comp I, you should expect to have the basic skills, both writing skills and critical thinking skills, necessary to be successful in Comp II. When you look back at the syllabus that you were given at the beginning of the semester, you should be able to check off the completion of all of the course requirements listed there. Furthermore, when you leave Comp II, you should have advanced your critical thinking skills to include writing more mature compositions with more depth and awareness to prepare you for literature classes or for other classes required for your major.

Expectations in a Nutshell

When you look at the charts that follow, you will see what skills, behavioral and academic, your teacher expects you to be able to have both entering and exiting your composition classes on both levels of composition. You'll notice that those expectations change as you move through the program and become a more mature writer, a more mature reader, and a more mature student.

Believe it or not, learning to write well is a skill that you will need in every area of your life. Your teacher's expectations for you are high; your expectations for yourself should be just as high.

Expectations for Students: Life Skills and Actions

	BEFORE COMP I	AFTER COMP II
SENSE OF RESPONSIBILITY	Comes to class, even in the rain Follows directions	Has few attendance problems Seeks direction from teacher via email and Blackboard, if necessary
WORK ETHIC	Submits assignments in a timely matter Lacks chaos-soaked excuses Shows discipline	Is a self-starter and does not have to be reminded to do his/her work
INTERACTION WITH OTHERS	Can work with others in a group setting Respects peers, teachers, and staff Participates in discussion without rancor	Is experienced and comfortable with fellow classmates and teachers
READING/ INTERPRETATION	Can read on a college level Can annotate and interpret the written word	Is ready for college literature courses Is prepared for work in college major Correctly assimilates outside sources for use in subject areas
IDEAS AND ORIGINALITY	Understands that independent thinking and interpretation must match a point of view	Understands the role of research and documentation in concert with original thinking and ideas

Skills: Composition and Writing

BEFORE COMP I	BEFORE COMP II	AFTER COMP II
Competent paragraph and essay organization skills	Competent essay organization skills, including formulation of thesis, use of topic sentences, and specific support with details and examples	Independent thinking coupled with the ability to follow directions
Using thesis and topic sentences and understanding their roles in the essay		Ability to use specific style manual for documented papers and projects
Supplying supporting details and examples to strengthen organization and ideas	Depending upon college access, familiarity with use of Word, document formatting, and flash drives	Use of argumentation or persuasion in academic writing
Understanding the difference between academic writing and informal writing	Level of knowledge about rhetorical modes' use in academic writing	Preparation for analytical writing in other disciplines or subjects, especially literature
No use of casual language like text messaging and slang	Use of the Internet for research, primarily through the library's databases	Understanding of workplace expectations about deadlines and time limits
Absence of aggravating major errors like comma splices and fused sentences	No major errors	
No fragments	Confidence with verb forms and tenses, including historical present and subjunctive	
Few errors with subject-verb agreement	Deliberate use of sentence variety and parallelism for interesting paragraph structure	
No errors with verb endings	Basics of multiparagraph essay form, especially paragraph structure	
Correct spelling, especially with homonyms	Use of transition words and internal paragraph coherence	
Correct use of basic commas	Original ideas and thoughts and adequate organization skills for presentation	
Firm grasp of capitalization and terminal punctuation		

You Are a Writer!

Read these words again; say them aloud to yourself; write them on your hand . . . whatever you need to do to remember them and make them meaningful to you. They are powerful words if you will only believe them.

Why powerful? Because the written word is powerful. Even in this world where a delete key is never far away, the written (or typed) word still carries power.

Think about it. Have you ever sent an email or a text message in which you accidentally typed the wrong word? Maybe you typed an email in a fury, calmed down, meant to hit cancel, and instead hit send. Those were probably some powerful words, right? Powerful enough to get you fired? Powerful enough to cause an argument? Words are important, and when you're the writer, you are responsible for what you write.

In conversation, you have the luxury of using hand gestures and facial expressions in addition to words to make sure that the person who is listening understands you. You can ask whether the person understands and then explain more, interject, or even modify your message, all to aid communication. However, when you are writing, you no longer have these luxuries.

When you turn in a paper, in most situations the teacher is grading your paper in his or her office or home when you are no longer around. He or she cannot turn to you and say, "Which sentence did you intend as your thesis statement? Did you mean to put this in quotation marks? What did you really want to say in paragraph three?" Essentially, what you have written on your paper is all the reader (teacher, friend, boss, etc.) has. Your typed or written words stand in the place of you; they are your voice.

You use this writer's voice in many different areas of life. Maybe you simply write letters or emails or text messages to friends. You also probably have to email your instructors. In your jobs, present or future, you have to use writing, perhaps more than you realize. Healthcare workers have to fill out charts on their patients, providing notes that other nurses on later shifts have to be able to understand, for someone's life may depend upon it. Contractors have to be able to compose bids and communicate with their clients; their success depends upon it. Psychologists have to be able to write extensive notes about their clients, and teachers of all subjects have to be able to write: to communicate with parents, with administrators, and most importantly, with their students.

At the very least, you are all writers right now—in the classroom, on the computer screen, or on your cell phone. Wherever you are—you are writers who have a voice. Writing is an opportunity. Let this class be an opportunity and let this textbook guide you.

Now That You're a Writer, You Actually Have to Write . . .

We have all had those moments when we look at the page we just typed and think, "That's not at all what I intended to say." What happened between the time your brain formed the beautiful, impressive thought and when your hands wrote or typed the words? This is one of the universal difficulties of writing—overcoming the disconnect between what we think and what we're actually able to write. At times, we may feel that an evil fairy has suddenly snatched our originality from us, or we may feel that we have nothing left to say. In fact, these are symptoms that show we are experiencing what it means to be a writer. Here are three universal pointers to help you along the way:

1. *Don't sit in front of your computer screen or notebook for more than ten minutes without writing something.*

   Writers often struggle for the perfect word, the perfect sentence, especially when they are just getting started. But really, you should just start writing and keep writing, even if it feels like nonsense. The more you write, the more you will have to say. Blank screens beget blank screens, whereas words beget sentences, sentences beget paragraphs, and paragraphs beget essays.

2. *Don't get too attached to your writing.*

Drafting and editing are wonderful processes, but you have to be willing to let go of your first draft before you can see the beauty of a second draft, a third draft, and the editing that goes along with them. You have to be ready to embrace the fact that the first draft that you write will not be the best draft you write. Think about it this way: You're much smarter now than you were when you were five, right? So what you write two days from now should be better than what you wrote two days ago.

3. *Don't wait too late to get started.*

In the movie *The Great Debaters*, Denzel Washington's character tells his child, "Do what you gotta do in this life so you can do what you wanna do." This is obviously a difficult lesson to learn, but the bottom line is, you "gotta" pass your composition classes because you "wanna" be able to graduate from college, have a career, and receive a paycheck. In pointer number two (above), I told you to be prepared to write more than one draft of your papers. You will not be able to do that if you wait until the night before the paper is due to begin writing. More likely, you will turn in mediocre or poor work that does not accurately reflect your writing ability, or worse, you'll turn in nothing at all. And one more point: Giving yourself time to write gives you a very important luxury—the luxury of thinking about style.

Style

I have style. Do you have style? Urban, hippie, goth, hip-hop, skater, preppie, country/western—these are all styles, styles of dress, that is. Having a writing style is based on the same principle. Just as your style of dress can represent your identity, your style of writing represents your voice—how you want to portray yourself as a writer to your readers.

Those readers, your audience, should also direct your stylistic choices. Often, students simply assume that the only logical audience for their papers is their instructor. While this is certainly true on one level, writing papers becomes much more interesting when you move beyond considering your instructor as your intended audience. Let's say you have decided to write a paper on the parking problems students experience on your community college campus. Whom do you want to read this paper? What do you want to accomplish in your paper? What do you want your audience to feel or do in response to your paper?

Perhaps you want to address the paper to your peers, the other students on campus who are also experiencing the parking problem. If this is your audience, you should keep in mind that they are already well aware of the problem, so your goal might be to garner support and get other students involved in an organized effort to effect change. Your overall style in this paper may be casual since you are addressing your peers and trying to get them to support a cause.

On the other hand, you might consider your college administrators as the audience. After all, they are the ones who need to be aware of the problem so that positive changes can occur. In this case, your style might be much more formal, elevated, and fact-based because you are trying to convince administrators that the problem exists, that you have thought seriously about the issue, and that it deserves their attention.

Style can be comedic, mysterious, dramatic, serious, casual, formal, or journalistic. These styles can be achieved through word choice, sentence structure, tone, and mood—to name a few.

Let's take a look at a couple of examples of different styles of openings on our topic of student parking:

> After a leisurely drive to my eight o'clock class, I arrive on campus a full ten minutes before classes begin. As I pull my car into the campus, I notice this is certainly a popular time to arrive; nevertheless, there are more than enough parking spaces for everyone. And then I wake up! In my three semesters at the college, I've never had this experience. Have you? The more realistic version is something like this: I arrive on campus after a not-so-leisurely drive through eight o'clock traffic only to be greeted by an onslaught of other students, all of us seeking one thing—a parking space. We don't just need a parking space; we need it fast. Suddenly, we're all enemies on a single battlefield, and only the strong survive. On the days when I am not one of the lucky ones, I find myself circling the parking lots as time ticks by. I've been at school for fifteen minutes, but I'm late again.

The above example was intended for an audience of student peers who are attuned to the problem of student parking. Notice the use of humor, the use of "I" to describe personal experience, the use of contractions or second person, the use of questioning, and the appeals to emotion. These are all elements that contribute to the more casual style of this paragraph.

Now let's look at a more formal example:

> The current student population of this campus is around 2,350, including day and night students. Of that number, approximately 1,650 are on campus every Monday and Wednesday morning for eight o'clock classes. However, there are exactly 1,435 student parking spaces on this campus. Even with an allowance for absences, this is not adequate; it does not meet the basic needs of the students. In order to give all students the greatest opportunity for success in their classes (especially their early morning classes) as well as to achieve optimal student satisfaction with the campus, a sufficient number of parking spaces need to be formed. This issue needs to become a priority for school administrators. Students who register and pay for their classes should at least have the opportunity to attend them.

Here, the audience was to be the college's administrators; therefore, the style is noticeably more formal. The members of the audience are not addressed directly as they are in the first example. Instead, in this paragraph, the readers are given specific figures and facts in an effort to prove the validity of the complaint. No second person or contractions are used, and in general, the vocabulary has been elevated for the professional audience.

Now, whether you choose to imagine your friends, classmates, parents, employers, administrators, or the President of the United States as your audience, they will certainly be more interesting to think about than simply imagining your instructor reading your paper. Having a designated audience gives your paper a purpose; it gives your paper a style; and most importantly, it makes you feel more like the writer you are.

Many students who avoid their writing classes, procrastinate writing papers, or even just fail to turn in papers are those who truly believe they cannot write well. Perhaps they believe this because of years of poor grades and negative comments. Maybe they're just insecure about their background in grammar and mechanics. Whatever the reason, they're afraid.

While a little fear can be good, it should not keep you from achieving your goals. As someone who loves writing and reading, I'll be the first to say that writing can sometimes *feel* magical for both writer and reader. However, the writing process is not about doing magic tricks. It's about hard work. Writing papers is going to require your time and effort, quite a bit of it. But it also means you don't have to be a magician who knows secret tricks to write a paper.

So go ahead. Put pen to paper. You might not be the next Toni Morrison; then again, you might. At the very least, you can pass your composition classes.

CHAPTER 2

Avoiding Chaos

Your Life: Your Chaos

Chaos has a number of definitions. It can come in the form of stubbed toes, flat tires, bad weather, corrupted flash drives, faulty printers, fallen tree limbs, Internet breakdowns, sick pets—the list is endless, and teachers have legendary stories about students' last-minute crises. Have you ever heard the old cliché, "The dog ate my homework"? That's chaos—fictional chaos, of course.

Overall, chaos is drama—mostly self-inflicted drama—that stops students from getting work to their teachers by the required deadline. Chaos is inevitable if you put off doing the work for *any other* activity. Writing assignments, especially, issue forth moans and cries of "chaos, chaos" from all corners of the globe.

One time-tested, surefire cure exists. You need a **schedule** in order to complete your school work on time and not lose your sanity. If you are not organized and are not aware of personal deadlines, then you will be smacked hard by chaos. And chaos hurts more severely the longer you procrastinate.

> Only one rule about chaos is certain: It will happen if you slack.

Since no one—not you and not your teacher—wants last-minute drama, you should get the inoculation against it—planning.

Planning Is Not Rocket Science

Did your teacher assign a research paper the day before it was due? Of course not. If a teacher assigns a due date of March 15, you should have that paper printed and ready to go on March 14.

Are you laughing? If you are, then you are unaware of this fact: Some people actually do just this—have their work ready before the very second that it's due. These organized students have other deadlines and must prioritize seriously. Most are careful, thoughtful souls who strive for excellence.

Time-management self-help books have one mainstay: Plan backwards. If your paper's due date is March 15, you should have a schedule that looks a bit like this:

MARCH 15	turn in paper and other required materials
MARCH 14	print final draft and get other materials ready for tomorrow
MARCH 12	final draft review
MARCH 10	corrections and additions
MARCH 8	rough draft edited and ready for teacher conference (if possible)
MARCH 1	rough draft written and proofed
FEB. 26	research and notecards turned in for grade
FEB. 22	research and notecards completed
FEB. 19	thesis finalized
FEB. 15	research through library Internet databases almost completed/ notecards pending
FEB. 7	term paper topic and stance/argument chosen

Between deadlines, you should, *of course,* work on your paper.

What the Working World Does

Standard practice in the business world is having goals with timelines for each employee. In addition, government jobs and nonprofits operate by delegating goals and deadlines to their employees. What do they do to help their employees achieve those goals and meet their deadlines? The answer is *office supplies*!

When you walk into any office supply store, you will see every type of calendar imaginable. One popular calendar contains a year's listing of months and days in grid form. It's laminated so that the employee can make notes with erasable pens or markers. Employees' offices all across the globe are lined with wall and desk calendars that keep them on task.

Students should use this system or their phones' calendar to keep both long-term and short-term goals and tasks present at all times. Graduation, exams, and final projects should be prominently noted. In addition, students should highlight smaller deadlines like homework assignments.

Since many students work, their employee schedules can also be included. Maybe even a few birthdays can be tossed in for good measure!

Your calendar can be overwhelming once everything is collated, but it's reality and it gives you an idea of what to expect.

Of course, you can also block out holidays and school vacations. Students who work and go to school (and even have children!) need to have a break *every once in a while!*

Yikes! My Calendar Is Crushing Me!

Setting priorities is vital. You have to let go of YouTube, video games, Netflix, trash TV, Snapchat, hangin' and chillin', and calls from friends who want to Facetime. ***But it's not forever. Just do the work first. Then have fun.***

Getting it all done seems almost impossible, even with the most organized person on the planet, but you can do most of it by **establishing a routine**.

ESTABLISHING A ROUTINE

Hint #1: *Get up Early*

This means getting to bed early. Say goodbye to TV, phone, and computer at a decent hour.

This step requires discipline. A lot. No one wants to let go of electronics, but you have to.

Hint #2: *Use the Alarm and Timer on the Cell Phone*

Give yourself a time limit for studying for one course and stick to it. Then switch to another task. Set the alarm to keep yourself motivated and on task.

Hint #3: *Organize the Annoying Stuff*

Can't find the socks that match the khaki pants? Pull the drawer or basket out while watching your favorite trash TV and organize it. You will eliminate the future need for profanity and sock tossing. You will also keep chaos away by completing small bits of personal organization.

Hint #4: *Multitask Only When It's Safe and Smart*

Many students claim that they can't study unless music is playing or the television is going. A large percentage of those who are most adamant about this are also the ones who cannot concentrate on serious tasks, especially on higher-level writing skills. Compose words without other words coming at you. Multitasking is dangerous for your GPA.

Teachers and Chaos

Teachers live with quite a lot of chaos. Our lives are no less complex than yours, our families no less important than yours.

Students whom we adore bring us life-altering stories almost every week. Our hearts never stop breaking for their tragedies, and we are ecstatic when our students triumph! By the end of the year, however, we feel completely empty and brainless. We have given our hearts away so many times that we need transplants, and endless nights of grading papers have forced us to get new eyeglass prescriptions.

We are not asking you to understand our lives or to sympathize with our plight. We are paid for what we do, and most of us love our jobs, but we have gone to college and graduate schools and beaten back our own time-management demons. So when you come to us with last-minute chaos over printers, we react first based on our own experiences and accomplishments.

You need to be organized and to meet deadlines. We had to do it for seven or eight (or more) years of higher education. Yes, we sometimes got breaks, but we didn't ask for them often. Don't wear out a teacher's sympathy with chaos stories—we didn't.

In the working world, your employer will not be generous about chaos. Your boss will not grant extensions and will not tolerate late work. You will, in many cases, simply be fired.

Learn how to manage your time while in college. The lesson will travel with you up the employment ladder.

Chapter 4

The Audience

Writers always need to keep their audience in mind. Offending the reader is unwise and unacceptable, as is catering to him or her.

English teachers are not squeamish, and most of us are not prudes. We have limits, though; you should respect us by not exploring your illegal or immoral activities and by not using profanity in your writing. However, most of our students have high morals and use good judgment in their work, so these offenses are not often a problem.

Your audience for any essay, however, is not just the teacher. Your audience is the reader, which includes the teacher but also includes your classmates and YOU.

Many students make the mistake of thinking that they must write to please the teacher's point of view. Responsible teachers do not want students to cater to their political beliefs and emotional needs and do not want to be considered the primary audience.

Also, we are a temporary audience. The next teacher, boss, or coworker will adjust the focus of a student's writing, so to gear writing to one person is relatively useless.

The Big Picture

Teachers want to be considered part of a larger audience, that of an educated citizenry. We want our state and country to prosper and feel that our students are our investment in the future.

As authority figures, we represent future employers who want you to have strong skills as writers and as workers. We try to take the long-term view of writing.

Students should listen to their teachers and follow their directions, but they should make their own choices in topics, organization, and content. A paper lacking originality is boring and redundant.

Your Own Worst Critic

Fine students often worry greatly about their essays. In doing so, they fret over their words and how their ideas affect their audience. Many students even agonize over their essays. For some, this mental exercise is as necessary as an outline or a keyboard.

Don't allow this introspective process to become detrimental to your writing. It can. Perfection is illusive and almost unknown, even in Yoknapatawpha County, Amherst, or Stratford-upon-Avon. These are references to William Faulkner, Emily Dickinson, and William Shakespeare, brilliant writers who had flaws but were completely original.

They wrote novels, poems, and plays. You are not writing in these genres.

As an essay writer, you are not using the same tools that writers in these genres use. Your strength has to be your ability to organize and to present your point of view and ideas logically and coherently to the reader. Your original, creative ideas must be organized.

Don't overdo it; flowery prose and stilted, inflated diction need to be trimmed. For instance, never say that someone has "become nonliving" when that person has died.

Members of Your Class

In class, teachers do not read or show bad essays to students while the authors sit in the same classroom. If the teacher asks to read your essay aloud, it will not be to humiliate you. Don't be shy. Allow other students to share your experience. Students often benefit most from the lessons they learn from each other.

Write your papers using strong, educated opinions that you develop from research or from serious contemplation. You can convince all of us to respect or to adopt your opinion if you write well and speak convincingly.

Speech Class, Too!

Public speaking and college writing are completely intertwined. Many teachers and students admit that they are more comfortable with one or the other, not both. However, both have a common factor, nervousness, which drives us in odd ways. For some, knees knock together while standing in front of a class; for others, writing the first paragraph of an essay creates stomach cramps.

Confident, bright students often become breathless as they walk to the front of the classroom. Talking in front of a class or to any group, whether friends or strangers, can humble even the most arrogant extrovert.

Composing an essay can be just as stressful. Even great writers fear a blank page. The strategies for success, whether through paper or in front of a podium, are very similar. The differences are also worth noting because they can be used effectively in each one.

Emphasis on Audience

Speech and English classes are not as divided as your class schedule and college catalog indicate. Both of them emphasize audience. In speech classes, the audience sits in front of the speaker most of time. Gauging the reactions is often the key to effective delivery.

This is also true for the written word. Anticipating the audience's objections and addressing them, especially in argumentation, is necessary to a well-argued composition.

Notable Terms in Speech and English Classes

VOICE	This word has separate meanings for the two disciplines. In college **writing**, you need a distinctive point of view with convincing evidence—voice. Your original voice on any subject brings a fresh view, even to tired topics.

Speeches also need to have this definition of voice, but the strength of an individual's words mixed with the sound of her/his voice can sway even the most biased audience. |
| **TONE** | This word is best applied to making speeches, but it is also important when composing essays. "Tone" is the attitude the writer has toward the material. Sarcasm brings one tone, encouragement another.

Words should convince, sway, or argue—without hotheaded, emotionally charged language. However, strong emotions are great when channeled into **well-constructed essays and speeches** and when married with solid evidence and vivid detail. |
| **AUDIENCE** | This term is more concrete in the discipline of **public speaking**. Speakers should not only know their audience, but they should also be familiar with the physical layout and environmental conditions surrounding their audience. An audience in a hot, humid auditorium will not be tolerant of theoretical, lofty speeches—not for very long.

Writers cannot be concerned with air conditioning or comfortable chairs for their readers. The writer must focus on crafting a thorough, well-organized essay that will appeal to a broad spectrum of educated readers.

Readers of an essay will not care if you wear baggy jeans or torn shorts when you write an essay. The audience for public speaking will care and will often judge you first based on your appearance. However, effective, well-crafted speeches can negate unfavorable first impressions. |

Attention to audience, even with its divergent meanings, is crucial. In both disciplines, guesswork and shoddy preparation are disastrous.

Preparation, editing, and respect for audience are vital.

The Communication Triangle

In writing, one point of the Communication Triangle is your audience, on a second is your setting, and on the third is your message. You are always in the middle.

Imagine that class has ended, and you are still in the classroom with your friend. Other people are in the classroom, including your instructor, and can hear the conversation you are having about the test you will have in your next class. You are anxious. In this situation, your audience is your friend and everyone else in the room, the setting is the classroom, and the message is that you are anxious about the test.

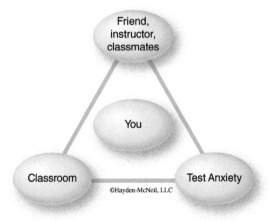

Because you are in the classroom and your classmates and instructor can overhear your conversation, you are more likely to speak in a more restrained way. Perhaps you will even whisper. When you and your friend get outside, your message is still the same (test anxiety), but your audience has changed (your friend and passing students who will catch only snippets of the conversation),

as well as your setting (outside on a college campus). Now, you will probably speak more freely. You may use words that you would not use in front of your instructor. You may say negative things about the next class. You may speak in a louder tone.

Imagine that you meet with the instructor whose test is causing you to have anxiety. You meet in the instructor's office. Now, your audience is the instructor, your setting is the office, and your topic is still test anxiety. But imagine how much different your tone and your language will be now.

As you write, this triangle stays with you. **You cannot write into a void.** You have to identify who and what is on each point of the communication triangle. Often, in a composition classroom, unless you are writing an assignment that calls for a specific audience (newspaper editor, future employer, school administration), you are typically writing for an academic audience in an academic setting.

Writing for an Academic Audience

"Academic audience" is a phrase that means that the person who is reading your paper has a college education and expects to see a certain type of organization, a formal dialect (word choice and sentence structure), and a more formal tone. Sometimes, people confuse academic writing with other types of formal language—language they find more familiar and comfortable, such as what they hear from politicians or preachers. Then, they write their academic essays as if they are delivering a speech or making a sermon. But those are forms of *spoken* language, not *written* language.

When you read an academic essay aloud, it should not sound as if you are delivering a speech. Instead, it should sound like you are reading an academic essay aloud.

Academic writing is also not the same as business writing: business writing is short and to the point.

Academic writing explores as many sides of an issue as possible. It does not get to the point quickly because the writer realizes that the reader needs to be taken on a journey. The reader needs time and opportunity to develop trust in the writer and, therefore, in the writer's words.

While academic writing is formal and will use more elevated language (*concede* instead of *give in*, *irritate* instead of *get on my nerves*), it should still be easy to read. The reader should not have to work to figure out what the writer is trying to say. The reader should not have to read a sentence two or three times in order to comprehend it.

With academic writing, you can write about basically any topic, but if you write about it in an academic structure, using an academic dialect and tone, your reader is more likely to be receptive to your message.

A Word on Grammar

People often think they are not good at writing, and that holds them back from writing an academic essay. But it does not hold them back from texting. It doesn't keep them from posting to social media. It doesn't cross their mind when they make a shopping list. So, why do they think they're bad writers when it comes to academic writing?

Usually, when people say they are not good at writing, what they really mean is that they are not good at editing. Editing is not the same as writing. Instead, it is just one step in the writing process—usually the last one.

Grammar affects your grade in a composition class, so you need to hone your editing and proofreading skills. A fear of editing, however, should not keep you from writing. Instead, familiarize yourself with your resources: the Writing Center on campus, NetTutor, and your instructor. Check with your instructor about using NetTutor, make an appointment in the Writing Center (if necessary), and consult your instructor during office hours.

If all else fails, review your old essays, and see what types of grammar errors are costing you points. The Internet (and this textbook!) is full of free resources. Do a search for your type of error. Make sure you understand what it is. Then read about how to spot it and how to fix it. Practice on your own work. Editing is a skill that you must develop over time. But having weak editing skills does **NOT** mean that you are a bad writer. Instead, it means that you have room for improvement.

R-E-S-P-E-C-T

Just as you should respect your audience without putting anyone on a pedestal, you can, in turn, expect respect from your teachers and fellow students—your audience.

The students who surround you are your audience. Get to know them and share the joys and struggles of composition classes together.

These two beautiful girls are daughters of Josh and Jennie Kidder. Josh and Jennie met in Ms. McCollum's English class while group editing an essay.

You may not have two cute children in your future when your teacher assigns group editing, but you never know.

Chapter 5

Prewriting the Essay

Starting

Students often say that not knowing how to get started is one of their reasons for not wanting to write. Staring at a blank page or computer screen can even trigger negative reactions, such as fear or procrastination. Sadly, many freshmen composition students find themselves in those positions because they have never exercised the muscle that is critical to success in the writing process—prewriting.

In the countless versions of composition textbooks available, standards for good writing have not changed over the years, which further repeats what teachers say: Staying true to the basics is essential. Fortunately, within the basics, there are still numerous approaches to fit a variety of learning styles. You should experiment with the methods described in this chapter to discover which ones best fit your writing style.

Another positive note on prewriting: Because this is the prewriting stage, you should have no concerns about errors—not typos, not commas, and not even sentence fragments. They do not matter at this stage. *Getting the ideas down on paper, or on the computer screen, is the objective.*

In addition, you should always adhere to the instructor's specifications for each writing assignment since rhetorical patterns and objectives will differ from one assignment to the next. Demonstrating attention to those details will certainly make a positive impression on an instructor.

Freewriting

Yes, it is as liberating as it sounds. What better way is there to fill the blank space than simply to begin with writing what you already know about a given topic? What is even better is that there are almost no restrictions—just a few simple guidelines.

For ten minutes you should write everything that comes to mind about your topic. Even if nervousness consumes your every thought, write that down. Often, getting those nervous thoughts out of the mind and onto the page will help untangle the jumble of ideas trying to break free. This takes practice. Be willing to freewrite until you are comfortable with expressing your ideas.

Then, underline ideas that are related to the given topic. (Most teachers do not mind if you do this on the computer or hand write and use a highlighter.) Next, circle or highlight those ideas that have the greatest potential for paper topics. Ask yourself these questions:

- Which ones are the most interesting?
- Which ones can generate more discussion?

For example, if the assignment is to write about America's prison system, begin with freewriting what you know, as in the student sample below.

I don't think I know much about this topic. I did visit a correctional facility on a high school field trip. It was a long way from the city, which seems good in case prisoners escaped. Plus, few people want to live beside prisons. We saw that it housed both male and female prisoners. I noticed there were areas where there were twenty women in one large room, bunk beds, sinks on walls by every bed and a small mirror. It was very loud in there and we walked straight through the middle of the room. Almost nobody smiled. There were no areas where the men were all together. The men were all in individual tiny cells. The barred side of their cells faced a dull beige wall. It seemed cold and there were no windows. The maximum security area was separate from the others. The cells were barred differently. They looked obviously stronger. I began to wonder about the people in that maximum security area. Were they really a greater threat to the others? Were they there for their own safety? That seemed the case with a blind prisoner. And there was a very young male there. I wonder what he did to be tried as an adult. The rec area was a basketball court. What if they didn't like basketball? Tables were outside in the rec area. Not everyone goes every day. Showers are not every day, humane? Prison seemed real to me for the first time. I was told to leave my purse at the check in. It is hard to imagine anyone taking something off a high school tour group with so much security around. What are problems with this place and other prisons? Does housing people like this lead to more problems? Does it do more harm than good to spend time in a prison for short-term stays?

First, let's be clear: this student knows quite a lot about prisons. Few people ever get to tour a facility as this student did. Freewriting about a topic will help to uncover a treasure trove of knowledge that you may never have considered.

The freewriting exercise can also help narrow the range of possible topics and could lead to an exploration of the differences between housing men and women prisoners. It could also lead to researching whether juveniles should be charged as adults. Continue freewriting or try another method listed below to generate content on the narrowed topic.

Brainstorming

This method resembles freewriting, but it suggests a little more focus be given to what goes on the page. Eventually, omit the rabbit trails, tangents, and off-topic ideas. Try to exhaust yourself of every possible lead.

Here is an example of brainstorming on the issue of free speech on college campuses.

College campuses are for higher learning. Free speech is connected to exploring new ideas, which seems inherent to the college environment. This is a topic that has come up repeatedly for decades, maybe longer. Colleges usually have a newspaper published. Many today have student Web and blog sites. These are forums for hot topics. Campuses must have policies in place regarding free speech or they may be confronted with lawsuits. Racial, ethnic, religious, political, social—all possible areas involving conflicts with free speech. Handled differently in regions of country considered liberal or conservative. How is it set apart from hate speech policy?

After underlining the possible options, you then highlight the better topics. This student sample may develop into a demand for a free speech policy update on a local campus, or it may generate a defense of free speech in a campus newspaper.

Questioning

Sometimes this process is referred to as the reporter's questions, or five Ws and an H. This prewriting exercise answers **who, what, when, where, why,** and **how** so that you are prompted to think about areas of a topic that might otherwise be overlooked.

Sample questions to get you started may look like this:

W#1	**Who** is involved in or affected by the discussion? **Who** are the participants in the situation?
W#2	**What** is the issue being discussed? **What** are the problems/benefits associated with the issue?
W#3	**When** does the issue become relevant to individuals? Society? The nation? The world?
W#4	**Where** is the situation taking place? Is the place contained in the past? Present? Future?
W#5	**Why** is this topic an issue at all? **Why** will it or will it not continue to be important in the future?
HOW	**How** might the situation be resolved? **How** will things turn out, considering several possibilities?

You will see how questioning is quite flexible as it is used in the next student sample of prewriting that explores the assigned topic of celebrity role models. This topic is too broad, but prewriting with questioning can help you narrow the possibilities down to a workable, more specific topic.

> **Who** is the subject of the discussion? Beyoncé, Taylor Swift, Dak Prescott, Kanye West, Justin Timberlake—the celebrities, athletes, singers, and the ones affected by the celebrity status (young tweenagers to college students).
>
> **What** is the issue? Celebrities/athletes/singers do make an impact on people. There are both negative and positive impacts, which I can list.
>
> **When** is this a problem? **When** is it a good thing? It is a problem when young people imitate bad behaviors they have seen in their role models. It is good when they are inspired to better their lives or the lives of others because of something good a celebrity role model has accomplished.
>
> **Where** does this take place? Not just in America, but America seems to have many examples of the issue. And more are added every day.
>
> **Why** is this happening? With bad role models, maybe people, especially the young, do not have good role models at home. (Absent parents, divorced parents—these are on the increase.) Same could be true of good role models. Perhaps, people are more impressed by star power these days. Maybe people are more vulnerable because

they don't know what they believe in or what their own talents are. Some say narcissism is on the rise and playing a factor in this.

How can this issue be resolved? The media should stop focusing on bad role models and spend more time on good role models. A shift away from celebrity power would be a good way to get back to identifying local unknown heroes.

After reviewing the answers that were generated in this Q & A session, the student highlights the best possibilities for paper topics, thus narrowing the search for topics. The above highlighted items indicate that the prewriting could lead to specific research on two different ideas, such as how female celebrities are negatively impacting young girls or what role the media plays in defining role models.

Clustering

This method of prewriting is more structured than earlier ones. Clustering prompts you to focus on an orderly arrangement of ideas as they come to you. While this may require more initial attentiveness to detail, it quickly reveals what areas have connections and what areas offer much information.

For example, when video games is the assigned topic, several organized possibilities arise from clustering. See the cluster in Figure 5.1.

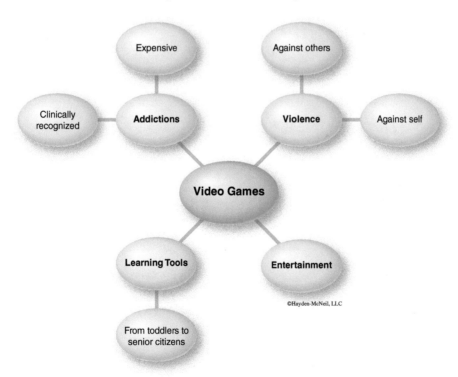

FIGURE 5.1. **Sample Cluster.** Topic: video games.

This effort may lead to a defense of video games by contrasting their benefits as learning tools and entertainment to their negative associations of addictions and violence. Of course, this clustering sketch can be expanded to include and further organize more specific information (i.e., naming specific learning tools and specific violent acts against self and others).

Outlining

This prewriting process is sometimes informal and sometimes classically formal. The differences between the two may be whether items are bulleted or set apart with Roman numerals. Another difference may be whether items are represented in words and phrases or in complete sentences. Ideally, this stage of prewriting occurs after you have used any of the previous prewriting methods and narrowed the possible topics. For instance, you may have freewritten on cloning and narrowed your ideas to animal cloning. The outline serves as an effective way to organize the information you have gathered and allows you to begin developing the actual structure of the paper.

To demonstrate these differences, the same topic of animal cloning is used for both informal and formal outlines.

INFORMAL OUTLINE

Animal Cloning

- defined as meat production
- types of cloning FDA approved
  - beef
  - pork

Benefits

- disease/quality control
- financial

Drawbacks

- ethical concerns
- consumers' caution over testing period
- vague policies

FORMAL SENTENCE OUTLINE

Thesis: Although animal cloning is detested by some, it will be in grocery stores soon.

I. Animal cloning is not a scientific dream; it is a reality.
    A. One type of animal cloning is for meat production.
    B. Two types of animals have been approved by the Food and Drug Administration.
        1. Beef cloning has occurred.
        2. Pork cloning is also possible.

II. There are proven benefits to animal cloning for meat production.
    A. Cloned-meat producers claim they will be able to control quality of meat by eliminating the threat of diseases.
    B. Cloned-meat producers also believe that cloned meat will regulate food production cost and make it more available to consumers at lower costs than traditional meat production.

III. However, there are also drawbacks to animal cloning.
    A. Consumer advocate groups have expressed ethical concerns about animal cloning, suggesting some producers may fail to label meat as "cloned."
    B. Potential consumers express concern over the length of the testing period for safety of cloned meat prior to FDA approval, stating ten years may not be enough.
    C. Some groups have concern over the implications of vague policies on future cloning endeavors.

Blank Page Gone

It is important to stress again that you should always follow the instructor's particular requirements for each assignment. However, remember that prewriting has considerable flexibility. Some of the possibilities have been explored in this chapter, but do not be afraid to alter and develop them according to what yields the best results for you.

Also, note that these methods are not always independent of one another. You may find that you like to freewrite first to generate ideas; then you organize your ideas with an informal outline or clustering. Be willing to explore the possibilities.

And, have no doubt—you will feel much better when you commit to getting started and begin to see the white space disappearing.

Chapter 6

Outline:
The Essay's Bones

Your instructor has given you an essay assignment. You have some ideas, maybe even a working thesis; however, before you begin writing, you need to organize your ideas.

I know, I know, you hate outlines!

You may never love outlining, but you must understand their purpose. Think about this for a minute. All humans have a skeletal structure. It is the framework of our body. It holds us up, keeps us straight, and maintains our stability. Without our skeleton, we would be a pile of goo slithering around on the floor. That would be so unattractive!

When you write, your outline is the framework of your writing. It keeps ideas stable and straightforward so that you can develop them fully. It will keep your essay from being a messy file of goo.

Once you add all your wonderful words, phrases, and clauses, your outline, your skeleton, will be unique to you, just like your fingerprint and just like you.

If you have a shorter writing assignment, you may have your topic and thesis mapped out already. With a more in-depth, longer assignment, you will need to spend more time gathering ideas, researching, and deciding on a focus for your essay.

Be sure to check the chapter on prewriting in this textbook, Chapter 5, for the steps that occur before outlining.

Scratch Outline: First in the Series

You can use one of three types of outlines. First, you can construct a scratch outline. In the scratch outline, you can jot down ideas in a basic listing framework. Here is an example:

Topic Idea: Reasons that I chose to attend a community college

I.   Financial
   - cost is half that of a senior college tuition
   - my college offers many scholarships
   - close to industry and retail so that I can work
   - many work/study opportunities

II. Educational
   - offers all of the core courses a university has
   - classes are smaller for more attention and individual help
   - allows me to decide if I want a terminal two-year degree or certificate or if I want to graduate and transfer to a four-year institution

III. Personal
   - close enough to my home to visit when I wish without having to wait until a holiday
   - parents and family are close to offer support and encouragement
   - keep in touch with high school friends and maintain my after school job

Notice the scratch outline lists ideas. They may not make much sense at first; but once the ideas are in place, then the writer can create a more specific outline to suit the needs of the assignment, especially if it is a long one. *When composing a scratch outline, avoid research and Google!* Use your brain! It is amazing! Think about what you already know: your life, your experiences, your perspectives, and your intellect. The more you jot down on your own, the more ideas you will have for your writing.

Basic Formal Outline

The next type of outline you can construct is a basic formal outline, which many instructors require. You've probably completed one of these at some point in your educational journey. The basic outline shows the thesis and the body components of your ideas. Here, in this format, you use A, B, Cs and 1, 2, 3s. Here is an example using the same topic as in the scratch outline. Notice that the ideas are more filled out, making the essay easier to complete. Also note that every A has a B (at least) and every 1 has a 2 (at least). This is a formal outline requirement.

Thesis: After much deliberation and discussion with my counsellor and my family, I chose to attend a community college because it offered me financial, educational, and personal advantages.

I. One reason I attended a community college is the financial advantage which it offered me.
   A. The tuition is very affordable at half the cost of a public university.
      1. In addition, my room in the dorm is quite reasonable.
      2. The school also offers several meal plans that fit into my budget.
   B. Because my community college has a superb reputation, many former students endow scholarships to help students like me.
      1. Some scholarships are based on need.
      2. Others target a particular field, several in my major.
   C. I also have the advantage of being close enough to business and industry to get a part-time job if I find I have time.

II. Another reason I chose to attend a community college is the educational opportunities community college affords me.
   A. Every course required in the core curriculum of any four-year institution in my state is offered at my community college.
   B. Instead of being a number in a classroom of 300 students in my freshman courses, I am an individual to my instructors.
      1. I can get extra help from instructors, who have office hours set aside to help me.
      2. My instructors work with me individually to make sure that I understand the material.
      3. I can go to the math lab or writing center for further help if I need it.
   C. Community college offers me the choice of getting a terminal degree of certificate or transferring to a university.
      1. My community college offers a variety of technical programs which will allow me to go to work right after graduation.
      2. In addition, I could enroll in a career program like truck driving, bricklaying, or diesel technology, which would put me on the fast track to a career.

      3. Besides those options, I could also finish my two-year core courses, graduate from community college, and transfer to a four-year school.

III. Finally, community college offers me a personal advantage.

    A. I am close enough to visit home without having to wait until a major holiday.

        1. I am the first in my family to attend college and sometimes get homesick.

        2. My family can offer support and encouragement if I get stressed.

    B. I can keep in touch with my former instructors and friends still in high school.

        1. They can offer support or help if I need it.

        2. I can be a positive mentor to younger family members and friends who are still in high school.

With this format, you use complete sentences that give a very brief and general overview of the essay. The topic of each paragraph is clear and concise, and the claims to support each idea show the direction the writer will take in order to prove his/her thesis. Notice that the more the skeleton/outline is filled in, the easier the first draft will be.

Extended Format Outline

The third type of outline is the extended outline. This format, which is more complicated and requires more planning, is covered in Chapter 25 in the "Strategy: Literary Analysis Puzzle" section. It is one that would require your instructor's explanation and permission to use.

The Skeleton Is Complete!

Many students view outlining as unnecessary, a step that prevents them from pouring their thoughts and ideas onto the page. However, the outline is one of the most important elements for any type of essay that you write in any subject, not just this one. It lets you know what you know or don't know; for instance, if you need three major ideas for three paragraphs of body but can think of only two to put into your outline, you should be forewarned that you don't know enough about that particular subject to write about it. Also, taking the time to build that skeleton for your essay requires that you think the process through completely before you attempt to develop those excellent ideas that you have. And besides, who wants to end up as an unattractive pile of goo!

Chapter 7

Bricks and Mortar: Building the Essay

Organize First, But . . .

Once you have finished brainstorming and outlining your essay, you actually have to begin writing your essay. Many students do not take the time in this part of the writing process to write paragraphs and/or entire essays that readers are able to understand.

Instead of following their outlines and writing sentences that flow together to support one main idea, students often abandon their outlines and just expect that whatever flows from their fingertips to the keyboard or to the paper will be fabulous and understandable to the reader. While this may be possible, that kind of talent is the exception, not the rule.

Writing an effective essay with strong paragraphs requires careful thought and consideration not only about your essay topic but also about your readers' ability to follow your essay.

As a writer, you are responsible for explaining your topic with clarity and for guiding your readers through your ideas so that they can follow your thought process. You must essentially become a tour guide who excites and educates at the same time. If you want your tour group, or readers, to follow your ideas closely, to learn from and be entertained by your ideas, and to come back yearning for more information, you must challenge yourself to be bound by clarity, coherence, unity, and development.

Clarity

The most essential part of your essay is that you stay focused on *one main topic* throughout your essay.

If you were on an Italian eatery tour in San Francisco and your tour guide took you to a museum celebrating the American Beat Generation, what would you think about this supposedly "Italian" tour? You would more than likely want your money back from that tour guide!

Remember this when you are writing: If you start an argumentation essay writing about the use of fantasy literature in English classes, you do not need to stray off topic and start writing about Algebra class. Your reader is going to wonder why anyone would ever be interested in the subject or even write about it, for that matter.

> **NOTE:** The author of the fantasy essay referred to here is a woman. The pronoun references in this chapter are "she" and "her" for a reason! See the essay at the end of the chapter for the entire argument.

The Thesis: Clarifying Your Tour's Focal Point

The best way to clarify and solidify the main point of your essay is to have a strong thesis statement. In the thesis, you should clearly state the main idea of your essay and the purpose you have for writing this essay. You state the main idea so that your reader does not get distracted by any point presented in your essay, and you state your purpose so that your readers can immediately see the importance of reading your essay. If your readers do not see these two important reflections of your leadership, they will not—probably because they cannot—follow you.

WRITING A THESIS

If a student were to write a paper about fantasy literature, as previously suggested, she would want to focus on the argument itself and how her evidence supports it. Moreover, her readers would expect her to give them a side of the discussion that they may never have seen. As a writer, she must consider all these facets of her topic when writing her thesis, and she might go through several drafts before she gets to that perfect thesis.

INEFFECTIVE THESIS STATEMENTS

Teachers always tell students to write a thesis that is **unified, restricted, and precise**, but what does that really mean? One way to explain this is to show you examples of thesis statements that do not meet these three expectations.

> No-No Example ·
> **Announcement**—This essay is about increasing the use fantasy literature in schools.

The student realized that this announcement thesis was ineffective because she was referring to her essay, which she does not need to do. Her readers know this is an essay without her pointing that out in her thesis. Her focus *should* be on her topic only.

> No-No Example ·
> **Bland Fact**—Fantasy literature isn't commonly used to teach.

The focus of the above thesis is now fantasy literature, but the thesis never tells the reader what the essay pertains to in relation to the topic or what the student's purpose for writing this essay is. As a result, her thesis is too vague.

> No-No Example ·
> **Unnecessary Question**—Is fantasy literature used in the classroom enough?

A thesis should never be a question because the writer, or tour guide, should be answering the readers' questions. Express your position to the reader based on your experience and your interpretation of that experience.

EFFECTIVE THESIS STATEMENTS

Three-Point Thesis

This type of thesis specifically states the three points that will be covered in the author's essay.

> Increasing the use of fantasy literature within the classroom is a necessity because students will be enjoy it more, build their vocabulary, and be inclined to read away at home.

Through this thesis, the author conveys the main point of her essay: increasing the use of fantasy novels in the classroom. She also tells her readers what her support body paragraphs for her argument will be focused on: (1) how students will enjoy the content, (2) how it will build their vocabulary, and (3) how it will encourage them to read at home.

Be certain to make the wording in all three parts parallel: just words or just phrases. The example about fantasy literature consists of verb phrases.

> **WARNING:** Some instructors do not want three-point thesis sentences. Check with the instructor.

Two-Point Thesis

Though utilized less than the three-point thesis, this type of thesis states two main points.

> Headphones should be banned in the classroom to cut down on potential cheating and to decrease the noise that emanates from them.

The writer can expound upon these points and write one paragraph about potential cheating and two paragraphs concerning the noise. Unlike the three-part thesis that seems to demand equal attention for all three points, the two-part thesis is less constrictive.

Again—be certain to make the wording in both parts parallel: just words or just phrases. The example about headphones contains infinitive phrases.

> **WARNING:** Some instructors do not want two-point thesis sentences. Check with the instructor.

Main Idea and Purpose Thesis

This type of thesis focuses strictly on the author's main idea and purpose for writing the essay without giving away the author's entire paragraph structure plan.

> Classroom English instructors should increase the use of fantasy literature in their classes.

Although she doesn't tell her three main ideas up front, she uses direct language to keep her readers engaged in her essay and in her argument.

> **WARNING:** Some instructors only want three-point thesis sentences. Check with the instructor.

DIFFERENT TYPES OF THESIS STATEMENTS

No matter the mode (or type) of essay, you need to state your main point and the overall purpose for your essay.

Comparison and Contrast Example ·
Although I thought choosing which university I would transfer to would be easy, my two favorite options, University of Mississippi and University of Southern Mississippi, are so similar that deciding became extremely difficult.

Cause and Effect Essay Example ·
Getting a speeding ticket can create serious monetary problems.

Classification and Division Essay Example ·
My iPod is overrun with southern rock music, classic country, and teenage pop because these types of music define my personality.

Process Essay Example ·
Planting a successful vegetable garden can be simple if a person is willing to follow the right steps the first time.

Narrative Essay Example ·
My journey across China taught me to value American freedom.

Introduction: Enticing Your Reader to Follow

Once you have pinpointed an effective thesis for your essay, you need to incorporate that sentence into an introductory paragraph that draws your readers into your essay and makes them see your point of your writing

The best way to do that is by writing an introduction that is both interesting and relevant to your readers. In the first sentence of your introduction, you should always connect your topic to your audience; you should then use the remainder of your introduction to build up the main idea. There are many effective ways to accomplish these two goals.

Suggested methods for beginning an essay:

- Background information about the topic
- Anecdote or story
- Question
- Quotation
- Definition

PLUSES AND MINUSES OF EACH METHOD

	PLUS	MINUS
BACKGROUND INFO	adds relevance to choice of topics	can get boring if the content is bland
ANECDOTE OR STORY	can draw attention to the topic if it's not too long and is on point	can sound preachy and can allow the reader to be confused about the thesis
QUESTION	effective when use sparingly	preachy and repetitious if used too much
QUOTATION	can be terrific if it's appropriate and not too lengthy; especially good if humor involved	stacking quotes wrong— loses writer's voice
DEFINITION	can clarify exactly what the author means	can bring an automatic F for plagiarism if copied from the phone or a dictionary

An author can entice readers in numerous ways as long as the author remembers that she must make her topic relevant to her readers. Also, the introduction must build up to the thesis, which is often the last sentence of your introduction. You want to focus your reader specifically on your main idea and purpose before you take off on your tour, explaining your points as you go.

Examples of Effective Introductory Paragraphs

Two examples from Appendix A, one from Appendix B, and another from Appendix C; the complete essays are located there.

Example #1 from Lauren Walker ·

In the summer of 2008, four hurricanes wreaked havoc across the country of Haiti. Over 800 people were recorded dead over a course of thirty days. Cities were deemed uninhabitable and thousands of Haitians were left homeless and starving. Many did not know if their families and loved ones were dead or alive. My extended bus ride returning to Haiti was filled with anxiety and nervousness, as the fear for the sake of my friend Patrick and his village weighed in on top of an anticipated reunion.

What makes Lauren's opening paragraph effective? The topic, the attention grabber, and the great thesis make the reader want to read further. The gruesome details and the familiarity of tropical storms to most of the readers also pull the reader's attention to the content.

Example #2 from Suhail Basalama ·

In my country, Yemen, the last grade of high school is the most crucial for two reasons. It reveals the outcome of twelve years of studying, and a student's future depends mostly on it. When a student wants to apply for a governmental scholarship or enroll in a university, the most important factor is the high school score. The final exams of high school are administered directly by the Ministry of Education to assure that students from all over the country have equal opportunities. Therefore, graduating from high school in Yemen with high scores requires discipline, diligence, and patience. The last year of high school was the most challenging grade that had a huge influence on my life.

What makes Suhail's opening paragraph effective? Finding out that the writer is from Yemen is immediately interesting. That's an attention grabber, but the subject matter about high school graduation from another country is fascinating and parallels our American experience.

Example #3 from Tyler Bass ·

One Lake House on Sea Island Drive is not quite like the rest of the houses in the area. Upon approach, the first noticeable feature is a house considerably larger than the rest. After further examination of the houses around it, other features make this house differ from the others on Sea Island Drive. The most dramatic dissimilarities are the three staircases descending to the lower level and a wraparound porch that connects to a balcony on the back. On the lower level of the house is the bar. Two grills are mounted into the bar, which is covered in bottle caps, old street signs, stickers from all the random tourist spots, and even the tailgate from an old Chevy truck.

What makes Tyler's opening paragraph effective? Tyler does not have an attention grabber; in fact, one is not needed when the writing is descriptive and clear. What Tyler does have is an amazing ability to build a picture of his house for us, the readers, and he closes the opening paragraph with a distinctive visual feature, a "tailgate from an old Chevy truck." Tyler picked the right topic for this rhetorical mode—description—and bit by bit, Tyler reveals the house to readers.

Example #4 from Charles Cannon ·

The Christian church has evolved a lot since its founding. Evangelism has become one of the most important goals, as has entertainment. As a young Christian who has been raised in church, I have gathered both from experience and through others' opinions about how modern changes in church, specifically those aimed at students, have affected church environment and young Christians. Modern youth group culture needs to be changed.

What makes Charles' opening paragraph effective? Because his topic and point of view are unique, Charles' paragraph stands out. This part journey/part argumentation essay is powerful. Additionally, his thesis is clear and to the point.

Topic Sentences: Guiding Your Reader through Your Points

In general, topic sentences are the most important tool in writing effective body paragraphs. These are usually the first sentence in each body paragraph, and they state the main idea of that paragraph. Its purpose is to present the main point that the body paragraph it is introducing.

Since the author's first body paragraph is about her exposure to fantasy literature within a classroom and what she has noticed about the works assigned to her by previous instructors, the writer's topic sentence needs to focus on these points.

BODY PARAGRAPH ONE: TOPIC SENTENCE

An extremely limited use of fantasy literature in schools and other places of higher learning exists today.

With this topic sentence, her readers know that she is going to write about the rare use of fantasy literature within a classroom.

The second job of the topic sentence is to relate back to the previous body paragraph so that your reader can see how it is transitioning to new ideas that are still connected to the thesis.

BODY PARAGRAPH TWO: TOPIC SENTENCE

The increase of fantasy literature in classes will not only benefit the students but will also help the teachers.

This topic sentence transitions from the previous paragraph by expanding on an idea previously mentioned and puts the focus on her new point: the benefits both teachers and students gain when fantasy literature is taught in class.

BODY PARAGRAPH THREE: TOPIC SENTENCE

> Interest in literature and literacy rates have been declining as the reading levels of students plateau at a young age.

This sentence introduces another valid point in the author's argument while providing a smooth transition between itself and the previous body paragraph.

These transitions are important to your readers because the readers need to see how your points connect. This helps them become part of your essay and helps them to understand your thought process as a writer. Remember that you are guiding them through your essay; you don't want to lose them.

> **NOTE:** This chapter's sample essay includes an opposition paragraph as the final body paragraph, body paragraph four. Argumentation essays typically include some form of an opposition paragraph either as the first body paragraph or as the last body paragraph.

Body Paragraphs: The Details Matter

UNITY AND COHERENCE

After creating a strong topic sentence to guide your readers in the right direction, now you need to make sure that your body paragraphs include enough detail to inform and interest your readers.

A major factor in writing effective body paragraphs is whether the paragraph is **unified**. Essentially, a unified paragraph is one that stays on topic. As stated earlier, a unified paragraph is easy to write if you have a detailed outline. You must follow that outline without straying off course. If you stray off course, you will make your topic sentences for the body paragraphs irrelevant and confuse your readers.

An essay cannot be unified unless it is also **coherent**. To write coherently, an author must present her ideas in a logical, organized way. In other words, the readers must be able to follow the writer's ideas without getting confused.

For example, since this author is writing an argumentation essay, she should present her paper in an order that focuses on her argument to keep from confusing her audience. It would be odd (and destroy the essay's unity) if her first body paragraph were about the limited use of fantasy literature in English classrooms and then later to retell the plot of one of the books.

In other essays such as cause and effect essays, some ideas logically build off each other to create a larger point. With other essays, an author might have some points that are stronger than others. If this is the case, it is logical to put the best point last so that your paper will end on a high note.

ORDER OF IDEAS: THE PYRAMID

In almost essays, the order of the ideas and points that the writer presents is determined by what the writer wants to emphasize. In one essay, the narration essay, the order is determined by a time line: beginning, middle, end.

In most essays, the writer must choose which pyramid he or she prefers: the regular one or the inverted one.

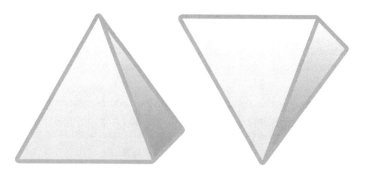

In the regular pyramid, your least important idea begins at the top and the most important ones appears near the conclusion. It's just the opposite for the upside down pyramid. The most important idea begin right after the introduction and the least important ideas come last.

Writers have distinct preferences. Many prefer the traditional pyramid— smaller to bigger idea. Some writers will begin their essay in this fashion and switch. Here's the point: Your ideas must be organized, not random.

Choose a pyramid and organize.

TRANSITIONS

To help create this unity and coherence in an essay, it is also important that a body paragraph have transitions throughout so that your readers can easily move through each detail and connect each idea presented. This is called *coherence*.

Transition Words—Words That Bring Coherence

TIME AND PLACE	CONTRAST/COMPARE	REPEAT/EMPHASIZE
Finally	Although	Most importantly
Occasionally	Though	Surely
Since then	Unless	Meanwhile
Beyond	On the contrary	Finally
Farther	However	Certainly
Near the middle	Similarly	Therefore
Shortly	Conversely	In fact
Since then	In spite of	Again
Wherever	In addition	As stated
At first	On the other hand	Consequently
Recently	On a similar topic	Furthermore
Eventually	Otherwise	In addition
Later	Likewise	However
Presently	To compare	Thus
That night	Unlike	Nevertheless
Immediately	Just as similar	In summary
Next	Despite	For example
For example	For example	

The best (and possible the simplest) transition phrase in the history of writing is "for example." Students often forget this very accessible phrase. Though it should not be overused, "for example" is a great way to follow up and give evidence of the prior statement.

> **Example** ·
> Banning headphones in computer labs is a good idea for most students, but they can be necessary in some instances. **For example**, some students need noise-cancelling headphones to concentrate on writing.

PARAGRAPH DEVELOPMENT

Even though an author may stay on topic and transition smoothly between points, s/he also must provide specific details so that the readers can feel as though they fully understand the author's point or can visualize an event that is being described.

If an author is too general, then readers will leave the essay feeling as if they learned nothing. The best way to add detail is to add specific values when writing about monetary issues; to use vivid descriptions when telling about a place you visited; to acknowledge people, places, and times by names and times specifically. Also remember the five senses and make the scene vivid with the smells and sights. Do not repeat the same details in later paragraphs.

These fresh details will make your readers feel like they have gained more information than what they originally expected and could possibly encourage them to take another tour with you.

REVISING BODY PARAGRAPHS

This is an example of our author's rough draft of her second body paragraph about the possible benefits of adding fantasy literature in the classroom.

> Most teachers use works that have been deemed classics and have been taught for many years due to that label. Teachers are then able to use notes from their educational predecessors to teach their current students. By using fantasy literary works, teachers can expand their own literary horizons. The students can then add their own perspectives on the content within the work to assist the teacher in annotation. As student participation increases, the interest level of the teacher will also.

Although this paragraph has some good points, it is missing some key details and transitions that would make it even stronger.

- Why do teachers typically use classics in the classroom?
- How is the inclusion of fantasy literature mutually beneficial to both students and teachers?

Also, the reader might be wondering why the author briefly mentions a focus on students. Though this may be a good point to include, it actually takes away from the paragraph's **unity** because students were barely mentioned.

This revised paragraph shows how the author added details and transitions and left out points that took away from her body paragraph's focus.

> The increase of fantasy literature in classes will not only benefit the students but will also help the teachers. Most teachers use works that have been deemed classics and have been taught for many years because of that label. Teachers are then able to use notes from their educational predecessors to teach their current students. By using fantasy literary works, teachers can expand their own literary horizons by teaching an unconventional work of fiction. The students can also add their own perspectives about the content to assist teachers in future classes.

The added details, ideas, and transitions give the readers an insight to the author's argument and allows them to develop an opinion, even if they hadn't previously considered the topic.

Conclusion Paragraph: Leaving the Tourists Wanting More

Once the author has completed her detailed body paragraphs, she must end her paper with a conclusion paragraph that finalizes her essay. This paragraph should be short but still interesting to the readers. You want to leave readers excited about your essay and what they have learned. You do not want them to feel as if they wasted time on your tour!

These are some different approaches to writing effective conclusions.

RESOLUTION AND RECOMMENDATION

You might offer an insight about what you gained from your experience and, then, challenge your readers to learn from your experience. The featured author could reiterate her past classroom experience in relation to the topic and encourage her readers to reflect on their own literary exposure.

PREDICTION

You could also end by telling what you think may happen in the future as it relates to your main idea. At the end of this essay, the author could express the interest she now has to make a change in classrooms all over to increase the use of fantasy literature.

QUOTATION

An author may want to end an essay with a quote that directly relates to her experience, or for this argument essay, the author could revisit the quote that she used in her introduction.

JUST PLAIN CLOSURE

Writers tend to want to say something profound at the end of an essay, and it's not always necessary. Leave the reader with a sense of closure—most of the time. If you want the reader to feel deliberately uncomfortable or you want to challenge the reader, do so! But never preach or get gooey.

A Successful Tour

Writing a good essay is much like giving a successful tour: hard work. An author must be willing to write and revise, write and revise, and write and revise again. Very few people write successful essays with perfect clarity, coherence, unity, and development with their first drafts of essays, but you can be successful at writing if you put in the work required and make a plan to guide your readers through your essay with a thesis, topic sentences, detailed body paragraphs, and an introduction and conclusion that keep your readers wanting more.

Your success as a tour guide is right before you; you just have to work hard to obtain it!

Final Note about Numbers

You'll see that some of the numbers in this chapter are not spelled out. Check with your teacher about stylistic preferences. Follow the directions you are given in regards to this very fluid rule.

Sample Essay: Argumentation

Victoria Mulqueen, Student

A Need for Fantasy

The importance of using literature in English courses is evident. The specifics, such as types of literature, vary from class to class based on mandatory requirements and the personal preferences of teachers. In my experience, one aspect that all of my previous English courses have in common is a lack of fantasy literature. English instructors in educational institutions should increase the use of fantasy novels in their classes.

An extremely limited use of fantasy literature in schools and other places of higher learning exists today. I have taken higher English courses since fifth grade and have only been assigned two books that fall into the category of fantasy, *The Giver* and *The Hunger Games*. In both instances, the class as a whole seemed more receptive to the lessons within the novels and to reading the assignment in general. Adding more fantasy assignments will ensure a larger variety of works being taught in schools and will then make the students more open to reading outside of the assignment's parameters. Exposing students to books within this category will expand the minds of all parties involved.

The increase of fantasy literature in classes will not only benefit the students but will also help the teachers. Most teachers use works that have been deemed classics and have been taught for many years because of that label. Teachers are then able to use notes from their educational predecessors to teach their current students. By using fantasy literary works, teachers can expand their own literary horizons and their minds by teaching unconventional works of fiction. The students can also add their own perspectives about the content to assist teachers in future classes. As student participation increases, the interest level of the students increases as well.

Interest in literature and literacy rates have been declining as the reading levels of students plateau at a young age. This tends to happen as the readers become uninterested in the assigned material. Adding a novel with the subgenre of fantasy will change the pattern of books assigned to pupils and will therefore increase their interest in basic reading. As reading increases among students, their literacy rates will increase as well. Although adding fantasy novels is beneficial to increasing literacy rates, renowned books are also important in accomplishing this goal.

Of course teaching well known books, such as *To Kill a Mockingbird*, is also necessary in educating individuals about literature. Works like Lee's novel are considered classic because they changed the world of literature and also contain timeless lessons. While the teachings of classic novels are essential, at the same time, teachers should still increase the variety of genres and subgenres, like fantasy, and use them in their classrooms.

The escalation of fantasy literature use within educational institutes is necessary. The addition of this category in the curriculum is beneficial to both students and instructors. Increased literacy rates will decrease frustration, especially for students. Expanded views regarding general literature will help to make students more open-minded and educators more in tune with students' interests. Because of the obvious advantages, teachers everywhere need to increase the use of fantasy works in their classrooms.

Chapter 8

Narration Essay

Essay writing in composition classes is not the same as writing for a creative writing class. The same applies to technical and workplace writing; they differ greatly.

Both creative writing and essay writing require a good deal more artistic creativity than most workplace writing. They communicate in their specific venues.

Restrictions to complete freedom—organization, thesis, topic sentences, transitions, paragraph unity, coherence, and on and on—are seriously calculated and produced in academic writing with essays but are less important in creative writing. They are very important in business writing.

However, academic writing without creativity is totally bland.

Here's the good news:

In narrative and descriptive essays, the writer has more opportunity to use her/his imagination and creativity. In fact, these particular modes of writing must have more carefully crafted creativity that works with the thesis, topic sentences, and organization.

Definition of Narration Essay

A narration essay is simply an essay that tells a story. Logically, then, a narration is centered around a sequence of events guided by a strong thesis statement.

Narratives are crucial in American culture, especially in the South. We tell stories all the time, and we pass on family history through their telling. Without stories, what would we do at family reunions other than eat?

But knowing and hearing those funny stories, sometimes stories that make us look foolish, endear us to family. Of course, sharing stories about the hard times is a way of creating or strengthening relationships that sustain us in difficult times.

English teachers hear many older people brag, "I'd make a million dollars if anyone wrote down my story." We tell these folks to get busy writing on a computer or on loose-leaf paper, but to do it for their families, not for some dream of making big money. For students, teachers suggest keeping journals, diaries, notebooks, blogs, or anything that could be useful years from now when the itch to write about their lives hits them. Holding fast to stories keeps family heritage alive. Writing a narrative essay is one way to take a family story and make it poignant and appealing to a larger audience. See Hammons' "Growing up Poor" at the end of this chapter as an example.

Uses of Narration in College Writing

Writing a narrative essay is a common assignment for English classes; however, you likely will also be asked to use your narrative writing skills in several other college courses. For example, in a history class, your professor may ask you to write a discussion response that explains the sequence of events that led up to King Phillip's War. Your psychology professor may ask you to explain how Sigmund Freud developed his theory on dreams. Both require a sequence of events in time order—the essence of a narrative essay.

EMBEDDED NARRATIVES

In many other essays—especially with argumentation—you may need to use a narrative (story) as a part of your evidence to support your stance or opinion. For example, a student supported her essay's thesis that African-American teens are sentenced more harshly for petty offenses by her research and by the story (narrative) of her brother's experience in court. The narrative embedded in her argumentation essay strengthened her thesis and added to the other evidence found through research in her essay.

What to Do *First* in Narration and Description: The Topic

Choosing a topic can be aggravating, but you must pick a topic that appeals to you, especially with narration and description! Because you have a bit more artistic freedom with these two kinds of writing, you should choose a topic that will inspire fine writing.

> **WARNING:** If you choose a topic that is too painful and/or too fresh, you might not be able to write about it without losing your sense of organization and balance. When the pain floods into your mind, you tend to lose track of the topic. Sometimes, hurt and pain have to wait until they have been sufficiently processed before they can be discussed through essay writing for a class. Know your limitations with personal heartache as they apply to essay writing. Grief can overwhelm the writing process.

Many teachers will provide a list of topics. Work with and play off the list; perhaps combine two topics. Check with the teacher before altering the topic list.

Choosing the right topic is mandatory. If you start your essay and feel that you cannot use the topic as well as you initially thought, tell the teacher and work out a schedule for making up the time you've lost.

Practice Now: Don't Wait

Practice writing your essays by choosing a topic listed at the end of this chapter and running through all the steps suggested in this chapter. You can study for essays! It's called practice. Both the teacher and the Writing Center (if available) will be glad to look at your practice work and make suggestions. Please don't ask the teacher or Writing Center personnel to grade your practice work. It's practice, not a final product.

> **IMPORTANT:** Never ask anyone in any Writing Center to proofread your work. They are not proofreaders! They will help you a lot but will not proofread.

SUGGESTED PRACTICE STEPS

1. Choose one or two topics from the list in this chapter. Put both topics side by side and start freewriting, clustering, brainstorming, listing, etc. Let the winner name itself. The one that has the most information and is more interesting simply wins!

2. Organize using any method you'd like—an outline with bullets instead of Roman numerals, a set of index cards, or blank boxes for inserting info. Just organize in some form.

3. Ask yourself what the point is. If you have a lot to write about a wreck you had last year, you must have a central idea. What was so important about the wreck to you?

4. Determine one MAIN idea about the wreck, though several may apply. The thesis contains only one main idea, so run with the ONE that applies.

5. Start composing the essay. When finished, take a break and go back to it for proofreading and editing.

6. Show the essay to a tutor at the Writing Center or to your teacher.

7. Take feedback from the professional without hurt feelings.

8. Revise it! Now get ready for doing almost the same process for a graded essay.

Thesis for Narrative and Descriptive Essays

Each narrative essay must answer the vital question: *Why is this story/narrative important?*

Simply relating the events of your recent vehicle accident is mostly uninteresting if the reader does not know what the point of this story is. Did the accident cause you to be in a cast for months? Did your mother have a similar accident when she was 18 that damaged her leg? Did a deer's antlers almost impale your cousin who was next to you in the truck? If you are writing an essay on the State Fair, is the State Fair magical to you? A nightmare? The reader won't want to read your narrative unless you also know why the story is important and can convey that to the reader.

Make the reader want to read your essay.

No accident or prom or graduation story is interesting unless it has a main point/thesis. If it does not, the writer rambles in many directions, writes entirely too much, and lacks focus for her/his work. Many teachers have read stories about the prom that deteriorated into a listing of colors in the prom dress. No, get a point: Was the prom an amazing night or the worst night of your life? Did the prom live up to the hype? Why should your reader care about a story that is about you?

One way to figure out what the point of your story is that you want to convey to the reader is to figure out what the story means to you.

- Did this event make you realize something about yourself, your family, your community, or your past?
- Did it help you make a decision about your present or your future?

Those sorts of realizations might be your point because they will help your reader understand why the story is so important.

Again, the key question is: **What's the point of the story?**

And any reader—especially the teacher—will appreciate a story that is well told and interesting.

Crafting the Thesis

In both the narrative and descriptive essays, you need to follow the basic rule of thesis sentences:

MAIN THESIS FORMULA FOR ALL ESSAYS

| Topic | + | Main Idea/THE IMPORTANCE | = | **THESIS** |

Examples for Narrative Essays

TOPIC	+ MAIN POINT	+ BIT OF DETAIL
Going to the fair in Jackson	has always been thrilling for me	because of the rides.
Prom night of 2016	became the worst night of my life	as a result of my date's careless driving.
My car accident last July	was so frightening and painful	that I refused to drive for six weeks.
The Jackson Zoo	is still my favorite place to take my daughter	even though they no longer have elephants.
Watching a Hitchcock movie at the Stand Theatre in Vicksburg	was a fantastic new experience	because I had never seen any of his films on the big screen.

NO-NO LIST FOR THESIS SENTENCES

1. **The mysterious thesis.** These thesis sentences hint that something will be revealed later on in the essay, but they hold back on what it is. Unless your instructor specifically tells you that this kind of thesis is acceptable in a narrative essay, stay away from it.

   No-No Example ·
   The events of January 15th were never to be matched.

   The above thesis hints at something interesting. You must be clear, not mysterious.

2. **The many-parts thesis.** This is the long, ponderous thesis that painfully won't end.

   No-No Example ·
   My grandmother's death was so overwhelming to the family that we lost contact with each other for two years, and my Aunt Edna's death two years later was the only thing that brought us together again under the same roof.

   Fix this monster sentence with focus on one main detail. EX: My grandmother's death split my family apart for years.

The Beginning Bones

GETTING TO THE POINT

Be sure to arrange details around the focus of your story. If you have ever listened to someone ramble on in a story and have gotten lost trying understand the point being made, you know how important it is for a writer to get to the point in an essay.

In writing a narrative essay, you will be asked to state the main point in your thesis of your essay. In most college composition classes, the main point appears in the first paragraph.

Ask your instructor if she or he has a preference for the location of the thesis. Some will say to put it in the first sentence. Others will say to put it as the last sentence of the first paragraph, while others say to put it anywhere in the first paragraph.

> Don't get hung up on the teacher's preference about thesis location. It is based on the way that teacher was trained; all of the ways listed above are valid.
>
> As a student, you must be flexible because different disciplines will vary their requirements. Get used to it early in college.

Any English teacher will know if you do not have a thesis in your essay. That's what a student should really be concerned about!

GIVE GOOD DETAILS/DESCRIPTION

Once you have a good plot/outline planned, focus your energies on providing details. Make your story come to life with vivid details, such as description, names, dates, and dialogue. When you describe something or someone, think of using the five senses: sight, sound, smell, taste, and touch.

Never say, "I went to the store to get some stuff."

Instead, you should say, "I went to Kroger to get hummus and pita."

Next, make the specifics of the Kroger trip relevant without rambling on endlessly or padding the content. Was the food for a midnight snack or for a school event the next day?

Examples of Effective Use of Details

Victoria Pagan's narrative/descriptive essay contains vivid description and detail about her family trip to Loch Ness, Scotland:

> The museum staff showed us a short documentary on the castle. As the film finished, they drew back a thick red curtain, revealing the most amazing view. What was left of the castle was located on the side of a rocky cliff that overlooked the loch. I first noticed the towers of the castle that were still standing. They were surrounded by what used to be great walls, now reduced to rubble. The walls only stood about two feet high, but I could see where separate rooms were still visible. As I looked to the end of the castle, I noticed that one of the towers was stable enough for people to go into and had an open space at the top. From about fifty feet in the air, I could see the length of the entire loch. Because we went in the morning, the sun was just past the peak of the hills and was casting light on the water. It looked like a scene from a romantic movie.

Notice how Victoria plays with the images related to light. They are so vivid that the attentive reader can almost see an abandoned castle on a large lake. Her entire essay can be enjoyed at the end of this chapter.

Emanuella Reyes's essay in Appendix B also utilizes description creatively:

> The sun and sand went hand in hand with its warmth, tickling our feet and rushing up the rest our bodies. The feeling seemed to ignite more excitement in us, making us jog and then run towards the water. All we could hear was the sound of the calm waves disrupted by our bodies being thrown against them. Nothing could compare

to it. The ocean's movement and coolness refreshed my skin and worked its way up to my mind. Even at a young age, the memories of bad divorce, the idea of starting over, and the reality of the separation seemed to be taken by the waves and no longer ate away at my thoughts. Although it wasn't church, the water seemed to baptize all problems within us.

Emanuella's words evoke a more emotional response because she is equating the ocean at Miami Beach to a spiritual reawakening. Without the great description, the emotional response would not be as powerful.

USING DIALOGUE

If you quote anyone in your essay, make very, very sure that it is important. Ordinary conversation is boring unless it leads to a monumental event.

Another giant problem with quoting in narrative essays is that most writers have difficulty with using quotation marks and punctuation correctly. <u>Put commas and periods inside quotation marks</u>.

Don't overuse dialogue. It is not just another way to slap words into an essay and create a higher word count.

Keep these rules in mind when writing dialogue:

1. Format each line of dialogue from a new speaker as a separate paragraph.

2. Use quotation marks appropriately.

3. Because you are quoting the way people actually speak, feel free to use slang, regionalisms, the word "you," etc., in lines of dialogue. Do not, of course, use them in the body of the essay if your teacher does not allow use of second person.

4. Most importantly: Don't quote needlessly. **No-No Example:** "Then she said that we could go to the mall," adds nothing to your essay.

5. Do not use incorrect punctuation in your quotes. **No-No Example:** "You can't go over to anyone's house, you have not done the dishes." This sentence contains a comma splice, and no one adds commas to conversations—not even English instructors! We do, however, know when they occur.

Last word on using dialogue: Use it sparingly.

GENERATING IDEAS

Use the strategies provided in the "Prewriting the Essay" chapter. Once you have completed your prewriting routine, you must organize your ideas. Using an outline is one of the very best ways to see your vision on paper. Some English instructors and professors do not care if you use automated bullets or Roman numerals. However, many teachers still prefer the traditional outlines. Follow the teacher's instructions.

The General Order of Events

The three parts to any story/narrative are the beginning, middle, and end. In general, the beginning should provide background and set the reader in a specific time and place. The middle should have a climactic event where some conflict takes place. The end should show how that conflict is resolved and provide a sense of closure.

OUTLINE

Thesis: My most embarrassing moment occurred when I scored a goal for the opposing team in a basketball game.

I. Beginning
   A. I arrived at the gym.
   B. The team cheered in the locker room.
   C. We warmed up on court.
   D. We began the game.
II. Middle
   A. We played the first half.
   B. We began the second half.
   C. I stole the ball.
   D. I scored a goal for opposing team.
III. End
   A. I realized my mistake.
   B. I heard comments from teammates and coaches.
   C. I received support from parents.
   D. I faced students at school the next day.

This outline is average, at best. Most teachers do not want "Beginning," "Middle," and "End" as part of the organization in the outline. MLA also does not want these headings.

Always make sure that you have the teacher's complete instructions and directions for outline form and content.

INTRODUCTION

The introduction should include the following parts and use the following order to give these parts:

1. **Creative element at the beginning**—a story, quote, definition, question, etc. Do not copy from the dictionary! This is plagiarism, and who really wants to read the dictionary? Don't make your reader read the dictionary either. Use quotes sparingly in description.

2. **Background**—your age at the time of the story, the location of the story, names of people featured in the story, etc.

3. **Thesis**—stated clearly. Some instructors will allow an implied thesis, but the vast majority prefer a clearly stated thesis.

BODY

The body of the narrative essay is merely the story itself, in whatever order you have decided to use. You need a structured set of paragraphs with transitions between them, just as you would in other types of essays.

If you use dialogue, you will have several extra paragraphs because you will begin new paragraphs every time a new speaker has a line of dialogue.

Remember to use creative details that appeal to the five senses. Also remember that each paragraph covers one particular unit—of time, of the action in the story, of the people involved, etc. Do not begin a paragraph about how a wreck occurred and go off on a tangent about the police during the paragraph.

The tangent should be cut out of the essay. Save that outrage for another essay! Stick to the wreck and just refer quickly to the police barking orders to those watching the tow truck.

CONCLUSION

Never, ever end any essay with a giant pink bow. A bow occurs when the writer falls into the age-old habit of having the prince and the princess ride off into the sunset together; the story is all wrapped up nicely with a bow. It's also called the Happy Ending Syndrome (HES). Resist HES.

The other popular form of ending an essay is the Walk Away Syndrome (WAS). This involves not having any conclusion, leaving the reader shaking his or her head and asking what happened.

Your narrative is not complete until your concluding paragraph. It explains how you feel about the story you just told or how it eventually had an impact on your life (or your child's health or dating habits—whatever the subject of your essay is). There's no need for a bow. The reader simply needs a sense of closure, even if that sense of closure is an uneasy or uncomfortable feeling. It depends on the writer's intentions and her or his creativity.

The essay does not have to end with all loose ends tied up; that's unrealistic. But it does need to end clearly.

> **HINT:** Think of the introduction and the conclusion as framing your story. You introduce the story and then reflect on it. The last sentence in your conclusion should be creative but without a bow.

Choosing the Direction of the Essay

Many different types of narrative essays exist. In most college composition classes, however, two types predominate: the one-story topics and the journey topics.

The one-story type centers around single story—a car wreck, a move, a job interview, an athletic accomplishment.

Journey topics trace a history—car wrecks, moves, job interviews, athletic accomplishments, etc. See the examples below.

SINGLE-STORY TOPICS	JOURNEY TOPICS
The worst trouble I have ever been in	Troublemaker child
My first breakup/rejection	Failure at relationships
A terrible/great job interview Remember not to write a process essay here!	Winning jobs through my interview skills Remember not to write a process essay here!
An event that reaffirmed my faith/shook my faith	Surviving hard times with stronger faith
A valuable lesson about money	Learning to save money
Joining the military	A family history of service to the country
A move to a new place	Military life and moving again
A cell phone mistake	Bad luck with cell phones and texts
The time I scored the winning goal, touchdown, etc., in a ball game	Developing my athletic skills
Worst day working at Happy Day Play Daycare	Taking care of two-year-olds at Happy Day Play Daycare

Hybrids combining these two strategies are also common. Just remember to make transitions between them and to make the timeline clear.

Argumentation and Narrative Essays

The majority of the writing that college students will complete during their years of classes will fall under the heading of argumentation because this mode of writing incorporates serious critical thinking skills that college professors strive to improve. It also involves taking a stand, looking at the alternatives, and drawing conclusions based on examining the evidence. Research is involved with many of these essays.

Students will sometimes get to choose their topics for these projects and papers. When they choose a topic, they often choose topics that are meaningful to them—for a variety of reasons.

For example, if you choose to write on federal aid for victims of natural disasters and lived through Katrina or another violent weather outbreak, adding a part of your story to your research paper or project is a good idea. In this instance, you can use first person, I, we, me, and us.

Don't overshadow an argumentation essay or project with the narrative, but adding your experience to the content strengthens it if you do not stray too far from your argumentative thesis. If done well, your story becomes part of the evidence used to strengthen your argument.

Sample Essay: Narration

Laura Hammons, Instructor

Growing up Poor

My family dislikes my saying that we were poor. It is too embarrassing, too confessional. We are no longer poor, and those difficult days contain harsh memories, many of which are painful to recall. Growing up poor is more dangerous now, but it was and still is, humiliating. No one forgets.

We were a fairly typical struggling middle-class family in the 1960s until we had a tragic setback. When I was eleven, my mother had a stroke that almost killed her. She survived, but she was not the same; she lost much of her eyesight, which affected her ability to drive, to sew, and to read—all crucial needs for the mom of her time and her intelligence. Tragically, she also developed epilepsy, had seizures in public, and became a prisoner of her disabilities and of depression. On the other side was my dad; he had hospital bills that overwhelmed his meager state employee's salary. We would have been members of the "working poor," a term that is used a lot now, if we had known what it was.

Our parents shielded my brother and me from the worst of the disasters, but even as a child, I thought that never getting new clothes and always wearing tight shoes were unfair. Friends went on back-to-school shopping trips and took music lessons. I had the best of the free world for any child—my imagination and a library card. Our family also had a rabbit-ears television set that got one channel which, thankfully, played old movies on the weekends. Humphrey Bogart and Katherine Hepburn fit well in my world.

Unlike many disadvantaged people then and now, we had the stability of one home. We lived there for many decades, though Mama and Daddy could not afford to buy the home until I was grown. While renting, we saw the house deteriorate with neglect. We could see the ground under the tub while sitting on the commode. This gaping hole was, no doubt, part of the source of the rats that invaded us. One of my scariest teenage memories involves my mother beating huge field rats to death with a broom while they ran over her feet and I screamed.

Those who have never known poverty politely quake at these stories, and those who know the experience tend to romanticize it, saying (among other blather) that love triumphs over the pain. Those of us who have been through it and have come out the other side know that poverty is not particularly noble and that the church ladies who hugged us and bought gifts embarrassed us. As an adult, I can appreciate the kind church ladies and have filled their shoes a few times, but as a child, I wished that they had left the gifts on the front steps and walked away, quickly.

Friends who do not understand poverty are amazed that my gregarious, successful family sometimes went without food and slept on mattresses on the floor. I try not to sugarcoat or overdramatize the experience, but I never know what to say to expiate their guilt or cover up my small sense of shame at confessing my past. Once in a while, I tell my story to students to connect with our lessons, especially when teaching literature, and I see heads nod quietly. Poverty is too familiar. My wish is that students see that people like them can make it out, without any extraordinary talent and with dignity. But maybe I just need to tell the story.

Sample Essay: Narration/Description

Victoria Pagan, Student

Loch Ness

Three summers ago, my family and I took a vacation to Scotland. My favorite place that we visited was the famous village of Loch Ness. In Scotland, they have words that mean the same as other, more American words. For example, "law" is another word for "hill," and "loch" is another word for "lake." All of the scenery in Scotland was beautiful, but nothing could compare to this legendary sight. We spent an entire day driving around the village and visiting important places there. It was a breathtaking experience.

During our first few days in Scotland, my family and I decided that we wanted to visit the sight of the infamous Loch Ness monster. It was so much more than I had imagined; I never thought of Loch Ness being such a beautiful place. The drive there was just as exciting as the museum and castle we visited. It was a fifty-seven-mile drive north that took about two hours. We woke up at 7:00 that morning and headed north. We were staying in a city called Dundee that is known for its rolling hills and rainy days. As we drove through the countryside, we stopped seeing the urban homes and found more that were styled like cottages. The hills slowly turned into mountains and the rain changed to a light mist. The temperature was dropping as we traveled north.

When we got into the village, we stopped to eat the array of different sandwiches that we got from a little coffee shop on the way, and it was cooler outside the car than I had expected. We also stopped halfway up to where the castle and museum were; I could smell the damp air and the loch was surrounded by lush green hills. Recent rain had caused a light mist to roll over the surface of the loch. It was a beautiful sight that I could have looked at for hours. We continued to the small museum that they had, which was focused on the legends surrounding the Loch Ness monster and the history of the castle. As we approached our destination, we could see from the road that the castle was mostly in ruins.

The museum staff showed us a short documentary on the castle. As the film finished, they drew back a thick red curtain, revealing the most amazing view. What was left of the castle was located on the side of a rocky cliff that overlooked the loch. I first noticed the towers of the castle that were still standing. They were surrounded by what used to be great walls, now reduced to rubble. The walls only stood about two feet high, but I could see where separate rooms were still visible. As I looked to the end of the castle, I noticed that one of the towers was stable enough for people to go into and it had an open space at the top. From about fifty feet in the air, I could see the length of the entire loch. Because we went in the morning, the sun was just past the peak of the hills and was casting light on the water. It looked like a scene from a romantic movie.

All of the scenery from my family's trip to Scotland was beautiful, but nothing compared to the misty hills of Loch Ness. Even the long drive didn't make seeing the change of the landscape any less exciting. The view overlooking the loch from the top of a tower was breathtaking. I would love to go back someday, but it is not a trip that I will forget any time soon.

Sample Essay: Narration

Naylet Bustos, Student

I Am Not Ashamed

No matter how much people smile or how happy they may seem in public, we will never know what they go through behind the closed doors of their home. Taking a step back and looking at my own experiences, I realize that this statement also applies to my life. I was born in Grenada, Mississippi. Thanks to this fact, I am a United States citizen and do not have to fear or worry about being deported, but I remain concerned over my parents being deported because they were not born in Ameria. Growing up with immigrant parents helped me become the mature young woman I am today.

Coming to the United States was not for vacation or for pleasure; my parents came to the United States illegally to give birth to me. They knew if I were born in America, I would have more opportunities and a better future. After living in America for two years, my parents decided to move back to Mexico. Living in Mississippi was foreign to them, and not knowing anyone made them feel like Mississippi was not the right place for them. As a result, we got on an airplane and headed back to Mexico. A year later, they discovered that once again they were expecting. They wanted to give their unborn child the same opportunities I had, so they decided to cross the border once more when I was a toddler.

Most people may not have memories from the time they were three years old or from their childhood. When I look back at my memories, nothing is more vivid than the time my parents and I crossed the border from Mexico to the United States. It was a cool, early morning. The grass was moist from the dew and my eyes were blinded from the rising sun. My parents and I were lying flat on our stomachs in a ditch as we waited for my uncle to pick us up.

Living in an unfamiliar country brought many difficulties as well as opportunities. My parents did not speak English and therefore communicated with others through hand gestures. When I was old enough to go to school, they enrolled me into Head Start for four-year-olds. They wanted me to learn how to speak English so that I would not have to go through the struggles they did. At the age of four, I became their personal interpreter. I translated anything from the total balance at the grocery store to what the doctor said during appointments. As I got older, my responsibilities grew. When my brother was born, I helped my mom take care of him when she and my dad were at work.

After the day at school, I would make us snacks and help him with his homework while my parents were at work. My parents could not even attend most of our school events because they worked endless shifts. They worked five to six days a week so that my brother and I would have everything we needed and wanted. My parents spoiled us; we had the best clothes and the latest technology. I never realized the pain they went through or the motivation behind their hard work until we were separated for the first time.

My parents were forced to move in with my aunt in 2010. I was devastated when they left. I saw my parents only once a week because they moved closer to their job nearly forty-five minutes away. The long drive put them at risk of going through numerous roadblocks that the police were having in an attempt to deport all illegal immigrants. Without a license, they could have been taken to jail and deported. During this time, I grew, matured, and realized that my life could change in the matter of minutes.

At the young age of fourteen I learned how to hide pain and fear of losing my parents behind a smile. I am thankful for the struggles I have faced. I am blessed to have parents that put our well being before their own lives. I have immigrant parents, and I am not ashamed.

Sample Essay: Narration

Victoria Mulqueen, Student

What Isn't Killing Me

I am well aware that people all over the world suffer from various diseases, illnesses, and complications every single day. Some are dying from their diseases, hoping for a cure that will eliminate their death sentence. Others have to take medication to treat their symptoms or block the illness completely. However, the gastrointestinal ailments I have, gastritis and IBS, cannot be blocked. No cure for IBS exists; it is a widespread disease that affects the bowels of its host, and medicine can only treat the symptoms. Although the illnesses I have aren't deadly, I have struggled daily to endure the symptoms of my stomach conditions since my diagnosis.

I was first diagnosed with gastritis, Irritable Bowel Syndrome (IBS), and a mild case of lactose-intolerance in 2012. The news about being lactose intolerant did not affect me as much as the IBS because I was lactose intolerant in infancy and had never gotten over my sensitivity to the particular sugar found in dairy. However, I was concerned about the gastritis and IBS. Both irritate my gastrointestinal tract, and their symptoms strike fear in me when the IBS decides to flare.

The absolute worst case of these flare ups occurred about two years after my diagnosis. My family and I were in Sumrall, Mississippi, visiting my grandparents. For nine hours straight, my body was completely rejecting my dinner, trying to expel all sustenance out of my system in any way possible. Unfortunately for me, that meant vomiting profusely into the bathtub while sitting on the toilet and praying for the double-ended nightmare to be over. The next day, my parents took me to the Emergency Room so various medical staff could pump me full of fluids. That was my fourth trip and worst to the Emergency Room after my diagnosis.

Although the physical aspects of this sickness are quite gruesome, I would rather endure them than the mental toll they have taken on me. I am terrified to eat when my stomach feels anything other than normal.

As a result, I often confuse hunger pains with gastritis pains and think that if I eat anything, I will be sent to the hospital again. I fear that if I eat even one bite before I am scheduled to be with my friends, I will have another IBS episode and will have to disappear from them and run to the bathroom for extended periods of time.

Some doctors believe that certain symptoms attributed to my IBS are caused by anxiety for various reasons. My mother believes this as well, and I don't disagree. I wish there were an explanation as to what causes these flares. If the diagnosis were anxiety, I would welcome that because I can take medication to treat it, but no daily medication for my stomach conditions exists. The only relief I have occurs when I go to the doctor and am given shots for the nausea and sporadic headaches. The prescribed medicines offer no relief because by the time I need them, my body has already started to wage a war on itself. The only solace I find for the mental effects is praying to God. I know that my suffering has a purpose, even if I am blind to it.

By the grace of God alone, I have not yet given up. I have seen worse suffering in others, but I will conquer my own illness. IBS affects a countless number of individuals all over the planet, and, I am sure, like myself, they are hoping for a cure. My gastritis and IBS may inhibit me at times, but I won't let them affect me as greatly as they have in the past. I will continue to endure and to pray until I no longer am scared of my own body and of my own mind.

Chapter 9

Comparison and Contrast Essay

Comparing and contrasting items is a natural activity that people use to make choices and ultimately to make sense of their world. We conduct daily business based on choices; those choices often revolve around judgments we have made through comparing or contrasting two or more items.

You may have contrasted two items this morning when you got dressed: "Should I wear the white shirt with the black stripes or the solid blue shirt?" You may have contrasted two choices when you decided what to eat for lunch: "Should I eat a sandwich at home or a hamburger from McDonald's?"

You probably even chose your college based on two or more choices. Perhaps you contrasted community college with a university. Perhaps you contrasted Holmes Community College versus Hinds Community College or Northeast Mississippi Community College versus Itawamba Community College.

The point is that you are already familiar with the concepts that this chapter will expound upon. That's good news. Now all you need to work on is refining your skill in comparison/contrast. Don't get too complacent. Understand that comparison/contrast is one of the most important rhetorical modes you will learn in freshman composition because it will help you in your entire college career (and far beyond).

Comparison/contrast is so important because its format encourages the writer to use critical thinking skills. When you match one item against another, you are analyzing information. When you write your judgments based on that analysis, you are synthesizing information. The concepts of "analysis" and "synthesis" are important to educators. Analysis and synthesis are the highest levels of thinking and writing that you will conduct. When you correctly analyze and synthesize, you are indeed performing at a college level.

So how will you analyze and synthesize later in your college career? Whether it is comparing or contrasting major authors of American literature, major periods in history, foreign policy in developing countries, artistic movements, or theories of mathematics, comparison/contrast helps students make sense of information by enabling them to draw parallels, make connections, and eventually evaluate subjects using relevant criteria or points.

Remember that the reason you are taking freshman composition is so that you will be able to write appropriately whenever you are asked to do so in other college courses, in work situations, and in life choices. Thus, it's up to you to remember to use the comparison/contrast format when necessary.

The history teacher may not tell you ahead of time that s/he expects you to use a certain format when answering a comparison/contrast question; however, that teacher certainly expects your information to be organized well.

Additionally, literature teachers know that students who make the highest grades on discussion tests are those who remember how to format information based often on comparison and contrast guidelines. The other modes that include giving examples—division and classification, and definition—are often necessary, as well.

Definition

Many people use the word "comparison" to mean both "similarity" and "difference." Of course, we know "comparison" means "similarity," but it also often implies "difference." When you write a comparison/contrast essay, however, you should make it clear to your reader whether you intend to discuss just similarities or just differences or both. Therefore, you may want to use the word "contrast" to discuss differences.

In some cases, English teachers want you to discuss only similarities OR differences, not both, in your assigned essay. Good advice in general is to pay close attention to the topic's wording if the teacher assigns topics. If the topic says to compare OR contrast items, clearly the teacher wants you to decide whether to discuss similarities OR differences. If the topic says to compare AND contrast, clearly the teacher wants you to discuss both. If you are unsure how your teacher wants you to write the comparison/contrast essay, be sure to ask for clarification.

Generally, it is tough to discuss more than two items in a comparison/contrast essay, especially in a freshman composition class. Therefore, you want to limit the items you wish to discuss to two.

Types of Comparison and Contrast

Planning and prewriting are even more essential when you are writing this type of essay because you have to classify the categories you are using to compare/contrast the two subjects. To help them figure out what to say about their two subjects, some writers find it useful to create a Venn diagram about the two items. Filling in the circles with details about your subjects can help you determine whether the two subjects have a lot of similarities (everything listed in the intersection of the two circles) or differences (everything listed in the outer circles). The list of characteristics can also help you decide what points to make about each subject.

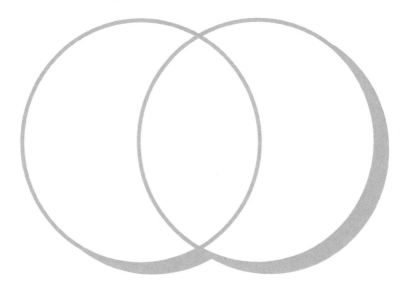

Once you have chosen the subjects you want to compare and have classified the points you want to make, you must decide on which structure to use to organize what you want to say about them. The two types of comparison/contrast structures are **subject-by-subject** and **point-by-point**.

CHARACTERISTICS IN SUBJECT-BY-SUBJECT FORMAT

If you use the subject-by-subject format, you will develop the body of the paper by organizing all the details and information around the two items. If your essay is about the differences between your two best friends, the topics of your body paragraphs will be your two best friends. In other words, you would describe all the points you wanted to make about Friend #1 before moving on to describe the points about Friend #2.

CHARACTERISTICS IN POINT-BY-POINT FORMAT

On the other hand, if you use the point-by-point format, you will organize all information around the characteristics of the items being compared and contrasted. For example, in your essay about the differences in your two best friends, your body paragraphs will discuss the three or four ways in which your two friends are different. See the sample outlines that follow.

Formulating a Thesis

It's vital in the comparison/contrast essay to give a **detailed thesis**. Whether you use the subject-by-subject format or the point-by-point format, your thesis will need to include the two items you will compare or contrast and whether you will focus on similarities or differences. You may want to name your body paragraph topics as well. However, it is not a requirement that you do so.

Lastly, an important part of the thesis is the **judgment**—why you are comparing or contrasting the two items. It is in fact the purpose of writing your paper. You should think about the overall message of your essay.

- What is it in particular that you wish to say about your subjects?
- What larger meaning can be derived from your discussion of the two subjects?
- What is the purpose of making your comparison or contrast?

You may want to discuss the judgment briefly in the thesis, but it is possible to postpone discussion of the judgment until the conclusion. Or you may state the judgment in the thesis and elaborate on it in the discussion.

Read the sample thesis sentences listed below:

- Mississippi State University differs from the University of Southern Mississippi in campus life, student body, and size; however, I enjoyed my educational experiences at both colleges.

- Even though New York seems quite different from Mississippi, my New York cousin and I are alike in our hobbies, our sense of humor, and our work ethic.

- Situational comedies are more entertaining than reality television shows.

- The changes from the Obama administration to the Trump administration have been drastic.

Writing an Outline

Once you have written a thesis, you should decide what type of **organizational structure** you want to use in the essay. In the subject-by-subject format, you will discuss your two items as separate entities. Therefore, you must be careful to point out to the reader how the two items match up against each other.

In the point-by-point format, the structure automatically forces you to match up the items side-by-side. Also, this type of format encourages you to give a lot of supporting details to prove your points. Each point is a different characteristic or category that you use to compare/contrast your two subjects.

Order: In the sample outlines that follow, notice the importance of order. Be consistent in discussing the details in the same order in each body paragraph. Organizing your details in a parallel order will help your reader follow your line of thought. Discussing the details in a haphazard order confuses your reader.

SAMPLE ORGANIZATION PLAN: SUBJECT-BY-SUBJECT

Thesis: Though Grandmother Viola and Grandmother Cordelia do not look alike, in their relationships with their grandchild, their socioeconomic backgrounds, and their talents, both are wonderful grandmothers.

- Grandmother Viola
  - Physical appearance
  - Relationship with grandchild
  - Socioeconomic background
  - Talent
- Grandmother Cordelia
  - Physical appearance
  - Relationship with grandchild
  - Socioeconomic background
  - Talent

SAMPLE ORGANIZATION PLAN: POINT-BY-POINT

Thesis: Grandmother Viola and Grandmother Cordelia are different in their physical appearances, their relationships with their grandchild, their socioeconomic backgrounds, and their talents; they both are wonderful grandmothers.

- Physical Appearance
  - Grandmother Viola
  - Grandmother Cordelia
- Relationship with Grandchild
  - Grandmother Viola
  - Grandmother Cordelia
- Socioeconomic Background
  - Grandmother Viola
  - Grandmother Cordelia
- Talent
  - Grandmother Viola
  - Grandmother Cordelia

Transitions

Transition words are important in every type of essay, but if possible, they are even more important in the comparison/contrast essay. In this type of essay, you should use transitions to help match up items so the reader clearly understands that you are describing how they are the same or how they are different. Common comparison/contrast transitions are listed in the box below:

TRANSITION WORDS— FOR COMPARISON	TRANSITION WORDS— FOR CONTRAST	
also	otherwise	yet
likewise	on the other hand	even so
similarly	in contrast	on the contrary
in the same way	conversely	however
in addition		although
by the same token		

In the subject-by-subject format, you should use comparison/contrast transitions in the **second body paragraph** to show the reader how the second item matches up to the first item. Using these transitions will alleviate the problem of the essay having the appearance of two separate topics that don't belong together.

In the point-by-point format, you should use comparison/contrast transitions in the **second half** of each body paragraph. Again, using these transitions will help you prove to the reader that the two items indeed are alike or different. In other words, the transitions will help your readers make sense of all of the details you have provided for them.

Referencing. You use these types of transitions only when you discuss the second item; therefore, you are referring back to the first item. You can refer back to an item only after you have discussed it previously. For example, if you were writing the essay about Grandmother Viola and Grandmother Cordelia, in the latter part of body paragraph two, you might say, "Grandmother Cordelia, *unlike* Grandmother Viola, is short and stocky." You can refer back to Grandmother Viola's appearance only after discussing it.

SAMPLE TOPIC OUTLINE: STRIBLING'S ESSAY

Thesis: While both the online and classroom settings offer opportunities to learn, online education falls far short of traditional classes.

I.   Changes in learning techniques
II. Control
    A. Extra responsibilities
    B. Schedule
    C. Workload
III. Organization
    A. Physical media
        1. Handouts
        2. Digital files
    B. Virtual media
        1. Handouts
        2. Digital files
IV. Relationships
    A. Student-teacher
    B. Student-peer

Notice that when you can write a topic outline, you don't write complete sentences. Normally, it's a good idea to put as much detail as possible in your outline. A detailed outline will make writing the rough draft manageable.

A great outline will also ensure that your essay is organized and well-supported.

Organization of the Comparison and Contrast Essay

The **introduction** of a comparison/contrast essay is the same as the introduction for any academic essay. You should begin with a creative statement or "**hook**," such as a quotation, a story, a question, a definition, or a shocking statement. Next, you should give some **background information**. Introduce your topic to the reader and explain why your topic is important or relevant today. Lastly, state your **thesis**.

In the **body** of the essay, follow your outline. Begin each body paragraph with a **topic sentence**. Next, address your first subheading on your outline by **providing proof**, **examples**, and **details** to explain your ideas. In your proof, be as specific as possible. List names, give brief narrative examples, or state specific places.

Remember to use comparison/contrast transitions when you are discussing the next item or items of your essay. In the subject-by-subject format, the second item will be the second body paragraph. In the point-by-point format, the second item will be in the second half of each body paragraph. As always, you should use other relevant transitions whenever necessary throughout the essay.

In the **conclusion**, again follow the usual format for concluding paragraphs in academic essays: restate your thesis, offer general closing information, and end either with a clincher, a catchy phrase that sums up your essay, or a sense of closure for the reader.

For more reminders about paragraphing and organization, see Chapter 7, Bricks and Mortar: Building the Essay.

Comparison and Contrast Topics

Most of the following topics can be varied in several ways to fit your personal opinion or experience. Use the list to help you think of ideas for your essay, and change your topic accordingly.

Do not use the wording of the topics/prompts in your paper. *This is called plagiarism.*

1. Compare or contrast two sports teams, two musical groups, or two television shows.

2. Contrast two teachers, two role models, two preachers, two coaches, two parents, etc. Stick to people you know—not celebrities!

3. Compare or contrast two good friends. Do not emphasize the obvious by writing endlessly superfluous external details like hair color.

4. Compare or contrast two video games or two gaming consoles.

5. Compare and contrast the pit bull dog with another canine.

6. Compare and contrast the influence of the Mississippi Delta Blues and New Orleans Jazz on modern rock 'n' roll.

7. Compare or contrast the PC and the Mac or a Kindle and a Nook.

8. Compare or contrast two towns or cities with which you are familiar.

9. Compare and contrast two communities or neighborhoods where you have lived.

10. Compare and contrast then and now—music, manners, raising children, farming, sports.

11. Compare and contrast your church at two different services.

12. Compare and contrast two family members' attitudes about grades.

13. Compare and contrast two facets of working at day care—the children's eating habits, their sicknesses, times of parents' arrivals and departures, etc.

14. Compare and contrast city and country living.

15. Compare and contrast types of e-sports.

16. Compare and contrast two types of art—painting, ceramics, photography, etc.

Checklist: Group Editing Criteria for Comparison and Contrast Essays

Check each box to indicate that you have worked with that particular area of the paper.

CONTENT: THESIS AND FIRST PARAGRAPH

☐ No use of "similar but different" in thesis.

☐ Thesis contains the main idea and purpose of the paper.

☐ First paragraph draws the readers' interest to the paper.

CONTENT: PARAGRAPHS

☐ All points and paragraphs relate to thesis.

☐ Topic sentences introduce each paragraph's content.

☐ Good transition between paragraphs/subjects.

☐ Content is unified.

☐ Good details and examples are included.

☐ Comparisons and contrasts are clear.

MECHANICS

☐ Mechanics of paper are correct: paragraphs, margins, spacing, MLA form, and title.

GRAMMAR

☐ Commas are ok.

☐ There are no big sentence errors.

☐ Good work with punctuation.

_____ Proofreader

_____ Paper's Author

Note to the proofreader:

- Do not rewrite the paper.
- Do not fix the writer's problems.
- Communicate with the writer. Mark problem spots and explain them.

Sample Essay: Comparison and Contrast

William Stribling, Student

Paper v. Technology

With the rise of new technologies, the ways in which students and educators teach and learn have changed significantly over the past decade. Chalkboards have been replaced by smartboards, assignments are completed and submitted online, and even public high schools have started issuing computers to every student in order to utilize online tools. In college, not only are online classes offered for nearly every subject, but thousands of online degrees are available for those who want to continue their education outside of the traditional college setting. While both the online and classroom settings offer opportunities to learn, online education falls far short of traditional classes.

Online classes certainly have advantages. One of their largest selling points is the flexible schedule they allow for students. Since the life of a college student is a hectic one, any extra control is almost always welcome. With an online class, students have extra control in regards to completing assignments and proctored exams. This can allow them to keep a job or to join extracurricular activities, and they may have been impossible before. On the other hand, the consistent schedule found in the classroom makes it easier to keep that workload from becoming overwhelming. It's easy to procrastinate online assignments and end up in a situation where students have a mountain of work that is nearly impossible to get over. For example, a friend of mine took a Programming II lab online and with five weeks left in the course, he realized he'd fallen behind on over 21 hours of homework assignments. He then had to work endlessly for days on end in order to catch up on work that should have already been done. With extra control inherent in online classes, extra responsibility comes along. It's up to the students to determine whether he or she can manage the load.

Another way these two settings provide distinct contrast is through the organizational skills required of the student. I am inherently an unorganized person, which can make keeping up with all the physical items for a class a little overwhelming at times. Handouts can be lost, textbooks can be misplaced, and any number of deadlines can be lost in the shuffle. Online classes remove this stress through materials being located online. It is much more difficult to lose a digital file because another another copy can be quickly downloaded. This has brought the classroom into the 21st century and removes unnecessary stress from the shoulders of students. That being said, digital media will never be able to match the benefits of physical materials. As annoying as it may be to keep track of so many papers at times, taking actual notes in a classroom is the best way for most students to maintain what they are taught. The ways in which students interact with the material they're learning is where the differences occur in both of these settings.

Finally, online courses and the classroom offer different experiences in regards to student and teacher relationships. The online class does provide a safe, stress-free environment for students who have problems with being called on in class or interacting with other students. On the other hand, college is just as much as about giving students the skill set to function in the real world as learning the information found in textbooks. Being present in the classroom will force a person to take on those problems. In addition, the relationships that students have with their professors change depending on the setting. While students can still receive video lectures and can email their professors with any questions, there is still immense value found in face-to-face interaction. My most treasured college experiences so far have not only come from what my professors have taught me in class but the wisdom they've shared outside of the classroom and the bonds that have formed from those interactions.

Sample Essay: Comparison and Contrast with Sources

Nathan House, Student

Socialistic and Capitalistic Forms of Government

In our modern age, many forms of government and economic systems are on display in the world at large. In many cases these systems are in direct competition with one another in the world market to gain the top monetary standing. Among these economic systems, two types stand prominently for consideration: socialism and capitalism. These systems are incorporated into the top economic nations and social societies of our time, and both present challenges.

Socialism, according to *Britannica*, is defined as a "social and economic doctrine that calls for public rather than private ownership or control of property and natural resources" (Ball). Socialistic forms of government are based on theoretical utopia originating in the late 19th century with the main goal of becoming more like communism. Socialism was the philosophical invention of Karl Marx and Friedrich Engels, who were the main proponents of social and economic reform of the time. Developed to change social order and bring economic equality, socialism claimed that all live in community and are, therefore, fundamentally dependent on one another. When all people in a community work on an individual product, that product becomes the property of all people who were involved in its production. In extreme forms of socialism, the only possession that an individual is allowed the "privilege" of owning is his or her own personal clothing. Therefore, the social control of property and ownership of goods insures the equal distribution of resources to all people but leaves little incentive for personal achievement or development. Socialism is considered by many to be a more noble form of social economics, and in a perfect world devoid of human emotions and shortcomings, socialism would be an ideal form of government.

Regrettably, every time socialism has been enacted, by force or otherwise, it has failed. Many supporters of socialism do not recognize its intended purpose of an eventual shift to communism, upholding the idea that it can be a stand-alone form of government. Socialists refuse to see the very simple reasons that this form of government is doomed to failure. For instance, certain people will always abuse the system for personal gain, resulting in a net loss of product or resources. Greed, selfishness, impatience, and laziness are fundamentally present in the human condition and impede the socialistic system in a diversity of ways. A potentially dangerous issue occurs when all resources and products are placed in a centralized location creating the need for an organization of individuals or singular representative to be placed in charge of its distribution. Eventually, that organization or representative will acquire enough power to subjugate the "commoners," leading to a breakdown of socialism into totalitarianism.

Capitalism, or free market economy, is defined by Britannica as an "economic system . . . in which most of the means of production are privately owned and production is guided and income distributed largely through the operation of markets" ("Capitalism"). Capitalism developed naturally over thousands of years by the transfer of goods for goods or services rendered, but the rapid growth and development of the free market economy started in the 16th century. People living in capitalistic communities are dependent upon each other for the continued progress of the system, but unlike socialism, ownership of property and products begin in the hands of an individual or corporation and is dispersed based on individual desires. Most forms of modern capitalism have essences of socialistic ideas, but this is counterproductive. Capitalistic societies are responsible for more advances in technology, higher average median wealth, lessening of gross poverty, and better social equalization than all other societies combined. Capitalism, though flawed, is a working model of economic and social principles, and the free market system is extremely robust and capable of enormous leaps in prosperity for individuals who excel. Capitalism is the normal flow of work for profit: do the work well and get the reward. Abusing the system is difficult to do. Traits such as honesty, integrity and hard work often garner very beneficial results, while greed, dishonesty and laziness are shunned and often punished. However, income gaps can become very wide, which often leads those less advantaged to believe they are second class citizens. Even worse, the wealthy can become so powerful that they may use their influence to control members of government to facilitate the unethical use of legislation to their benefit.

Socialism and capitalism are fundamentally different in their applications. Capitalism is the natural order of events that follow from individuals exercising their right to barter and behave in a free society, while socialism seeks to control this order and force an outcome that is desirable to one group or individual. No form of government is perfect, and capitalism, when corrupted, can become just as despotic as socialism. However, while capitalism encourages individuals to produce, socialism leads to the eventual collapse of work ethic. Mankind is predisposed to selfishly seek out his own gratification and success, even at the expense of others. Because of this, socialistic forms of government are at a distinct disadvantage to capitalistic governments because of the inherent human element. When all people receive the same amount of reward, regardless of the amount of effort put forth, they lose the motivation for achievement and self-improvement. This lack of motivation eventually leads to the breakdown of socialistic systems into either totalitarian or capitalistic societies.

Works Cited

Ball, Terence; Dagger, Richard. "Socialism." *Encyclopedia Britannica,* www.britannica.com/topic/socialism. Accessed 24 Oct. 2016.

"Capitalism." *Encyclopedia Britannica,* www.britannica.com/topic/capitalism. Accessed 24 Oct. 2016.

"Property." *Encyclopedia Britannica,* www.britannica.com/topic/property. Accessed 24 Oct. 2016.

Chapter 10

Cause and Effect Essay

Understanding Cause and Effect

It is human nature to ask questions. We always want to know why an event occurred. As children, we ask questions such as "Why is the sky blue?" or "Why do birds fly?" Then, as adults, we are faced with questions such as "Why did you choose that career?" or "Why have you chosen to marry your spouse?"

All of the questions that we ask point to one phenomenal fact: Our lives and the world around us are made up of a series of causes and effects.

Cause and effect writing, otherwise known as causal analysis, is the attempt to understand how certain events connect to create an outcome or several outcomes. Often several different causes can create a specific effect, and those same causes can also create different effects.

A successful cause and effect writing explores the past, present, and future in an attempt to gain answers to questions that we as humans continue to ask.

Getting beneath the Surface

In a cause and effect analysis, a writer must know the difference between causes and effects and may use brainstorming as a way to dissect the question that needs to be answered. We can think of causes as reasons why an event occurred. Effects are simply the consequences or results of something that happened.

> Since the writer of the essay at the end of this chapter is a female, the pronouns used to describe her journey and her writing will be "she and "her."

For example, an incoming student may be asked why she decided to attend a particular college. The decision to attend that college is the effect for which the questioner wants to know the causes. She may have chosen to go to that college because of the school's excellent reputation, because of scholarship inducement, or because of a specific program that the college offers. These causes are all based on the school itself, but there may be other personal considerations that have factored into that student's decision. The school may be close to her home, her friends may be attending that school, or her parents may be forcing her to go there. By brainstorming all of these options, an author can write an essay that does more than just scratch the surface of why this student made this huge life decision about college.

All Causes Are Not Equal

Once an author has finished brainstorming, s/he can begin to place the causes identified into categories. One way to sort the causes is by designating them as either **main causes** or **contributory causes**. **Main causes** are the most important factors that have created the effect, and **contributory causes**, although still important, are just not as important as main causes.

If the author writing about her school choice decided to designate the causes of her choice this way, she may note in the paper that the contributory causes of her choice were the school's proximity to her parents and the scholarships offered by the school. The author could then identify her main cause as the school's highly rated nursing program. Classifying contributory and main causes allows the author to guide the reader through her decision-making process.

Although distinguishing between contributory and main causes can be an effective tool when writing a cause and effect essay, some topics require the author to examine **immediate** and **remote causes** to explain an effect. An **immediate cause** occurs closely in time and space to the effect; therefore, these causes are easy to identify. **Remote causes**, on the other hand, happened in the past and, as a result, are difficult to associate with the effect, even though they do connect.

For example, the student who wants to attend her school of choice because of the nursing program might explain her desire to be a nurse by explaining how she loves helping people and how she has recently begun fostering this love by volunteering in an assisted-living community. She might also emphasize how she recently took human anatomy and physiology in high school and thoroughly enjoyed learning about the different functions of the body.

Both of these causes are immediate because they have occurred recently in her life. Although these causes are important, they are both connected to her experiences as a child when she had to help her mother take care of her ailing grandmother. This remote cause has created in her a desire to volunteer, to excel in her classes, and ultimately to become a nurse. Making these distinctions between causes can help a reader to see the big picture of how all of the events tie together.

Traveling the Causal Chain

Just as making a distinction between various types of causes is an effective way to structure a cause and effect essay, creating a causal chain is an effective way to showcase how causes and effects can relate and interchange. In a causal chain, the cause produces an effect. This effect results in a subsequent cause, which produces another effect. This sequence continues on down the chain.

If a student wants to identify why he made an A on a test that most of his other classmates barely passed with a C, he might use the causal chain to track his road to an A. When signing up for his human anatomy and physiology class, he specifically chose the 9:00 a.m. time slot so that he would not be late for class and because he could work at his job later in the day and not miss his class. As a result of this time choice, he was always on time to class and always in attendance. Because of his excellent attendance, he never missed the notes and always heard the lecture. Therefore, when he began to study for the test, he had already learned a large portion of the information, so he had only to review some points that he was either unsure about or had forgotten. Since he had made good choices about his schedule and worked hard in class, he was able to make an A on the test easily.

The following chart is a depiction of the same causal chain of events, with the effect becoming the cause in the next link of the chain.

9:00 a.m. class

    (cause) → on time and never absent

      [effect] ↓

    (cause) → complete notes

      [effect] ↓

    (cause) → only review needed

      [effect] ↓

    (cause) → A on test

By using a causal chain, the author can guide his reader through the events of his chain logically and can easily organize the essay by following the chain and placing the separate events into distinct body paragraphs.

The *Post Hoc* Pitfall

During the brainstorming process, it is important that an author realizes when she or he is falling into the *post hoc* fallacy. *Post hoc* reasoning occurs when a person assumes that just because A preceded B, then A must have caused B.

Superstitions are classic examples of *post hoc* reasoning leading to illogical thinking. For example, if the student writing the above causal chain assumed that he made an A on the test because he wore a particular shirt on test day, then he is not taking into account his hours of preparation attending class and studying his notes. Instead of putting emphasis on the true causes for his high test grade, he would have identified an incorrect immediate cause that did not relate at all to his grade.

Starting a Cause and Effect Essay

As you begin the essay, you must let your reader know that you are writing this essay for a specific purpose. No reader wants to think that you are just listing causes and effects. If you are writing an essay about why you have chosen a particular career such as nursing, you do not want just to list the reasons why. Instead, you want to explain how these reasons have been shaped by your life. You want to make a real connection with your readers.

The thesis statement is the most effective place to make this connection with your reader. In your thesis, you should identify your topic, whether your focus is on causes, effects, or both; you should also concentrate on your purpose for writing the essay. Draw your reader in with this information so that the body of your paper is easy to follow.

Example with Cause as the Focus ·
Working as a ward clerk for two years motivated me to become a pediatric nurse.

Example with Effect as the Focus ·
My hours of observation in the pediatric ward inspired me to study harder in my phlebotomy classes.

Example with Cause and Effect ·
Working twelve-hour shifts in the emergency room forced me to budget my time more wisely.

Structuring an Effective Essay

Once you have brainstormed about the various causes and effects and then categorized those causes as contributory and main or immediate and remote, you must now put the essay in an effective order for the reader.

In an essay about contributory and main causes of an event, the final body paragraphs should always be focused on the main causes, and the preceding paragraphs should be focused on the contributory causes. This structure allows the causes to build upon each other.

The same effect is needed when an author focuses an essay on immediate and remote causes. Put the remote cause in the final body paragraph so that the reader can identify how the immediate causes are related to the historically relevant remote cause. Your job as an author is to explain an effect and all its causes fully to the reader. These structures will give the reader a strong foundation to follow.

Creating a Detailed Outline

Consider using the pattern of providing *a claim, pieces of evidence,* and *interpretation of that evidence* in your body paragraphs. The following sample outline develops each body paragraph by giving two sets of *claim, evidence, interpretation* as a discussion of each topic sentence. Decide the level of detail that you wish to give your reader when outlining your essay. Some topics would need to be developed more (and therefore include more sets of *claim, evidence, interpretation*) than other topics.

Thesis: Working as a ward clerk for two years motivated me to become a pediatric nurse.

I. Cause One: One reason being a ward clerk helped me find my career is I discovered that I handle hospital paperwork efficiently.

   A. Claim—I quickly learned how to pay attention to detail in completing the paperwork.

   B. Evidence—The other clerks who worked during my shifts often asked me to help them fill out the paperwork for certain procedures. I was glad to help and was pleasantly surprised to learn that I had mastered the forms.

   C. Interpretation—Helping my peers gave me confidence to seek out even more duties to perform in my position. Therefore, I took on additional paperwork that only a few clerks felt skilled enough to complete.

   D. Claim—In addition to being noticed by my peers, my efficiency at paperwork was noticed by my supervisors as well.

   E. Evidence—One afternoon a nurse with whom I worked needed paperwork for an emergency situation. Normally, the nurses check over the paperwork, but in this instance, the nurse simply grabbed the papers and sped off to the patient's room.

   F. Interpretation—It was at this point that I realized how meticulously I had been preparing paperwork. I didn't know that my supervisors had noticed my work, but this example proved to me that my hard work had been appreciated. Also, this example made me begin to wonder if I could one day work in a higher level position at the hospital.

II. Cause Two: Another reason the job as ward clerk helped me along my career path is I realized that I manage nurses' schedules well.

   A. Claim—Not only did I enjoy completing procedural forms, but also I liked scheduling the work of the nurses on my shift.

   B. Evidence—One nurse in particular—Miranda Jones—asked me to be in charge of her schedule for every shift that we shared. I readily agreed, and I ended up working solely for her by the end of my term as clerk.

   C. Interpretation—Because of the specifics that I learned while scheduling Nurse Jones' day, I saw the hands-on work that she performed. The more duties that I saw her perform, the more I became enamored with the nursing profession.

   D. Claim—When emergencies caused the nurses' schedules to change, I oversaw the changes.

   E. Evidence—During the first emergency that occurred when I was managing Nurse Jones' schedule, I helped the other clerks rework the patients' procedures planned for that day. Furthermore, I communicated with the lab to reschedule the blood work necessary for upcoming patients' visits.

F.   Interpretation—By getting to know the particulars of various departments in the hospital, I saw the bigger picture of the ward where I worked.

III. Cause Three: The main reason that I pursued the job of pediatric nurse is that I love caring for infants and children.

    A.   Claim—My favorite duties as a medical clerk included assisting patients.

    B.   Evidence—When I had the chance to work in the maternity unit, I assisted the mothers before and after their labor. Also, I assisted the nurses in their caring for the infants. Once I had to monitor several infants in the newborn baby room while the nurses were in a meeting. At first I was terrified, but after I changed a couple of diapers, I came to realize that I was a natural caring for the infants.

    C.   Interpretation—My instincts relating to nurturing babies showed me that pediatric care would be a good fit for me.

    D.   Claim—The opportunities I had to interact with children in the hospital showed me that I can make them feel safe and calm during their hospital visits.

    E.   Evidence—During a late night shift, I walked into the room of an eight-year-old boy. He reminded me so much of my little brother that I was overcome with emotion. Yet I managed to take his vital signs without his even knowing I was doing so. I talked to him about video games, school, and friends, and before I left the room, he asked when I would return. I made a special point to go back and read him a story later in my shift.

    F.   Interpretation—The moments I spent with the babies and the children I encountered made it clear to me that I was destined to be a pediatric nurse.

Writing the Essay

INTRODUCTION

In writing the introduction, consider the definition of the word "introduction." The purpose of your introductory paragraph is to introduce the essay to your reader. In order to do so, you should begin creatively so that the reader will be engaged. Next, you should tell the reader what your topic is and why it's an important topic. In addition, you may want to give the reader a brief history or background relating to your topic. Last of all, end the introduction with your main idea—your thesis.

- Give a creative start (attention-getter).
- State the topic and give necessary history or background on the topic.
- State your thesis.

BODY PARAGRAPHS

If you have written an extended outline as shown previously, you have a detailed guide in writing your body paragraphs. Therefore, simply follow your outline and develop your ideas wherever possible.

Furthermore, add transitions and other forms of connections to help each body paragraph's coherence. End each body paragraph with a sentence that gives closure to the paragraph and helps the reader make sense of the details you gave in the body paragraph. The ending could include one sentence or several sentences.

CONCLUSION

The conclusion is often the inverse of your introduction. In this instance, you would begin the conclusion by restating the thesis in different wording from the introduction. Then, you would discuss general closing information relating to your topic, and you would end with a creative phrase (the opposite of the attention-getter from the introduction).

However, the conclusion paragraph is flexible in its parts. Your two goals in the conclusion are to give meaning to your topic—what the reader is to learn/believe from your essay—and to give the reader closure. Be sure the reader feels that you have concluded your discussion in a satisfactory way.

- Explain why it's important to discuss the causes/effects.
- Give closing information about the discussion.
- Optional—make a prediction or state a solution relating to the causes/effects if relevant.
- End with a clincher—a catchy phrase that sums up your essay.

Transitioning between Points

Writing an effective cause and effect essay is dependent on your reader's understanding the connection between all of your causes and/or effects. As a result, it is important that you use transitions to show the causal relationships you are presenting. You can use the following transition words to help you in your writing.

Transition Words

FOR EFFECTS:		
as a result	hence	because
thus	therefore	for this reason
consequently	as a consequence	resulting in
FOR CAUSES:		
because	caused by	root of
stem of	source of	for this reason
beginning of	for several reasons	

Equality in All Points?

The writer should not fret over splitting causes and effects into a 50/50 pattern. In many cases, the causes are more familiar or important to the writer. In others, the same principle applies to the effects. For example, smoking is a contentious but popular topic. It should certainly be significantly narrowed before attempting a short essay. Once this topic is focused, it can be the subject of an effective, passionate essay. For nonsmokers, the effects may be more prominent; for smokers, the causes may be more significant.

Thesis Example for Effects. . . . .
Smoking has so many deadly consequences that it should be banned from public places.

Thesis Example for Causes. . . . .
Growing up around cigarette smoke makes a child more likely to smoke.

No writer should forget to discuss the cause or causes when concentrating on the effects—likewise with causes as the focus. For the reader's understanding and clarity, the writer can focus either the introductory or concluding paragraphs on the other side of the coin. If the essay concentrates on causes, the concluding paragraph can effectively discuss the final point of the paper, the effects, before returning to its original point as stated in the thesis.

The writer is under no obligation, however, to give either the causes or the effects a 50/50 consideration. Equanimity of opinion is not a necessity unless the writer feels tremendously compelled.

SPECIAL NOTE: Appendix D contains more examples of cause and effect essays.

Sample Essay: Cause and Effect

Leah Spencer, Student

My Journey to Becoming a Pediatric Nurse

It could be mindless and boring. It could make me sleepy. It could make me feel unimportant. It was my summer job after high school graduation. My friends were working in clothing stores at the mall or as lifeguards at the pool, but the only job I managed to get was a desk job at a hospital. My job did not provide me with stylish clothing or a good tan; however, it did change my life. Working as a ward clerk for two years motivated me to become a pediatric nurse.

One reason being a ward clerk helped me find my career is that I discovered that I handle hospital paperwork efficiently. In the first few weeks of the job, I learned how to pay attention to details in completing the paperwork. The other clerks who worked during my shifts often asked me to help them fill out the paperwork for certain procedures. I was glad to help and was pleasantly surprised to learn that I had mastered the forms. Helping my peers gave me confidence to seek out even more duties to perform in my position. Therefore, I took on additional paperwork that only a few clerks felt skilled enough to complete. In addition to being noticed by my peers, my efficiency at paperwork was noticed by my supervisors as well. One afternoon a nurse with whom I worked needed paperwork for an emergency situation. Normally, the nurses checked over the paperwork, but in this instance, the nurse simply grabbed the papers and sped off to the patient's room. It was at this point that I realized how meticulously I had been preparing paperwork. I didn't know that my supervisors had noticed my work, but this example proved to me that my hard work had been appreciated. Also, this example made me begin to wonder if I could one day work in a higher level position at the hospital. Now that I look back on my early days as a ward clerk, I understand how the mundane task of completing paperwork started me on the path to my dream job.

Another reason the job as ward clerk helped me along my career path is that I realized that I managed nurses' schedules well. Not only did I enjoy completing procedural forms, but also I liked scheduling the work of the nurses on my shift. One nurse in particular, Miranda Jones, asked me to be in charge of her schedule for every shift that we shared. I readily agreed, and I ended up working solely for her by the end of my term as clerk. Because of the specifics that I learned while scheduling Nurse Jones' day, I saw the hands-on work that she performed. The more duties that I saw her perform, the more I became enamored with the nursing profession. When emergencies caused the nurses' schedules to change, I oversaw the changes. During the first emergency that occurred when I was managing Nurse Jones' schedule, I helped the other clerks rework the patients' procedures planned for that day. Furthermore, I communicated with the lab to reschedule the blood work necessary for upcoming patients' visits. By getting to know the particulars of various departments in the hospital, I saw the bigger picture of the ward where I worked. Having this broad vision of the department showed me that I indeed wished to pursue a career where I would work with more than one area and with various staff and patients.

The main reason that I pursued the job of pediatric nurse is that I love caring for infants and children. My favorite duties as a medical clerk included assisting patients. When I had the chance to work in the maternity unit, I assisted the mothers before and after their labor. Also, I assisted the nurses in their caring for the infants. Once I had to monitor several infants in the newborn baby room while the nurses were in a meeting. At first I was terrified, but after I changed a couple of diapers, I came to realize that I was a natural at caring for the infants. My instincts relating to nurturing babies showed me that pediatric care would be a good fit for me. Interacting with children in the hospital showed me that I could make them feel safe and calm during their hospital visits. One memorable instance stands out. During a late night shift, I walked into the room of an eight-year-old boy. He reminded me so much of my little brother that I was overcome with emotion. Yet I managed to take his vital signs without his even knowing I was doing so. I talked to him about video games, school, and friends, and before

I left the room, he asked when I would return. I made a special point to go back and read him a story later in my shift. The moments I spent with the babies and the children I encountered made it clear to me that I was destined to be a pediatric nurse.

I don't know where I would be without that job as a ward clerk. I probably would not be getting up early every morning and happily driving to the hospital to take care of people's children. I am thankful that the hospital hired me for an entry-level job that led me to my ultimate career. The journey to my dream job was worth it every step of the way.

Chapter 11

Argumentation Essay

The Internet changed education forever. Information is everywhere.

As a result, the need for report papers—informative essays and informative research papers that were the mainstay of writing classes in the past—has diminished and even disappeared.

Many teachers now prefer writing that makes a point and takes a stand. We need to see that you can take information, analyze it, and make valid recommendations and conclusions. We also want you to know how to cross-pollinate information: to take ideas from history and sociology and apply them to English. Of course, we want you to take your solid writing skills into other classes.

We want you to do all this without cheating and by basing your opinions on substantial, truthful information. Your opinion is important, but in essay writing, it is secondary to the accuracy of the facts and to truth.

College teachers want you to have a strong voice. Rather than just spitting back information from cyberspace, you should make a convincing argument with a specific purpose in a well-written Standard American English (SAE) essay. This is the heart of argumentation writing.

Truth Matters, Even Now

Much of the information that floods our lives is deliberately wrong. Many have learned to use the Internet as a way to mislead the public with half-truths and full-blown lies.

This "fake news" is often done for money or political gains. This sort of writing and thinking has *nothing* to do with academic writing, especially with argumentation writing. Stooping to new lows with fake news and fake websites is abominable.

As a writer and researcher, your job is not to accept information from sources or websites without carefully scrutinizing it. Watch for bias. Everyone has opinions and has some bias, but the vitriol associated with extreme bias has no place in academic writing or research.

What Argumentation Is *Not*

Students sometimes think that argumentative writing, like television talk shows, entails assaults on the reader. Absolutely not.

They sometimes think that argumentative writing should be insulting or should attack others' beliefs and opinions. Completely wrong.

Argumentation is logical and thoughtful, not angry or malicious. Good argumentative writers deal with both mundane and powerful subjects with ease. They examine and evaluate while supporting the main idea, the thesis.

Argumentation requires a healthy respect for the reader. This does not mean that the writer has to be politically correct or nonoffensive. Academic writing sometimes hurts others' feelings but should never be deliberately malicious. You want the members of your **audience** to continue reading your paper, even if they disagree. Under the best circumstances, you want the audience to accept your opinion and/or adopt your proposals.

> Should this book be printed on blue paper? Your response for or against is your stand, your argument. Is this topic boring? Try this one instead: Should rapists be chemically castrated? Your response constitutes the core of your argument.

Whether a subject is boring or shocking, deciding a stand and organizing a solid argument are necessary for argumentative writing.

The Dark Side of Argumentation

Those who can debate any side of an issue—even one that is a lie or one that is morally repulsive—are called **sophists**. It's a term from Ancient Greece for the teachers who were paid to argue well, without any consideration for the public welfare or the truth, in order to sway public opinion. They often utilized dirty tricks and logical fallacies when they spoke or wrote. Then and now, sophists stop at nothing to win an argument.

You, the writer in a college English class, should never take on the role of a sophist. Examples of sophists are all around you on the Internet and the news, but **you must have evidence, details, and examples to back up any opinions**. And you will not tell lies or be malicious in academic writing. Again, this does not make your writing bland or generic. When done well, argumentative writing stops wars, creates democracy, and promotes essential human rights.

College writing calls for decency and thoughtfulness.

Avoiding the Sticky Appeals in Writing

Good writers do not try to win the readers' approval by tugging at their heartstrings or appealing to a sense of ethics that mirrors the writer's own belief system and upbringing. In fact, good writers avoid sticky emotional and logical appeals while writing or they address them in a clear, honest way. However, most writers try to avoid using both the emotional and ethical appeals altogether.

Avoiding the Emotional Appeal

The logical, serious writer does not divert the reader's attention from the argument by appealing mainly to her/his sympathies. We are all too familiar with those who do so: animal rights' groups, AIDS and cancer organizations, and even greeting cards and insurance companies. They pull at our heartstrings to market a product. Good college writing does not involve extreme emotional outpourings with clichés and drama.

One classic example of the emotional appeal in students' papers will explain the most common problem with the emotional appeal. Students have often begun papers by making this kind of statement: No-No Example: "Imagine a small child left in her crib with a pink blanket and an empty bottle. The baby screams at the top of her lungs because she was born addicted to drugs." Then the paper/argument/essay proceeds without facts or details, but with plenty of preachy clichés and phrases.

This topic and first sentence are not effective because they draw too much from the emotional appeal.

College papers should avoid the sensationalism of the emotional appeal.

Ethical Dilemma: Fair v. Unfair

Appealing to the reader's sense of fairness can also be a trap. What one writer thinks is unfair and unethical may make little or no sense to another.

Here's a typical example of a split in ethics:

> If you are the victim of a recent crime, you may believe that the authorities should lock up all criminals and throw away the keys. If you have a relative in prison who is treated inhumanely, you may hold the opposite point of view.

A writer must not assume that the audience is pro-law enforcement or anti-law enforcement. Instead, the writer should take a strong stance using the best argumentation tools—logic, evidence, examples, organization of ideas, and solid thesis—and present her or his point of view in an essay.

However, assuming that any person reading your essay will have the same set of ethics with which you are imbued is a terrible mistake.

Both points of view about crime and prison might be too close or too personal to handle objectively. When the writer starts imposing a sense of outrage over fairness or the lack of it, s/he becomes illogical and, some of the time, irrational.

At other times, hot topics are too controversial and too clouded by rancorous debate from talking heads on television and radio. Sensible, logical reasoning, often lost in these discussions, is very important in college-level argumentation writing.

Avoid the ethical appeal. "Fair" is a sticky, relative term. Think about a topic from many angles before developing your argument. Have empathy while still holding true to your argument.

On the front end of the writing process, be wise. Choose a topic that you want to learn about, one that will not make you slip into emotional and ethical rants.

Best: The Logical (or Intellectual) Appeal

To move the audience best, a writer needs to speak to the reader's intellect, not just to the heart or to familiar knee-jerk opinions. No writer should forget that the audience in a college-level classroom is intelligent. Readers do not respond well to a condescending tone.

A more practical problem for most writers is that they constantly make the same or a very similar statement paragraph after paragraph—most of the time without any evidence, details, or examples. If the statement had been fully supported the first time it was made, we got the point then. *Move on to another point in your outline.*

When writing so that the reader will respect you—and after all, is that not what you want, at least?—remember that you first and foremost must have convincing evidence to impart to the reader. The reader's attention will then stay focused on your argument if it is well-developed and logical.

The biggest downside to the intellectual appeal is that it requires the reader to think and to reason. Many readers prefer to be inspired by the emotional appeal or to hear the often one-sided rantings of ethical appeals. However, though the intellectual appeal requires more thought, it is the approach that a mature reader will most appreciate.

Logical Fallacies: Faulty Thinking

All writers get weary, and when we do, we often resort to the tried-and-true ideas that ring in our heads. Unfortunately, these ideas may not be useful; in fact, some have been recycled for many generations:

No-No Examples . . . .
Those Italians sure can cook.

My best friend and her sister are Lithuanians. They can dance well. Lithuanians are just born with a sense of rhythm.

Mormons make fine FBI agents.

How many hundreds of statements like this have you heard—or perhaps even said? They and many like them are called logical fallacies. **College writers should completely avoid logical fallacies. They are mistakes in thinking that become more glaring when put into written form.**

OVERGENERALIZATIONS

Statements like the prior ones lump groups of people—Mormons or Italians, for example—into large categories.

Types of Overgeneralizations

- **Hasty generalization.** Quick judgments based on gut reactions, rather than on solid evidence, are good examples of hasty generalizations.

    Teachers are sometimes guilty of hasty generalizations, especially when tired. If a teacher catches two plagiarized papers in one class, in his/her exhaustion, s/he may loudly declare that plagiarism has skyrocketed in composition classes. More evidence is needed to support that generalization, even for weary English teachers.

- **Allness.** When **all or none** of any entity **is stated or implied**, all-ness has occurred. If someone writes or says, "Students at my school hate the food at the college cafeteria," s/he is implying that every single person dislikes the cafeteria's food. Those who really think about that statement know that some people will like the food in the cafeteria, even when it consists of canned corn and reheated chicken. The implied "all" is thus untrue.

Watch for these words: *all, most, none, no one, anybody, everyone, everybody,* and *nobody.* Replace them with *some* or *many.* Overstatement and exaggeration are not effective in formal writing.

FAULTY REASONING

Most logical fallacies fit into the following umbrella categories:

- *Post hoc, ergo propter hoc.* This Latin phrase means, "After this, therefore because of this fact." It is a favorite tool of parents who imply that driving at night will inevitably result in disaster. Correct this problem in your writing with solid evidence.

- **Either/or.** Very few decisions boil down to two choices, but an either/or argument would have you believe that only two options are available: "Either you take this vitamin or you'll never grow tall." Many, many tall people have not taken vitamins. It is not an either/or proposition.

  Some argumentation essay writers make rash statements like this: "Either we build a wall between Mexico and the United States or we will ruin our economy." Be careful to avoid either/or statements in your writing; they are easy to make because of their familiarity.

- **Red herring.** This fallacy is based on stink. If you create a diversionary stink, you will take the reader's attention from the subject/argument in question and lead him/her in another direction. It often masks a lack of solid evidence. A red herring in any argument diverts the reader's attention.

- **Circular reasoning, or begging the question.** This is popular in freshman composition essays. It involves the writer folding back on his/her own words in an argument: "Making paper airplanes is a waste of time because it squanders a lot of valuable time." Don't repeat yourself. Don't repeat yourself.

- *Ad hominem.* This Latin phrase means "to the man/person." This may be the cheapest of all the dirty tricks, and it is used in the media all the time. For example, two commentators' debate about the environment turns malicious, and they begin a character attack on each other based on divorce scandals. This is a classic *ad hominem* attack where the issue of environment is forgotten and personal attacks take place. It is another way to hide ignorance of an issue. It does not work in essays.

- **Hypotheticals.** Don't construct "pretend" scenarios and suggest possible solutions. You cannot predict the future and should not try to manufacture one to fill a page with words in an essay.

Fix these problems by avoiding personal attacks. Stick to the issues and to well-organized evidence.

Formulating a Thesis for Argumentation Essays

Your teacher will direct you on organizing your ideas, starting with a pain-free flow of ideas—no spelling or grammar considerations in this prewriting phase. As you start to organize, you will develop a line of reasoning that will begin to swirl around a main idea, your thesis. The thesis will help to keep your thinking on track and organized. Getting there requires having an airtight thesis.

Argumentative thesis sentences must be solid. Here's a typical one that is not:

No-No Example ·
There are problems with closing military bases.

This thesis sentence does not take a stand—a necessity in argumentation. It is, at best, an elementary report thesis.

Revised No-No Example ·
Problems with closing the military bases in Mississippi have occurred.

This is more specific, but it is still not argumentative. The writer must persevere, even when frustrated. How about this?

So-So Example· ·
Mississippians should fight to keep all the military bases that are located here.

It is better, but it is still rough. What does the writer mean by "fight"? Could that be replaced with a better word or phrase? Yes, but the writer does not need to be caught up in micromanaging every single word at every single minute. It can kill creativity and the flow of ideas. The last thesis sentence of the three listed above is a *good start*.

NO writer should have a perfect thesis in the prewriting phase. When the paper is submitted to the teacher, however, the thesis should be rock solid.

When to Write a Thesis

Writers get far too impatient about wanting a great thesis statement almost as quickly as they chose a topic. This is unwise and works in only a few isolated cases.

Don't try to skip the steps: Prewrite first, even if you hate doing so. After that, start with a working thesis, and call it a "working thesis." Make sure that you are aware that a working thesis will change four or five times, in many cases.

You can also wait until you have gone further in the drafting process before starting a thesis. You must do what's comfortable for your style of writing. But come what may, start with prewriting before building a thesis.

The thesis statement is so important that you will need to review it one last time before submitting your essay. Make sure that it's accurate and really is the center of the ideas in your essay.

Sample Argumentative Thesis Sentences

All of the thesis sentences below are argumentative thesis sentences. Some are better than others. Based on your instructor's directions and the department or school's requirements, which one fits your needs best?

- Americans' fascination with celebrities is having a negative impact on culture and attitudes.
- While both the online and classroom settings offer opportunities to learn, online education falls far short of traditional classes.
- Headphones should be banned in the classroom to cut down on potential cheating and to decrease the noise that emanates from them.
- Modern youth group culture needs to be changed.
- By integrating creative writing and fantasy literature into the curriculum, a remedy to this epidemic is possible.
- Government, industry, and even average citizens need to realize the threat posed to the environment and should take every precaution to protect it.
- Pressure to develop into the smartest, the fittest, the fastest, the strongest, the prettiest, and many other "-ests" suppresses children in ways that often cannot be reversed.
- With the rapid increase in Spanish speakers moving from the overpopulated southwestern region of the United States towards the Atlantic Coast, Mississippi is experiencing numerous nontraditional changes, which are affecting our social structure.

- Veterans should be given better opportunities for stable employment.

- Clanton High School should offer a college preparation class so that the staff and teachers can more efficiently prepare students for college.

- Obsessive Internet usage in our culture has weakened creativity, opened the door to abuse, and weakened learning skills.

- If prevention methods are not increased, then the teen suicide rate will continue to rise and more of our young will die needlessly.

- English instructors in educational institutions should increase the use of fantasy novels in their classes.

These thesis sentences, though of mixed quality, have clear stances—one of the hallmarks of strong argumentative writing.

The Three-Part Thesis Question

Some teachers advocate using the three-part thesis. Which of the students' work in the examples does this?

----- NEWS FLASH -----

Teachers do not agree on everything. Styles differ; schools differ; departments differ. Employees—even English teachers—almost always have to bend to the will of their bosses, and that includes (in many teachers' cases) a department chair, a division chair, an academic dean, a Vice President, and the President of the college. The teacher may not be able to set his or her own guidelines about thesis sentences, deductions of points, or consequences of plagiarism.

In addition, like accountants and doctors and engineers, English teachers are not all alike and have been trained by different colleges and schools of thought. Students should know how to adapt to these styles because the world of work mimics this chaotic pattern. Be ready.

Some teachers despise the three-point thesis. As a student, you should follow the directions that you receive because *ultimately* you will, most likely, use every type of thesis statement if you stay in college long enough. And the rules will change. Flexibility is required.

Changing the Thesis and Content

Finding a good thesis can often be terribly frustrating. Students sometimes have a total change of heart just a few paragraphs from the thesis. They begin with one main idea and flip-flop. *It's quite all right to change your mind while writing, but the problem occurs when you do not go back and change your thesis and revise prior information.*

Because no one is chiseling words in stone, the writer also has the option to rearrange paragraphs by cutting and pasting content. If the writer feels that his or her new argument is weaker, s/he can change the paper again!

It is a crazy process at times, but we writers must do what works best for the argument and for the reader without compromising our souls. Often, moving a sentence or two strengthens a paragraph immensely.

> Here's how to cut and paste quickly in Word:
>
> Highlight any sentence or passage that you want to move. Once highlighted, press Control + X simultaneously. The sentence will disappear; don't panic.
>
> Place your cursor in the spot where you want the sentence to reappear. Press Control + V simultaneously. The sentence will reappear. Be sure to check your capitalization and spacing before and after the sentence.

Epiphanies often occur when a student closely examines his or her order of ideas in a paragraph. **Don't be shy about adding transition words or changing the order of your sentences to match the order of ideas in your paragraph. Make it flow!**

The Opposite Side or the Alternative View: Respecting the Opposition

Very few arguments have no opposition. The few that do include child abuse and murder. Almost every other subject has at least one other side.

Ignoring the other side means that you have not really done your job of thinking seriously and thoroughly about your topic.

In order to ask and answer all or most of the anticipated questions that your essay raises, you need to discuss the other side or an alternate view of your argument in your essay.

A person who writes on any topic must show the reader that s/he has examined the other side and has answered the reader's questions about the other side's relevance to the essay.

With a topic like the death penalty—a hugely controversial topic—the argumentative writer will, in most essays, take a stand for or against it. Whatever the viewpoint/thesis is, the writer must acknowledge that opponents' views are valid without falling into logical fallacies (especially *ad hominem* attacks) and sensationalized emotional appeals.

When any topic related to criminal justice, many alternative views can be offered. This topic is incredibly personal to many students and is a huge societal concern. If researched and handled properly, the topic can be handled thoughtfully and can serve to educate the writer and the members of that writer's class.

In most short argumentation essays, a writer generally devotes a paragraph to discussing the opposite to his/her thesis. Sometimes, this paragraph contains the pro to match a con or vice versa.

If you write an essay that advocates abolishing the rugby program at your college, the opposition paragraph would contain substantive reasons why it should stay in place. You may have a personal vendetta against the coach, the players, or the sport. *Never* let that attitude permeate your argument. See the logic section of this very chapter!

WHATEVER THE CASE MAY BE, **make the opposing viewpoint or the alternate way of thinking a part of the strength of your essay.** If you do not incorporate the opposite view or alternative views, the reader will wonder if you really thought seriously about your topic. It will seem incomplete.

Classic Organization of an Argumentation Essay

From Socrates to the 21st century, the classic organization for an argumentation essay has not changed:

FIRST SECTION	Introduction, background, and thesis
SECOND SECTION	First major point (pertaining to your thesis) with examples and details
THIRD, FOURTH, FIFTH SECTIONS	Major point (pertaining to your thesis) with examples and details
NEAR THE END	Opposition/alternative view paragraph
LAST SECTION	Conclusion

This order can and should be changed.

The writer can work with this classic organization, just as Socrates did, to make the essay and argument stronger. The opposition/alternate view paragraph can appear earlier. The opposition can be spread throughout the paper if you really want to be like Socrates.

Just organize it well. See Chapters 6 and 7 for organizing and building paragraphs.

Editing: The Best Tool in the Box

No one ever wrote a great paper without extensive editing. Just as diamonds do not roll out of the earth already cut and polished, papers, especially argumentative papers, require extensive editing.

BUILD COHERENCE

Internal transitions between sentences, coherence, can be most troublesome for students. The writer understands the connections between ideas and sentences; the reader cannot. Oftentimes, an additional sentence that may seem somewhat childish or obvious to the writer is just what the reader needs. For many writers, adding transition phrases and sentences is often the last step in the polishing/editing process.

BUILD TRANSITIONS

Moving from one major paragraph to another requires some shuffling. *One idea must connect to the idea before it*. Use transition words and phrases; they are indispensable. Because the readers are not in the mind of the writer, we need WORDS to lead us from one idea to another, especially at the beginning of paragraphs. For that reason, transition words and phrases are absolutely critical.

TRANSITION AND COHERENCE MARKERS

Admittedly	In case that	Obviously
As a result	In fact	Oddly enough
As I have heard	In order that	Of course
Assuredly	In other words	On that account
Because	In particular	Once more
Certainly	In spite of	Similarly
Consequently	In this way	Since
Emphatically	In truth	So that
Equally as important	Indeed	Surely
For example	Inevitably	Therefore
For instance	Just as surely	Though it is true
For this purpose	More specifically	To be sure
For this reason	Most importantly	Under these conditions
Granted that	Naturally	Undoubtedly
In as much as	Nevertheless	

SPECIAL NOTE: Examples of argumentation essays are in Appendix C.

Visual Analysis Essay

Why Visual Analysis?

We live in an age of visual communication. The people who left behind cave paintings and those who sent smoke signals also lived in ages of visual communication. Our digital world is more complex in that:

1. Our communications are often more complex.

2. They have the capacity to reach more people in a much faster way, instantaneously.

3. Our communication tools change more often.

4. We are saturated with visual signals in ways people who lived before digital TV, Internet, and smartphones simply could not have been.

In our age, visual literacy means being both a proficient reader and producer of visual information.

Television came into its own in the 1950s, bringing visual communication to the forefront of our lives. Although we had newspapers, photography, radio, and movies before that, the combination of picture and sound brought directly to the home captivated audiences in its own unique way.

Since that time, media of all kinds, including everything from billboards to magazine ads, has become extremely sophisticated. Marketing campaigns have managed to embed certain images associated with products so deeply into our collective consciousness that they're nearly universally recognizable. Some examples include the Nesquik bunny, the Nike "swoosh," and the Pillsbury Doughboy.

We are bombarded with images that are designed to embed themselves in our memories and create certain reactions in us, such as the desire to purchase products or support causes.

Smartphones and other electronic devices ensure that even the least digitally engaged of us are almost constantly exposed to visual stimuli and, consequently, attempts at visual persuasion.

What does this mean for us? What does it have to do with a need to study visual analysis or to incorporate visual analysis into college writing assignments?

It has plenty to do with it, as it turns out.

1. **Basic literacy.** There are certain shapes, symbols, and images that the average person is expected to be able to easily identify. As you could imagine, it'd be difficult to scrape along in the world if you didn't know what a stop sign or restroom sign meant. Likewise, some images are iconic to a culture. All Americans are expected to recognize the American Flag or the Statue of Liberty. The ability to recognize these symbols, shapes, or images instantaneously, without having to put any thought into deciphering the meaning or purpose, means you have basic literacy.

2. **Consumer savvy.** A large percentage of the images we encounter in a typical day are attempts to sell us something. Awareness of what these images are trying to sell us, how they are going about it, and what impact the images actually have on our desire to purchase is essential. In digital media, this is particularly important. It's unimaginably easy for online advertisements to be disguised as informative pieces. A greater understanding of how we are manipulated through image and design can make us smarter navigators in this environment.

3. **Intellectual savvy.** Because information is so readily available, the importance of memorizing vast quantities of material has been replaced with memorizing methods of finding information. As people learn these methods, they also develop criteria for sorting, evaluating, and prioritizing what they find. This is one version of critical thinking; it requires visual analysis. Much of the information available online is either visual

by nature or couched in a visual design that communicates its meaning. If there is a picture introducing an article, for example, that picture will influence the way we read the article. Understanding these influences is essential to developing real intellectual savvy, which is, after all, what you come to college to do.

4. **Design savvy.** Being design savvy is a necessity considering that many professional jobs require presentations of some kind. Nowadays, people expect visuals alongside speeches—think of it as a package deal. The last thing you want is to be guilty of presenting an ineffective PowerPoint.

In Shakespeare's *Hamlet*, Polonius tells Laertes, "Neither a borrower nor a lender be." It's an archaic ideal to think it would even be possible to say "neither a consumer nor a producer be" in relation to digital media. The fact is that it is unthinkable; if you function at all in the age of digital media, you are both a consumer and a producer of digital media.

If you have a Facebook or Snapchat account, have ever sent an email, taken a photograph with a digital camera, or even created an avatar in an online game, you are a producer of digital media.

The degree to which you'll be expected to be skilled at utilizing digital devices and navigating digital spaces increases exponentially each year. If you are a college freshman this year, there is a very high likelihood that you will not be able to get some professional jobs by the time you graduate from college, unless you are highly proficient as both a consumer and a producer of digital media.

That's why visual analysis is so important; image is everywhere in the digital world. You won't really be proficient as a digital consumer/producer without some finely honed visual analysis skills.

Does this mean you need to be an artist? Not necessarily. But you do need to learn to think like an artist to a certain extent.

What Is Visual Analysis?

Analysis is the process of breaking something down in order to understand it better. Thus, visual analysis is the process of breaking down images for observation, explanation, and enhanced understanding. This basic definition can mean many things.

1. **Critiquing artistic composition.** At its core, visual analysis makes value judgments about the designs of images as works of art. It looks at the elements of visual art—line, texture, perspective, tone, balance, contrast, etc.—with a critical eye. You might do this in order to write art reviews or to critique a successful artist for the purpose of learning from that artist. You might also do it in combination with one of the approaches mentioned here. The artistic composition of a piece informs the way we understand its meaning. Although you don't have to be an artist to engage

in visual analysis, you do have to know a little bit about how art is made. The design principles for putting together works of art are the same for putting together advertisements. Knowing how to analyze the design of any image is the stepping stone to understanding and learning a great deal about the purpose and meaning of the image.

2. **Developing greater design savvy.** Design savvy is obligatory in the digital world. Critiquing the designs of others is a crucial step toward improving your own designs and becoming a more professional communicator.

3. **Marketing analysis.** If you want the kind of consumer savvy that means you won't easily be taken advantage of due to slick advertising, you need to engage in some marketing analysis. Likewise, if you hope to own a business or promote an organization or product, you're going to need to analyze markets and marketing campaigns. This means you'll need to break down the images, words, and sounds in order to understand how they all work together to influence consumer behavior. Not all visual analysis is strictly visual. A critique of a television commercial or website might involve an analysis of the ways in which the visual plays against words and sounds in order to form meaning. *More often than not, in fact, visual analysis is multimedia analysis.*

4. **Rhetorical analysis.** Rhetoric is the art of persuasion or the art of making meaning. Thus, rhetorical analysis means breaking down a text to its individual parts in order to examine how its meaning has been made. What strategies have been used? What tools, devices, or designs have been employed? Why are those choices effective or ineffective? Why have they been used at all? If you understand that images can be used to persuade or to establish ideas, you can use the same kind of analysis that you'd apply to a speech to examine a poster or other visual.

5. **Political analysis.** It's important as a citizen and potential voter to understand political propaganda and rhetoric. You can do so by analyzing campaign speeches and political marketing campaigns, many of which involve visual persuasion.

6. **Digital citizenship observations.** Being a good citizen holds the same meaning and significance in the digital world that it does in the real world. You must pull your own weight, be considerate of others, and do your part to solve the problems around you. What that really translates into online isn't always obvious unless you take the time to analyze your surroundings.

7. **Memoir/reflection.** Sometimes visual analysis is something we do simply to understand more about ourselves. By examining the influences of various media on our lives, we can understand more about how we think, why we've made certain decisions, and how we feel about certain topics.

8. **Studying images as cultural narratives or icons.** Cultural narratives are stories that help define the identity or collective character of a set group of people. These stories don't have to be told in words; a collection

of quilts, a slideshow of a family reunion, a yearbook, or even certain types of dances can form a cultural narrative. Studying cultures through analyzing their narratives—visual, textual, or otherwise—can be a fascinating way to enhance your understanding of history, literature, or any other academic disciplines.

These are just a few examples. You might think of other ways to engage in visual analysis, or you might think of a way to combine some of the ideas mentioned here. Visual analysis skills are both necessary and commonly used in digital settings.

What to Look for in Visual Analysis

In order to determine what to look for in visual analysis, you must first determine your purpose. Are you looking mostly at design? Are you looking at the message or the story of the image? Do you expect the piece to have an agenda? Do you expect it to reflect the attitudes or character of a person or group?

You won't have one magic checklist to go through for every case of visual analysis because what you need to look for depends on what you are examining and why. The best plan is to make your own checklist for each particular analysis so that it will fit what you need.

However, some general approaches can apply.

DESIGN

Look at colors, shades, and tones. Study lines, shapes, focal points, the ways in which items are balanced within the frame, and the ways in which a sense of perspective is created. Look at the degree of particular detail or the lack thereof. What techniques were used to create the picture? How do those techniques matter to the overall impact or meaning of the picture? Examine where items in the image are located. What is located above other items or below other items? Does the location of certain items say something about the purpose or meaning of a part of the image or the image as a whole?

STORY

A description becomes a story when it has action—when something happens in it. It becomes a better story if there's a sense of conflict or tension and if it is told in an interesting way. Look for elements of storytelling in the image. What is happening? What has happened? Where is the tension? What's unique or interesting about it? If someone were telling you the story in the picture, what tone of voice would be used? Is this tone apparent in the image? If there are people in the story, what are their attitudes, moods, and/or motivations? Be careful not to make up a story that isn't actually in the image, but definitely use the clues in the image to determine what the story actually is.

AGENDA

Is the image attempting to persuade you of something? Is there an agenda behind it? Does the agenda affect the way you read the image? How do you know what the agenda is? Is the evidence in the picture itself, or do you need to know something else in order to understand the agenda? How does the image attempt to manipulate your emotional reactions and ethics? In order to find the agenda, you may need to do some digging to find out who commissioned the image and for what purpose; was it a person, company, organization, or government?

CONTEXT

Is there something outside the frame of the image that you need to know to understand its meaning? Is there a historical or political context? Is there a cultural context? Would researching the background of the image help you to understand it? Does that work both ways? Can the picture help you to understand the context? Does the picture complement or enhance your research on the subject?

RHETORICAL APPEALS

Every attempt to persuade a viewer uses the three rhetorical appeals: logos (appealing to logic and reasoning), ethos (appealing to the viewer through the image's or the creator's credibility), and pathos (appealing to the viewer's emotions). To be savvy about images, you must look carefully to determine which appeals are being used in an image and recognize how a particular part of that image is using one of the rhetorical appeals. Think about the animal abuse commercials that show pathetic animals and ask for monetary support; the animals are being used to create the emotional appeal to persuade viewers to donate. When looking at other images or even multimedia visuals, the emotional appeal is often easy to find. The logical and ethical appeals can be harder to locate but add important information about the argument of the image, mainly the facts or reasoning and the reason why the viewer should believe what he or she is seeing.

Thirteen Ways of Looking at a Picture or a Poem

Wallace Stevens wrote a poem called "Thirteen Ways of Looking at a Blackbird," with at least one point being that any given image or idea can be viewed in any of a dozen or more ways. Remember this concept when you look at any image, read poetry, or find yourself exposed to new ideas. Anything can be seen in more than one way as long as you stay within the context of the work being examined.

If you are trying to decipher the meaning in a picture or poem, consider at least these thirteen ways of seeing it:

I. VOICE	Essentially, this means personality. Is there a strong sense of personality? If so, how is it indicated?
II. PERSPECTIVE	From what point of view do you see the scene?
III. SETTING	Where is the poem or picture located? What place, culture, and historical reality surround it?
IV. TEMPORALITY	At what rate is time passing in the picture or poem? How much temporal distance exists between the speaker and the events or between the viewer and the events? How does time matter?
V. LINE	Where are the lines? How are they divided? How do they work in relation to one another? What does this mean for the way you see/hear/feel the work?
VI. METAPHOR	What in the work is meant to suggest something else? How is the suggestion relevant? Does it attempt to influence you in any way?
VII. FORM	What shapes and rhythms are employed? What's deliberate about the form? How does this influence the way you read the work?
VIII. TONE	What is the general attitude or atmosphere of the work? What kind of "vibe" or "feel" do you get from it? Is the work dark, light, moody, comic, sinister, sarcastic, or witty? How do you know?
IX. PURPOSE	What is the creator's intent? What point is he or she trying to convey? Do you know what you are being told and why it matters?
X. TENSION	Is there conflict of some sort in the work? Is there emotional risk or a longing for something that can't happen within the confines of the poem's or picture's reality?
XI. INTERSECTION	What are the cross-points of the work? Where do ideas, images, or associations overlap? Do these cross-points complement each other? Do they add to the tension? How are they important?
XII. SPECIFICITY	Are the details precise? Are multiple senses engaged in reading? Is the image presented detailed enough to make it unique?
XIII. RESOLUTION	Does the work provide a sense of completion? Do you feel you've been told what you were meant to be told? Have you been left with something worth pondering?

You may not include all thirteen in any given visual analysis. You could write a whole essay using just one criterion for analysis, or you might combine two or three criteria. Nevertheless, spending time working your way through thirteen ways of seeing anything—image, poem, or idea—will truly help you to understand it so that your critique might be more fully formed, or more aware and insightful.

TIP: For more ideas on writing about images, do a search on "photography techniques" or "design principles" to gain additional information about visual composition from an artist's perspective. Also, check out the websites listed at the end of the chapter for more help.

Writing the Visual Analysis Essay

A visual analysis essay should be organized like any other essay—with an introduction, a body, and a conclusion. Your introduction should establish a point about the image, your body should support that point by examining the image based on a set of criteria, and the conclusion should pull it all together while reestablishing how and why the point has been made.

From there, the visual analysis essay might take on the organizational pattern of any of the rhetorical modes listed in individual chapters in this book. For instance, two political campaign posters could be examined together in a comparison and contrast essay. A persuasive essay might be made out of a critique of an advertisement. Perhaps you could attempt to persuade teenage girls not to fall prey to cosmetic ads by critiquing the way in which a particular ad misleads women about what it considers attractive.

You might write a description essay based on a photograph of a disaster zone or a narrative essay based on looking through a family photo album. You could write a division and classification essay on the types of political cartoons published on a given day and on a given topic.

How about a definition essay about a piece of art that represents a particular style or movement?

You get the picture (pun intended). A visual analysis essay could be any type of essay as long as it also happens to break down the elements of at least one image. You could even use the same types of approaches to visual analysis that are used in the Critical Approaches chapter by employing psychological, historical, or reader–response theories.

What you need to write visual analysis is (1) a purpose (see listed possibilities under "What Is Visual Analysis" in this chapter); (2) a thesis (an overall point, judgment, or position about the image); (3) criteria by which to analyze or critique (see "What to Look for in Visual Analysis" and "Thirteen Ways of Looking at a Picture or a Poem" in this chapter); and (4) an organizational pattern or plan (see chapters on modes in this book).

Taking the time to plan those four items, as well as spending some quality time with the image you want to analyze, should put you well on the way to an excellent analytical essay.

WEBSITES WITH IMAGES FOR ANALYSIS

National Gallery of Art: http://www.nga.gov/onlinetours/index.shtm

Museum of Modern Art: www.moma.org

The Tate Gallery: http://www.tate.org.uk/collection/

PHOTOGRAPHY

Life Magazine: http://www.life.com/

National Geographic Photo Galleries: http://ngm.nationalgeographic.com/more/photography

Time Magazine Photo Essays: http://www.nga.gov/onlinetours/index.shtm

UNICEF Photo Essays: http://www.unicef.org/photoessays/index-pe.html

POLITICS

Association of American Political Cartoonists: http://editorialcartoonists.com/

Marshall Ramsey's Blog: http://blogs.clarionledger.com/mramsey/

Sample Essay: Visual Analysis
Sandra Currier, Student

Poster: Humanizing Hitler

After World War I, Germany was in a complete state of disarray. The country needed a saving grace—someone who would carry the broken people of Germany out of the ashes and into a new age of prosperity. The person that the Germans thought they needed was Adolf Hitler. His ability to motivate the German people was an amazing feat; speaking to crowds appears to be rather simple, but Hitler's effectiveness in doing so transcended that of others. Although his beliefs were unquestionably un-American to the United States, that was not the case for the German people. In a propaganda poster of Adolf Hitler and a young girl, the intent is to humanize Hitler. Regardless of whether this message intended to make Hitler appear more human to the German people or to the American people, it succeeded only mildly. The propaganda poster employs the use of body language and color to convey the idea that Hitler wanted to be emotionally invested in the needs of his people.

The most prominent aspect of this propaganda poster is the body language of Hitler and the young girl. Body language provides cues to understand how a certain person feels in a given situation. If a person's body is visibly tense, it is unlikely that the person is comfortable. If a person's body is relaxed, it is understood that the person is very comfortable. In the propaganda poster, Hitler is bent down toward the little girl; his body is positioned this way to exemplify that he is on an equal standing with his people, he cares for them, and that they reciprocate fully. His hands are cradling the girl's arm in a very protective manner, which shows the audience that he is acting as a peacemaker of sorts. It is implied that by extending his arms to the girl, Hitler is essentially doing the same to the people of Germany. Moreover, Hitler and the girl are engaging in very persistent eye contact, which is a sign of mutual respect and trust. This aspect of the poster indicates that Hitler is worthy of the respect and trust of the people of Germany. All in all, the poster employs varying forms of body language to portray to the German people that Hitler was a trustworthy leader and compassionate human.

In addition to body language, color is a prominent aspect that further allows this poster to humanize Hitler. Despite the fact that the poster is black and white, color is utilized in the most useful ways. The little girl practically shines; the way her face is illuminated draws a sharp contrast between her and the soon-to-be leader. Most of the light is focused on her cheekbones, which highlights her youthful innocence. Her apron is white, which symbolizes purity and innocence and her hair is adorned with a pretty bow. All of these specific elements surrounding the little girl depict her as the prime picture of the German youth. Although the photo is done in black and white, one can tell that the young girl has blonde hair, which is a prime physical attribute of Hitler's master race. The fact that her lovely innocence shines so brightly makes Hitler's attempt at extending his hands to her particularly powerful. When thinking about color in regards to Hitler's appearance, the main focus is his suit, particularly one area that looks blindingly white. In the background of the poster are trees, implying that the sun is shining on Hitler and the young girl. The strong focus of the lighting on Hitler's back attempted to show people that Hitler would brighten the future of Germany; that he was their light and hope.

The propaganda poster of Hitler and the little girl aimed to humanize Hitler, which it likely succeeded at for the German people during World War II. Hitler gave them a voice and a scapegoat and justified the hatred of the Jewish population. Germans saw Hitler as a human who loved them and their children. For most Americans now, this poster likely instills disgust. The fact that this young girl is even smiling at Hitler is utterly horrifying. As Americans, we only see the darkness of what Hitler did to the Jewish population. This poster attempts to humanize one of the most horrific dictators this world has ever known; the use of color and body language is powerful, but only when one takes into consideration the audience and the time in which this poster was made.

Work Consulted

Hitler and Young Girl Poster. *ICC Canvas.* Classnotes, Bowers. Spring 2016. Accessed 4 April 2016.

Additional Rhetorical Modes

Description, Exemplification, Definition, Problem and Solution, Division and Classification, and Process

What's a Mode?

Mode means way or method. If you tell a story, you are writing in narrative mode, and you will therefore be writing a narrative essay.

English teachers, like any other teachers, have their own ideas about what rhetorical modes they want to teach in their freshmen composition classes. This chapter will highlight some of the modes that may not be taught as commonly as some of the other modes and therefore do not warrant a separate chapter.

Description Essay

Good writers paint pictures for their readers with their words. As a writer, you are trying to transfer the images and ideas that are in your mind directly to the minds of your readers. One effective way to achieve this goal is through description.

You will use description in many different types of writing throughout your college career. Even if you are writing a process essay or an argumentation essay, you may find it appropriate to describe. In the process mode, you may describe what type of firewood is most effective in a campfire. In argumentation, you may describe the demeanor of an instructor who was so lazy that she should have been fired.

Description, probably more than any other rhetorical mode, is one that you will use almost every time you write. If you are not using description in most of your essays, you should consider how much better your writing could be if you did so.

For this reason—its importance—there's an entire appendix devoted to descriptive essay examples. See Appendix B.

When using description, you must consider the five senses:

- sight
- sound
- smell
- taste
- touch

Try to get your readers to experience the subject of your writing. For example, if you are writing about walking on the beach on a summer's day, it is not enough to describe how the beach looks; while this is a good start, you should also describe the smell of the air, the feeling of the sand, the taste of the salt water, and the sound of the waves. The more senses you involve in your description, the more your readers will experience and remember.

When describing, it is also important to consider how much description is too much. If you are writing about a classroom, your readers probably want to know about the people in the room, the sounds of different discussions, and the smell of the freshly mopped floor; however, they may not need to know how many bricks are on the walls or the exact number of desks in the room. You want your readers to feel as though they are there, but you do not want them to be bored. Use details that seem significant.

Finally, decide the **order** of your descriptive details. Sometimes it is easiest to begin with what you see first when entering a place; if you are describing a person, you might begin with a physical feature that stands out to you. If you are writing from memory, you could begin with the detail you remember above all others. Many writers choose to act as the camera for their readers and scan the area, left to right, up and down. Again, however you decide to arrange details, do not forget all of the senses. Even though you may choose to begin with sight, the other senses are equally as important.

While it is true that all adjectives describe, not all help to paint a clear picture to your readers. Choose adjectives that are clear. For example, what does a pretty house look like? While "pretty" is an adjective, it does not help you adequately convey an image to your reader. The same rule applies to "fun." Like "pretty," it is too vague. Be as specific as possible. You may also try using figurative language, such as similes, metaphors, hyperbole, and onomatopoeia.

SAMPLE DESCRIPTIVE SENTENCES

The following sentences are examples of bland or vague sentences that can be improved with appropriate descriptive words. Notice that some sentences are not really wrong or bad but can be better with revision. However, some sentences are just plain wrong.

> BAD—few adjectives: The house where I grew up is located on a deserted street.

> BETTER—more adjectives: The white-washed, wooden house where I grew up sits alone on a gravel road ten miles from the nearest town.

> BAD—vague adjectives: We went on a garden tour and saw lots of pretty flowers.

> BETTER—specific adjectives: During the pilgrimage, we toured six gardens and saw many exotic plants, such as hibiscus and periwinkle.

> BAD—too many adjectives: The stern, bespectacled, gray-haired teacher stood staunchly at the front of the meticulously organized classroom and began her lengthy lecture on the reasons that being tardy was the one greatest downfall of the new generation.

> BETTER—adjectives not overdone: The stern teacher stood at the front of the classroom and began a long lecture on her idea that tardiness is the greatest downfall of our generation.

> BAD—stilted diction with overused thesaurus: The diverting entertainment at the establishment made the patrons at the enterprise venerate their excursion that evening.

> BETTER—adjectives without pretense: My friends enjoyed hearing the band Widespread Panic at Rick's Café that evening.

Any time you revise an essay, whether it is a description essay or another type, check for sentences that you can improve with descriptive words. Also check to make sure that you have not overdone your description with flowery language, clichés, or stilted diction.

SAMPLE THESIS SENTENCES

The thesis in a description essay is very much like any other thesis sentence. It states your main idea, and it may list or omit the body paragraph topics. Consider rewording your topic into a statement that reflects your opinion of the topic.

- The loud sounds, the unnaturally bright colors, and the whir of worn-out machinery at a county fair make me feel so afraid that I avoid it at all costs.

- My idea of a perfect evening consists of family, food, and fun movies.

- Watching my grandmother work in her ancient, outdated kitchen taught me invaluable lessons about preparing food and caring for family.

SAMPLE TOPIC OUTLINE

Thesis: My idea of a perfect evening consists of family, food, and fun movies.

I. Family
    A. Comfort of my wife and children
    B. Oversized, soft sofa
    C. My dog at my feet
    D. Soft lighting in my den

> This is a topic outline. Check with your instructor on the type that you are required to complete.

II. Food
    A. Chips and spicy salsa
    B. Salty peanuts
    C. Orange Crush soda
    D. Oatmeal raisin cookies

III. Fun Movies
    A. Latest blockbuster
    B. Family comedies
    C. Animated children's movies
    D. Home movies

Notice that the subheadings list specifics, and most of the specifics provide the writer with the opportunity to address the five senses. Think of how you would describe the comfort of the oversized sofa. Next, think of how you would describe the taste of spicy salsa and salted peanuts. Lastly, think of how you could describe the sounds of the latest blockbuster movie or an animated children's movie.

Exemplification Essay

Exemplification is simply an example paper. When you *exemplify* something, you give an example of it. Sometimes English teachers assign the exemplification essay as a way to teach their students the basics of writing college-level essays, which require a lot of proof. Often in freshman composition essays, the best way to prove a thesis is to give examples. Without specifics, you haven't proven anything. Thus, the exemplification essay helps you learn to develop your ideas by providing concrete evidence in the body paragraphs to prove your thesis.

In addition, you can apply the exemplification format to almost any college essay and almost any other rhetorical mode. Some topics that could be exemplification topics are listed below:

- Characteristics of a good sister, brother, parent, etc.
- Characteristics of a typical Civil War, World War II, or Vietnam War battle
- Stereotypes of Americans (or any group) disproven or proven

SAMPLE THESIS SENTENCES

In your thesis, you may name your body paragraph points or not. As long as you name your topic and what you will say about your topic, you have a good thesis.

- Good parents share a number of similar qualities.
- The battles of the Vietnam War included many of the same elements.
- Although Southerners are often viewed as lazy, dumb, and prejudiced, that is not the case.

SAMPLE TOPIC OUTLINE

Thesis: Good parents share a number of similar qualities.

I. Dedication
   A. The motivation to learn about child development
   B. Books on parenting
   C. The will to discipline the child appropriately
   D. Books, videos on discipline
II. Patience
   A. The ability to see problems as growing pains
   B. The terrible twos
   C. The ability to control their tempers
   D. The teen years

III. Creativity

    A. The ability to relate to a child's imagination

    B. Coloring, singing, dancing

    C. The ability to let a child be unique

    D. Allowing pursuit of activities the parent did not choose

Notice that the outline subheadings consist of general ideas and general examples. However, when you write the body paragraphs, you need to make your examples as specific as possible. That means you should **give an example of something that happened one time**. For instance, if you were writing body paragraph two from the sample outline, you could discuss an encounter that you had with your parents when you came in late one Saturday night. That example would relate to a parent's ability to control his or her temper with a teenager.

A good rule of thumb for examples is to give at least two specific examples per body paragraph. If you have this level of detail in each body paragraph, you probably have a well-developed essay. You might find it helpful to list your examples on your outline.

Definition Essay

According to the *Merriam-Webster Online Dictionary*, "to define" means "to determine or identify the essential qualities or meaning of."

Dictionary definitions are usually concise for publication purposes. However, you may find that writing an extended definition of a term is necessary in your academic career. Teachers want to know that you thoroughly understand specific concepts. You might need to explain the definition of a term in biology or history. Thus, when you write a definition essay, you will elaborate on the condensed dictionary or textbook definition of a term. You may even be asked to give your personal interpretation of the term's definition along with examples studied in the text and in class.

When asked to do so, you may want to begin with the concise, formal definition of your term in the introduction and then expound on it in the body. When you state the formal definition, name the term (your topic), its class, and its specific characteristics. For example, you might give the following formal definition: "Hope is a feeling that makes people look forward to the future." The term is "hope," the class is "feeling," and the specific characteristic is that it "makes people look forward to the future."

CRITICAL FACT ABOUT DEFINITIONS IN ESSAYS

Use the dictionary definition *only* if you have the teacher's permission to do so. If you use the dictionary, put the **exact wording in quotation marks** and cite it.

Similar to the exemplification essay, the definition essay lends itself easily to possible topics in several different academic areas. Some topics that could be definition topics are listed below:

- Define Romanticism. How does it differ from the generic term "romantic"?
- Define mitosis.
- What are the defining characteristics of alternative rock music?

Notice that all of these topics could be written by using the format of another rhetorical mode. The first topic on Romanticism could be a comparison/contrast essay. Secondly, because defining mitosis would require a student to discuss *how* something works, it could be a process essay. Lastly, a student could use the exemplification format to write about the characteristics of alternative rock music.

SAMPLE THESIS SENTENCES

A good way to develop a thesis of a definition essay is to give the formal definition as your thesis. However, giving the formal definition as your thesis is not a requirement. As always, you may name your body paragraph points in your thesis or omit them, according to your teacher's instructions.

- Romanticism is a literary era that emphasized intuition or feeling over rational thinking.
- Mitosis is a process by which a cell divides into two identical parts.
- Alternative rock music is a genre of music that breaks from mainstream rock in several ways.

SAMPLE TOPIC OUTLINE

Thesis: Alternative rock music is a genre of music that breaks from mainstream rock music in several ways.

I. Lyrics
  A. Negative lyrics
  B. The group "I Love You but I've Chosen Darkness"
  C. Politically incorrect lyrics
  D. Beck's song, "MTV Makes Me Want to Smoke Crack"
II. Vocals
  A. Screaming sound
  B. Nirvana
  C. Raw, throwback sound
  D. Kings of Leon

III. Instruments

    A. Use of a variety of instruments

    B. Classical instruments

    C. Muse

    D. Organ/piano

    E. The Hold Steady

As with any other essay, you should give specifics in the body paragraphs. Notice that the above outline lists two examples of alternative rock groups in each of the body paragraph subheadings. If you don't list examples in your outline, be sure to add them to the body paragraphs when you write your rough draft.

Problem and Solution Essay

The problem/solution essay is a variation of the cause/effect essay and the argumentation essay. In the problem/solution essay, you address a problem and offer solutions to that problem. The discussion of problem and solution does not have to be equal. If you know more about the solution, then discuss it more thoroughly.

In the problem/solution essay, you may want to address the problem in the introduction and use the body paragraphs to discuss solutions. In this case, discuss one solution per body paragraph and give specifics about your ideas. Another option would be to discuss the problem in the first body paragraph and then discuss the solutions in the remaining body paragraphs. Use this format if you think that the problem needs to be justified or explained in more space than an introduction would provide. Again, be sure to discuss one solution per body paragraph and give details about each solution.

A third option in formatting the problem/solution essay would be to discuss the problem in the body paragraphs and touch on the solution in the conclusion or the final body paragraph.

Some topics that could be problem/solution topics are listed below:

- How can we combat obesity in the United States?
- What steps do you suggest in combating the problem of teen smoking?
- What is your plan for improving the economy?

You may be able to use the problem/solution essay format in many different academic courses. Any time you have a criticism of some issue, you may use this type of essay to expound on your opinion of how to fix the problem you have highlighted. For example, if you have problems with saving money, you can come up with a plan to stop spending based on a long-term evaluation of your financial needs.

SAMPLE THESIS SENTENCES

Remember that you do not have to list your body paragraph topics in your thesis, but you may wish to list them if your sentence seems to gravitate naturally toward your topics.

- Obesity has become a widespread problem in the United States and will continue to be a problem until we implement several key solutions.

- Three steps that may help combat teen smoking are to begin discussing the problem in elementary schools, to provide intensive educational programs about smoking's hazards, and to enforce dire consequences for teen smoking.

- My plan for improving the economy involves creating jobs, providing tax incentives for small business, and retraining displaced workers.

SAMPLE SENTENCE OUTLINE

Thesis: Obesity has become a widespread problem in the United States and will continue to be a problem until we implement several key solutions.

I. We should overhaul our school cafeterias.
   A. Cafeterias should not provide candy.
   B. Cafeterias should not provide sodas or other sugary drinks.
   C. Cafeterias should hire nutrition experts as cafeteria managers.
   D. Cafeterias should make lunch a culinary experience for students.
II. We should give incentives to businesses that allow exercise at work.
   A. Businesses could provide office exercise space and exercise equipment.
   B. Businesses could promote employee exercise groups.
   C. Businesses could emphasize the connection of productivity to employee health.
   D. Businesses should get tax incentives for promoting exercise programs.
III. We should encourage parents to limit children's inside play.
   A. Communities could create bike paths.
   B. Communities could build more neighborhood parks.
   C. Parents could install timers in their home computers.
   D. Parents could enroll their children in environmental programs.

As always, you should give specifics in your body paragraphs. You may want to discuss negative examples before you provide positive ones. For example, you may want to describe the food choices you had in your elementary school cafeteria and then say what choices you should have had.

Division and Classification Essay

Try putting people or events into little boxes and naming them. You may be called narrow-minded, bigoted, naïve, or something even harsher.

Take a chaotic pile of information and organize it, and you may be called efficient, dedicated, smart, or something even more flattering. You may even be called a scientist. Genus and species' names are scientific chaos organized.

Some teachers hate this mode because they do not want their students to put people into boxes; they say that it oversimplifies a complex, diverse world. However, this mode is extremely useful in the workplace.

Because the division and classification mode is so useful in real-world applications, you should be familiar with it. It has, in fact, been extremely useful (and impressive) for many who can think on their feet in **job interviews**. If a potential employer asks how you handle stress, you can start dividing and classifying stress quickly in your head and answer, "When I am on time deadlines, I make extensive lists and go through them in order of most important to least serious. When I am working in a group with others, I try not to react negatively to offhand negative comments that I hear."

Dividing is the act of whacking any subject into pieces and classifying is the act of naming those pieces. The pieces need to be **parallel**; for instance, you should *not* tell an interviewer that you make lists, work well with others, and don't eat carbs. Eating habits don't match the other two office-related items.

If your music instructor gives you the topic *music*, you can divide and classify music by genres: jazz, blues, rock, and classical.

If your American history instructor gives you the topic *explorers*, you can divide and classify explorers by nationalities: French, British, Italian, Spanish.

Division and classification essays can also show how clever or humorous you are. If the teacher gives you a topic like *sports fans*, you can divide and classify baseball fans by their seating preferences in the stadium: bleacher bums, money men, true fans, and casual observers. One student took this topic and used it to describe NASCAR fans by the litter at their campsites. The possibilities are endless.

Example #1 ·
teachers → how hard their tests are →
    discussion-only tests
    ridiculously easy
    tricky

Example #2 ·
students → posture in their seats →

eager overachievers

cool slouchers

nervous leg movers

Remember that your classifications should not be boring. Dividing teachers by subject matter—math, English, reading, science—is definitely boring. Once you have clever and innovative classifications, you should switch from classifying and dividing to description. You will also need some exemplification, and you might be able to use comparison and contrast, as well.

None of the modes that are in this book are meant to be used in a vacuum. All are related and all are tools to be used for writing effectively.

SAMPLE THESIS SENTENCES

- Teachers' personalities are reflected in the styles of tests that they give.
- Of the vacations I have taken (a family bonding getaway, a luxury cruise, and a mission trip), the mission trip was the most gratifying.
- When attending a high school basketball game, parents show their true colors: the good, the bad, and the malicious.

SAMPLE TOPIC OUTLINE

Thesis: Teachers' personalities are reflected in the styles of tests that they give.

I. Knowledgeable teachers
   A. Long discussion
   B. Relevant applications
   C. Tests reflecting the material
II. Lazy teachers
   A. Reverse matching ABCs like junior high
   B. Standardized tests
   C. Tests lacking material emphasized in class
III. Unprepared teachers
   A. Recycled tests
   B. Open-book tests
   C. Tests reflecting material covered in class

Process Analysis Essay

No form of composition has as many real-life and workplace applications as the process essay. Children have to know the steps for tying shoes; employees need to know how to operate machinery. Both of these require the telling of a process in the correct order with adequate description in each required step.

Two types of process essays exist. In one case, the essay writer speaks directly to the recipient of the process, using second person and imperative mood. The steps are often short and numbered. All of this is done for a reason: giving too much information can stymie the urgency involved with these projects, especially in the workplace. This **directional essay** is you-directed and you-centered.

When an author explains the process—even for readers who will never actually duplicate the actions—the essay adheres more to formal writing procedures. Paragraphs are longer and more developed. Instead of being chock-full of short sentences that get to the point quickly, **informational essays** generally contain more depth in content and paragraph structure.

If you have ever assembled a piece of furniture from a package, you know how important this mode is!

DIRECTIONAL	INFORMATIONAL
• great for workplace writing • uses second person—"you" and "your" • contains short paragraphs and (sometimes) short sentences	• often used in academic writing • avoids use of second person, just as other formal writing does • has longer, more developed paragraphs and sentences
EXAMPLE: Recipes; furniture assembly directions; self-help books; employee manuals	EXAMPLE: Explanation of your understanding of a process or product; academic use— essay exams that ask for a recap of class notes on how a rebellion began or how an author or musician affected her/his colleagues' work

FORMULATING A THESIS

Both types of essays require thesis sentences. For each type, the thesis will be similar, if not identical.

One classic topic for directional essays is changing a tire. The thesis sentence needs to reflect the importance of this task and of the essay:

Directional or Informational Thesis ·
Knowing how to change a tire could save a stranded motorist considerable time and money.

In an informational thesis about the importance of regular maintenance on a vehicle, the writer taps into his/her main purpose, the importance of this work.

> **Directional or Informational Thesis** ·
> Simple, regular maintenance by the owner of any vehicle is cost effective and shows initiative.

Here's what a student should NOT do with a thesis for any process paper:

> **No-No Example of Process Thesis** ·
> There are four major steps to changing a tire: preparing, removing, changing, and replacing.

The above thesis sentence is too simple, too obvious, and too repetitious.

ORGANIZATION OF A PROCESS PAPER

Dr. Bill Durrett, a brilliant Mississippi English teacher and mentor, once said, "I like a recipe that starts with, 'Go to the refrigerator and open the door.'" His point was obvious: Most of us need very clear directions. This fact is crucial in directional essays. Not explaining that a knob is turned counterclockwise can ruin an important project and frustrate the worker endlessly.

Body paragraphs in informational process papers should follow the logical pattern involved with the steps. For writers, the tricky part of this paper is bunching too much information into one paragraph. Every paragraph requires a clear direction and/or clear topic sentence, so bunching or packing scattered bits of information is unnecessary. The steps should be clear, sequential, and detailed.

In directional papers, shorter paragraphs are generally accepted. Be sure to check with your teacher.

SAMPLE: FORMAL TOPIC OUTLINE
FOR A DIRECTIONAL PROCESS ESSAY

Thesis: Hanging laundry outside requires sophisticated skills.

I. Hanging clothes outside
   A. Time-honored skill and not new
   B. Money saver
   C. Sloppy work ruining clothes
   D. Proper way to hang clothes
      1. Mama's lessons
      2. Neighborhood pride and gossip
II. Washer to line
   A. Sorting by type from the washer
   B. Last in basket—first on the line

III. Order on the line
   A. Pyramid or reverse pyramid order
      1. Personal preference with small to large items
      2. Exceptions with linens
   B. Hiding the unmentionables with bigger laundry
IV. Drying time
   A. Summer in Mississippi
      1. Quicker on line than in dryer
      2. Shameful waste of money and electricity
   B. Cracked hands in cold weather
      1. Dryer use in bitter cold
      2. Frozen shirts defrosting
   C. Inside drying
      1. Clothesline in laundry room
      2. Curtain rods as clotheslines
      3. Drying racks
V. Great way to save clothes
   A. Evidence—lint trap on dryer
   B. Shirts lasting a decade
   C. Improved ironing and crispness
   D. Eco-friendly and frugal

PROCESS FOR DEVELOPING AN INFORMATIONAL PROCESS PAPER THESIS AND OUTLINE

First Working Thesis ·
~~Learning to sew was supposed to mean new clothes for me, but I only learned a limited number of skills.~~

Second Working Thesis ·
~~Sewing was very important when I needed new curtains.~~

Third Working Thesis ·
Though I had good sewing teachers, I got only a few valuable sewing skills.

Fourth Working Thesis ·
I had good sewing teachers who taught me valuable, moneysaving skills.

How I learned to sew

- Mom
- home economics
- repairs on jeans
- fixing friends' clothes
- saving money

Starting with small projects

- first lessons on sewing machine
- apron in home ec
- working with patterns
- valances with Mom
- shirts I never wore

Mastering the finer skills

- lining curtains
- only did 2 windows
- matching patterns on plaids
- buying my own machine

Skills that I use constantly

- sewing for friends
- teaching the kids in my life
- saving money
- enjoying a project

Note the clipped words and phrases like "home ec" and "kids" in this rough draft. They will be edited from the formal outline and final paper.

Also notice the lack of parallelism, numbering, and formality. They will be integrated into the final draft of the outline, which follows.

SAMPLE: FORMAL SENTENCE OUTLINE FOR AN INFORMATIONAL PROCESS PAPER

Notice how some of the items listed above are not used. Cutting while editing is normal!

I. Learning to sew was one of the best skills I acquired in high school.
   A. My mom taught me how to sew buttons and simple seams.
   B. Taking home economics helped me to operate a sewing machine.
   C. I have used sewing skills my entire life to repair my own clothes.

II. The home economics class was difficult.

   A. The machine was entirely different from my mom's.

   B. I was uncomfortable with patterns and intricate craftsmanship.

   C. Mom had emphasized sewing for household items like curtains and valances.

   D. The first shirt I made for class was ugly and poorly constructed.

III. After I left high school, I abandoned the finer work involved with patterns and reverted to the materials that my mom had used.

   A. Even though I was never a great seamstress, I bought my own machine for $100 and used it for many years.

   B. My strength as a seamstress was not with yokes and buttonholes; it was with simpler projects.

IV. My best work has been with window coverings.

   A. Brown and beige valances were the absolute cutest valances I have ever seen, and they only cost $3.00 per window.

   B. My crowning achievement was lined curtains for the living room, though I ran out of patience after two windows.

   C. I tried to make Roman shades but failed miserably because it was too complex.

V. Since high school, I have used my sewing skills in many useful ways.

   A. Besides doing window treatments, I have resewn seams and patched hundreds of shirts and pants.

   B. Sewing is a wonderful gift for others; it saves them the cost of new clothes.

   C. Younger members of my family are beginning to sew because I have taught them the basics.

   D. Sewing is a great skill that I have never mastered, but I have learned enough to satisfy most of my needs.

Always make sure that you have the teacher's complete instructions and directions for outline form and content.

Final Note about Rhetorical Modes

Remember that you are required to write essays in a freshman composition class so that you will be prepared to write appropriately whenever you are called to do so in other classes and in the word of work.

Remember, too, that most essays combine elements from several rhetorical modes.

Checklist: Group Editing Criteria for _____ Essay

CONTENT: THESIS AND FIRST PARAGRAPH

- [ ] Interesting first sentence—no mention of "society" or "world" or "today."
- [ ] Thesis contains main idea of paper.
- [ ] First paragraph draws interest to the paper.

CONTENT: PARAGRAPHS

- [ ] Topic sentences introduce each paragraph's content.
- [ ] All points in each paragraph relate to the topic sentence.
- [ ] Good transitions between paragraphs.
- [ ] Good coherence within each paragraph.
- [ ] Good, specific details.

STYLISTIC CONCERNS

- [ ] No expletives—there is/there are/there have been, etc.
- [ ] No unnecessary questions.
- [ ] No excessively wordy sentences.
- [ ] No information language/diction.

GRAMMAR AND SPELLING

- [ ] No major errors.
- [ ] Good work with punctuation.
- [ ] No misspelled words.

MECHANICS

- [ ] Paragraphs are clearly tabbed.
- [ ] Title is centered correctly.
- [ ] Header contains last name and page number.
- [ ] MLA format is correct.

_____ Proofreader

_____ Paper's Author

Note to the proofreader:

- Communicate with the writer. Mark problem spots but also explain your corrections to her or him.

- Do not rewrite the paper. Make notes on the paper. It is not your job to revise every word of the paper.

- On the left side of the checklist, check each box to indicate that you have worked with that particular area of the paper.

Note to the writer:

- The proofreader is *not* responsible for your grade.

- Correct or ignore any and all suggestions based on your best judgment.

Topic Lists

DESCRIPTION TOPICS

1. Sunday morning at your house
2. Favorite place to study
3. Protected land you have visited
4. Military training exercise
5. Family vehicle
6. Workshop
7. Restaurant after closing
8. Favorite baby _____
9. A concert
10. A day care center

EXEMPLIFICATION TOPICS

1. Characteristics of a good sibling, parent, preacher, basketball player _____
2. Lessons I learned in high school
3. Reasons I like band, football, chess, drama _____
4. My favorite band, book, movie _____
5. The benefits of having a dog, cat, bird _____
6. Reasons for the popularity of reality TV shows
7. *Life in Pieces* (or some other TV show) is the best show on television.

DEFINITION TOPICS

1. Family
2. Joy
3. Hurt
4. Bullying
5. Harassment
6. Parent
7. Real
8. Seeing
9. Work
10. Discipline
11. Pain
12. Cell phones
13. Friends

PROBLEM AND SOLUTION

1. Sexual harassment
2. Single-parent households
3. High cost of living
4. Nontraditional students' needs
5. Internet addiction
6. Safety on campus
7. Recycling
8. Loss of wildlife habitat
9. Verbal or physical abuse
10. Peer pressure in high schools
11. Facebook or Twitter use
12. Cell phone contracts
13. Fast food
14. Student jobs
15. Treatment of older students
16. Commuter students

DIVISION AND CLASSIFICATION TOPICS

1. Children at a nursery or day care center
2. Coaches
3. Tools of a specific trade
4. Different brands of a musical instrument
5. Politicians
6. Slackers
7. Supervisors
8. Fellow employees at your place of work
9. Liars
10. Sycophants
11. High school cliques

PROCESS

Combined with Narrative

1. How I survived _____
2. How I avoid trouble in my neighborhood or community
3. How I learned to be a good babysitter
4. How I kicked a bad habit
5. How I learned to do landscape or yard work
6. How I learned to live without _____
7. How I avoid harassment

    ☐ in the workplace
    ☐ on campus
    ☐ at the mall
    ☐ at a party

8. How I chose my college major

9. How I study for a _____ test

10. How I taught a child to _____

11. How I learned to play _____

12. How I have kept a job

13. How I balance my hectic schedule

14. How I live on a fixed income

15. How I survived a difficult time in my life

16. How I maintain my Facebook account

17. How I treat customers

18. How I survived a bad family vacation

19. How I avoid trouble on campus

Chapter 14

Grammar and Language Review

By the time a student reaches college, he or she has worked hundreds of practice exercises, chosen thousands of correct verb forms, and identified countless prepositional phrases. In a perfect world, you, as one of those students, would remember everything that you've learned from those grammar lessons and could apply all that knowledge to your essays.

Unfortunately, that dream world does not exist. To help you remember and build your skills, this chapter provides a review of the most important elements of grammar and style as they apply to composition. You will need to consult a college handbook or a grammar site on the Internet for more detailed information.

Appropriate Use of Person in Formal Writing

Standard American English (SAE) should be used in all formal academic writing. In SAE, third person pronouns (*he, she, it, they, one—and all their forms*) are considered more formal than either first person (*I, we*) or second person (*you*) pronouns. For that reason, you will be directed to write most of your essays in third person. In formal criticism, "one" or a noun such as "the reader" or "the student" works best.

USE OF *I* AND *WE*

The first person pronouns are appropriate when giving an example of something that you have done, but first person is generally not appropriate in other situations.

> No-No Example ·
> For instance, **you should not write "I believe," "It seems to me," or "I think."** The fact that your name is on the paper is enough.

USE OF *YOU*

Although *you* is often used in speaking, it is not appropriate in formal writing (unless for process essays) for grammatical, rhetorical, and semantical reasons.

However, it is appropriate to use second person pronouns in writing a process-analysis (how-to) essay when the writer is giving directions or instructions.

Check with your instructor about using second person. Some are adamantly opposed and others are more lenient.

IMPERATIVE MOOD

The imperative mood is involved with use of the word *you*. This mood is the command mode in English.

> Get some sleep. Brush your teeth three times a day. Stand up straight.

All are commands, the imperative mood. All have *you* as the understood subject.

Deal with the imperative mood as you would with any use of second person: avoid it except with process writing. Ask your instructor if you need more information! And beware, some imperative mood sentences do not sound bossy: "Consider the actual number of carrots used in their recipe." This sentence is polite, but it still uses the imperative mood. Avoid imperative mood.

> Be sure to know your teacher's preference about second person, imperative mood, spelling out numbers (including percentages), and abbreviations. Styles and preferences change constantly.

Appropriate Use of Active and Passive Voices

Voice is a term used to identify the relationship of a transitive verb to its subject.

Transitive verbs are distinguished as either **active** or **passive** voice depending on whether the subject of the verb performs the action expressed by the verb (as in example 1), or whether the subject receives the action expressed by the verb (as in example 2).

Example 1 (active voice) ·
On Friday, the students conjugated the verbs.

No-No Example 2 (passive voice)· ·
On Friday, the verbs were conjugated by the students.

In most cases, the active voice construction, in which the subject performs the action of the verb, presents a more concise expression, as the example above shows.

However, there are occasions when shifting the emphasis from the subject as performer of the action of the verb to the subject as receiver of the action is necessary. For example, when you don't know who or what performed the action, passive voice is necessary (as in example 3). Also, when you want to place the emphasis on the receiver of the action, the passive voice is preferable (as in example 4).

Example 3 ·
The Natchez Trace was finished in 2005.

Example 4 ·
Corn is processed for multiple purposes.

In the above examples, the writer is not claiming who/what built the Natchez Trace or who/what processes corn. The writer may not know or the fact may be irrelevant. Passive voice is preferred with these limited exceptions.

Using active voice is much preferred by most instructors. Using strong, specific, active voice constructions can empower your essay and make the message more clear.

Sentence Variety: Making a Change from the Ordinary

Like other aspects of revision and editing, rewriting sentences to improve variety comes after you have completed a paper for strong content and correct format. When you are satisfied that your paper says what you want it to say, then you must consider how you are saying it.

The standard format of an English sentence is subject-verb-predicate. However, if every sentence in your essay is in that format, your writing will be as boring as a child's textbook. **You want your writing to be interesting and to sound as if a college student, not an elementary student, wrote it.** Two ways to do this are to combine sentences that are repetitious and to change the sentence format.

It is not enough to have profound or important ideas in a paper. Those ideas must be stated in a way that makes the reader want to read more and to appreciate your thoughts. That means not only writing in Standard American English (SAE) with correct grammar, but also composing sentences that vary in structure in order to avoid boring, formulaic writing. In SAE you will also avoid any use of slang terms or phrases.

Good writers use a variety of sentence types to make their writing more interesting. Just as an essay that contains all simple sentences would be monotonous to read, so would an essay with *only* compound or *only* complex or *only* compound-complex sentences. Varying sentence length—some long, some short—will also add a more mature dimension to your writing.

COMBINING SENTENCES

Read over what you have written, looking for words or phrases that are repetitious. If you find that you have repeated the same word or a pronoun in two consecutive sentences, you can improve those sentences by combining them.

> No-No Example ·
> **Repetitious/Needs Combining:** Many college students live in dorms. Dorms can be noisy. It is hard to study in a noisy dorm.

Notice that the above sentences have repeated words such as *dorm* and *noisy*. These three sentences are also very short and choppy. While it is tempting to write short sentences so that you do not have to worry about punctuation problems, these sentences do not sound as if they were written by a mature writer.

One way to combine the sentences is to change the repeated noun into a pronoun, either a personal pronoun (he, she, it) or a relative pronoun (which, that). Another way is to combine the sentences using a coordinate, subordinate, or adverbial conjunction.

> **Corrected with pronoun:** Many college students live in dorms that can be noisy which hinders studying.

> **Corrected with conjunction:** Because college dorms can be noisy, college students often have difficulty studying in them.

If you find that your sentences are consistently short (ten words or fewer) or that you repeat nouns or verbs, try combining some of these sentences.

CHANGING SENTENCE FORMAT

Because the usual format is subject-verb-predicate, any time you change that order, you are giving variety to your writing.

You can make a simple change by adding a transition word or conjunctive adverb to the beginning of a sentence. Words such as *next*, *then*, and *however*, followed by a comma, give a quick, easy change, and provide transition between thoughts. You do not, however, want to use such a word at the beginning of every sentence; you no longer have variety when every sentence begins with a transition word.

> **BIG HINT WHEN USING A SCREEN TO WRITE:** If you feel that you may be using one particular word too often, press Ctrl + F at the same time. This will bring up a navigation window. Type the word you'd like to see highlighted in your essay, press enter, and the word will appear highlighted every time you used it. Don't do this too often while first typing. Wait til the editing and proofing process. You don't want to micromanage too severely.

The second method mentioned on the prior page uses a conjunction to combine sentences. Subordinating conjunctions at the beginning of a clause will make that clause a dependent one, so you must have an independent clause in the sentence as well. Dependent clauses can come either at the beginning or at the end of the sentence. Changing the position of the clause is a way to give variety to your writing.

Remember, though, that a dependent clause at the beginning of the sentence is technically an interrupter, so it is followed by a comma. A dependent clause at the end of the sentence is in its standard location, so it is not preceded by a comma.

Correct with comma: Because college dorms can be noisy, college students often have difficulty studying in them.

Correct without a comma: College students often have difficulty studying in dorms because they can be noisy.

While "and" is a coordinating conjunction and can be used to join two clauses, use it sparingly. Try a variety of conjunctions to improve your writing.

Be sure to use the appropriate transition for the statement you are making, and be sure to punctuate your sentence correctly.

USING PARALLELISM

One way to add variety to your essays is to work on utilizing parallelism in sentence structure. Just as parallel lines are equal, running side by side, parallel constructions are equal, meaning that they are of the same type.

For instance, in a description, you can use all adjectives or all adverbs or all prepositional phrases to add unity to your work. Likewise, you can use gerunds, infinitives, or participles to make your sentences flow smoothly. What you would not want to do it is to mix these elements; the result is discordant to the reader.

No-No, Unparallel ·
I enjoy cooking, to go to the movies, and a nap.

Parallel
I enjoy cooking, going to movies, and napping.

No-No, Unparallel ·
I went to the store, the mall, and dropped by Sonic.

Parallel
I went to the store, to the mall, and to Sonic.

> **BEWARE:** The last element in a list often contains the source of the problem with parallelism.

Professional writers and speakers understand the value of parallel structure in their sentences. It adds a powerful boost to the written word when done well.

ELIMINATING EXPLETIVES

Another way to strengthen your writing is to eliminate weak constructions that begin with expletives, which just delay the real meaning of the sentence. Most of us use "there is," "there are," "there have been," and a dozen other versions of "there" + verb to start sentences. It is a weak, overused phrase for formal writing.

Phrases like "there is," "there are," "there were," "there have been," and "it is" add nothing to a sentence.

No-No Example ·
There is a game at 10:00.

So much better
The game begins at 10:00.

Eliminating expletives can also cut wordiness:

No-No Example ·
There are three dogs lying in the road.

So much better
Three dogs lie in the road.

The poor writing examples listed above are acceptable in middle school but are not considered to be even close to college-level writing. Avoid them and click Ctrl + F to check and make sure that you do not have them. Reword the sentences that do contain "there" + verb constructions.

Inappropriate Language for College Writing

Different kinds of writing use *different* kinds of language and format to fit the needs and expectations of *different* audiences. Business writing, technical writing, personal writing, research writing . . . each has its own conventions.

When you write an academic research paper or formal essay, you must speak the same "language," Standard American English. This is the language of the essay, not of the street or of the family conversation or of television.

This formal language and structured format meet the expectations of those in your academic field. Usually, that format applies either to MLA or APA. Both demand strictest uses of English—Standard American English.

INFORMAL DICTION

The way you speak to friends, coworkers, and family members is acceptable language to use in your everyday conversations, emails, and correspondence.

However, informal language is not what your college English instructor, nor future employers, will deem satisfactory. Research papers and formal essays require formal language. Avoiding the blunders from the list that follows will assist you in maintaining college level diction.

Conversational Diction

Never forget that a formal essay is not a conversation between friends. When you choose words that are more conversational and not correct for formal English essays, you are using informal diction. Here are just a few examples.

INFORMAL DICTION	CORRECT VERSION
alone time	solitude
warmness	warmth
lemme	let me
gonna	going to
hafta	have to
a must	necessity or requirement
hanging out	spending time
bug out/freak out	become hysterical
leave out	left or leave
pricey	expensive
pretty much	very
aha moment	epiphany

Slang

Slang is a part of our culture and our everyday conversations. However, slang has no place in research papers or in academic writing.

Slang is tied to vocabulary fads that come and go. In fact, almost as soon as they go from the street to print, they become old and unpopular. For instance, in the 1950s your mothers and grandmothers were *having a hissy over the latest flick*. Later on, these same females were *rapping with the studs*.

Even current and popular slang terms are not appropriate for college writing. Keeping up with the latest slang can certainly reflect how cool you are, but using slang in a formal essay is never appropriate.

Clichés

These phrases have been used so often that they are completely worn out and unacceptable in higher-level writing. More importantly, your reader might think that you are too lazy to think of more creative ways to make your point.

Using specific words and phrases that hold the reader's attention ensures a better essay. Good academic writing contains concrete details without relying on clichés.

The list of clichés is infinite, and the following is only a sampling from recent student essays:

GENERAL CLICHÉS			SPORTS-RELATED CLICHÉS
was all in	off the chain	give him some space	got on the right track
straight and narrow path	had a positive (or negative) vibe	got his head on straight	went the whole nine yards
there for me	back in the day	relationship went south	step up his game
was all business	was big on	eaten out of house and home	set the record straight
jump down his throat	go-to moment	stay on top of the books	get the ball rolling

Euphemism

A special type of cliché is the euphemism: using a more pleasant, gentler word to avoid a hard reality. Referring to someone who died as "going to her/his reward" or as "passing away" might be appropriate to spare someone's feelings in a conversation, but these phrases are not acceptable in formal essays.

Colloquialisms

Colloquial language is the casual language of everyday speech. Therefore, it is difficult to remedy because we use it so often. Colloquialisms, no matter how useful we find them in conversation, are not appropriate in college writing. Words such as *yep, sorta, gonna, fixin, kinda,* and *y'all* are too informal for essays.

Contractions

Another colloquialism that falls into our writing is the use of contractions—*can't, didn't, won't.* Take the time to write out the contractions.

Check with your teacher for specific instructions! Some forbid contractions and others tolerate them sometimes. Know your instructors' requirements and preferences.

Clipped Words

An additional colloquialism to avoid is clipping or abbreviating words. The following are examples of clipped words.

INCORRECT DICTION: CLIPPED	CORRECT DICTION
ad	advertisement
limo	limousine
fridge	refrigerator
burger	hamburger
TV	television
doc	doctor
teen	teenager
info	information
kids	children
kid	child

A serious writer uses formal diction in academic writing.

Profanity

Although you may choose to use profanity in everyday speech, it is extremely important not to slip those "four-letter" words into your academic writing. The use of profanity can insult or even infuriate your audience.

Cell Phone Text Language

If U R texting N college writings, *stop*! You are creating a "text mess." In the age of cell phone madness, college students who constantly text on their cell phones are letting *text language* slip into academic writing, a practice which has writing instructors reaching for their red pens.

Cell phone texting language is not appropriate for college writing. Avoid those that follow and the hundreds of others that populate your world.

TEXT LANGUAGE	CORRECT VERSION
U	you
cuz	because
2	to/too/two
4	four/for
R	are
N	and/in
i	I
bc	because

Jargon

Jargon is a vocabulary specific to a particular group or profession. Using jargon to communicate with someone in that particular group or profession conveys your meaning clearly *only* if you are currently working in that profession. However, using jargon to communicate with your general audience is often viewed as haughty and snobbish.

While computer aficionados, sports fans, and Harry Potter enthusiasts all have a language that they understand, throwing around phrases like "bits and bytes," a "double play," or "the Ministry of Magic" might confuse or agitate your audience.

AVOID PRETENTIOUS LANGUAGE

Just as nonstandard English is inappropriate for college writing, so is pretentious language. A writer should strive to write in his or her own voice in language that is understood by both writer and audience. For instance, in a current television series a forensic examiner says, "Because the precipitation is about to commence, we quickly need to amass the paraphernalia."

While the language is appropriate for that particular television character, the language would be pretentious for a college student. More appropriate would be, "Since it is about to rain, we need to gather all the evidence now." Pretentious language has the capacity to make a writer appear foolish rather than intelligent. Sprinkling your essay with as many multisyllabic words as you can glean from the thesaurus will not improve your grade.

AVOID BIASED LANGUAGE

When you are writing a paper for an academic assignment, you can generally assume (unless clearly stated otherwise) that your intended audience will be both male and female; therefore, **inclusive language** is appropriate. By referring to both your male and female audience, you avoid alienating readers of either sex. Although writers sometimes try to avoid gender bias by use of **he/she** and **his/her**, the practice makes for awkward sentence structure. The whole issue can be simplified as exemplified:

No-No Example, Biased. . . . .
A student should attend all of his classes.

> *Unbiased*
> Students should attend all of their classes.

No-No Example, Biased. . . . .
A teacher should prepare for her lecture well in advance of the class meeting.

> *Unbiased*
> Teachers should prepare for their lectures well in advance of the class meeting.

Biased language is a result of inaccurate generalizations or thoughtless habits. Because accuracy is one of the goals of all academic writing, working to eliminate biased language is important.

Addressing your audience in an inclusive and respectful way is a basic form of good writing etiquette. For most biased language, there is a nonbiased alternative:

- **Race/Nationalities.** When discussing ethnicities, use language that is appropriate for formal writings, such as Asians, Native Americans, African Americans, or Hispanics.
- **Age.** When utilizing terms concerning age, do not use insulting terms, such as old man, granny, or old folks.
- **Class status.** When referring to socioeconomic class, do not use offensive terms, such as redneck or country hick.

Challenge yourself to learn to recognize and eliminate biased language from your speech and writing.

STYLISTICALLY WEAK WORDS AND PHRASES

Much of the easy, relaxed way we speak creeps into writing. In formal English, it should not.

Three vague words are particularly bothersome and ineffective for teachers:

ISSUE/ISSUES	This is a terrible substitute for more powerful words like "problems" and more accurate terms like "mental illness." **Issues** is a generic word that says nothing.
THINGS	Overused! A "thing" is an object that has no name. No one has "things" on the brain. We have ideas! We have daydreams and concerns, NOT **things**.
DIFFERENT	If nothing good or positive can be said about anyone or anything, then the word "**different**" is applied. It is a catch-all word that has no clear meaning and absolutely no depth of thought.

Etc.

Another very popular abbreviation is etc. In technical writing, use of etc. is acceptable and expected. In formal writing, actual details, not "etc.," should be used.

No-No Example· ·
We had turkey, dressing, etc. for Thanksgiving.

So much better
We had turkey, cornbread dressing, garden vegetables, and pecan pie for Thanksgiving.

So much better
We had a traditional Southern Thanksgiving dinner with all the fresh vegetables and baked goods that my mom always cooks.

Listing every single item on the menu is not necessary. It's padding for the paper, and the teacher is aware of what you are doing. However, substituting "etc." for details is never a good idea. Learn to describe well and to condense information, instead of leaving it out with a mysterious "etc."

Infernal Gripes

Almost every writer wants to start an essay with a variation of these words:

Most instructors despise these sentence beginnings.
- In our world today
- In today's society
- In our society today
- In our society
- In our country
- In our country today

Avoid infernal griping about the world, society, and country. It makes you sound like a grumpy old codger. Avoid these phrases!

Human Beings Matter

When referencing human beings of any type—teachers, students, parents, children, convicts, shoppers—use the relative pronoun *who*. When referring to objects or non-humans, use *that*.

> **No-No Examples** ·
> Teachers that, students that, women that, men that
>
> *Correct*
> Teachers who, students who, women who, men who
>
> *Also correct*
> phone that, printer that, drone that, situation that, tree that
>
> **No-No Examples** ·
> anyone that, no one that, everyone that
>
> *Correct*
> anyone who, no one who, everyone who
>
> *Special note*
> SIPs also take "who," (see pp. 164–165).

Major Errors Review

Whether you are enrolled in an institution of higher learning or working in the business world, you will be expected to use Standard American English for both speaking and writing when in formal situations.

As stated before, SAE involves using standard forms of verbs and standard punctuation. In most English departments, instructors count off heavily for errors in a number of areas, referred to as the *major errors*. These include **sentence fragments, run-on sentences, agreement errors, verb form errors**, and **shifts in construction**. You should pay close attention to your instructor to determine what his or her guidelines are in these areas.

As with the other academic conventions discussed in this chapter, you need to proofread for the standard forms of grammar when you prepare your final draft. When you revise a paper, you may alter, omit, or add sentences. For that reason, before you turn in your final copy, you must proofread and correct any errors that are not in Standard American English.

SENTENCE FRAGMENTS

A sentence fragment is a group of words that is punctuated as a sentence but is incomplete as a sentence. Hinds' student Tommy Paige so aptly defined fragment as "a piece of a sentence."

Generally, there are two types of fragments: those that do not contain a subject or a verb and those that do not make a complete thought.

Fragments that are missing a subject or a verb can be corrected by providing the missing part, as seen in the examples below.

No-No, Fragment ·
Proving my point.

> *Correction*
> Proving my point was my goal in the debate.

No-No, Fragment ·
And eat lunch.

> *Correction*
> On my break, I exercise and eat lunch.

No-No, Fragment ·
The students in the quad.

> *Correction*
> The students in the quad are my friends.

The second type of fragment may contain a subject and verb but may not express a complete thought. This error is sometimes caused by last-minute separations of sentences.

These fragments can be corrected by joining the group of words to an adjacent sentence or by omitting the subordinate conjunction or changing the relative pronoun to a personal pronoun.

Other fragments are more common and complex, dependent clause fragments.

No-No, Fragment ·
Although my cousin and I were late. We were seated before the movie actually began.

> *Correction*
> Although my cousin and I were late, we were seated before the movie actually began.

No-No, Fragment ·
My roommate went to my high school. Who is my best friend.

> *Correction*
> My roommate, who is my best friend, went to my high school.

No-No, Fragment ·
Because I could not eat Mexican food with bell peppers. I asked her not to include them on my order.

> *Correction*
> Because I could not eat Mexican food with bell peppers, I asked her not to include them on my order.

Common Ways to Avoid Some Types of Fragments

No definitive list exists, but two very easy reminders may help:

1. Do not start sentences with "which."

    No-No, Fragment ·
    Which was the best breakfast I ever ate at her house.

2. Do not write sentences with an –ing verb as the main verb.

    No-No, Fragment ·
    His point being that he was tired of seeing violence on television.

    No-No, Fragment ·
    She thinking about going to college in California but not knowing about tuition there.

RUN-ON SENTENCES

A run-on sentence is created when independent clauses are joined incorrectly. Run-on sentences fall into one of two categories: comma splices and fused sentences.

> **No-No, Comma Splice** ·
> My high school was very crowded, the two thousand students in the halls between classes could scarcely move.

> **No-No, Fused Sentence** ·
> My high school was very crowded the two thousand students in the halls between classes could scarcely move.

You can correct run-ons in a number of ways:

1. a period—Ex.1

2. a semicolon—if you know how to use it correctly—Ex. 2

3. a FANBOYS (see p. 170)—Ex. 3

4. a subordinating conjunction—Ex. 4

Corrections

Example 1 ·
My high school was very crowded. The two thousand students in the
halls between classes could scarcely move.

Example 2 ·
My high school was very crowded; the two thousand students in the
halls between classes could scarcely move.

Example 3 ·
My high school was very crowded, so the two thousand students in
the halls between classes could scarcely move.

Example 4 ·
Because my high school was very crowded, the two thousand stu-
dents in the halls between classes could scarcely move.

Identifying and correcting run-on sentence errors in a composition can be
difficult tasks for many students. If run-on sentence structure is a problem
for you, proofread your papers carefully for possible errors and practice using
Internet grammar sites for reinforcement.

Here's What is *Not a Run On*

Incorrect use of a comma does not create a run on. It's accurately called a
comma fault (or error). *Know* the difference.

Not A Run On ·
Janet and Thomas smelled the roast burning in the oven and they
called 911.

Not A Run On ·
When we first went to the Grand Canyon, my sister and I were amazed
at the sights but we were not able to hike into the area that day.

Both of these sentences should have commas before the FANBOYS (see
p. 170). This is an error, but it is—by no means—a major error.

SUBJECT-VERB/NOUN-VERB AGREEMENT ERRORS

Businesses report that subject-verb agreement errors raise red flags in hiring
or in promoting an employee. Correcting verb error problems in your writing and speaking will improve not only your composition grade but also your
future employment options.

Errors in agreement occur when there is lack of correspondence between
related words. In writing, agreement errors can occur between **subject and
verb** or between a **pronoun and antecedent**.

This error is better understood by example than by definition:

Agreement Errors

No-No Example in Bold #1 ·
The two thousand **students** in my high school eat at the same time
and **goes** back to class together.

No-No Example #2 ·
We was at the game with our friends.

In the first sentence, the subject of the sentence, *students*, is plural in number,
but the second verb—which also modifies *students*—must also reflect a plural
subject.

The *S* Fight

Lots of SINGULAR verbs in the present tense end in s. Examples:
tests, contacts, plants, goes, looks, eats, stands—and tens (if not
hundreds) of thousands of verbs also end in s when singular. Exceptions
to this rule do exist, but this is the overall identifier.

Here's the confusing part: nouns.

Nouns that end in s are plural. Examples: tests, contacts, plants, looks,
stands. Some of these words are in the verb section, and as verbs, they
are singular. AS NOUNS WITH S ON THE END, THEY ARE PLURAL.

To recap:

- **Verbs ending with s—singular**
- **Nouns ending with s—plural**

Noun-Verb Agreement Errors (aka pronoun and antecedent errors)

These occur within dependent clauses embedded in the sentence (the independent clause).

No-No Example #1 ·
My teacher told me to take all the **students who was** in the class to
the gym.

No-No Example #2 ·
The **animals** at the Jackson Zoo **that needs** medical care are in the
veterinarian's office.

These verb agreement errors are often difficult to detect. Make sure to know
what the subject is and you'll be able to add the correct verb.

Noun-Pronoun Agreement Errors

As the editor/writer types these words onto the screen, the rules for nouns and pronouns are in the process of changing. With singular indefinite pronouns (SIPs), the rules have almost completely morphed.

Here's a quick listing of singular indefinite pronouns using the acronym SANEBOT:

S	SOME	Combine with all three words below.	somebody someone something
A	ANY	Combine with all three words below.	anybody anyone anything
N	NO	Combine with all three words below.	nobody no one* nothing
E	EVERY	Combine with all three words below.	everybody everyone everything
B	BODY	Add to the end of the four words above.	*There are more indefinite pronouns, but these are the main ones that give all of us trouble.*
O	ONE	Add to the end of the four words above.	
T	THING	Add to the end of the four words above.	

*the only one with 2 words

Here's what is changing with indefinite pronouns: the use of "their" with "everyone" and everybody." Other changes are on the way, but this one is growing wildly outside of the Petri dish.

> Classic/Old Way of Using "Everybody" or "Everyone" with SIPs . . . . .
> **Everyone** in the class got **his or her** textbook from the bookstore.

> New Way of Using "Everybody" or "Everyone"
> with SIPs for SOME TEACHERS . . . .
> **Everyone** in the class got **their** textbook from the bookstore.

> **Warning for all Students over SIPs!**
>
> Do not expect every teacher to accept the newest changes. It's not that we are dinosaurs. It's just that permanent changes in our language only occur over decades of use. Some teachers may be hesitant to accept this change because of the many trends that we have seen disappear, but grammar handbooks are now discussing its acceptability.
>
> There is also another possibility: your instructor may mark these noun agreement errors on your essay but not reduce your overall grade. Clarify this with the instructor.

The REAL, Unchanging Pronoun-Noun Agreement Errors

Though SIPs present a problem, other instances of agreement are clearly incorrect:

> No-No Example #1 ·
> The **students** eat **her** lunch at noon.

In this example, "her lunch" should be "their lunches." Otherwise, one girl is being horribly bullied at lunch.

> No-No Example #2 ·
> When **students** go to the library, **he or she** is usually looking for a quiet place to study.

In the above example, "he or she" should be the simpler version, "they," to match the noun it modifies, "students."

OTHER PRONOUN PROBLEMS

Unclear pronoun reference involves the reader not being able to distinguish to whom or what the pronoun refers. The most popular unclear pronoun is "it."

> No-No Example ·
> I went to the play at school and later went to Waffle House with friends. **It** was great.

In the above example, the reader is confused: What was fun? Was it the play, Waffle House, or the entire experience? Clarify what you mean.

Incorrect pronoun case errors occur mostly with objects of the prepositions.

> No-No Example ·
> She gave the money to **Mama and I.**

In the above example, "I" should be "me" because "me" is the object of the preposition "to." Often times, using "I" instead of "me" sounds fancy and sophisticated. It's not. It's wrong, even when rich people and celebrities say this.

Pronoun placement errors are simplest to correct. Remember this rule: always put yourself last. In use of "I" and "me"—in any list—put these words last.

> No-No Example #1 ·
> **I and Mama** ate dinner at Joanie's Rainbow Diner.

> No-No Example #2 ·
> My sister gave the gift certificate **to me and Mama** on New Year's Day.

To repeat the rule: *always put yourself last.* In use of "I" and "me"—in any list—put these words last.

VERB FORM ERRORS

Regular verbs end in *-d* or *-ed* in the simple past and the past participle forms. Irregular verbs have different forms in the past and the past participle. If you need more information on irregular verb forms and their uses, check a grammar handbook, a grammar site on the Internet, your school's writing center, or a good dictionary.

The misuse of verb forms is one of the most common major errors and, unfortunately, can be difficult for students to spot.

> Incorrect Verb Form· ·
> He seen the dead dog in the road.
>
> *Correct forms*
> He saw the dead dog in the road.
>
> He has seen the dead dog in the road for the last two days.

Verb Tense Consistency

As stated before, verb tense refers to time, specifically the relationship in time between the action of the verb and the speaking or writing about it. The two most common tenses that you will use are present and simple past.

The present tense is used in writing about a literary work, in signal phrases introducing a paraphrase or direct quote, and in discussing ideas that continue to be true. In using present tense verbs, you must be careful about subject-verb agreement because of the "s" that is always added to the third person singular verb.

I see	we see
You see	you see
He, she, it sees	they see

The simple past tense is used to indicate events that happened in the past and are no longer happening. The simple past verb form is the same for both singular and plural, so you do not have to worry about agreement.

In an academic paper, you should be consistent in your use of tense. In a literary paper, for instance, always maintain present tense. If you are using simple past, do not slip into past perfect (using *had* as an auxiliary) or past progressive (using *was* with the *-ing* form of the verb). As you proofread, look at every verb to check for tense consistency.

In fact, proofreading carefully is the cure for many of the writing errors discussed in this chapter.

Appropriate Use of Verb Tense

Verb tense refers to the *time* in which the action of a sentence occurs. Although there are many verb tenses, each with a specific use in writing, the two tenses used most often in academic papers are **present** and **past** tenses.

Present Tense

Present tense verbs are usually formed by using the base form of the verb. They are used to indicate action occurring now—in the present.

Present tense is used for three applications: literary papers, citations in research papers, and actions or ideas that are still in force.

Historical present. Whenever you are called upon to write an essay about a work about history or a piece of literature, academic article, poetry, nonfiction, fiction, drama, and film, use of the present tense is appropriate for most of the essay. Present tense is used because, although the author might be dead, the work of literature lives on. Therefore, the character of Phoenix Jackson "walks" down the path in the short story by Eudora Welty. Romeo and Juliet *are* star-crossed lovers.

Use present tense when discussing the author in relation to his or her work.

Example••
Shakespeare demonstrates the qualities of true love.

Use present tense in discussing the piece of literature.

> **Example.** . . . .
> *The Waste Land* presents Eliot's views of life in postwar Europe.

However, use past tense to refer to some aspect of the author's life or the work's publication that occurred in the past.

> **Example.** . . . .
> T. S. Eliot wrote parts of *The Waste Land* while in an asylum.

To express habitual action or current ideas, use present tense.

> Advances in medicine are made every day.
>
> Changes in documentation form are necessary because of the many changes in technology.

Past Tense

The simple past tense is used to indicate events that happened in the past and are no longer happening. Use either the one-word form ending in *-d* or *-ed* for regular verbs, shown in Example 1 below, or the past tense form for irregular verbs, shown in Example 2.

> **Example 1** . . . .
> The boy **wanted** to pass the class, but he **failed** because of his work schedule.

> **Example 2** . . . .
> The class **left** at recess and **went** to the zoo.

Using past tense in narrative essays is particularly important. If you are writing about a football game in middle school, you should use past tense because that game was in the past. Therefore, you "threw" or "ran" the football. You did not "throw" or "run" the football. Don't get caught up in remembering the event and forget that you are writing a formal essay for English class.

Wordy Verbs

In an attempt to sound sophisticated or mature, many students will create elaborate verb constructions. Wordy verbs are generally unnecessary. In fact, simplifying verb tenses often strengthens essays.

The worst offender in the wordy verbs category is "would." Instead of saying, "She would go to church," simply say, "She went to church."

CONTRACTIONS

Check with your teacher about using contractions in any essay.

Here's what the problem about contractions is in the 21st century. Meaning to say "we will" on a text message, you will often get "well," when the obvious contraction is "we'll." This lack of attention has bled through to English classes.

Before the problems associated with autocorrect, students overused and misused contractions like "she'll," "Janet'll," or "students've." They are still used incorrectly, as are "we're" for "were" and a hundred over incorrect variations.

What teachers really want students to avoid are the NAME + VERB contractions: "Louise'll."

We do not object to a normal contraction, two verbs combined, but allowing a normal contraction often invites horrible misuse of contractions in general. In order to calm the chaos involved, most teachers simply do not allow contractions.

Again, check with your teacher about using contractions in any essay.

Punctuation Review

Nothing baffles students like commas. While not a complete list, the rules that follow comprise the great majority of what needs to be studied.

COMMA RULES

1. **Commas in a series.** Use commas to set off items in a series.

   Example·······································
   In my office, I have three **pictures, a bookshelf, and a filing cabinet**.

   The comma after bookshelf is not optional in SAE.

2. **Compound sentences.** Use a comma between two complete sentences joined by a coordinating conjunction.

   Example·······································
   I have never seen the Lady Volunteers play a basketball game in **Knoxville, but I have** seen them in Starkville when they came to play the Lady Bulldogs.

   In order to use a comma with a coordinating conjunction, you must have two complete sentences with a subject and a verb. In the first sentence in the example above, the first subject is *I* and the verb is *have seen*. In the second sentence, the subject is also *I* and the verb is also *have seen*.

The coordinating conjunctions are also known as FANBOYS.

F	for
A	and
N	nor
B	but
O	or
Y	yet
S	so

3. **Introductory clauses.** Use a comma after an introductory element at the beginning of a sentence.

Dependent Clause··
When I go to the **gym, I usually stay** for two hours.

Verbal Phrase···
Running toward the **bus, I tripped** and fell to the ground.

Prepositional Phrase··
In the middle of the **woods, the boys** built a fort.

4. **Transitions.** Interrupters that can be taken out of a sentence without changing the sentence's meaning but also show a connection between the sentences they are connecting.

Example···
However, I would like for you to wash my car today.

Example···
I **would, however, like** for you to wash my car today.

Example···
I would like for you to wash my car **today, however**.

Some comma transition words or phrases are *however, therefore, moreover, also, then, next, for example, first, second, third,* and *as a result.*

5. **Appositive.** A word or group of words that defines or explains the word or phrase that comes before it.

Example···
I am excited to see what **Dan Mullen, the head coach of Mississippi State's football team**, can do next year for the Bulldogs.

6. **Nonessential and essential elements.** Essential elements are needed to understand the full meaning of the sentence. Nonessential elements are not necessary to understanding the meaning of the sentence.

Nonessential Example ·
I really need to go to **the store, which** is on the corner of Main and Gloster in Tupelo.

Essential Example ·
The **students who work really hard** will definitely do well in this course.

Even though the extra information about the location is not necessary, the fact that only students who work hard will do well is important to the sentence. If I had put commas around "who work really hard," that would have made that phrase extra, just an afterthought.

Do not stop using nonessential elements just because they have this label! They add valuable content.

SEMICOLON RULES

1. A transition word used to combine two sentences:

   Example. ·
   I went to **the store; however, when** I got there, I realized that I had forgotten my grocery list.

   The transition words used for this rule are the same as the ones used in the comma rule. However, this time the transition is used to combine two sentences that each have their own subjects and verbs. Now, if you only put commas around "however," you create a run-on.

2. Combining two similar sentences:

   Example. ·
   I went to Mississippi State when I got out of high school; my major was International Business.

   Do not get crazy with this rule and combine three or four sentences with semicolons.

3. Separating a series that already includes commas:

   Example. ·
   I have lived in Southaven, Mississippi; Gainesville, Florida; and Ridgeland, Mississippi.

   Example. ·
   The new officers have been elected for the next fiscal year of the Accounting Club: James Freeman, President; Erica Royal, Vice President; Juan Nunez, Parliamentarian; and Ginna Parsing, Secretary.

COLON RULES

1. Introduce a list with a complete sentence or putting emphasis on a particular word.

    Example. . . . .
    When you go to the store, please pick me up some items: eggs, bacon, and grits.

    Example. . . . .
    All of these ingredients focus on one important meal: breakfast.

2. Introduce a list with the phrase *the following* but make sure that a complete sentence precedes those two words!

    Example. . . . .
    If you want to succeed, you have to do the following: study hard and read your assignments.

3. Introduce a list with the phrase *as follows* but make sure that a complete sentence precedes those two words!

    Example. . . . .
    The plans for the trip are as follows: leave at 8 a.m., drive to the beach, and stay in a condo for three days.

4. Introduce long quotations in an essay or research paper.

5. Do not use a colon after *such as* if this phrase is in the middle of a sentence. In fact, colons are almost never used after *such as*. Avoid this!

USING MODIFIERS CORRECTLY

Misplaced Modifiers

A modifier is a word/phrase that changes the meaning of the word directly beside it. If a writer does not put the modifier beside the word it is meant to alter, then the meaning of the sentence could change.

No-No Example . . . .
The plates are on sale only tomorrow.

The use of the word *only* in this sentence implies that the sale is only tomorrow. However, if you mean only the plates are for sale you would say the following:

Example. . . . .
Only the plates are on sale tomorrow.

Just one word—*only*—changes the entire sentence.

Dangling Modifiers

A dangling modifier is a word/phrase that does not connect to anything in the sentence.

> **No-No Example** ·
> When working out at the gym, running and sit-ups are always done.

This sentence looks and sound strange because it is strange. Who is working out at the gym? Certainly, "running and sit-ups" are not working out at the gym. Put who is actually doing so right after the intro clause or phrase.

> *Correct*
> When working out at the gym, Ashley always runs and does sit-ups.

Now, we know who is at the gym: Ashley.

> **No-No Example** ·
> While turning the corner on two wheels, Granny smashed the mailbox.

Here we have a grandmother who has two wheels growing out of her thighs. Instead, the sentence should read:

> *Correct*
> While turning the corner on two wheels, the car that Granny drove smashed the mailbox.

CORRECTING APOSTROPHE ERRORS

Among other culprits, text messaging has killed the apostrophe. Unfortunately, you really need to know how to use apostrophes correctly. Apostrophes show ownership. They are like little tags on items that show they have been sold, and you will not know an item has been sold if it does not have a sold tag on it.

Singular Possessive

> **Incorrect** ·
> the girls bike

> *Correct*
> the girl's bike

Without the sold tag, *girls* looks like an adjective to describe how the bike looks. With the sold tag, we know that the bike belongs to the girl.

Plural Possessive

Incorrect ·
the horses's feed

That does not even look right, does it? That is because, when you have a plural noun owning what comes after it, you do not need the extra s at the end.

Correct
the horses' feed

Just one s is all you need—and the sold tag, of course.

Incorrect ·
womens' work

Women is the plural of woman, so adding an s to the word does not make sense.

Correct
women's work or men's work or children's work

If the plural word does not have an s on the end, then you should add the 's to show ownership.

Titles with MLA

MLA, the governing body that controls format of English essays, recently changed one of their oldest rules—one about underlining. No longer are writers allowed either to underline or to italicize titles of longer works: we must italicize whenever we type these titles.

When handwriting, however, you must underline the names of longer works. That rule has not changed.

TITLES TO ITALICIZE

Books—*Go Tell It on the Mountain* by James Baldwin

Plays—*Fences* by August Wilson

Television Shows—*The Big Bang Theory*

Movies—*Star Wars*

Long Poems—*The Inferno*

Websites—*YouTube, Facebook*

TITLES WITH QUOTATION MARKS

Song Titles—"Wonderwall" by Oasis

Short Poem—"Birches" by Robert Frost

Short Story—"The Man Who Was Almost a Man" by Richard Wright

Article in a Journal—"Are Undergraduate Students Ready for Online Learning?: A Comparison of Online and Face-to-Face Sections of a Course" in journal *Aura Special Education Quarterly*

Page or Work on a Website—"Spring Style" on website *Tupelo Bloggers*

TITLES WITH YOUR OWN ESSAY

Students are often confused about the different rules pertaining to their own titles. They do not seem to follow the MLA guidelines about quotation marks. Students are right! The rules do change for entitling their own work.

General Rules for Titles in Students' Essays

1. Do not use the teacher's prompt or topic.

2. No quotes (single or double) around your own essay's title.

3. No ALL CAPS in titles.

4. No **bolding** in titles.

5. No large fonts in titles.

6. No funky or **CRAZY** fonts in titles.

7. No *italics* unless you have a book title in your essay's title.

8. No periods at the end of titles.

9. Capitalize the first word of every title.

10. Capitalize the last word of every title.

11. Capitalize the first word after a colon.

12. Capitalize every **major word** in a title.

    a. See rules 9, 10, and 11.

    b. Capitalize verbs, including tiny "be" verbs like *is*, *am*, or *are*.

    c. Capitalize subordinating conjunctions like *because*, *although*, *when*, etc.

    d. Do *not* capitalize prepositions, even long ones like *against* or *beyond*.

13. Always capitalize proper nouns; this rule never changes, especially within titles. Examples: Chicago, June, Lauren, Easter, English, French, Harrington, Deputy Director, Apple (iMac, iPhone—these are exceptions), etc.

Chapter 15

The Library Speaks Volumes

Becoming Information Literate

In this electronic age, you may wonder why the library is relevant. Although libraries have been around for thousands of years, they are more relevant today than ever before because of the information overload in today's world. The libraries and the librarians who work in them carefully select content and provide guidance and direction to users who are looking for relevant and authoritative resources.

Going to college is not only about reading textbooks and attending classes; it is also about learning how to research and where to find information. To be successful in today's world, you must be

information literate. This does not mean knowing everything: it means knowing where and how to find the information that you need when you need it.

Get to know who the librarians at your college library are and ask them for help. Librarians are knowledgeable about many disciplines and are experienced in locating information on a variety of topics. They assist in locating reliable sources, and they understand how information is organized. The librarians are there to help!

Do not be intimidated or overwhelmed by an unfamiliar library. Once you learn to utilize the resources and wealth of knowledge that your college library provides, you have a gateway to an immeasurable amount of information from the web and on databases. You learn by doing, and this is especially true of research.

Books: Some Old, Some New, but All Useful

But wait—aren't books dead? Nothing could be further from the truth.

Books remain the most comprehensive, thorough, and reliable sources of information available, even with all of the current emphasis on electronic sources. Books go through a careful vetting/editorial process that results in reliability. In addition, the author cites sources used for writing the book so the reader can check the original information.

Unlike much of the information on the web that is often created by someone who may or may not have any knowledge of or expertise in the subject, books are often written by experts or by authors who have researched their topics and checked their facts.

Don't Judge a Book by Its Age!

While a book is not as current as an article in this month's magazine or something on last night's news, for some disciplines older books may contain more reliable and relevant information than newer sources.

But books, like any type of source, should be evaluated before you utilize them. For information in fields such as medicine and science, new discoveries are constantly being made. For that reason, the most current medical or scientific journals would provide the most current information. For example, if you were researching medicines used to treat breast cancer, the information in a book written ten years ago would be outdated. However, if you were doing research on theories of King Tut's death, a book on ancient Egypt might be an excellent source for background even if it was written before you were born.

Background Information: Reference Resources, a Good Place to Begin

Reference resources are often good for background information on a topic or for an overview of your subject. Before you start looking at magazines and periodicals that are shorter than a book and often cover only a tiny aspect of your topic, use a reference book to find out about your topic.

For example, if you are considering writing on genetic engineering and do not know much about it, an encyclopedia will usually give some history of it, describe what it is and how it is done, give areas that use genetic engineering, and explain positive and negative aspects of it.

Most libraries have reference resources online as well as in print.

Topic Too Broad?

Reference resources are also good for helping you narrow a topic so that it is more manageable for you. For example, genetic engineering is much too broad a topic for a freshman composition paper.

> TIP: Some teachers say that if you locate a whole book on your topic, it is too broad for a research report or paper.

Here's the good news: Reference resources about genetic engineering will provide ideas to help you choose some small aspect of the topic. For example, after a little background reading, you may decide to write on genetic engineering of corn and its benefits to Africa.

Library Classification Systems

Universities and community colleges use one of two classification systems for cataloging their books: the **Dewey Decimal** or the **Library of Congress**. Dewey Decimal uses numbers (110 B27P) to classify books. Library of Congress uses letters and numbers (DT61 .S57). Both are referred to as **call numbers**.

Both of these classification systems have the same purpose: to arrange books on the same subject together on the shelves. Having the call number helps you locate a specific book. Once you locate one book on your topic, the area around that book on the shelf should contain more books on the same topic.

Online Catalog: The Key to Locating Books in the Library

To find library books, you will need to look in the library's online catalog. Using a computer in the library or any place that you have Internet access, you can locate what books a library owns, where the books are located, and whether a book is checked out or on the shelf.

In the old card catalog (long wooden drawers), you could look up books by author, title, or subject. Now, in the online version, you can search for all of these at once by using the "words or phrase" search. This really speeds up your searching.

> TIP: Use the "words or phrase" search instead of the "subject" search for your topic unless you know exactly which subject headings were used in cataloging the book.

For example, if you look in the online catalog under "subject" for books on "abused child," you will not locate anything if the subject heading used is "child abuse." But "words or phrase" will locate the books. Also, think of other terms to use for your topic, such as "abused children" or "family violence." The information is there; be patient in searching for it.

After locating a book, you must write or print its call number (found in the online catalog) and go to the library stacks (shelves) to locate the book. When writing down the call number, note if the book is housed in a special location such as the reference room or the reserve desk. Never hesitate to ask someone in the library to help you—the catalog and library shelves can be overwhelming for anyone.

> TIP: Be careful to copy the call number exactly or you may have to begin the process all over.

PLACED ON RESERVE

With extremely popular topics, you may find that the books are unavailable for checkout but placed instead on "Reserve." The Reserve collection can generally be found at Circulation (or the front desk). If the books are on reserve (which means that use is restricted to the library premises), be ready to photocopy (bring money) and ask a librarian for help if you are not familiar with the photocopy machines.

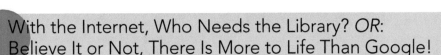
With the Internet, Who Needs the Library? *OR:* Believe It or Not, There Is More to Life Than Google!

Your university or community college library resources are usually much more reliable because these libraries endeavor to select resources that have gone through an editorial process involving experts and scholars. Research for term papers is best done first through the library databases rather than through a search engine like Google, because these databases contain collections of quality magazine, journal, or newspaper articles selected and paid for by the library (and your tuition dollars!). Make no mistake—Google is great for buying shoes, reading gossip, and locating fake news.

However, in many cases, you will have to work with the library databases to find sources that are reliable, factual, and in-depth.

Kick the Habit!

- Fight your addiction to Google.
- Reroute your first impulse and go to the library's databases instead. They have better information!
- The library's resources are selected for college research projects. Use them!

THE LIBRARY'S DATABASES

Library databases are collections of magazines, journals, newspapers, or book articles that have been digitized and categorized together by subject. The great majority of the information in the databases is still available in print. Libraries often choose to buy electronic instead of print subscriptions to these articles to provide students with "any time/any place" access.

> TIP: Don't let the term "database" scare you. *A database is just a collection of material bundled by subject.*

There are different databases for disciplines and/or subjects. For instance, students in a literature course looking for criticisms of Shakespeare's *Hamlet* might choose a database called "Literary Reference Center." The same principle applies to nursing, psychology, history, etc. All require different databases. The library also provides databases for controversial or political issues. These are often found under the subject "Pro/Con."

Are Library Databases a Web Source?

Be clear on directions your teacher gives about the types of resources you are allowed to use for your project. Some teachers may specifically direct you to use *only* library resources and prohibit resources found through Google or other search engines. This doesn't mean you have to use only print resources at the library or that you have to go to the library to use their resources.

Many students are understandably confused about the distinction. For clarification: Because so many of your library's resources (books, articles, videos, etc.) are online, they can be accessed *through* the Internet whether you are at the library, home, or visiting relatives in Florida. So when a teacher directs you to use library resources and not to use Google or Internet sources, what he or she means is that you should gather rather resources found at the library or from the library's online databases, not from the Internet.

Trust the library databases, rather than random information from the web. Make sure you understand exactly what the teacher's directions are for your assignment before using information from the web.

So Many Databases, So Little Time— Use the Library's "Discover" Tool

Students usually need to search through two or three databases when beginning research into general topics for English classes. Academic Search Premier, MasterFILE Premier, and Newspaper Source are excellent *general* databases that contain information on an array of topics.

There are *subject* specific databases as well; they contain information on specific subjects such as environment, business, religion, or health.

Be realistic when choosing which databases to use. Before you begin using any of the subject-specific databases, look at their titles and decide which ones seem best for your topic. No one should expect the nursing databases to have information on building skateboarding parks, unless articles about treating skateboard injuries are in the nursing databases.

Most libraries also provide a "Discover" or "Discovery" database as their central search tool. Discover(y) is a compilation of all the library's online resources— ebooks, articles, and evideos. By searching a library's Discover(y) search engine, you are searching **all** the library's databases plus its online catalog of books and videos. Of course, you will likely find more than what you need, so learn to *narrow* your search in a variety of ways. Here are some tips:

1. When putting in your search terms, don't use big phrases. Use two- or three-word terms that describe what you are looking for and join the terms with "and": adolescents *and* suicide OR teens *and* drugs *and* addiction.

2. If your first set of search terms doesn't garner the results that you want, use synonyms to produce new or different results. For example, use "adolescent" instead of "teen" or try "climate change" instead of "global warming."

3. All library Discover(y) search engines have a menu of "limiters" that you can select in order to limit your search results in a variety of ways. You can limit your search to full-text only or by the format of materials you want (books, article, video). You can also specify the type of material needed (academic, news, trade publications), subject area, geographic location, or language of the article.

Citations and Bibliographies

Students not only have to become proficient in finding good information, but they must also learn to cite resources used to develop a paper. One of the advantages of using library databases is that these databases provide "citation" information and the ability to "save" and/or "email" bibliographic information used in papers. These citation aids can be found in the detailed record of articles you choose to use. "Cite" or "Citation" (which also appears when you email, print, or save a record) provides all the pertinent information, and in the necessary order, for citing the article in MLA, APA, or a dozen other style formats.

NOTE: Though "Cite" provides all the correctly ordered citation information, it does not always capitalize, italicize, or punctuate in the required format. ALWAYS consult the appropriate style guide required by your instructor. Style guides can be found at your library or on their website.

TIP: MLA, the Modern Language Association, is the organization that writes the rules for documentation used for disciplines described as the humanities including English courses.

Passwords

Be aware that you must have passwords to access library databases when you are not on campus. Be aware, too, that colleges do not share the same passwords; each is unique. Most academic libraries are set up so that you can access online library materials from off-campus using the same student ID and login information you use to register or check your grades. However, some databases may require a unique login that you can obtain by contacting your library.

Last Word on Librarians

Librarians work hard to keep up with the constant changes in the electronic world. Most have a special gift for helping students in their research, regardless of the fields of study. Relying on librarians for their talents and knowledge is the same as relying on teachers.

Part of receiving an education is becoming information literate. No one can know everything, but if we are information literate, we know when, where, and whom to ask for what we need. This includes knowing when to ask a librarian for help! Librarians have access to knowledge that you will need and may not even know exists. Rely on them.

Remember, they may be good shushers, but they are even better helpers.

Chapter 16

Reading for Research

Reading is a form of thinking. Just as you must think about what you write, you must also think about the words you read. Consider your behavior when you watch a movie or a ballgame that captivates your attention. Instead of passively sitting and watching the characters on the screen or the playing field, you become emotionally and even physically involved with the characters and the players.

Reading a novel for pleasure at the beach and reading an article for a term paper are completely different. If a novel gets boring or has too many technical details, you can often skip ahead. In research, skipping content means undermining learning. You must be willing to follow the writer's chain of ideas and examples to understand and fully appreciate the work.

Get a Dictionary

Get a dictionary. Experts say that you need a new dictionary every few years to keep up with our evolving language. Though this statement is true, don't let it hold you back from using an old dictionary. They have plenty of words, and they are spelled correctly.

> When I just skipped those words, of course, I really ended up with little idea of what the book said. . . . I saw that the best thing I could do was get hold of a dictionary—to study, to learn some words.
>
> —From Malcolm X's *Autobiography*

Having a dictionary app on your phone will suffice for most people. Others want to flip around in a dictionary or thesaurus to get a better idea of word choice and spelling.

Organization of Materials

The most effective method of dodging any reading assignment is distraction. Some check their phones constantly while others clean the room or watch awful YouTube videos. Whatever your favorite distraction is, put it aside and get your computer, books, highlighters, pens, and notebooks in order to work in a quiet place.

No one reads successfully in chaos. No one, no matter what you have read or heard, can put 100 percent of her or his brainpower into serious reading while other noises are occurring.

WHAT *NOT* TO MARK

1. Do not mark, write on, or highlight any library books.

2. Do not mark, write on, or highlight any books that you can sell back to the bookstore. Use sticky notes when necessary.

3. Do not mark, write on, or highlight any material that the teacher tells you not to touch. Use sticky notes when necessary.

WHAT YOU *SHOULD* MARK

1. *Please, please mark up photocopied material that the teacher gives to you.*

2. *Please, please mark up computer printouts that you run off from the computer at home or public places on campus.*

3. *Please, please highlight and mark your notes.*

All teachers appreciate students who do not want to mark books out of respect. However, the truth is that a book you use, know, and understand IS RESPECTED.

A minister once said, "The best version of the Bible is the one that you actually read." The same is true for books—read them and mark them, especially if they belong to you.

Read for Content, Not Speed

Be willing to sacrifice fast page-turning action for comprehension. Slow down. You are busy, but so is everyone else.

Understand that you will read an article several times, especially if you are writing an analysis or an annotated bibliography. If you read for content, you will not have to repeat the process as often. If not, get ready to repeat this process over and over.

If you are reading a biology or psychology text, you need to slow your pace to allow extra time to identify the information needed for study. An article on a familiar subject like paying students for good grades requires similar concentration, even though you know a lot more about money than you do about botany.

Patience, Even When Discouraged

Many students feel cheated about their previous education after they have been in college for a few weeks. They voice strong resentment for former teachers who smothered them with handouts and worksheets that were never checked or discussed. Many say that they didn't get the background needed in math, science, or English.

Students who are patient with themselves and with their reading can often advance many grade levels just by reading carefully and looking up words. *Be patient and learn.*

Active Reading: Mark It Up!

Reading is an active process that requires the use of a pencil to record your thoughts. Annotating the text is a form of note taking that occurs while you read to promote critical thinking and knowledge of the material. Use prereading strategy questions to guide you. Write questions in the margins to focus your attention on the main ideas of the selection.

This process improves your comprehension because you are actively engaged in the reading process. By annotating the chapter, you are identifying the important information you need to review and study. As you practice this skill, you will find a system that works for you.

Consider the following suggestions for annotating a chapter:

- Write questions in the margin to guide you in identifying the key concepts or main ideas. Use these questions to create study guides for review.

- Identify important definitions within the text by writing "def" above the word.

- Identify key terms or concepts by circling them.

- Highlight unknown words, look them up in the dictionary, and write definitions in the margins.

- Number steps in a process or series.

- Identify transition words and phrases.

Concentration: The Key

Have you ever read an entire section of a chapter only to realize that you cannot remember a single concept that you read, except a few isolated words or phrases? Oftentimes, after experiencing a reading disaster, we console ourselves by saying that the material was boring.

Perhaps our minds wandered, our phones blew up, or family problems burdened us. No matter what the cause, understanding and remembering the material we just read did not occur, and, as a result, academic achievement will not occur either.

Concentration is a skill that must be developed through practice and patience. You must plan to concentrate when you read and study if you are to understand and remember the information. Decide to take an interest in subjects and courses that may not be your favorites. In addition, you must commit to consistent study times that take priority in your schedule.

One vital step to improving concentration is to take notes in your own words. Notes should be brief and should address the main ideas and the most important supporting details. Sometimes it is helpful to include an example to promote understanding of difficult concepts.

Finally, you must improve concentration when you make a connection between the idea being introduced and the entire concept being studied. If you are unsure of how the smaller idea fits into the larger subject area, reread the material and ask questions until you understand the relationship between the two.

Avoid Distractions

Internal and external distractions often sabotage our efforts for success. Internal distractions are personal, physical, or psychological problems that distract us from studying or focusing during class. For example, having a headache, feeling hungry, or worrying about a relationship or money are all internal distractions. Preventing internal distractions is the best plan of attack.

Keep a notepad to jot down personal worries as they come to mind while you study. Realize that you can solve these problems at an appropriate later time. Put them out of your mind for now and return to study. In addition, eat properly and get adequate sleep.

Articles from Periodicals

Taking on the task of dissecting articles from scholarly journals is time consuming. In technical fields, articles often have 30 to 50 pages and require specialized dictionaries. For the most part, you will not have to use too many of these articles in your composition class.

Most of the articles that you will use come from daily, weekly, or monthly periodicals. Topics involving literary-based subjects can come from specialized journals which, while not simple, do not rival most technical journals with jargon, charts, and complexity.

You will need to read each article closely. Some instructors will require notecards.

Summarizing Articles

Your instructor may ask you to submit a summary of an article as homework. When this happens, follow these suggestions for writing a thorough summary.

1. **Absolutely *do not plagiarize* in any form.** You will make a zero on this assignment if you plagiarize. See Chapter 17 in this textbook for information on plagiarism and its consequences.

2. Organize your summary, especially the topic sentence, extraordinarily well. *Do not use the author's organization* of her/his ideas when writing your summary. Mimicking another writer's structure and organization is plagiarism.

3. For the topic sentence/first sentence, include these elements:

   - The author's full name
   - The title of the article
   - The title of the periodical in which it appears (if one is indicated)
   - The main idea of the article—in YOUR words

Refer to the author by his/her full name when *first* mentioned; in any other references, refer to the author *by last name only*. This applies to other authors, Rick Bragg and Eudora Welty included. Never call an author by first name when analyzing his/her work.

4. Do not let personal issues or grievances creep into the analysis. Keep personal commentary completely out if the teacher indicates that this summary does not involve your reaction or response. Use of "I" is unnecessary in this assignment if you are not writing a response.

5. Article summaries (and articles themselves) are not fairy tales and do not have to end happily. Do not force a happy ending, especially by adding a personal comment.

   • End your paragraph by mentioning the author or the article. This will pull the reader back into the main idea of the paragraph, the thesis.

6. Don't read anything into the article that's not there. Never "go off" on an issue or person. Never, ever preach.

7. Do not ask questions. Since your job is to analyze and summarize, the need for questions does not exist.

8. Use quotation marks when needed, but do not overquote. Teachers know the material without your recopying it.

9. Use the present tense when discussing the content of the article. In formal writing, this is called the historical present. In the text of your summary you would write, "Smith says" or "Jones asserts."

10. Do not write more than the teacher assigns.

11. Remember that you are writing a summary of the assigned article, not of the topic of the article. Refer to the article and author.

12. Do not refer to an article, play, poem, or epic as a "story."

13. Proofread and edit for common errors.

Chapter 17

Integrity for Writers: Avoiding Plagiarism

Casual dishonesty is often admired, especially with a player who talks a good game. However, college writing and research require a rethinking of casual morality.

Ideas are commodities. For that reason, you cannot legally videotape a movie while you are sitting in a theatre. That's stealing someone's creativity and work. In English class, if you take an idea, a sentence, or a passage from an article in a magazine (or any source) and never indicate that you have done so, you are also stealing. That's plagiarism. The writers who poured their hearts and talents into that work are trying to make their impact on the world; you are stealing their experience, their education, and their sweat equity.

To steal casually by copying and pasting is a serious way to destroy your character and reputation in college, as well as your college career in some cases.

More than likely, though, you just want to get through this course with a decent paper. You are not a thief and would never dream of stealing.

Anyone who has been in college for several semesters understands how powerful words are. They determine everything. But when you have to write your own words in a disciplined fashion, you can feel some pain. Writing is tough, and good writing is both tough and incredibly rewarding. If you can effectively transfer what's in your head to paper, you have gotten an education from somewhere—your high school, your college teacher, your mom.

Know Your Style: MLA and APA

Our governing body for rules, MLA, has tough, rigid guidelines. The Modern Language Association (MLA) is a real organization that creates rules for writers. We follow their directions with margins, Works Cited pages, and just about everything else pertaining to writing a documented paper. However, they are not the only organization with rules about papers. The American Psychological Association (APA) is another organization with stylistic guidelines. It is used in many areas of science and education.

These organizations do not exist to annoy us, though that often seems the case for both teachers and students. They exist to level the playing field around the world. If you moved anywhere in the world and did a paper in an English class, you would probably be expected to follow the rules of MLA or APA. Each standardizes procedures and rules for writers.

With MLA and APA, the form and emphases are different, but their purpose is identical. Both are geared to help writers to create a clear, coherent paper with sources that can be traced back to the originals. If you can use either one of the style manuals comfortably, you can switch back and forth to accommodate the requirements of the assignment. The principles remain the same, regardless of the style choice.

Rules for MLA and APA can be mastered if you pay attention to details and follow the guidelines.

In Case You Missed the Point

People who have gotten off track (for whatever reason) while writing research papers often become desperate. They have a deadline and an empty screen. What is best for filling a blank screen? The Internet, of course, is the answer for many, many students. "Everyone else does it" has been repeated and repeated as justification for cheating.

Plagiarism can change your life in ways that you cannot imagine. Here are some true, real examples:

- A prominent Boston newspaper man gets fired for plagiarism.
- A young Navy officer has his master's degree revoked, has his commission taken away, and is dishonorably discharged from the service for plagiarism.
- A candidate for president is humiliated when the press discovers that his stirring speech had been given years before by an English parliamentarian. He is humiliated for years by plagiarism.
- A young author with a major book contract is discovered to have dipped into her photographic memory and copied passages from her favorite author into her work. She loses her book contract and a sizeable chunk of her future for violating rules about plagiarism.
- A prominent SEC football player is kicked out of college for plagiarism.
- Several online students are found to have plagiarized after they graduated. Their degrees are revoked for plagiarism.

And these are just the tip of the iceberg.

In the real world, people will sue you if you plagiarize their work. In college, plagiarism can result in an F or a zero on an assignment, expulsion from a class, or even expulsion from school.

In order to understand why our society deals with plagiarism so harshly, you must understand what intellectual property is.

Intellectual Property

Consider that the word "property" in this phrase indicates ownership. Although people cannot copyright or own every idea, they can copyright the way they write about an idea. In composition classes, you will have several opportunities to work with sources, so you must pay close attention to the rules about documentation.

RESPECTING OTHERS' PROPERTY

Thus, when you begin to research a topic, you will encounter intellectual property—your sources. As a person with integrity, you need to respect intellectual property rights and to learn the appropriate ways to use the sources in your own work.

PROTECTING YOUR PROPERTY

Your mind and your creativity are a huge part of who you are. You may choose to share them through your faith or your talents. You may choose to keep your ideas to yourself and live a quiet private life. It's your choice.

When someone takes your ideas and presents them as his or hers—not yours—that person has stolen your intellectual property, your ideas. Creativity and original ideas are the source of endless inspiration. No one should steal your talent.

Consequently, you should have no difficulty understanding why deciding to steal someone else's ideas and presenting them as your own is never acceptable.

Can Plagiarism Ever Be Accidental?

"I didn't mean to."

"I didn't know that it was plagiarism."

"I didn't know what to do."

This words are too familiar and often very sad.

Because ignorance of the law is no excuse, the answer to the above question is "NO!" In fact, this question has been raised by the courts, and the courts agree: Accidental plagiarism is by legal definition *plagiarism* and is subject to punishment.

You should not cheat, even accidentally, and plagiarism occurs often if you are not careful. Doing an assignment at 2:00 a.m.—not careful. Having your girlfriend come over to "help" with your notecards—not careful. Doing sloppy research and not identifying your notecards carefully enough to document the information properly—not careful.

Glancing at the wording from the original source while you type or write—*not careful.*

"I'm Confused": Defining Plagiarism

Plagiarism is:

1. Copying a passage from another student's essay.

2. Turning in another student's essay as your own.

3. Copying a passage from a professional work (such as a poem, novel, short story, newspaper or journal article, etc.) and putting it in your paper as your own.

4. Using exact wording from a printed work and not putting quotation marks around the passage.

5. Quoting or paraphrasing a passage from a printed work and not documenting the passage correctly.

6. Paraphrasing a passage from a printed work and using too much of the original wording.

7. Altering the meaning of a printed work in your paraphrase.

8. Imitating the structure of a passage in a printed work.

9. Reading an article online or in print and writing your own paper, loosely using ideas from the article that you read.

10. Imitating the overall organization of a printed work.

Plagiarism is not limited to the above examples, so be sure to check with your instructor if you have questions about your work.

"Sloppy documentation" is plagiarism. One example of sloppy documentation is omitting a parenthetical page number after a quote—even when the quote is accurate and the quotation marks are correct. It is still plagiarism, though many teachers choose to place this form of plagiarism in a separate category, one that does not yield instant failure.

Because of the proliferation of the Internet, today's students have an even more tempting situation regarding plagiarism than did their predecessors. Now students can find free essays on the Internet. Also, students can type in their subject matter on a search engine and find material in a matter of seconds. Most instructors encourage their students to use online material because it is the most current and timely.

The line "To whom much is given, much is asked" is relevant to your college writing courses. Even though you have such convenient access to information, it is your responsibility to learn the skill that accompanies that technological advancement.

Helpful Plagiarism Prevention Websites

Instructors and students now have websites that help them avoid and detect plagiarism. You should know that your instructor very likely will upload your essay into a plagiarism detection website. In order to avoid any problems in your essay, you should consider checking your essay through plagiarism detection programs in Canvas or the Internet.

Beware of the plagiarism detection sites on the Internet, however, because they will charge you.

Avoiding Plagiarism in Research Paper Writing

You normally have the following options when you integrate source material into your essay:

- Quoting
- Paraphrasing
- Splicing
- Summarizing

QUOTING

Following is the original passage from page 2 of a book by Spencer Moore. The examples that follow are based on this passage.

Original Passage #1

Writers often struggle for the perfect word, the perfect sentence, especially when they are just getting started.

Example #1: Plagiarized ·
Incorrect Use of Quotation in Student's Paper
According to author Spencer Moore, writers often struggle for the perfect word (2).

Because the above passage doesn't use quotation marks, it is plagiarized.

Example #2: Incorrect/Plagiarized ·
Use of Quoted Material (also known as sloppy documentation)
According to author Spencer Moore, "Writers often struggle for the perfect word."

The above example has been only partially corrected. It is plagiarized because the author omits the page number in parentheses after the quotation.

Example #3: Incorrect/Plagiarized ·
Use of Quoted Material (also known as sloppy documentation)
According to author Spencer Moore, "Writers struggle in many ways for the perfect word" (2).

The writer has altered the quote by adding words.

Example #4: Fully Corrected ·
According to author Spencer Moore, "Writers often struggle for the perfect word . . . " (2).

The student puts the author's name in the lead-in, uses quotation marks, and cites the page number at the end. Because some of the original quote was excluded, the student uses ellipsis marks to indicate that the quote is incomplete. The quotation marks follow the three ellipsis marks.

Example #5: Fully Corrected ·
According to one expert, "Writers often struggle for the perfect word . . . " (Moore 2).

The student uses quotation marks and cites the author's last name and page number at the end. Again, ellipsis marks are used at the end with the quotation marks following them.

Example #6: Fully Corrected ·
According to author Spencer Moore, "Writers [frequently] struggle for the perfect word . . . " (2).

The student gives the author's name in the lead-in, uses quotation marks, and identifies a changed word in the quotation by using brackets. Ellipsis marks are used to indicate an omission from the original material.

Example #7: Fully Corrected ·
According to author Spencer Moore, "Writers . . . struggle for the perfect word . . . " (2).

The student gives the author's name in the lead-in, uses quotation marks, and omits part of the quotation by using an ellipsis. Changing the spirit of the quotation, even if you use an ellipsis, is still plagiarism. Because material is left out, ellipsis marks are used at the end of the quote, too.

Follow these guidelines when quoting rather than paraphrasing your source material.

Quote when you are using statistics, defining a term, or emphasizing an expert's opinion. The most appropriate time to quote occurs when you cannot and should not ruin the beauty of the quotation; this is rare, as direct quotes should be.

In all other instances, you should paraphrase.

> **WARNING!** At 3:00 a.m. the day your essay is due, you might be tempted to proclaim, "I couldn't have said it better myself" and quote everything you see. Do not procrastinate or avoid paraphrasing. Paraphrasing is necessary for a well-written paper.

PARAPHRASING

You should paraphrase as much of your research as possible so that your essay will be presented in your own voice and will be coherent and unified. Consider this bit of advice.

> **GENERAL WISDOM:** Read the passage that you wish to paraphrase. Reread the passage. Put away the original work for a moment. Write the passage from memory using your own words. Do not glance at the source, even for a small hint.

Specific Directions for Paraphrasing

- Use your own language to reflect the idea of the passage.
- Do not simply vary a few words in your version; reword the entire passage.
- Do not use quotation marks when paraphrasing—only when you quote.
- Document by citing author and page number at the end of the paraphrase.

Check the paraphrase in three ways:

1. Does the paraphrase accurately reflect the original passage?

2. Is the paraphrase totally in your own wording?

3. Is the structure of the paraphrase your own and not too closely related to the original passage?

The following passage is from page 24 of an article by Bill Smith. The examples below are based on this passage.

Original Passage #2

DNA evidence has revolutionized the previously broken criminal justice system.

Example #1: Incorrect Paraphrasing with Plagiarism · · · · · · · · · · · · ·
According to author Bill Smith, DNA evidence has drastically changed our previously broken criminal justice system (24).

This paraphrase follows the original source too closely and copies some of the sentence structure of the passage. It is, therefore, plagiarism.

Example #2: Paraphrasing without Citation—Also Plagiarism · · · · · · ·
The criminal justice system, which once had problems, has been tremendously changed by DNA evidence.

This sentence, which is an adequate paraphrase, lacks documentation and thus is also plagiarized.

Example #3: Paraphrasing and Plagiarizing
(also known as sloppy documentation) ·
The criminal justice system, which once had problems, has been tremendously changed by DNA evidence (24).

This paraphrase does not cite the author's name. It is also plagiarized.

Example #4: Correct Paraphrase ·
According to author Bill Smith, the criminal justice system, which once had problems, has been tremendously changed by DNA evidence (24).

In this paraphrase, not only does the student correctly give credit to the author and page, but he or she also completely rewords the original source and accurately reflects the meaning of the original source.

Paraphrasing correctly can often be the most mysterious task for students. The most effective key is not looking at the source. If the writer knows the material, she or he should work from the ideas generated by the article, not from specific wording.

Looking away from the material is absolutely vital for avoiding plagiarism while paraphrasing.

SPLICING

You should use the technique of splicing as often as possible when you are writing a research paper. Splicing is a combination of paraphrase and quotation. When you are paraphrasing and are unable to reword a phrase, quote the phrase and leave the rest of the material as a paraphrase. This combination, when done correctly, makes your writing easy to read. It encourages you to quote the absolute minimum amount of wording from the original passage, instead of quoting large chunks of information, while also paraphrasing most of the material that you wish to put in your research paper.

The splice is not a summary; it gives specific information, rather than main ideas, from a source. The splice blends your words and the author's words. Follow the instructions for paraphrasing and quoting regarding avoiding plagiarism.

The following passage is from pages 126–27 of an article by Logan Mullen. Example #1 on the following page and Examples 1–4 on pp. 200–201 are based on this passage.

Original Passage #3

Members of the Oxford High School football team recently began practicing in the summer heat. Although several players suffered from stomach cramps and dehydration, the coaches continued the practice into the late afternoon. The coaches gave the players frequent breaks and urged them to drink a lot of water. Head Coach Tyler Phillips praised the achievements of the first day and guaranteed a win over in-county rival Lafayette High School at the end of the season.

Example #1: Good Splicing of Materials ·
The head coach of the Oxford High School football team "guaranteed a win over in-county rival Lafayette High School at the end of the season" (Mullen 127).

The splice in Example #1 combines paraphrased material from the first part of a sentence in Original Passage #3 and a quotation from the last part of the sentence in Original Passage #3.

Example #2: Good Splicing of Materials ·
Ignoring the chain of command and protesting to the head boss is "a gimmick that works best only on television" (Hammons 66).

The splice in the above example combines paraphrased material and quoted material from Original Passage #4 (see p. 202).

PARAPHRASING VERSUS SUMMARIZING

While paraphrasing is rewording the details of a passage, *summarizing* is stating the main idea of a passage. A paraphrase may be as long as or longer than the original. An original passage may be three sentences, but the paraphrase, in some cases, may be four or five sentences—depending upon the researcher's purpose and emphasis. In general, you should paraphrase material when it is important to give specific details from a source. Quoting is necessary only when the original source is so fresh and relevant and timely that it cannot be paraphrased.

Organizing a paraphrase much differently from the original is essential to avoid plagiarism. When you do so correctly, the reorganization may require more words than the original.

Often in research papers, writers will give examples, arguments, explanations, etc., from their sources, and paraphrasing will be the technique used to relay that information. Writers need to use paraphrased information from their sources when developing body paragraphs.

SUMMARIZING

You probably will paraphrase much more often than you will summarize. If you want to give a conclusion, and only that conclusion, from a source, however, you should summarize the information.

A *summary* by definition is shorter than the original passage.

Example #1: Insufficient Summary ·
The Oxford High School football team practiced in the heat (Mullen 126–27).

This summary does not cover the entire paragraph, even though the parenthetical citation erroneously indicates that it does.

**Example #2: Plagiarized Summary
(also known as sloppy documentation)** . . . .
The Oxford High School football team overcame problems from practicing in the summer heat to impress its head coach enough for him to promise a win over the team's rival Lafayette High School.

This summary has better content than the first example, but it does not include the parenthetical citation at the end of the summary. If not corrected, it will be counted as a plagiarized passage.

Example #3: Good Summary . . . .
The Oxford High School football team overcame problems from practicing in the summer heat to impress its head coach enough that he promised the team would beat its arch-rival Lafayette High School (Mullen 126–27).

This summary is effective, and it includes the parenthetical citation at the end.

Example #4: Good Paraphrase . . . .
Several Oxford High School football players experienced problems from the heat during the team's first practice. The coaches encouraged the players to take breaks and hydrate themselves; however, practice continued to its duration into the afternoon. Head Coach Tyler Phillips was so pleased with his team's performance that he vowed to beat Oxford's arch-enemy Lafayette High School (Mullen 126–27).

Notice that the summary in Example #3 is one sentence, and the paraphrase in #4 has three sentences. Also, the paraphrase includes more details than does the summary.

More Summary Examples

Your summary length should depend on the assignment that you are completing. When you are writing a research paper, you may be able to determine the length of summary that you wish to use in your paper. In other assignments, your instructor may require you to write a summary of a certain length. For example, your instructor may tell you to summarize a short story in the introduction of your critical analysis of that short story. In that case, your summary would be only a few sentences long.

Keep in mind that the majority of the material in a research paper should be paraphrased or spliced. When you give details in the body of your research paper, you should use those two techniques. Use summary only when you really just need to give the main idea of the original passage.

Consider the following examples of various lengths of summaries.

The following passage is from an article by Laura Hammons. Example #2 on p. 200 and the examples on p. 203 are based on this passage.

Original Passage #4

Common complaints about parking decals and dirty bathrooms should be directed to the deans, not a higher authority, even if the student is upset about plumbing in the dorms. For problems with the dorm, the student should work first with the dorm staff, but if that does not work, the Dean of Students, not the president, should be the point of contact. The college president may be on his/her way to an Appropriations Committee hearing at the Capitol to secure millions of dollars to fund the school, and the vice president might be working on plans to expand the campus or revamp the curriculum. When students are angry or hurt, they often want to see the person in charge and sometimes head to the "top guy's" office. When they do, however, most high-ranking college officials will advise overwrought students to follow procedure—to see the teacher or dean first. Going straight to the top is a gimmick that works best only on television. In serious business or academic settings, a student needs to work through the process respectfully and diligently.

When upset about a problem with a class, students tend to run to the closest office of the highest official. This is unwise. After calming down, the student should see the teacher about the problem. If an office conference does not resolve the issue, the student should turn to the teacher's immediate boss—the department chair. In addition to administrative duties, many of these instructors teach five or more classes, which means that they are not available at all times. Of course, this can be a big disadvantage for students who may be frantically searching for immediate help; however, they should not skip this vital person. The Chair is often able to resolve the problem without the student's having to climb the ladder of job titles. Not starting further up the chain of command is ultimately advantageous to both students and instructors; jumping straight to the top creates stress and ill will. If the student does not feel that s/he has received satisfaction from the teacher or Chair, the student should then go to the Academic Dean.

Example #1: Correct One-Sentence Summary · · · · · · · · · · · · · · · · · · ·
If students experience problems on campus, they should follow the chain of command in order to make a complaint (Hammons 66).

Example #2: Correct Brief Summary ·
Students who experience problems on campus often take their complaints to senior administrators at the college. However, those officials usually will send the students back to the person in charge of the area in question. Therefore, students should respect the chain of command when they are lodging a complaint (Hammons 66).

Example #3: Correct Long Summary ·
Students who have complaints about their campuses sometimes handle the grievance process inappropriately. Often, students are tempted to go to the highest official on campus to protest an issue that is relatively trivial; however, students should understand that college presidents and vice presidents have many serious matters that they deal with on a daily basis. Complaining to the highest official on campus may not yield positive results. The best practice is to see the person in charge of the department that relates to the complaint. Then, if necessary, the students should take the complaint to the next person in command until the issue is resolved (Hammons 66).

Chapter Exercises: Integration of Sources

In this section, you will complete several tasks relating to the integration of sources, such as quoting, paraphrasing, summarizing, and splicing. You will use one excerpt from an article as the original passage. Notice that the individual page numbers are listed so that you will be able to document your parenthetical citations correctly.

Original Passage

This passage is from a narrative essay by Ashley Lancaster. The underlining has been added for the exercises that follow.

Note that sections of the passage are labeled at the ends of sentences.

Why do people tend to do crazy activities on their thirtieth birthdays? Do people really think that having a wild weekend in Vegas, buying a brand new convertible, or jumping out of an airplane is going to make them feel better about passing into a new decade of their lives? (#1) Apparently I did because the only present I wanted when I turned thirty was to skydive, and this seemingly irresponsible act did so much more than make me feel young again. (#2) My experience with skydiving on my thirtieth birthday is my most memorable experience because of the overwhelming sense of fear and exhilaration that it created in me and because it ultimately taught me that conquering my fears is always a great personal present. (#3)

I had never been bothered by age before, so I never imagined that I would be bothered by my thirtieth birthday either. To prove that turning thirty was just going to be another day, I refused to have a party or make plans with my friends. Making a big fuss about the day would only make it more important. (#4) I did, however, decide to increase my workout routine the entire week of my birthday just to prove that I could still physically do whatever I wanted. (#5) So, instead of running two miles, I ran four, and instead of doing fifty sit-ups, I did 150. By the middle of the week, I was so tired that, one night when my husband came home from work, he found me weeping in bed. "I am old," I cried when he walked into the bedroom. "In college, I could run for hours, but now I'm so exhausted. It's only Wednesday." Cory had no idea what to do, and he was even more shocked when I said, "I know what I want for my birthday. I want to skydive." My reason for choosing this present was not logical. Basically, I had always dreamed of doing it but had always been too scared. Even if I could not run four miles, I knew I could jump out of an airplane. I had to do it! (#6)

Complete the following tasks related to the previous passage:

1. Quote the sentence labeled #5. Lead in to the quotation by stating the author's name. Document parenthetically.

2. Quote the sentence labeled #5. Lead in to the quotation but do not state the author's name. Document parenthetically.

3. Quote the sentence labeled #5. Change a word in the quotation and use a bracket to reflect the change. Document parenthetically.

4. Paraphrase the section labeled #4. All of the underlined sentences are part of that section. Document parenthetically.

5. Paraphrase the section labeled #1. All of the underlined sentences are part of that section. Document parenthetically.

6. Write a one-sentence summary of the entire original passage. Document parenthetically.

7. Write a brief summary of the entire original passage. For an original passage of this size, your brief summary could be three to five sentences long. Document parenthetically.

8. Write a long summary of the entire original passage. For an original passage of this size, your long summary could be six to ten sentences long. Document parenthetically.

9. Write a splice that incorporates part of the sentence labeled #2. Paraphrase part of the sentence and quote part of the sentence. Document parenthetically.

10. Write a splice that incorporates part of the sentence labeled #5. Paraphrase part of the sentence and quote part of the sentence. Document parenthetically.

Chapter 18

The Net-Savvy Writer

The past few years have seen enormous change in the way people communicate. Because of social media sites like Instagram, Facebook, and Twitter, along with other Internet tools like blogs and wikis, everyone is a writer. Everyone is a reporter, a commentator, a marketer, and a storyteller. Lives, opinions, and attitudes are chronicled online. YouTube has more content than a television network could produce in decades. Twitter is an always-on stream of information, ideas, and reactions. Texting is now the primary means of private communication among people.

So much writing now takes place now in the public sphere that few jobs can be done without the ability to write at a nearly professional level. No employee can assume that someone else will take care of the writing and editing that goes out to the public. Even an email sent to a coworker might be forwarded numerous times. Therefore, it's more important than ever before to be a good writer.

The ability to complete certain technological tasks is all well and good, and basic literacy of common tasks will always be required. Beyond that, however, you need the ability to adapt to new technological situations and demands.

More than knowledge of a specific technological application, you need confidence, willingness to try new things, awareness that everything is learned through a process of trial and error, and acceptance of change.

That said, the characteristics of good writing don't change much from situation to situation. Nor do certain fundamentals of Internet savvy. Concentrating on process, presence, presentation, and people skills (the 4 Ps of digital composition) will make you a long-term net-savvy writer.

Process

When we speak of process in writing, we usually mean the process required to produce a piece of writing: brainstorming, drafting, revising, editing, and so forth. Becoming a net-savvy writer means becoming more aware of process at multiple levels, including observation, experimentation, and problem solving.

OBSERVATION

In older models of broadcasting such as television, radio, and newspapers, most people were consumers of information but not necessarily producers. In the Internet model, the general populace becomes both producer and consumer. The news is now broadcast not in a straight line from reporter to reader but in a series of loops from reporter to blogger to tweeter to YouTube commentator and back again and again. In the end, thousands of people are responsible for creating the story.

Many forms of information are now disseminated to the general public through just such a looping process. If you post a Facebook status update on a topic or comment on someone else's update, you are part of that system as both a consumer and producer of digital media.

Being net-savvy means taking what you produce up a notch from status updates. It might mean you make a website or keep a blog. It might mean you maintain photo galleries on Flickr or have your own YouTube channel. Maybe you will run a Facebook group for an organization and post regular information to it. Maybe you will find yourself in the position of sending out group emails from work or making digital scrapbooks for your family. Regardless of how you go about it, when you engage in these forms of communication, you are a producer of digital media.

Writers have always learned to be good writers and then better writers by studying other writers. Students are encouraged in school to do close readings of texts so that they can break down the elements of good writing in order to copy the techniques.

That approach is necessary to develop any kind of writing skill, especially digital skills.

When you find a website, blog, wiki, video stream, photo gallery, or any other kind of digital communication that seems well done to you, study it. Examine how it was put together and how you might copy the techniques. Study good examples that you know were put together with tools you have on hand. If you want an excellent Blogger blog, roam through Blogger looking for examples. If you want to make a website using Google Sites, find successful Google Sites to examine.

Do more than examine. Analyze. Critique. Look at the writing, the design, the layout, the incorporation of images and multimedia elements. Ask yourself three main questions: What doesn't work? What works? How can I use the same technique?

Be an observant consumer, always on the lookout for ideas to apply to your own writing. Remember that writing in the digital age is more than text. It is image, sound, layout, and so much more. Observing all of these elements and how they work together in successful examples of digital communication is the first step toward becoming a net-savvy writer.

EXPERIMENTATION

We might as well face it: there's no quick and easy path to becoming a good writer or to becoming net-savvy. If you're now more aware of how others are doing it, you've made the first step, but that's just one way to begin.

We learn any talent through a process of trial and error, of repeated trial and error over time. We can learn how to put a bookcase together by following a set of instructions, and as long as the bookcases don't change, those instructions will see us through to keep completing the same task again and again just by following a set of rules. However, digital composition is not a bookcase. Instead of a product, it's a performance more akin to a musical or athletic performance than to baking "fail safe" brownies by a recipe or putting together the same type of bookcase over and over again exactly the same way. Successful musicians, artists, athletes, and writers all have at least one characteristic in common—they keep trying and adapting.

Developing talent means experiencing ups and downs. It means seeing an individual success as an opportunity to push yourself to become even better and seeing an individual failure as an opportunity to learn. It means practicing, practicing, practicing.

Be willing to try and you will find and develop your talents for digital communication over time.

Experimentation means:

- Learn as you go. Don't wait until you fully understand a task before attempting it, because you may never fully understand it before you've actually done it. Learn enough to get started, and just jump in.

- Let go of anxieties. Remember that there is nothing you can mess up in a digital composition that can't be deleted if need be. Many of the tools for digital communication are designed for general consumers. If you can type an email, you can make a website. If you can create a Facebook profile, you can set up a blog. You won't accomplish anything if you don't try, and confidence alone can truly yield fantastic results.

- Apply your own creativity. Originality matters. Even when using templates to design a piece of digital writing, find ways to make it your own. Infuse the writing and the layout with your own personality and purpose (see more on this under "Presentation" in this chapter).

PROBLEM SOLVING

You can count on two things regarding technology: It constantly changes, and it will fail you at some point. Light bulbs go out on projectors during presentations, blogs go down just as you are about to submit a lengthy post that you have not saved elsewhere, and cell phone service fails just as someone else is waiting for your important reply.

You will also fail the technology. You will hit *send* on an email before it is complete. You will post broken links on websites. You will forget to format an image to the appropriate size for your blog post. You will spend hours working on a project only to forget where and how you saved it, or worse, you will lose the flash drive on which it is saved.

These mistakes and failures happen to everyone, and they don't mean total disaster. However, acquiring good problem-solving skills and good problem-solving attitudes is necessary if you are going to be net-savvy.

Consider these examples of technological problems and ways to solve them.

Situation 1

You've been given an assignment to create a project site for a class, and you do not know how to begin.

Problem-Solving Strategies for Situation 1
- You read through all of the information provided about the assignment to be sure you understand what's expected.

- You ask your instructor and/or other students about any parts you don't understand.

- You Google "how to _____" to explain technological tasks you don't understand.

- You search YouTube for video tutorials on tasks you don't understand.
- You Google "apps for _____" to find out if there is an application or tool that will help you with the tasks required.

Planning-Ahead Strategies for Situation 1

- Start the assignment as early as possible. Don't procrastinate on a job you have never done before.
- Read ahead on handouts and textbook assignments to be sure you understand what is expected of you.
- Find a partner or a group of people in the class you can work with to help you keep up with assignments and troubleshoot any problems you encounter.

Situation 2

You are giving a PowerPoint presentation, and the projector fails.

Problem-Solving Strategies for Situation 2

- Continue the presentation without the PowerPoint.
- Provide contact information so that the audience can email you for copies of the slides they missed.

Planning-Ahead Strategies for Situation 2

- Take handouts in case of technology failure.
- Print out copies of your slides for yourself so that you will have them to refer to in case of technology failure.
- Practice your presentation so that you can give it without referring to the slides if need be.
- Arrive early and do equipment checks before the presentation begins so that potential problems can be fixed ahead of time.

Situation 3

You've been working on a class project or major research paper for weeks, but when it is time to turn it in, you experience a technology failure of some sort. The printer doesn't work. Canvas (or the course management system your particular class uses) goes down. Your computer crashes, or you lose your flash drive.

Problem-Solving Strategies for Situation 3

- First, in this scenario, there may be nothing left to do but hope and pray. Your assignment is due when your instructor says it is due, and it is the instructor's prerogative to refuse to accept it late no matter the reason. In fact, you should expect that technology failures will not be counted as excuses since you have most likely known about the assignment long enough to make allowances for any potential problems.

- In the case of a printer failure, go immediately to a computer lab or printing service—as soon as it opens that morning—and print out your paper.

- If Canvas goes down, email a copy of your assignment to your instructor the first time you try and fail to access the assignment through Canvas. Continue trying to upload it to the appropriate place, though, every 15 minutes until the system comes back up. The email to the instructor is just to document that you did complete the assignment on time. It isn't meant to substitute for submitting the paper the way the instructor requested.

- If your computer crashes, go to another computer and keep working. Borrow a computer from a friend, use a computer lab or a library, or go to a copy center where you can pay by the hour for computer time. It's your responsibility to find a viable alternative.

Planning-Ahead Strategies for Situation 3

- Follow the 48-hour rule. A major chunk of your grade rests on one assignment that you've been given weeks to complete. Make a habit of completing assignments at least 48 hours in advance so that any problems that arise can be solved before it is too late.

- Save early, often, and in multiple locations. Save to your computer and to a portable drive. Email to yourself and/or upload the file to a document storage space online. Give yourself multiple ways to access your work so that if something happens to your computer, you can still access it.

- Print the first finished draft. If all else fails, a hard copy of your work can save you from having to start over.

- Keep a backup ink cartridge for your printer on hand in case you run out of ink during a major project.

Situation 4

You've filmed a video interview for a class project, but when you play the video back, you realize the sound is distorted.

Problem-Solving Strategies for Situation 4

- If possible, redo the video.

- If you cannot redo the video, ask your instructor if you can substitute some of your own voice-overs for the sound track on the video in places where it is particularly distorted.

- Break up the video into segments, and insert text slides between segments to help clarify what was said.

- Lay short snippets of text over the video to help clarify what was said.

- Practice using your camera ahead of time so that you know how to get the highest quality sound and video before using it for your class project.

- Practice editing video ahead of time.

- To warm up for your official interview, do a short test run with your camera after you sit down with the person being interviewed. Play back your test clip on the spot to make sure the camera is working properly.

- Charge all equipment ahead of time and carry extra batteries.

- If possible, take a backup camera with you. Perhaps even record from more than one camera at more than one angle. This will allow you to do some interesting edits even if a backup for quality is not necessary.

A net-savvy person takes problems in stride, realizing that there is always a solution to a problem. Remember you are always only one Google search away from finding out how to do anything you need to know.

PROCESS AND THE INDIVIDUAL DIGITAL ASSIGNMENT

Good writers are always mindful of the fact that writing develops through a deliberate process, never at its best on a first try. Like music, writing needs a few practice runs before becoming a top-notch performance.

In truth, every writer has an individual process that works for him or her. For some, consuming Mountain Dew is an integral part of the writing process. For others, nothing happens until just the right pen has been selected.

For a less experienced writer, learning standard steps in a writing process and then adapting those steps to individual needs over time is useful, as is paying attention to advice on process.

The inexperienced writer can learn from the teachings of those who have come before. The best writing does develop through a process. For traditional assignments, the process includes steps like brainstorming, drafting, sharing, revising, and proofreading.

Digital assignments follow much the same process. Consider following steps along these lines:

- Read the assignment thoroughly.

- Ask questions about anything you don't understand.

- Look at samples of how others have completed similar assignments.

- Brainstorm ideas.

- Do a preliminary search for tools that might help you complete the task.

- Find and watch (or read) tutorials for any unfamiliar applications you will use in the assignment.

- Sketch out the layout of your project on paper first to help yourself envision it.
- Start building the layout of your project.
- Write a first draft of your text.
- Plan your multimedia elements.
- Create your multimedia elements.
- Integrate the media and text into your project.
- Review for mistakes.
- Make corrections.
- Seek feedback.
- Make notes and brainstorm ways to revise.
- Revise.
- Proofread.
- Publish.
- Proofread again.
- Make any necessary corrections.

Note that these steps include time to plan for the multiple elements of digital writing, and they include time to go back and rethink earlier steps again and again along the way. All writing is better when the writer doesn't just pass by a step but also circles back around to revisit it a few more times as well.

Perhaps the most significant difference here is that the process for digital writing says to proofread and correct after publishing. That's not possible in print; changes can't be made until a new edition comes out.

On a blog or a wiki or a regular old website, however, you can indeed proof and correct after publishing. Take advantage of this fact and appreciate it.

Presence

A fact of life in the new millennium is that almost everyone Googles. If you set up a couple of friends on a blind date, they might take your word for how wonderful the other is, but they'll also go online to see if there is anything unsavory posted by exes to random websites. A boss interested in hiring you will do the same. Be aware of that, and make it work to your advantage.

This means that you should not only avoid a trail of bad impressions in your digital wake but also that you should be sure that there is something good about you for others to find. These days everyone going into the job market needs an online presence. That presence should be polished, professional, and personable (the three Ps of pitching yourself to an employer).

Create a website, a blog, an online résumé, or an e-portfolio to promote your skills. Whatever you do should be polished in appearance, make use of impeccable grammar, and show you to be a well-rounded person with varied interests and abilities. Let it show some personality.

People want a sense of who you are, not just what you've done. However, don't go overboard in crafting your online persona. Appearing to be too cutesy or silly or snarky or angry will make a bad impression.

At the same time, be careful not to let potential employers find things you don't want them to see. Remember, they've all heard about Instagram and Twitter. They'll look there first. What's on your profile?

Most people do and say things in the presence of their closest friends that they wouldn't share at work. However, online, personal lives and public lives are not always automatically separate. You have to take steps to assure that they are.

If you're on Facebook and you don't want your boss, or your teacher, or your sweet old aunt to read what you and your friends are up to, set your status to *private*. Use anonymous screen names on public forums, and don't share enough personal information about yourself that people could identify who you are.

If you don't want your coworkers to see pictures of you at your friend's 21st birthday party, make sure these images aren't out there or they might follow you for years. Though lots of students live by the saying we learned from *South Park*, "There's a time and place for everything. It's called college," that doesn't mean that you won't pay for what you do in college. The Internet just makes it even more likely that you will keep paying for long years to come. Make the trail of information you leave about yourself online work *for you*, not *against you*.

Presentation

Perhaps the biggest lesson of becoming a net-savvy writer is that writing doesn't stand on its own and never has. From cave walls to clay pots to 8 ½" × 11" semigloss paper, part of the impact of writing has always been created by the medium of its transmission.

In a print version of an essay, margins, fonts, paragraph structures, headings, graphics, and other formatting options matter as a part of your writing. Online, they matter just as much and maybe more. Plus, in online writing additional design considerations become paramount.

On paper, for example, convention dictates that most writing will have a plain white background. Not so online. On paper, paragraphs without pictures look perfectly normal, though they seem barren online. On paper, references are written out, whereas a link often suffices online.

Internet writing is tied to its presentation design in a much more immediate and significant way than print counterparts often are. That shouldn't hold you back. Templates are available for almost anything you might try to do online, and a few simple design considerations can really make a big difference.

Whether writing a blog, designing a presentation, writing a photo essay, or laying out an electronic newsletter, follow these guidelines:

- **Avoid crowds and gaps.** Don't leave gaping spaces between separate elements in a piece of digital writing—such as between a picture and the text describing it—but at the same time, don't scrunch it all together. Leave just enough room for the eye to sort out easily how the pieces fit together.

- **Avoid design clashes.** If you wouldn't wear two particular colors together or paint them together in a room in your house, they may not be right for your web writing either. Try not to make your readers dizzy with unfortunate choices in colors, lines, or shapes. Be mindful of what you are doing as a piece of design and as a piece of writing.

- **Avoid distractions.** Some people like flashing, moving parts on web pages, and other people find them very annoying. Sometimes they serve a purpose in drawing attention to elements that need emphasis. Other times they only distract from the real purpose of the page. Use any such visual distractions sparingly and to good purpose.

- **Choose to be original.** Clipart is bad. Original designs are better. Your own original designs are best. Using clipart in a presentation, web page, or other digital medium gets attention, but maybe not the kind of attention you want. You don't have to be a design expert to find more original options. To start, take your own photographs. If you want a stop sign used to call attention to a warning message, instead of using clip art, take a picture of a real stop sign. You can crop it and make your boxing around it so that it becomes an original.

- **Choose simple.** William Safire once said, "Never use a long word when a diminutive one will do." Irony aside, this is usually good advice. You could also say, "Never use a fancy font when a plain one will do." Just as you can easily overcrowd a digital composition, you can also easily overclutter one with attempts at being too fancy. When in doubt, err on the side of simplicity.

- **Draw attention where you want it.** Experiment with headings, font sizes, bold print, italics, and other design considerations to call attention to important points in written documents. Use shapes, perspective, and other visual elements to draw the eye where you want it in more visual texts.

- **Emphasize readability.** Sometimes design choices such as background colors and images can look good but also end up obscuring the text. Some very pretty fonts are difficult to read, especially for prolonged passages. Don't avoid using background images, which can truly enhance the impact of a digital composition. Just make sure they do complement what you have to say if you are overlaying them with text.

> TIP: To learn more about design for presentations and other digital compositions, read *Presentation Zen* by Garr Reynolds, or visit the site http://www.presentationzen.com.

People Skills

SHOWING RESPECT

We live in a contentious world in which political campaigns are down and dirty, news commentators are often insulting, and trolling is the order of the day on blogs and message boards. All of this can make it seem as though being angry is the only way to be heard. Not so.

As a student, you'll communicate in writing in a variety of ways, including essays, peer responses, discussion board activities, and emails to other students and to professors. You might even have blog assignments or other forms of public writing. Regardless of the means of delivery, keep in mind that the diction of power is not by definition the diction of friction.

You'll win much more respect by showing respect rather than trying to prove that you too can be as rude as anyone else. You may think that this doesn't matter, but one day you'll need letters of recommendation from your instructors, or you'll need that person who sat next to you your sophomore year to put in a good word for you when you apply for a job. You do not want these people to remember you as the loudest person in the class with the most creative ways of slamming other students.

In the workforce, the impression you make in your writing will matter even more. One of the most common reasons cited for not promoting employees is "does not work well with others." That kind of reputation can follow you around for years, particularly in the age of written communication that never really goes away. The age of smartphones and online customer service makes this an even more vital lesson.

Before you click *send*, read aloud what you've written and think about how it sounds. Be sure it makes the impression you want. In fact, if the message you've written is the first draft, it probably isn't the best draft, especially if it is angry. The old saying that "you catch more flies with honey than with vinegar" may not be accurate, but the concept behind it certainly is. People will be more willing to listen or to help a person who does not sound angry.

To garner respect for yourself in and out of electronic classroom settings, consider these tips:

1. **Always write grammatically correct sentences.** The classroom is not a YouTube response or a Twitter post, and your teacher is not your text buddy. "R we hvn tst 2day?" might make sense to your friends, but in the classroom, that kind of expression says you are lazy and disrespectful.

2. **Be aware of "netiquette" conventions.** For example, ALL CAPS MEANS YOU ARE SHOUTING. Don't shout in classroom interactions. It's rude. For more on netiquette, go to the following website. http://www.albion.com/netiquette.

3. It shouldn't have to be said, but we'll say it anyway. **Always avoid obscenities.**

4. **Identify yourself fully in all electronic classroom conversations.** When emailing your instructor, tell what class you are in and what assignment you are referring to before asking your questions. When posting to class discussion boards, remind people of the context for your comment before making it. You will not get a response if no one knows what you are talking about.

5. **Pay attention to your tone of voice online so that it is not misinterpreted.** For example, last-minute panic over an assignment can come across to your teacher as anger or resentment if you aren't careful. People who might be willing to help you with problems might not have much sympathy if your tone makes them think you are just being a bad sport. Be straightforward and matter of fact about your requests rather than ranting or going off on tangents.

6. **Be patient.** Online communication doesn't always mean instant gratification. When you email an instructor or post a question to a discussion board, a day or more may lapse before anyone is available to help you. Your instructor could be stuck in meetings all day or have the flu or simply be buried in grading. Your classmates could have sick children or car trouble or tests for other classes. For that reason, don't wait until the last minute to ask your questions.

7. **Keep your own tone helpful in working with peers online.** Don't try to make them feel stupid or inadequate. Remember that some people are just shy, and some people have abilities that don't come across at their best through the written word. In any case, all members of a classroom are equally valuable. Treat them as such.

8. **Respect the fact that people have different perspectives.** Your audience is the entire class, not just your friends or the people who will most readily agree with you. The classroom is made up of people with various religious beliefs, political leanings, genders, races, and cultural values. Don't assume that everyone agrees with you, and don't demean those who might disagree. This doesn't mean you have to be afraid of expressing

your perspective. It does, however, mean that you should respect the fact that people have the right to differ. Once you've offended others, they no longer care what you think, and you've already lost the argument.

In other words, be polite. That's what it all boils down to, and that's not so difficult, is it?

CONSIDERING ETHICS

All writing requires certain ethical choices. Whether deliberately or automatically, writers work through checklists of decisions.

- Am I using original words, ideas, and organizational patterns?
- Am I documenting everything that I borrow from someone else?
- Am I refraining from telling anything confidential that affects other people?
- Am I using language that will not offend my audience?
- Have I considered multiple perspectives on the information?
- Have I considered my own bias on the information and the bias of others?
- Am I being fair-minded in my presentation of the information?
- Have I avoided taking anything out of context in a way that might skew the meaning?

These choices and more should be considered with each new piece of writing. Ethics are always important, but online their significance is magnified many times over. Online writing is public writing; therefore, online ethics are public as well. Infractions can matter to a lot more people. And because many people write online now, the average student in a writing class is more likely to write publicly and to face public ethical considerations in writing. That's why it's so important to develop early habits of being honest, fair, and considerate in all writing.

Sometimes what it means to be honest, fair, and considerate is not as easy to recognize as we might think. If it were, there'd be no need for the large array of classes in ethics offered to people going into professions of journalism, law, medicine, business, and so on. Sometimes we make unethical choices just because we haven't thought through all of the implications. We are particularly susceptible to doing this when we are in new situations, as we so often are online.

For example, consider the ethics of incorporating multimedia elements, such as images, music, and video, into your online writing. It's easy to make digital copies of any of these elements to remix into your own work. If you want a song to use as background to a podcast or as an introduction to a presentation, the easiest thing of all to do is to think up a song you like and go looking for an MP3 of it to download and import into your own project.

But what if that puts you in copyright violation? What if that is expressly against the wishes of the artist?

Although we would never consider stealing a credit card from a friend, we so easily forget that taking a digital picture or song and using it for our own purposes might also be stealing.

Legally, copyright protects an artist's rights to make reproductions of a work, to make derivatives of the work (or new works based upon the original), and to display, distribute, or perform the work. An artist might sue if he or she believes any of those rights have been violated, and the court may or may not agree. Copyright issues are amazingly complicated and amazingly confusing.

U.S. copyright law does contain fair use principles that make it possible for journalists and scholars to write about a copyrighted work and to share parts of that work in the criticism or reporting of it. The amount of the original used, the reason it was used, and the degree to which that use affects the artist's ability to profit from the original are all considered to be mitigating factors within the law.

So using a clip from a copyrighted song in your PowerPoint presentation for a class and presenting it only to a class is protected by the parts of the fair use law that allow for reproducing small amounts of a copyrighted work for educational purposes.

If, on the other hand, you sync the entire song to your PowerPoint, convert the PowerPoint to a video format, and upload it onto YouTube with full public access, you may be cited for copyright violations.

The law is complicated and subject to a variety of interpretations in the courts, and you should read up on it at www.copyright.gov if you have questions about whether what you are doing is legal.

Putting legalities aside, let's just think about ethics. Your ethics are the system or the set of guiding principles through which you decide what is right and wrong. How do you decide what is right and wrong when you borrow from another person's work to enhance your own?

It isn't enough to say, "It was on the Internet and easy to download." Stores are full of merchandise that is easy to shoplift, but that doesn't mean it is right, fair, or legal to do so.

If you say, "I was using it for class," that puts you a little closer to right, considering classroom use is covered under fair use law, but it doesn't entirely excuse you. Turning in someone else's images or sounds as your own is as bad as turning in someone else's words as your own.

If you say, "I used only a small portion of the original, and I properly documented it," you arrive at a practice that is both legal and ethical.

With audio editing software, you can reuse only a small portion of a song. However, that's not so easy with a picture. Photo editing software will let you crop out only a piece of an image, but what do you do with it from there? How do you use only a corner of a building instead of a whole building as an illustration in your own work about something that happened in a particular place? How do you write a response to a political cartoon without showing the whole cartoon?

The answers aren't always easy. You might be able to get away with sharing the whole cartoon in an essay for which your audience is limited only to your own class. Posting that same copyrighted cartoon as part of a blog essay on a public blog, however, would be a problem. You've then distributed the work in a way that is unfair to the artist. You would be better off in that case simply linking to the cartoon where it is posted on the artist's own site.

One way of handling these ethical questions is to circumvent them wherever possible by creating most or all of your own content. Take your own photographs instead of copying them from other places. Make your graphics. Record your own music. However, in the case of music, you still have to be sure the musical score is not copyrighted before you record it.

Another way of handling these questions is to use materials that are available in the public domain or in the creative commons.

Copyright does eventually expire. The terms of copyright expirations have changed at various points in the history of the law, but if you are working with a piece of art that is more than 120 years old, you can probably assume it is in the public domain. Currently, copyrights are protected for the lifetime of the artist plus 70 years.

The Library of Congress has also archived a large number of photographs and musical recordings that are in the public domain either because the artist is unknown, the work was never copyrighted by the artist, or the work was originally contracted by the government (as were many photographs of American life during the Great Depression). Visit www.loc.gov to search the Library of Congress archives.

Creative Commons works are those copyrighted under special conditions to allow others to reuse them or to create derivative works from them. To find these works and to learn more about Creative Commons copyrights, go to www.creativecommons.org.

You will find a large number of photographs, graphic images, music, and video clips in the Creative Commons. Using these to enhance your own work is ethical because you are doing so with the express permission of the artist.

However, always read the copyright license, even on Creative Commons works. CC offers different types of licenses so that artists can select exactly how they are willing to share their work. Some may have indicated that they are willing for their work to be reused only for noncommercial purposes. Others may have indicated that the work may be reused only in its original form and is not available to be remixed or manipulated in any way.

Always respect the artist's wishes, just as you respect your neighbors in your non-digital life. Even though technological possibilities have developed far faster than our capacity to think through the ethics of new situations, it is not okay to download, copy, manipulate, and redistribute online content however we want.

Nevertheless, with a little extra thought and care, we can usually find ways to accomplish our own goals without behaving unethically.

NAVIGATING ONLINE POLITICS

If you have a social networking account, you've probably faced some personal dilemmas over friending practices. Do you limit yourself to close friends? Do you turn down people from work or from school? Do you turn down your grandmother? Or do you friend most people who ask and just hope for the best?

These are choices of audience, something all writers face. Even on paper, the question of who will read your writing has to weigh into your style, tone, and content. If you have no awareness of how the writing might be received, you can't hope to communicate effectively.

Still, on paper you can often physically restrict who sees your writing so that the "wrong people" never have to find out how you really feel. Would you rather your grandmother didn't know you are secretly in favor of legalizing marijuana? Simple solution. Don't show her the paper you wrote on the topic for sociology class.

That solution isn't so simple online. Even if your grandmother still doesn't know how to check her text messages, there's no guarantee she isn't reading your blog, and it is almost guaranteed that potential employers are viewing it. Online, you have to be prepared for any eventuality. You have to decide your public stance politically, socially, and professionally for one and all to see.

On a blog, the sites you link to your post say something about who you are. On Facebook, when you become a fan of a page, or when you join a group, that says something about what you believe. No one is asking you to be untrue to yourself for the sake of being politically correct, but it would be prudent to spend time thinking about the impression you make, not only with your writing, but with the elements that frame that writing as well.

Suppose a friend leaves an offensive comment on your blog article. Do you delete the comment and anger that friend, or do you leave it in place and allow someone else's feelings to be hurt? This is your choice. No one can make it for you, but people will be watching to see what you do. People will notice how you conduct your own personal and social politics.

BEING PERSONABLE

This section might also be titled "Being Engaging" or "Being Interesting" or "Impressing Your Audience." The way in which you need to be personable in establishing your online presence is all about voice and audience awareness.

When we talk about a writer's voice, we mean the kinds of energy and personality that infuse the writing. We mean that element of written voices that captures and expresses the personalities and moods of speaking voices. We mean the particular spark that makes your words on the page or screen sound like an actual person said them.

Be mindful of voice in all writing, not just online writing, but be extra mindful online because you never actually know who your audience might be. Something you post online for a class might one day be read by someone considering you for a job. That extra spark in your writing might be just what it takes to tip the scales.

And because digital writing is generally more visually oriented than its print counterparts, think about how your use of images, embedded video, and design elements also express personality and character.

When you go to a job interview in person, you know you are supposed to look your best, to wear business attire, and to remove any excess body piercings. You are also supposed to speak and behave in your most impressive manner.

Your online presence should do the same. If you have a portfolio of work available online for potential employers to peruse, make sure your work grabs attention through an engaging writer's voice and an engaging appearance. At the same time, remove the digital equivalents of tattoos and body piercings. You have a skull and crossbones picture on your site and a tarot reading widget in the sidebar? If that makes you happy, that's fine. No one cares except your grandmother and the people who are thinking about hiring you for a job.

If you care about getting that job, dress up your web presence to impress the same way you'd dress up yourself. Keep blogs and e-portfolios and project sites in a place that you can happily point out during interviews. And don't assume that if you haven't pointed them out, they haven't been seen. If it's out there, someone who wants to know more about you has looked it up.

More than just cleaning up, though, think about what it really takes to impress. In an interview, you know that looking the part is never enough. You also have to sound and act the part. That's basically all about confidence and enthusiasm.

You want to capture that same spark of vitality, that same confidence and enthusiasm, in your web writing. Put yourself into it wholeheartedly, but make it your best, most impressive, job-seeking self. Even if you aren't currently looking for a job, put that version of yourself forward as your public presence. Then, when you need to be impressive, you'll always be prepared.

Some Basic Mechanics of Being Net-Savvy

A few skills do come in handy to be net-savvy. However, this chapter is not going to provide step-by-step instructions for those skills. Because programs are often different from each other, you can find instructions for the ones you use easily enough just by doing a simple web search.

What we will do here is offer some tips to get you started and some advice about how to think about tasks you might be asked to do.

WRITING AN EMAIL

Email is a very easy essential skill required in all professional jobs. You can't get away with not knowing how to do it, and there's no reason you should want to. Most of the time, you have to know only how to "compose" and then "send" in order to operate it.

You should, however, keep in mind a few protocols.

1. Give your email a title that makes sense and clearly identifies the purpose of the message. If you are writing to a teacher, for example, your subject line might say "Definition Essay, ENG 1113, B Period." That lets the teacher know which class you are in and which assignment your question is about up front. It also identifies you as a student with a question. This makes it less likely that your email will go unnoticed if your teacher happens to get a lot of email.

2. Get right to the point. The person reading your email should know what you want in the first three or four sentences. Tell what you want first. After that, you can go back and tell your reasons.

3. Be succinct but not so succinct as to appear rude or vague. In other words, don't send a lengthy email where a shorter one will do, but at the same time, don't leave out pertinent information or write such clipped sentences that you sound angry. Tone is very difficult to interpret in an email. Taking a little time to establish good will can be important.

4. Be polite at all times. Even if you are angry, don't send angry emails, especially in professional or academic situations. Don't name-call or threaten. Just calmly and politely explain what your issue is. If you are too angry to be nice, write a draft of an email just to vent. Delete it when you are finished. Wait a few hours and write another one when you have calmed down.

5. Provide any information the person needs to know to respond to your email. If you have a question about your cable service, for example, no one can help you before you first tell your address so that your account can be looked up.

6. Write in grammatically correct sentences with properly spelled words. Email is now a formal means of communication and should be treated as such, particularly in professional and academic situations.

SENDING AN EMAIL ATTACHMENT

If you need to send an essay to an instructor or submit an application letter for a job or send any other type of document as a separate document rather than part of the email text itself, you must learn how to attach files to emails.

In most programs this is accomplished by clicking on either the word "Attach" or an icon in the shape of a paper clip. From there, the program will walk you through the steps of browsing through your computer for the document and attaching it to the email. If you cannot find the correct way, remember that one skill of a net-savvy writer is to know when to Google the instructions for how to accomplish a task.

SAVING TO A PARTICULAR FILE FORMAT

Hit "File" and "Save As" in most word-processing programs (Word, Works, Open Office, etc.), and you will see several places to choose how you save your document. There will be a place to give it a title and a place to choose the location you want to save to, whether on your computer or on a flash drive or other plug-in device. You will also see a category that says "File Type." Pull the menu open next to "File Type," and you will see many choices.

The main reason you want to be aware of this is to make your files accessible to those who use a different program. The ".docx" files created in the current version of Word don't open even in earlier versions of Word unless a file converter has been installed. Documents created in Open Office often don't open in other word-processing programs.

This can be remedied if you know how to change file type. Choosing ".rtf" or "rich text format" will almost always assure that the file can be opened in other programs. Choosing to save as "Word 97-93" will assure that people using older versions of Word can open documents created in newer version of Word. Likewise, Open Office users often need to change the file type to .doc or .rtf in order to share with people using Word or other programs.

For a Mac user working with Pages, the process is similar. To change a file type in Pages, select the "File" tab from the menu at the top to open the drop-down menu. Then, select "Export to" and choose from the options listed. The device will then walk you through saving the copy in the new format. Most computers will be able to open Word documents, rich text format documents, and PDFs.

Finally, many writers use Google Docs to ensure that they may access their writing online, making it available practically anywhere. Google Docs generally do not attach well to emails or Canvas, so writers should download a copy of the document and save it on their device before trying to attach it or upload it to another platform. To download and save a copy from Google Docs, select the "File" tab from the menu at the top of the page. Then, select "Download as," and you will see several options for different file types. Once you select one, the device will walk you through saving the new copy.

> **TIP:** If you try unsuccessfully to upload a word-processing file into Canvas or some other online site, one of the most common reasons for failure is that you are trying to upload an unsupported file type. Try saving as .rtf or a PDF to correct the problem.

CREATING A BLOG

Blogs can provide some of the best ways online to express yourself, hone your writing skills, document your progress on projects, respond to ideas and information, integrate multimedia elements into your writing, and so on.

You may be asked to create a blog as a class assignment. If so, your class might use its own blogging platform. If you want to create a blog on your own, though, you might start with a free blogging service. Two of the most popular are Blogger (www.blogger.com) and WordPress (www.wordpress.com). Go to one of these two sites, create a free account, and follow the instructions provided to make your first blog.

Another blogging site that operates a little differently is Tumblr (www.tumblr.com). This site lays claim to being the "easiest way to blog," and it is easy. It allows you simply to email in your blog entries, and it formats them for you. Tumblr also allows you to set your blog posts up to publish automatically to Facebook, Twitter, or other social media accounts that you may have, and it comes with a smartphone app so that you can blog by phone.

Some of these free sites make it incredibly easy to create the kinds of blogs that would have seemed complicated only a few years ago; photo blogs, podcasting blogs, and video blogs are no more complicated to set up and keep up than email and text messaging.

Sign up for an account on the site of your choice, or on several accounts if you want to experiment to find your favorite. Once you've followed the instructions provided by the site itself, all you need to do to start blogging is just to start typing.

CREATING A WIKI

A wiki is a website that has the potential to have multiple pages by multiple authors. Thus, you are most likely to use wikis for group projects in class.

Some places for creating wikis are PB Works (www.pbworks.com), WikiFoundry (www.wikifoundry.com), and Wix (www.wix.com). On these sites, you might create a website as a group project where you research a topic, advocate a cause, or even simply share materials to be used for school, work, or personal purposes.

Sign up for a free account, and follow the instructions provided by the web service to create your own site. Once you've done that, you can invite others to collaborate. As the site administrator, you can choose which people are invited to view, to add content, or to edit as well as add materials.

Google Sites can also be used as wikis, and even WordPress blogs can be used as wikis. A WordPress site can become a wiki because it allows you to add pages as well as posts; it also allows you to invite others to join your site as either readers, writers, or editors. This makes WordPress different from some of the other popular blogging utilities, as well as a good place to learn if you want to create a combination of blogs, wikis, and other types of websites.

Another option is to use the wiki tool within Canvas for class assignments. Some versions of Canvas include blogs and wikis. The difference in using this and using a web service is that Canvas takes care of security issues for you. You will not have to worry about who sees your wiki if people have to log into your class to view it. On the other hand, you will have to export all of your materials at the end of the class and import them somewhere else if you want to keep them on display.

The service you use will likely be up to your instructor, but it is a good idea to start experimenting with some of these online tools on your own so that you will be comfortable with them when you need them for class assignments and other projects.

CREATING A PROJECT WEBSITE

You have several options for creating a website for a class project. You could use a wiki platform like PB Works, which can be multiauthored but doesn't have to be. You could also use a WordPress site. Likewise, though WordPress can be used for blogging, it doesn't have to be. A WordPress site with a single post and multiple pages becomes a regular static website.

You might want to consider using something like Google Sites, which is designed for creating easy websites to which a variety of types of content can be added.

Access to Google Sites comes with a gmail account. Log into your gmail and click on "Sites" at the top of the screen (you may have to click on "more" first before you see "sites" as an option). This will take you to a page that allows you to create a new site. If you don't see a short cut to Google sites in your Google menu, just go directly to sites.google.com.

Webs.com appears to no longer have a free option.

ADDING YOUTUBE VIDEOS AND FLICKR IMAGES TO BLOGS OR WEBSITES

With WordPress and other blogging platforms like it, you are able to access and edit the HTML (HyperText Markup Language) associated with your blog. This is also the case in Canvas Discussions and Canvas Pages.

If you want to embed a YouTube video or a Flickr image into your blog post on a blog that allows you to format your own post, you need the HTML code for that video or image. Embedding in this case means that the image shows up as if it is part of the post even if it is actually hosted on another site. This is different from linking, in which your blog visitors would have to click on a hyperlink to go to the other site to view the image.

To embed, go to YouTube (or Flickr), find the video (or image) you want, and copy the HTML provided for embedding. On YouTube, this is labeled "embed." On Flickr, you will find it under "Share" and "Grab the HTML."

Once you have the HTML, go to your blog post and switch your text editor over to the HTML version rather than the visual version. Once you are in HTML mode, you can simply paste in the code you have copied from YouTube or Flickr.

That's it. You're done. Your video or image will show up in your post once you've hit publish.

This works on other types of websites as well. You can copy and paste HTML for embedding into Google Sites by switching to HTML mode, and you can copy and paste it into Canvas in the same way.

Blogs, wikis, discussion boards, and almost any other application inside Canvas that allows students to create content has an HTML-editing mode that can be switched on so that HTML code can be pasted in.

In newer versions of Canvas, and in new versions of some blogging platforms, options are built into the visual editor for sharing video and images. In that case, you can just click on the button for inserting from YouTube or Flickr and paste in the link rather than the HTML. Regardless of whether this option is available, though, if you know how to grab the code, you know how to embed.

FINDING CREATIVE COMMONS IMAGES

The quick answer to how to find Creative Commons images is to go to www. creativecommons.org, click on "Find," and either enter a search term or click on one of the listed sites to browse through images licensed under Creative Commons. That's the easy part.

You have already read about copyright issues earlier in the ethics section of this chapter. Unless an image has a copyright statement saying that it is okay to use it in your work, don't take it.

Creative Commons solves this issue by giving artists an easy way to tell others whether it is okay with them for the image to be posted on someone else's site or used in someone else's brochure.

When searching through Flickr or other photo sites, look at the license on the picture you want to use. If it says, "All Rights Reserved," move on along and find something else. If it says, "Some Rights Reserved," this indicates a Creative Commons license.

Click on the copyright information to see the terms under which that artist has agreed to share the work. Do not violate those terms. Artists who feel slighted by people misusing their work will probably pull the images so that they are not available to the public at all. Worse, they might sue you.

MAKING AN AUDIO RECORDING

You may be asked to make an audio recording for a class for any number of reasons. You might record your writings, do multimedia presentations, keep an audio journal, or do audio peer responses. You might record interviews conducted as part of a research project. You might have a podcasting project.

Whatever the reason, you have two options to make a recording. You'll need either the right software for using your computer as a recorder, or you'll need a recording device.

Two of the most common pieces of software used to make audio recordings are Audacity and GarageBand. Audacity is an open source program available as a free download at http://audacity.sourceforge.net/. GarageBand comes packaged with most Apple computers.

Online tutorials are available for using both programs on their sites, or you can find tutorials on YouTube.

Using either program to make a basic recording is easy. You need only to figure out how to hit "Record," "Stop," and "Play" to get started. From there, the tutorials will guide you through anything else you need to do.

If you decide to use a recording device, you have a lot of options. A wide variety of audio recorders are available at a cost ranging from under $50 to over $500 (and even much higher than that). You get what you pay for in many cases, and the more expensive devices often do provide better sound quality.

However, you probably will not need the highest level of sound quality for your recording since you are not doing it for a professional broadcasting network. Also, if you plan to share online, using the highest possible sound quality would make the file sizes too large and impossible to upload and post.

Some of the moderately priced recorders are really quite good, but even they are not your only option. Do you have an iPod Touch or an iPhone? The voice memo feature works as well as anything in its price range to make audio recordings.

If you are doing your recording for a class that uses Canvas, you may have access to the voice recorder in Canvas. If you have a blog on Tumblr, you can phone in an audio recording from any regular phone. Likewise, there are audio apps available for both iOS and Android that will make the job of creating a recording a snap.

> TIP: If you want to share an audio recording online, you'll need to save it as an MP3 file for faster uploading and downloading.

> TIP: You'll need a microphone to make an audio recording on a computer. If your computer does not have a built-in mic, one option is a headset microphone. The best option is earbuds with a built-in microphone. These come with iPhones and many people already have them.

WRITING WITH HYPERTEXT

Hypertext is one of the primary dividing lines between digital media and print media. On a printed page, you cannot link individual words and phrases directly to other pages. The ability to do this on the screen is one of the great transformative developments in the world of literacy.

If you write for the web, take advantage of the opportunity to turn your words into hyperlinks wherever appropriate. Those links serve as references, and they are far easier to access and follow than the traditional references provided in footnotes and Works Cited pages in print-based essays.

To turn a word into a hyperlink in most blog or web editors, you highlight the word and then click on the word link (or perhaps an icon of a globe with a paperclip on it). That will open a place to insert the URL for the page you want to link to.

The HTML for hyperlinking looks something like this: <a href="http://www. clarionledger.com">Clarion Ledger</a>. In this case the words "Clarion Ledger" would link to the website for the *Clarion-Ledger* newspaper.

You probably won't need to know that because you'll be able to use a visual or WYSIWYG (what you see is what you get) editor. Still, it's useful to understand that when you do use those visual editing options, you are creating HTML code. Even a rudimentary knowledge of what the HTML looks like and what it is supposed to look like will help you hand-edit web postings as needed.

Either way, whether you write your own HTML or use a visual editor, remembering to link is essential. It accomplishes what any referencing system accomplishes. It helps you give credit where it is due, back up your own opinions, and refer people to additional information about your topic. Hyperlinking makes you a credible writer as well as a savvy writer.

WORKING WITH VIDEO

A video assignment could entail any of a number of media tools. You might use a camera to record video, a program like Jing or Camtasia to capture a screencast, or a program like MovieMaker (on a PC) or iMovie (on a Mac) to edit together a variety of elements into one movie. You might combine all three, sometimes in the same movie.

Start by selecting a camera. The easiest camera to select is the one that you already have, which is probably on your phone, tablet, or laptop. If you wish to purchase a camera, keep in mind that the camera you start out with now doesn't have to last you for life. Nor does it have to be the most expensive. Your best option might be a simple point-and-shoot digital camera that also records video. Compact and relatively cheap, it can be used to capture both still and moving images.

You may wish to purchase some other form of video camera, or in a pinch you may end up using the video camera that comes with a phone or other device. You may even use the built-in web cam on a laptop or netbook.

Once you have a camera, play around with it. Film family events. Make funny videos of friends. Start a video journal of your own thoughts and ideas. Do whatever you need to do to familiarize yourself with the process of recording video, transferring it to a computer, editing it, and uploading it to YouTube or another video-sharing service where others can view it. This way you'll be prepared when you do have occasion to work with video for class.

Every device will have its own set of instructions, so be sure to read the instructions that come with your camera to understand how to record and transfer video.

Next you'll need to pick an editing program. MovieMaker for PC and iMovie for Mac are the most common beginner-level programs. Watch the tutorials that come with your program to understand better how it works.

When you are finished tweaking your video, save to a file format appropriate for sharing online. This is important because some video formats create such large files that uploading, downloading, and streaming are nearly impossible. On the other hand, some file formats that compress the video or reduce its file size end up sacrificing so much in picture quality that the video is fuzzy or distorted. The format that is considered to offer the best compromise between size and quality is MPEG4.

If you want to share your own videos on your own website or blog, it's best to open an account with a video-sharing service (YouTube, Vimeo, Google Video, etc.). These sites are intended to share video and offer the easiest way to share it in ways others can easily play. They simplify everything for you. Just log into your account and upload your video and the share-the-link or HTML code for embedding on your own site. The video-sharing site does the rest.

Just as everyone can be a news reporter now, everyone can also be a movie-maker now. The technology is here for the general consumer to use cheaply and easily, and if the number of movies being uploaded to YouTube each day is any indication, the general consumer is making movies galore.

Record. Transfer to computer. Edit. Export to MPEG4. Upload to YouTube. Copy and paste the embed code from YouTube to your blog, and you are not only a moviemaker; you are also a video blogger. It's that easy, and it's a process that will serve you well for digital-age college projects.

CREATING AN ONLINE RÉSUMÉ

You have a whole spectrum of options for creating an online résumé, but we'll just cover a few.

VisualCV

This is a résumé-building site that allows you also to add portfolio items. It provides several ways to share the résumé, including emailing as a PDF file or sending a link so that the résumé may be viewed online.

Google Docs

With a free gmail account, you have access to a whole suite of online applications, including Documents. Choosing "create new" and "from template" from Google Docs allows you to select a résumé template. Once you've completed your résumé by filling in your own information on the template, go to "Share" and "Publish as Web Page." This gives you a public link for your résumé that you can share with others.

Box.net

This is a file storage site. Though premium membership is not free, the basic startup membership with 1 GB of storage space is free. Here you can upload files and choose to make them public or private. If you make them public, you will be given a link to share with others for downloading. Create a résumé in a word-processing program to upload here. If you plan to share your résumé file directly online, though, it is a good idea to save it as a PDF file. This way you can be assured that the formatting will not change when it is opened on another computer.

> TIP: The .pdf file format is the best way to share documents like résumés where the formatting is particularly important. If the .pdf extension is not an option in your version of Microsoft Word when you go to "Save As" and "File Type," you can download the Adobe plug-in by visiting http://office.microsoft.com/.

LinkedIn

LinkedIn is a social networking site for job seekers and professionals. While it isn't intended to serve as a traditional résumé, your profile can include all of the information a résumé might include. You can also add portfolio items and link to other sites, including a résumé posted elsewhere. LinkedIn provides a way to connect with others and a way for others to recommend you within the site.

MAKING AN E-PORTFOLIO

An electronic portfolio or e-portfolio is a collection of work by a particular person presented in electronic form. It might be assembled as a project portfolio, such as a website with research and other materials gathered on a particular topic; an artist's portfolio, such as a collection of artwork, writing, or music; or a career portfolio, such as a collection of original works and other materials put together for the purpose of applying for jobs or advancing a career.

Just as there are different types of e-portfolios, there are also different electronic formats they can take. A photographer's portfolio might be put together as a blog, a slideshow, or a series of online photo albums. A writer's portfolio might be put together as one large PDF file or as a series of PDF files posted to a blog, to a website, or even to a document-sharing site like Scribd (www. scribd.com). A career portfolio could be assembled on a site like VisualCV. It could be put together as a website or even take the shape of a presentation with embedded links to portfolio artifacts.

Some schools have adopted e-portfolio platforms for student use. Even Canvas has a portfolio feature. You may be assigned both a portfolio and the format it should take. If so, follow your teacher's instructions.

Portfolios, however, tend to develop over time. Even if you are assigned one in class, that doesn't mean you can't continue to work on it after the class is over. Indeed, you should continue to work on it. You should always have at least a career portfolio that you update periodically so that it never falls seriously out of date.

Let's assume that you want to create a career portfolio as a website. First, you need to decide where and how to set it up. If you are majoring in computer programming or some other highly technical field, build your own website from scratch. Nothing else really makes sense for you. Everyone else, though, will do just as well to use a free service.

Consider using WordPress (www.wordpress.com). This is a blogging platform, but it is one that lets you add pages as well as posts. One post with multiple pages turns a blog into a regular website. This is an easy and free way to go about building your portfolio. You could also use Google Sites, or any of a number of free online tools.

> TIP: For more extensive instructions on using WordPress to build a portfolio, visit http://makeafolio.wordpress.com/.

If you prefer to put your portfolio together as a presentation, think about how you are going to include your components and how you are going to share the presentation with others. You can make a writing portfolio as a Google Presentation by uploading your writings into Google Docs and linking to them in presentation slides that serve as introductions to each piece of writing.

Or you could make a career portfolio using PowerPoint by uploading the individual components in various places—YouTube, Scribd, Flickr, VisualCV, and so on, depending on what kind of components you have. The slides could introduce each element, and the whole thing could be posted on SlideShare (www.slideshare.net).

A potentially more dynamic way of making a presentation portfolio than either Google Presentation or PowerPoint, however, is through Prezi (www.prezi.com). This makes for a whole different presentation experience in which larger files can be embedded and people can zoom in and out to see what they want.

However you go about it, think of your career portfolio as a résumé that has been expanded to include examples of your work. You want to embed writing samples, presentations, video projects, and anything else that represents the best work you have done for school or a job.

As with a traditional résumé, your portfolio will change and grow over time. It will also become more specialized. When you are first starting out, you might include a wide variety of projects in your portfolio. Later, you'll include only projects related to your particular career or even to your particular specialty.

A teacher, for example, would put lesson plans, classroom handouts, and articles written about teaching in a portfolio, whereas a real estate agent might include a slideshow of houses sold and samples of promotional materials created to sell houses.

The simplest way to go about making a career portfolio is probably to make an online résumé to create hyperlinks to link to samples of your work. This can be done using a résumé template in Google Docs. You can also do something very similar (and maybe a little flashier and more impressive) on VisualCV (www.visualcv.com). There you can build an online résumé and upload portfolio artifacts that will show up on the same screen as your résumé.

Possibilities abound, and you should take advantage of them. Whatever your chosen career, you need an online presence in the digital age. An e-portfolio is the best way to make that presence both professional and impressive.

Chapter 19

The Net-Savvy Researcher

Whether writing and researching for school or on the job, success requires some net smarts, or an Internet-specific kind of awareness. Online research involves the same elements of searching, evaluating, and organizing as more traditional library research, but the potential for pitfalls can be greater.

Substandard resources may appear at first glance to be perfectly acceptable. Personal pages might come across as professional. Biased sources might market themselves as mainstream. Even advertisements can look like articles. Thus, it is particularly important that the online researcher develop certain key knowledge and skills.

1. Navigating efficiently
2. Choosing wisely
3. Getting organized in a digital world
4. Giving credit where credit is due
5. Finding a purpose

Navigating Efficiently

As a student researcher, the first skill you need to master is that of knowing how to find what you need when you need it. Anyone with a smartphone and a few seconds to spare can generally find something about any topic desired in this technological age, but net smarts go beyond opening up a Google app on an iPhone or Android.

In fact, you don't even need a smartphone to have net smarts. You just need to understand where else to look and how else to look if your first try isn't as successful as you wished. You need to know how to differentiate between different types of electronic sources. And you need to know how to sort out the good, the bad, and the indifferent.

For example, Internet articles and library database articles might both be found by sitting in front of a computer and using a web browser, but they are not published in the same way, nor are they documented in the same way. Understanding these distinctions might mean the difference in passing or failing if your instructor has assigned a particular kind of resource.

Understanding the differences in a blog article, an online magazine article, and a *Wikipedia* article is also necessary to success. Much of this understanding is about simply paying more attention to where you are and what you are reading while online. It's also about understanding the process necessary to successful electronic research.

Searching the Web

Most college students have probably been Googling for years. Google provides help topics on most features of web searches.

However, even students accustomed to web searches often have difficulty finding useful information. If you keep coming up empty-handed, ask yourself a few pertinent questions.

1. Did you spell the search terms correctly? This might seem overly simplified, but it really is one of the most common reasons students have trouble finding what they want.

2. Have you tried varying your search terms? Simple changes like making your word choices more specific or putting your keywords inside quotation marks can sometimes make a big difference.

3. Have you tried more than one search engine? If you don't find what you need through Google or Yahoo, try a meta-search engine like Dogpile (www.dogpile.com).

4. In addition to Internet searches, have you tried looking in a variety of library databases?

5. Have you tried using the library catalog to find out what print sources are available on your topic?

6. If you've tried all of these suggestions and are still having trouble, go to www.google.com/support/ and review the tips under "Web Search Help." Also remember to ask librarians, classmates, and instructors for suggestions.

Think of searching for sources as a process in and of itself just like all of the other steps in the research process as a whole, such as organizing, evaluating, drafting, and revising. As with any process, sometimes you need to stop, regroup, and begin again. One of the most important factors in finding what you need is to know what you're looking for. Often that's easier said than done. It can become far less frustrating, however, if you follow a clear process.

STAGE 1: SELECTING A TOPIC

This part of the process requires becoming familiar with the assignment, brainstorming for ideas, weighing your own interests, and learning enough about your possible topics to make a good decision. To begin, you need to conduct some general web searches in which you might want to read articles that give basic overviews to help you understand what you need to look for when beginning your research in earnest.

STAGE 2: FOCUSING YOUR TOPIC

Most people start out with topics that are too broad to make good essays. Those general topics are comprised of many potential angles and perspectives from which to narrow down. To do this, take one of the overviews found in a general search and break it down into subcategories. Pick a few of those narrowed down topics to do initial searches on so that you'll have a sense of what's out there. From there, choose the angle that most interests you or the one on which you believe the best information is available.

STAGE 3: OUTLINING YOUR TOPIC

Fairly early on in the research process, you need an outline of your topic. This may or may not end up resembling the outline for your actual research paper, and it may be no more complicated than a brainstorming list. The point is that planning what to research is just as essential as planning what to write. Once you have an outline, you have a list of specific pieces of information you need to find to complete a paper. That will give you ways to vary your searches, and it will assure that you are locating substantive information. It does no good to find twenty sources on a topic if all of those sources say the same thing. Outlining early and often is one of the best ways to avoid this dilemma.

STAGE 4: ORGANIZING AND EVALUATING YOUR MATERIALS

Once you've done initial research on each of the subpoints you want to make in your research paper, you need to step back to assess what you have. Organize your sources in conjunction with your outline, and evaluate them for quality. Determine where you have gaps in information. Make a list of questions you still have or information you still need. From that list, choose keywords to use in additional searches.

STAGE 5: DRAFTING YOUR PAPER

No matter how well you've planned or how well you've researched, you will discover places where you lack the best information as you begin writing a draft of your paper. This is normal. It happens to everyone. Use it as an opportunity to take good notes on where you need more information, and work from there. Remember too that starting your draft early enough to leave time for conducting more research is part of the process. If you put off working on the paper until the last minute, you will not be able to complete this step, and you will end up turning in a weaker assignment.

STAGE 6: REVISING YOUR PAPER

Yes, even as you revise your paper multiple times, you should keep looking for holes in your research and resources that might fill them in. The more you learn about your topic, the more you'll learn about how to research it. You may understand only a few keywords associated with the topic to help in your searches when you first start out, but by the time you reach the point of revision, you should have a long list of possible subtopics and related points. Each of these offers a new way to look for information. Take advantage of that. Plan time for it. Understand that writing, revising, and researching go hand in hand. One step in the process does not start where the other ends, and no step is finished until all are finished.

Choosing Wisely

When selecting sources for a research project, or even when simply trying to understand something on your own, evaluating materials for quality and usability is extremely important. Before deciding to use any source, consider some of the following questions.

1. Is it **timely**?

2. Is it **relevant**?

3. Is it **reliable**?

4. Is it **free from bias**?

5. Is it **thorough**?

6. Is it **professional**?

TIMELINESS

Often, good research demands that we find absolutely the most current information possible. The whole premise of a term paper might be inaccurate if it is based on outdated information. On the job, outdated research could be even more costly. None of us wants to imagine being treated by a doctor working from old research or being represented by an attorney who has not kept up with changes in the law. We know the consequences of these scenarios could be dire.

We should also know that even in less extreme situations, we still lose the respect of our readers by writing from outdated sources, and we certainly risk failure on assignments. Therefore, the first step to assessing a source is to determine whether newer information might have already rendered it inaccurate or irrelevant. Additionally, some writing instructors ban the use of sources published before a set date. Always make sure you are aware of the requirements for your own assignment.

Online sources sometimes identify a publication date and sometimes do not. The absence of a date should at least cause you to question whether the source is appropriate. The information may or may not be outdated, but attention to detail is a mark of professionalism, so a clear publication date can matter in more ways than one. Keep in mind also that dates are part of the documentation process. Be as cautious of using an article that isn't dated as you might be of using one that is outdated.

RELEVANCE

Relevance means it matters. Before selecting any source, ask yourself how much it matters. How important is the information to your topic and your purpose? It is always important to keep looking until you've found the most significant information possible. Too often, students are tempted just to gather the first information they come to and call it a day. This is not advisable. Try developing a ranking system for the degree of relevance of each source and keep looking until you've found plenty of sources that rank high on your relevancy scale.

Aside from the degree of significance to your overall topic, you need also to consider how much the information you are gathering matters to the individual subtopics you plan to cover. Computers and printers make it so easy to print large stacks of materials for later use without really reading them. This method, however, can easily lead to your accumulating large stacks of completely useless information.

One of the most common complaints from students when they get down to writing a research paper is that all of the sources say the same thing. This is a result of poor planning, evaluating, and organizing during the research process. By knowing your subtopics and knowing the relevance of individual sources to individual subtopics, you can avoid a great deal of last-minute research paper angst.

RELIABILITY

Reliability of sources can sometimes be incredibly difficult to judge. Before committing to using an article, you need to know if it was written by someone with authority on the topic, if it was written for professional purposes, and if it was published through respectable channels. This can be difficult to assess in print sources; it is often nearly impossible to gauge in online sources. However, Net-savvy researchers do have some tricks up their sleeves.

First, check to see if the credentials of the author are provided. Be extremely wary of using anything posted online that tells neither the credentials of the author nor the purpose of the organization. Also consider whether that person's credentials are related to the topic. A medical opinion by a person with "Dr." next to the name won't mean anything if that person's doctorate is in art history. It would simply be an opinion, not authoritative information.

Next, try to determine whether the information was written and published for professional purposes. With the proliferation of blogs and social networking sites, opinionated sites abound that may appear at first to be professional but are really just meant to express personal views. Ask yourself if the topic is related to the author's job and/or if the author had any career credibility to gain by writing it. Ask yourself if the author has any authority on the topic and what kind of authority. Does the authority come through academic expertise or through personal experience?

Last, look at the site to which information is posted. What kind of authority does the sponsoring organization have? What kind of agenda does it have? What kind of editorial process does it go through to determine what will be posted on its site? All of these criteria can help determine the reliability of sources. If the site does not tell much about the organization or about the authors, then you truly have to question its usefulness.

AVOIDING BIAS

Biased sources do not make good research (even when we agree with them) because they are often more committed to promoting an agenda than to presenting accurate facts. When we use sources with an obvious agenda, we undermine our own credibility by making it look like we too care more about promoting a cause than getting our facts straight. In order to be convinced of anything, a reader first has to trust a source. Avoiding bias is just one way to gain that trust.

That said, sorting out what is biased and what isn't can be challenging. In fact, very little information comes to us purely without bias, and often we find ourselves looking simply for the least biased resources. Facts rarely avoid being couched in opinion, and most types of evidence can be manipulated into meaning whatever people want them to mean. Therefore, our task as researchers is to make the most informed and evenhanded choices possible. Sometimes that means separating opinion from fact in the sources we consider. Other times, it means taking two biased sources from opposite camps and comparing them to analyze the discrepancies along with the common ground.

Advocacy sites for social causes or issues, such as the National Rifle Association website, are particularly challenging. They are often filled with statistics and news alerts that appear to be very useful information. They may, in fact, include a plethora of accurate, well-researched information. Yet they are still promoting a cause, and for that reason we know that they present only one side of the debate. If there is equally accurate, equally well-researched information that undermines the cause of an advocacy group, it will not be found on its site and we will have to find the other perspectives in order to get a complete picture of the topic.

Thus, as researchers, we need perspective on any information received through an advocacy group. Whether we agree with the group or not, we know their findings to be one-sided. We know they have interpreted statistics or research to promote their own cause. We know we should be careful to remain objective, and if possible, we should locate our information through more objective resources.

In short, be aware of what people are trying to accomplish with their writing. Is your source from someone clearly out to promote a cause or to win people over to one particular side in a debate? If so, look beyond that source and do a little fact-checking in other locations. If you agree with the source, but you're uncertain about how reliable the information is, ask yourself how convincing it might be to a person who doesn't agree. Will the person who doesn't agree find you to be a credible writer if you use only the one side to make your argument or explain your topic? Try to find information that can be verified to the point that it would be difficult even for a skeptic to poke holes in it.

THOROUGH SOURCES

When an instructor stands in front of a class and tells students to go forth and locate ten articles on a given topic, probably no one's first thought is, "I'm going to find the longest, most complicated articles I can." The natural impulse is to go for the most interesting and the easiest to understand. That approach is not entirely wrong, but it can mean we end up having little substance with which to work.

If all of your articles are short and sweet, it's guaranteed that you won't extract enough information out of them to write a decent paper. Save yourself some heartache and don't shy away from the longer articles, but remember that longer doesn't necessarily mean more thorough. Pay attention to how much depth of detail is included. If it's just a general overview, it will probably provide only the same information that can be found in a hundred other places.

Long, short, or medium, you want the articles that offer the most specific information possible. Look for those first, and you'll save yourself the pleasure of having to hunt down all new sources the night before the final draft is due.

PROFESSIONAL SOURCES

Professionalism should always be the bottom line when choosing sources, and this can mean more than one thing. First, is the author a professional in the field? Does this person (or persons) have real authority on the topic? Second, is the information presented in a professional manner? Is the article included in a reputable publication or website? Is it neat, organized, clear, and all of the other things we might expect of people who take pride in their work? Does it reference its own sources? Are links kept current? Is enough information provided so that the article can be easily documented? Does it look like it was put together for serious business and not just as a joke or as a hobby?

All of this matters. Your credibility as a writer rests on the credibility of the sources you've gathered. Choose carefully, and make yourself look good.

COMMON PITFALLS

Certain Internet sources just don't make good material for research papers. Among the bad sources are those used so often by students that writing instructors loathe and despise them and are expert at spotting them from miles away. If you learn nothing else in the research process, learn how to avoid common mistakes and teachers' pet peeves.

Wikipedia

Topping the list of sites to avoid is *Wikipedia*, an online encyclopedia written by an open community. It is so popular that it pops up among the first hits on almost any given web search. There are two main problems with using it as a source for a research paper. First, *Wikipedia* is an encyclopedia, and most college instructors do not consider encyclopedias to be college-level resources. Encyclopedias give only general overviews, and they are normally written on junior high levels.

Next, theoretically at least, anyone can post to *Wikipedia*. This means we don't know who wrote what or what the credentials are of the people who contributed to any given article. *Wikipedia* can be a useful place to start understanding a topic, but before even considering using an article from it in a documented essay, ask your instructor if it is acceptable.

Blogs

The next most common online research pitfall comes in the form of blogs and personal websites, like Tumblr. The problem with using blogs as sources is that they exist only to express an individual's opinion. That opinion may or may not be expert in nature. Before using a blog or personal website as a source, verify two things: (1) Will your instructor accept blogs as sources? (2) Does the person who created the blog and its content have any authority on the topic?

For example, some of the more popular blogs have dealt with life in Syria since the beginning of the civil war between rebel groups and the government of Bashar al-Assad. Three main groups of people keep blogs on this topic:

(1) Syrian people who want to share with the world what they see in their own country; (2) people serving in the military or working in Syria who want to chronicle their time in a place where history is being made; and (3) people who have political opinions about the civil war and the military forces in Syria and want a place to voice those opinions.

In all three cases, the bloggers are offering opinion more than fact, and all have some particular political stance through which their opinions are filtered. Those opinions, however, are informed in varying ways. Perhaps we can learn a great deal from firsthand accounts of the war, and perhaps the political commentator really is an expert in political and/or military matters. This is possible. It's also possible that the blogger is the guy down the street who came up with his diatribe while drinking beer and watching CNN.

The rule of thumb is to apply common sense and to realize that we can't assume anyone is an expert just because he or she had something to say and posted it online. Beware the blog. It might be the researcher's friend, but it is just as likely to be a problem.

Sometimes blogs can be so sophisticated in appearance that it is difficult to recognize them. Obviously, if it has the word "blog" somewhere in the title or the URL, this should tip us off. Failing that, take some time to assess the nature of the site. Blogs are set up in journal formats where the most recent posting usually shows at the top of the page and everything else falls beneath it. If it looks like a blog and talks like a blog, it probably is a blog.

Once that's established, try to find the name and credentials of the author. If the credentials are not provided, or if they have nothing to do with the topic at hand, don't consider the blog to be a credible source.

Social Networking Sites

Facebook, Instagram, and Twitter can be good places to keep up with what is going on the world, depending, of course, on whom you follow and what your friends' interests are. Information posted to these sites is not good research paper material, though.

You might follow a link found on Facebook and decide the original article is valuable and worth citing; however, it's unlikely that you would be able to use status updates written for Facebook. This is for the same reason you would not ordinarily use blog posts as sources. Posts to social networking sites are exactly that: social. They are opinions expressed casually for the benefit of friends. They aren't meant to be authoritative information.

The exception to this rule might be official profiles of organizations, government agencies, and people in authority. If your paper is about government regulation of offshore drilling and how that relates to environmental issues, you may actually find citable information on the White House Facebook page. That's a far cry from citing something an ordinary citizen posted for the amusement of a few friends.

Apply common sense as necessary in these cases and be discerning about who posted and why before using any information found through a social network in a research paper. That will usually see you through.

Forums, Chat Rooms, and Subscription-Based Groups

Discussion forums, also known as discussion boards, message boards, or bulletin boards, saturate the Internet. They are everywhere, and they exist on nearly any topic and/or interest. Do not use anything posted to a forum as a source. Likewise, chat rooms and discussion subscriptions like Yahoo Groups or Google Groups are equally prevalent and equally suspect. Whereas blogs are sometimes expert and sometimes not, web forums are so much more often not. By their nature, they are primarily anonymous. We do not know who "logicman56" is, nor do we need to know. He (or she) is not an expert and should not be accepted as such.

Advertisements

Advertisements can be so slick these days that sometimes we've already bought the product before we even know someone is trying to sell us something. Online, ads also are often set up to look like any other website or even any random news article. In particular, medical advertisements often appear to be informative articles. Be aware of this practice, and be wary of falling for it. Ask yourself if an article is pushing a product and/or if it is published to a corporate website with products to sell. If so, it is likely a promotional tool and may not be trustworthy as a source.

Student Projects

Some people think that if a URL has an ".edu" extension, the source is automatically valid. That isn't necessarily true. Often, students fall into the trap of citing other students as sources. Quite frankly, most instructors don't care what another student had to say in another instructor's class. It's particularly embarrassing to you if you've used a ninth grader's PowerPoint project as a resource for your college term paper. This has been known to happen more often than you might guess. The lesson in this is, *pay attention*. Most student projects are labeled as such. If you cite one, it says you were too lazy to notice what you were reading. Even on educational sites, all of the same rules apply. Look for the credentials of the author before opting to use a source.

YouTube, Podcasts, etc.

Owning a video camera or a smartphone does not make a person an expert. Apply caution as necessary. Valuable information is available on popular video and audio file sharing sites. Valuable pieces of clothing are also available in salvage stores. This doesn't mean it would behoove us to purchase the first pair of designer jeans we find without first checking them carefully for flaws and even forgery. The point is that we frequently don't know where video or audio sources come from when we find them online. This makes them impossible to verify as acceptable research materials. If we know who produced them and for what purpose, we might have something to work with. If not, we simply can't use the information.

Abstracts and Reviews

We feel much safer using library databases than general Internet searches because we know that articles published within EBSCOhost have gone through an editorial process. They were not randomly published by anonymous people and organizations. However, we can still run into problems with database materials if we do not recognize the differences in types of articles found there. Often, what we pull up is an abstract of an article rather than the article itself. An abstract is merely a summary and will not provide enough information to be useful. Likewise, a review article is not helpful without also tracking down the source to which it refers.

In either case, use the information provided in the abstract or review to determine if you can locate the original text. If it is not available through the same database, it may be available in your library. You might also be able to obtain it through interlibrary loan or even through searching other databases. If the abstract leads you to believe that the article will be important to your research and you are unable to find it on your own, ask your librarians for help in locating it.

Organizing and Note Taking in an Online World

Before the age of notebook computers, library databases, and laser printers, the most common way of organizing research materials in a classroom was with notecards. Many teachers still use notecards as an integral part of the research process, while others have moved away from them in favor of newer methods.

Regardless, the purpose of the notecard system is still essential, whether it is carried out by handwriting onto 3" × 5" index cards or not. We still need a way to figure out how much information we have at our disposal and organize that information into viable patterns. Thus, let's explore some of our alternate possibilities.

First, whatever method you use, it is important to keep a *working outline* and a *working bibliography* in progress at all times. In this case, the term "working" just means that you are still working on it. It isn't a complete product. It is something that changes as new information is found and new ideas are formulated.

A working outline is important because it helps you see where you are going, what your goals are, and how close you are to meeting those goals. Without an outline, you will find it difficult to know whether you have everything you need to put a paper together, especially in a more complex research document.

A working bibliography helps you keep track of the sources used in your writing. Some students like to wait until they've finished a paper to put the Works Cited page together. This is always a mistake.

Without documenting as you go, you easily lose track of which sources you've used where. This can lead to unintentional plagiarism, which is still plagiarism by any name and can still earn you a failing grade on the assignment and worse. Also, without compiling your Works Cited page as you use the sources, you don't know what to put in your in-text citations, and you don't know whether you have all of the necessary information to document the source correctly.

Particularly with online sources, it is so easy to print something out and forget where it came from. Without knowing where the source was found, the citation is often hard or impossible to complete, and you will need to find the source again in order to cite it properly. A working bibliography can go a long way toward avoiding last-minute panic attacks over problems like this.

> **NOTE:** A bibliography is a list of sources (formatted according to a given style) related to a particular topic. A Works Cited page is a list of sources used or cited in a particular piece of writing. They are compiled in the same way. The only difference is that the word *bibliography* indicates only that the sources have been consulted, whereas the term *Works Cited* means that the sources have been referred to in the attached writing. Therefore, while you are in the process of locating your research, your instructor might have you use the term *bibliography*. When you are actually drafting and completing the paper, *Works Cited* will more likely become the preferred term.

> **NOTE:** *Works Cited* is a term used by MLA to indicate the page used to list sources cited in a paper. If using a different documentation style, you might label the page by yet another name. Some documentation styles call it the Sources Cited page, and some call it the References page.

THE JOYS OF PRINTING

Once upon a time when entering a reference section of a library, you could leave only with information that you physically wrote down with pen and paper. This was tedious work and the cause of many cases of severe finger cramps. It had its advantages, however. Students actually had to sit down and read anything they thought they might use in a research paper. They certainly weren't going to sit for hours copying out unrelated information. Now that we can photocopy or print anything we want, it is too tempting to grab the first stack of articles we find and head for the door.

Making full use of the library printers has its good and bad points. We can organize our articles into file folders, or we can hole-punch them and put them together in a giant binder (complete with labeled dividers, color-coded sticky notes, and lots of bright highlighter markings). It feels like we've accomplished something to see all that paper stacking up, and maybe we have. Maybe sticky notes and highlighters do the trick for us.

Or maybe we are eating up a rain forest for no good purpose. Don't waste ink and paper printing out articles that aren't useful. Read the articles first. Find out if they really pertain to the topic at hand and if they have anything to say that you haven't found elsewhere. Not only are you wasting paper if you print out sources you haven't read, but you're also wasting your time and setting yourself up to experience unnecessary anxiety at the last minute when you realize you don't have nearly as much information as you believed.

Also, consider other ways of keeping track of electronic sources that don't require excess printing. Create folders in databases with items to download to a computer or a jump drive. Email articles to yourself. Bookmark sites and articles. You might even try a social bookmarking site like https://del.icio.us/ to organize items found online.

A great approach to electronic note taking is to use an online tool like Evernote (www.evernote.com). This site is designed to help you save, organize, and comment on resources found online. It also has applications available for smartphones, iPads, and other devices to make accessing your information more convenient from a variety of entry points.

Find something that works for you, but be mindful of where you are wasting time and money. Keeping a notebook of printed articles can be a great way to get organized if you have actually read the articles and know how they fit into your topic. If you don't, you're just fooling yourself by carting around a bunch of useless pages.

ELECTRONIC NOTECARDS

The electronic equivalent of the old index cards used by generations of student researchers can be created in a variety of ways. You can make an annotated bibliography. You can make electronic flashcards in PowerPoint. You can blog about your topic, commenting on sources one by one. You can read an article while you brush your teeth in the morning and use a voice recorder to talk to yourself about it in the car on the way to school.

Or you can simply type your notes in a word-processing file. As stated previously, this method has its advantages and disadvantages. Typing notes can streamline the research process and save time. It can also make it easier to be intellectually lazy and merely copy and paste information without really paying attention to what it says. Whether electronic note taking becomes an asset or a liability is entirely up to you. A good method is to type the citation of the source at the top of the document and then to take notes from the source underneath it as you read, making sure to use quotation marks where appropriate. This method will allow you to know where you found a particular bit of information and whether you paraphrased it or quoted it.

If you have a working outline and a working bibliography, you can type notes that are much more useful. Think of this as a predraft. Type in subject headings according to your outline. Heading by heading, type in the notes related to that subtopic from the resources you've gathered. Be sure to fill in your citations as you go. By the time you've typed in notes on what you know about each subtopic in your paper, you are well on your way to creating a rough draft. Save the notes to a new file, and you can simply type over, around, and among them to make a rough draft. You might get rid of your outline headings as you write so that everything flows together in paragraph form, but you'll have a basic shell to work with. This will help you see exactly where you are missing information.

However you go about getting organized and taking notes, you should do at least this much: (1) find something that works for your instructor and (2) find something that works for you. You can try every trick known to the web and beyond, but if you haven't met the requirements for your assignment, you haven't done your job. You can also spin a lot of wheels trying to learn new tricks when for you, simpler might be better. We should all make the effort to stretch our comfort levels with new media and the subsequent new possible techniques. That doesn't mean we should shatter them.

Put together a plan that works for you and your instructor, and get to work on it. That, in the end, is what being a student researcher is about.

Giving Credit Where Credit Is Due

In our country, we value individual property rights, and that's why plagiarism and copyright issues are such big deals. Words, ideas, and artistic creations belong to people, and no one has the right to take them without permission. You can look at your friend's car. You can talk about your friend's car. You can take a picture of it, and you can wish you had one like it. But you can't take it for a drive without the owner's agreeing. If you do, consequences will surely follow.

This same basic principle governs the fines against illegal downloading of copyrighted music and bans on pirated movies. No matter how much you might want to fill your iPod up with free tunes, the artists do have ownership rights, and one way or another, people who steal from them eventually end up getting busted.

However, the ease with which things can be and are shared online has made the ethical and legal boundaries for the thievery of creative products difficult to distinguish. It is easy to believe there is nothing wrong with illegally ripping a CD when lots of other people have done it, and even you've done it in the past and not gotten caught. Still, every time a CD gets ripped, someone loses money. It's important not to forget that when we make our choices and form our personal values. It's also important not to forget that the legal system is working to catch up with the technological possibilities and that not getting caught once is no guarantee of not getting caught again.

HOW IS THIS RELATED TO WRITING AND RESEARCH IN SCHOOL?

The same copyright laws apply to school projects as to anything else. Plagiarism is illegal for the same reasons that pirating is illegal. Intellectual property belongs to its creator. No one else has the right to take it for a drive without permission.

Nevertheless, technology has made what is and isn't okay confusing. Millions of emails are forwarded every day with no regard to where they originated. News articles are reposted by the thousands to blogs and message boards. Pictures are "borrowed" from one website to be used on another. The Internet can look like one big happy free intellectual playground full of so much good stuff that doesn't belong to anyone. This isn't true, however, and treating information found online as "free" can only be to your detriment.

Online, as well as anywhere else, responsible people give credit where credit is due for these reasons:

1. **To assure that no one gets cheated.** If it belonged to you, you wouldn't want anyone else taking credit for it either.

2. **To establish credibility.** You may not be an expert on your topic, but you've found someone who is. Give credit to that person. This only makes you look smarter and more reliable.

3. **To keep the system in working and productive order.** We have style guidelines in place that provide sets of rules for how copyrighted materials can be legally talked about by other people so that scholars can continue to share with one another without worry that someone else will take credit. If scientists conducting medical research believe they will not be credited for their work, they are less likely to share it. Thus, others are less likely to learn from and be able to build upon what's already been discovered. By recognizing and adhering to a system that allows individuals to retain ownership over property after it has been shared, we help maintain a scholarly community that is capable of advancing our world of information and ideas.

4. **To avoid the consequences of wrongdoing.** Ideally, we should be able to put into this slot "because it is the right thing to do," but that doesn't always motivate everyone. Regardless, the consequences of wrongdoing are the same. For stealing music, you could be fined. For stealing source materials for a school project, you could fail or be expelled. For stealing other people's work on the job, you could be fired or sued.

IS IT EVER OKAY TO COPY AND PASTE FROM A SOURCE?

If you copy only a small amount, put the copied portions in quotes, and properly document the source, then it is okay. Otherwise, absolutely not.

We have a grand tradition in American education of little elementary school children being given report topics that they complete by copying facts word for word straight out of an encyclopedia. Just because it is done doesn't make it right. One day some zealot is going to take an entire fourth grade class to court over this. The more easygoing types among us tend to cut the little ones some slack. Children do research this way because they don't know any better. College students don't have that excuse. If you copy word for word, you'll face the consequences.

Copying from sources has always been an issue. It's just never been so easy to do it before. Back when students had to slug away letter-by-letter on a Smith Corona typewriter, it was almost as easy to write a sentence as to steal one. Now that a couple of clicks of a mouse can mean entire articles move instantly from one location to another, we have to make doubly sure everyone knows and abides by the rules.

Most students know that copying and pasting whole articles is wrong and will earn them straight zeroes for a semester (at the least). But be aware that any amount of copying and pasting, even short phrases or one-word descriptions, without proper documentation is wrong and can result in equally dire consequences.

Also, note that even when you document properly, only a limited amount of one copyrighted source can be reused in another. The people who scanned chapters of Harry Potter books to post online found that out. They may have freely admitted that the writing belonged to J. K. Rowling, but that didn't stop her publisher from taking legal action against them. Sharing parts of novels or other intellectual works like that may seem harmless, but it can be quite costly to publishers if it prevents people from actually purchasing the books.

When referencing any source, be sure you've documented correctly. Be sure you've quoted and/or paraphrased correctly. And be sure you've taken only a judicious amount of the original without spoiling the need for your readers to go look up your source if they want to know all or most of what it says.

Copyright law can be very complicated, but essentially what matters is that you've done nothing to diminish the value of the original either by monetary or intellectual standards. While generally assumed guidelines do exist, such as not sharing more than 10 percent of an article, the only real way to know what you can "get away with" is to test your legal boundaries in court. No one wants to do that.

Therefore, it's best to follow the practice of just not pushing your luck. Stick to short quotes only. Be sure those quotes are properly documented. And do not overuse any one source. In short, use common sense and be respectful of the fact that you should be writing your own paper, not presenting someone else's all over again.

ISN'T THERE A COMMON KNOWLEDGE EXCEPTION?

Yes, but that still doesn't mean it's okay to take another person's words or ideas. You don't have to provide documentation for information that is common knowledge if it comes from your head and through your words. If you don't know that the government response to Black Lives Matter has been controversial, you've probably been living under a rock on Mars. You might be able to make a statement about the controversy in your writing without referencing anyone. However, if you did look up information about it and used the words and/or ideas of a source, it should be documented.

IF I GIVE A LINK TO MY SOURCE, ISN'T THAT ENOUGH?

That depends. Are you writing a blog entry, or are you writing a documented essay? In academic writing, you have to follow an academic documentation style (MLA, APA, or whatever your instructor assigns). A link isn't enough. Academics require specific information for specific purposes. Not everything a reader needs to know about your source is evident from simply looking at a link.

Furthermore, the Internet is not a stationary place. It is a system that is always in a state of flux. Links change. Information gets deleted. For this reason, even in personal writing a link really isn't enough to cover you from charges of plagiarism. Give the details of who wrote it and where and when it was published if you truly want to credit your source.

WHAT DO I DO IF MORE THAN ONE SOURCE SAYS THE SAME THING?

Now that we have library databases to help us locate newspaper and magazine articles, this is a common dilemma. An article goes out on a news wire service and is picked up by hundreds of newspapers and even television and radio stations. Various newspapers give the same article their own individual headlines, and the student on the run ends up printing out ten copies of the same thing, or at least very similar variations of the same thing. In this case, remember that you are responsible for documenting where you got the information, not everywhere it was ever published. Pick an article that gives you what you need, and discard the others. Sometimes it really is as simple as that.

HOW MUCH DO I HAVE TO KNOW ABOUT AN ONLINE SOURCE TO BE ABLE TO DOCUMENT IT?

Both MLA and APA have made significant changes recently relating to the citation of electronic sources. For resources concerning these changes and proper citation of web materials, visit The Online Writing Lab at Purdue (owl.english.purdue.edu/owl/) and click on "Research and Citation." Also, Chapters 20 and 21 of this text provide MLA and APA citation information.

Essentially, both formats ask that you know the author's name, the title of the article, the title of the website, the date that it was posted, the date that it was retrieved, and the URL or DOI number. Other items might be included, depending on what kind of source it is and how much information it provides about itself, but these are the basics.

Sometimes even the basics aren't easy to pin down, so it behooves us to examine them one by one.

Author's Name

Often, wire service articles are published anonymously. Sometimes information from reputable organizations is published anonymously. Even government documents can fall into this category. Yes, it is possible to document a source without an author's name, even though this isn't ideal. If there is no author listed, be doubly careful to decide whether or not you trust the site itself before using the information.

Title of the Article

Most articles have titles. If you don't see one, you may not be looking in the right place. Sometimes, you even need to back up to the home page of the site to which an article is posted and trace the links to it to figure out what the title is. If it still doesn't appear to have a title, you really have to wonder how much effort went into it and whether it would make a good source anyway. Therefore, while it might be possible to document an online source without knowing an article title, it isn't advisable.

Title of the Website

Skipping this would be like trying to document a magazine article without knowing the name of the periodical it came from. If you don't know the name of the website, look at the URL for your article and trim it down to the "short version," or the part that stops at the .com, .edu, .gov, or .org. By typing in just that part of the URL to the location bar on your browser, you should be able to go to the home page of the site and find out what it is named.

The Post Date

Not everything posted to the web is dated. Sometimes it is very hard to find this information. However, most mainstream news sources and academic journals do include post dates. This part can be skipped in the documentation if necessary, but that isn't ideal. Be sure you really need the information and can't find it elsewhere before choosing an article from a site that does not date its materials.

The Access Date

This date is important and shouldn't be skipped. In the first place, it isn't impossible to know. You were the one who accessed the information. You ought to know when you did it. In the second place, the date of access can really tell us something. With sites that continually archive new information, the access date can help locate an article in the archives. With sites that have gone defunct and/or have deleted information, the date of access helps to establish when certain information was available at that location.

The URL

MLA has returned to including a URL in a citation The Eighth Edition of the MLA Handbook says URLs or DOI numbers are needed when available.

ARE THERE ANY SHORTCUTS TO DOCUMENTATION?

There are help tools that make documentation easier. Try http://secondary. oslis.org/. Oslis can help you format a bibliography and take some of the pressure off getting the spacing and other details exact. However, they are not a substitute for following the style guides and/or following the instructions of the assignment. They are also not infallible. For the most part, Oslis, like other citation generators, will format a correct Works Cited page. This assumes, however, that the correct information has been entered in the correct locations in its online forms. It isn't a miracle worker. It can't fix what you typed in incorrectly in the first place. However, Oslis is easier to use and more accurate than other generators.

Always be sure to double-check your bibliographies against the samples in your style guide regardless of how you put them together.

HOW CAN I KNOW IF I'VE INADVERTENTLY PLAGIARIZED?

If you are set up in your class to submit rough drafts to Turnitin.com, you can check your originality reports and make the proper corrections before submitting your final drafts. If you don't have those options, try www.plagiarismchecker .com or www.articlechecker.com.

These are free sites that help detect plagiarism. They can't find everything, though. You are still responsible for cross-checking your own work line by line against your sources. Plagiarism detection services can do only so much to help. They have access only to information found online or in their own databases. An instructor looking directly at your sources might very well spot instances of plagiarism not detected by an automatic checker.

The best thing to do is to mark places in your paper where you've used sources and to go through them carefully, making sure you've either quoted or paraphrased appropriately.

DO COMMON PHRASES AND SAYINGS MATTER?

Phrases like "in our society today" or "the fact of the matter remains" may end up being marked by plagiarism detection software. This doesn't mean they are plagiarized. They are simply part of the vernacular. However, they still lack originality. If phrases like this are marked in your writing, use them as an opportunity to revise for a stronger writing style.

Finding Your Purpose

Students tend to dread research projects. Research is laden with rules of a tedious and nitpicky nature. If you fail to italicize properly, or if you inadvertently use a source published one year too early, everything might fall apart for your grade.

Teachers who have had years to learn the rules of documentation seem merciless in pointing out infractions on research paper drafts. What could be more disheartening?

It is disheartening when you think of it like that, but research isn't about setting students up to fail. It is an essential learning tool, one that is useful to your life as well as to your school and professional careers.

Once, research nearly always meant libraries and archives. If you were diagnosed with an illness, your best option for learning more about it was to drive to a medical library and hope to find articles you could actually understand. Now, you can look up the illness from your phone while waiting in line for your prescription to be filled.

Research of the sort that belonged almost exclusively to academics in the past is for everyone now. That means you can't afford *not* to learn how to do it well. It also means your life can be greatly enriched if you do learn it well.

You can look up anything you need to know from anywhere you happen to be. If you disagree with a friend during a lunchtime conversation, you can retrieve hard facts to back up your opinions before your friend has had time to pick up a sandwich and take a bite. This is something to be celebrated and embraced. Research is exciting. Research is empowering.

The trick to enjoying a research project for class, and in fact the trick to succeeding at one, is to capture that sense of excitement and empowerment. Even if the topics are assigned, and even if the resources found are not what you expect, find what matters to you in the research process. Find your own spark of interest that propels you forward. This will make everything not just bearable but pleasurable.

That spark will probably come from taking the time to consider what matters about your research. What can you accomplish with it (outside of receiving a grade)? What purpose does it serve?

If you know your purpose in looking up information, you're going to put more effort into it. If you know your purpose in sharing information, you're going to infuse your writing with more energy. That will make the paper more interesting to you, which consequently will make you more likely to pay attention to what you are doing and less likely to make careless mistakes.

A fortunate side effect of this is that other people will probably find your paper more interesting as well.

Research matters. It helps us make decisions. It helps us solve problems. It helps us manage our daily lives. It helps us persuade others to our way of thinking.

Think of it this way: If you aren't highly motivated to become a better researcher, and a more net-savvy researcher in particular, you are competing in every single thing you do with people who are. That matters.

Chapter 20

MLA: A Guide to Research and Documentation

For most of you, when a teacher assigns an MLA-documented research paper, your stress levels increase. In this chapter, you will learn the basic rules of research documentation. That should make you more comfortable with MLA documentation and more at ease about your research project.

Whenever instructors mention MLA, almost every student has the same question:

"What is MLA, and why do I have to use it?"

MLA stands for Modern Language Association, and its purpose is standardization of documentation rules to create uniformity and consistency in documented papers. All of us—teachers, published writers in many disciplines, and students—who are required to use MLA style have to follow the MLA rules listed in this chapter.

Research before Writing

Some instructors assign topics and require varying types of evidence, so pay close attention to your instructor's guidelines before beginning research or making a trip to the library. After you are sure about the guidelines, you can begin looking for credible sources for your research paper.

First, assess your library's available research tools. Make sure that you know what is available to you in the library, in interlibrary loan, and on the web. Then begin researching to find sources that are appropriate for your subject. Keep searching, even if think you have exhausted your search.

> GREAT HINT: When stuck on EBSCOhost, change the search criteria/words and start fresh.

Once you have enough sources for your paper, you must sort through them and decide how to use them in your essay. The main techniques for using sources within the text of your research paper are **summarizing**, **quoting**, **splicing**, and **paraphrasing**. Check Chapter 17 for guidelines on incorporating your sources into your paper.

> NOTE: All examples in this chapter are single-spaced here to conserve paper. However, in your paper, you should double-space everything, thereby complying with MLA guidelines.

Parenthetical Citations

"Parenthetical" means "in parentheses," so a parenthetical citation (sometimes referred to as an in-text citation) is a citation in parentheses.

When you incorporate information from a source into your paper, you must cite it parenthetically *regardless of whether the material is quoted directly*. Citing means providing information about the source, which is usually the *author's last name* and *page number*. The first time you refer to an author **in the text**, use the author's full name. Subsequent references to the author use the last name only.

Never refer to an author by the first name only, and never put a first name in a parenthetical citation unless you have two or more authors with the same last name. In that case, use the first initial plus the last name; however, if the two authors have the same first initial, use the whole first name. This rule applies with summarizing, quoting, splicing, or paraphrasing. Doing this correctly acknowledges your source and prevents you from plagiarizing.

STRUCTURES OF PARENTHETICAL CITATIONS

These structures will be used for summarizing, quoting, splicing, and paraphrasing.

1. A work by **one author** without his or her name in the lead-in, which is the short sentence or phrase leading to the quote:

   (Smith 26).

2. A work by **one author** with his or her name in the lead-in:

   Anne Smith explains . . . (26).

3. A work by **two authors** without their names in the lead-in:

   (Carlson and Weston 55).

4. A work by **three authors** without their names in the lead-in:

   (Cartman, Wiezman, and Sylvester 22).

5. A work by **two or three authors** with their names in the lead-in:

   Carlson and Weston state that . . . (23).

6. A work by **more than three authors** without their names in the lead-in:

   (Johnston et al. 40).

7. A work by a **corporate author** without its name in the lead-in:

   (American Heart Association 32).

8. A work **without a named author** without a lead-in:

   ("Golden" 7).

> **NOTE:** The whole title of the article is "Golden Girl," yet in your parenthetical citation, you use only part of the title to refer to the article.

9. A work **without a named author** with a lead-in:

   According to the article "Golden Girl," . . . (7).

10. Two authors with the same last name:

    John Smith says . . . (23), or without a lead-in: (J. Smith 23).

11. More than one work by the **same author**:

    (Harper, "Golden" 5).

12. An **indirect source**:

John Smith states . . . (qtd. in Handley 4).

13. An **Internet source** with no page numbers:

(Kimble).

14. An **Internet source** with page number:

(Chandler 27).

> **NOTE:** The *MLA Handbook for Writers of Research Papers*, Eighth Edition, directs writers to add the paragraph number for web articles that have numbered paragraphs. In that case, *par.* or *pars.*, along with the relevant number(s), will be cited in the parentheses: (Jeffreys pars. 1–2).

Cite page numbers in your *parenthetical* citations as follows:

- For three-digit page numbers, abbreviate the second number: (235–36).
- For two-digit page numbers or fewer, use all numbers: (22–27).
- For pages that are not consecutive: (2, 6).

Quoting from a Source

In some cases, you might need to include specific language from the source as evidence for your argument. Using proper punctuation and MLA documentation indicates that you have quoted the language from a source. Failing to do this properly means you have plagiarized!

Placement of Cited Material

Check with your instructor on his or her preferences for using cited material at the beginning or end of a paragraph. Many instructors want each body paragraph to begin with a topic sentence connected to your outline and main points. Consequently, using a quote would not be possible. Others prefer that each paragraph end with a summation, again in your own words.

Punctuation with Documentation

Punctuation is always important in writing, but in research-based writing, it is critical because it offers visual cues to the reader. MLA has strict punctuation rules that must be followed to help your reader understand the different forms of your research.

Quotations are particularly important. You will use two types of formats when quoting from a source: **inserted quotations** and **block quotations**.

The difference between these two formats is the length of the quotation and the punctuation required.

INSERTED QUOTATION

When quoting four lines of typed text or fewer (4+ lines), incorporate the quote naturally into your writing using correct grammar and quotation marks, and remember to use a lead-in—a short phrase or a sentence that comes before you begin quoting.

Cite the quotation using one of the two following methods:

- In the first method, include the author's last name and page number at the end of the quotation in a parenthetical citation.

NOTE: Be sure to use only the last name of the author unless you have more than one author by that name, and do not use titles (Mr., Mrs., Dr., Rev., etc.) in the parenthetical citation.

Example···
"Faulkner is the father of neologisms" (Bailey 56).

- In the second method, introduce the quotation with the author's last name and a verb (*Smith argues*) and then end the quotation with a parenthetical citation that includes the page number.

Example···
Bailey asserts, "Faulkner is the father of neologisms" (56).

NOTE: Punctuation is very important in MLA documentation. Place the period after the parenthetical documentation with a summary, paraphrase, and inserted quotation. If you are using a direct quote, the quotation marks come at the end of the quote, before the parenthetical citation.

BLOCK QUOTATION (LONG QUOTATION)

When quoting a prose passage of **more** than four lines of typed text (4+ lines), follow these guidelines:

- Begin quoting the text on a new line after the lead-in.
- Make sure your text is double-spaced.
- Do *not* use quotation marks around the quote (unless the original source has them).
- Indent the left margin by 1 inch, but leave the right margin alone.
- Punctuate *before* the parenthetical citation.

Example of block quotation· ·

Austen deliberately confuses the reader about Mary; in fact, the reader cannot understand her reasoning. The narrator of *Pride and Prejudice* also influences the reader's thinking:

> Mary had neither genius nor taste; and though vanity had given her application, it had given her likewise a pedantic air and conceited manner, which would have injured a higher degree of excellence than she had reached. Elizabeth, easy and unaffected, had been listened to with much more pleasure, though not playing half so well. (Austen 23)

In all cases except for block quotes (as in the above example), the sentence's period follows the parenthetical citation.

PUNCTUATING WITH ELLIPSIS POINTS

Ellipsis points (. . .) are used to indicate omission in inserted and block quotations. For omitting words in a quotation, use three periods with a space before each one and a space following the end point.

> Martin writes, "According to medical research . . . second-hand smoke has been shown to aggravate many individuals" (68).

For indicating that a sentence continues beyond the quote, or that one or more sentences were removed, use three ellipsis points after the period with no space between the last quoted word and the period. Include a space between the ellipsis and the sentence that follows. In a parenthetical reference, the period comes after the citation.

> Rivers notes, "The campaign for the highest office has become more than a political race. . . . The outcome will determine the future of the world" (57).

PUNCTUATING WITH BRACKETS

Use brackets to set off your editorial insertions in cited material.

Use a bracket to clarify information that the reader needs to understand the quote:

> Kaplan says, "If he [John Markham] wants to develop the theory, the research supports the arguments" (268).

Use brackets to alter any quoted material for grammatical correctness:

> Walker notes that "[t]he world is ready for another war" (3).

Use brackets to clarify vague or misleading information.

> According to Smith, "[The committee] found in favor of the new proposal" (96).

Use brackets to indicate an error in the original text of the quote:

> Smith notes, "Percy Jones is the most meaniest [sic] person in the world" (50).

"Sic" is Latin for "in this manner" and is used when an error appears in a quotation. It indicates that the writer did not make the error but is quoting accurately.

TRANSITIONING FROM YOUR LANGUAGE TO QUOTED LANGUAGE

Always connect quotes to your own words in the form of either a **lead-in** or a complete sentence. Fading out with your own words at the end is awkward and generally seen as a weak way to connect a quote. Simply inserting a quote into your essay without connecting it to anything is called "dumping" a quote. Dumped quotes are usually considered errors.

A **dumped quote** would look like this:

> Harriet Jacobs shows the harshness of a child being alone in *Incidents in the Life of a Slave Girl*. In the first chapter, the reader sees the story of a child being separated from her mother and learning that she is a slave. "When I was six years old, my mother died; and then, for the first time, I learned, by the talk around me, that I was a slave" (343).

You have two basic options for fixing the problem. First, you could simply connect the quote to the previous sentence with a colon.

> In the first chapter, the author tells the story of the child being separated from her mother and learning that she is a slave: "When I was six years old, my mother died; and then, for the first time, I learned, by the talk around me, that I was a slave" (343).

Secondly, you can add a lead-in before the quote.

> In the first chapter, the reader sees the story of a child being separated from her mother and learning that she is a slave. Jacobs remembers, "When I was six years old, my mother died; and then, for the first time, I learned, by the talk around me, that I was a slave" (343).

Use the appropriate punctuation. If the lead-in is not a complete sentence, use either a comma or no punctuation, depending on the circumstance. Be careful with "that" and "because." These are two words that do not require commas after them.

Sentences must remain grammatically correct even when they contain quotes, so ask yourself what you would do if those quotation marks weren't there.

> Holden Caulfield of *The Catcher in the Rye* describes "pills and medicine all over the place, and everything smelled like Vick's Nose Drops" (Salinger 7).

In the above example, no comma is needed before the quote because you would not separate the verb from its direct object with a comma.

> In *Sein Language*, Jerry Seinfeld writes, "I hated those little snack-pack cereals. Still do. Don't like portion control" (156).

In the above example, the comma is required before the quote because the lead-in is an introductory element, which always requires a comma.

> In the campus newspaper, Jamie Brown adamantly denied her involvement in the election scandal: "I did not have illegal relations with that ballot box" (qtd. in Moore 1A).

In the above example, the lead-in is a complete sentence, so you must use a colon to connect it to the quote.

Note also that the parenthetical citation contains "qtd. in" before the author's name. This is the format to use for **indirect** quotes. An indirect quote is a quote that the author of your source article did not originally say or write, but either borrowed or quoted from someone else. When you use an indirect quote, always lead in with the original speaker's name, and always use the "qtd. in" construction for your parenthetical citation.

In all cases except for block quotations, the citation comes before the sentence's period. Note that if the author is mentioned in your lead-in, you do not need to repeat the author's name in your citation. Likewise, if the author's name is not in your lead-in, it must appear in your citation.

When discussing a source, always use the **historical present** tense.

> Morris, in his answer to the reporters, states, "I did not intentionally harm the guinea pig. It was only collateral damage" (qtd. in Smith 2A).

Note that the lead-in is in present tense, "states," instead of past tense, "stated."

Use a variety of verbs when you are using a lead-in. Repetition of something like "Smith says" or "According to Smith" gets boring. Some verbs that can be used follow:

acknowledges	finds	reports
believes	indicates	states
claims	insists	suggests
concludes	notes	
explains	observes	

Be sure that the verb you choose is appropriate in the context of the source. For instance, "implies" means suggests or hints at. Do not use that word if the author is clearly stating the idea. *Never* use the word "quotes" unless the author of your source is quoting someone else. Completely avoid "prove" unless you have conducted a scientific experiment.

PUNCTUATING TITLES

Titles of most "short" works are put in quotation marks. This includes the titles of poems, short stories, articles, editorials, reviews, etc. Always capitalize the important words in a title, even if the source you are using does not.

"The Raven" by Edgar Allan Poe (a poem)

"A Rose for Emily" by William Faulkner (a short story)

"The Language of Feminism" by Susan Milton (an article)

Titles of most "long" works are italicized. This includes the titles of books, magazines, journals, newspapers, plays, long poems, etc.

The Sound and the Fury by William Faulkner

USA Today

The Clarion-Ledger

The Glass Menagerie by Tennessee Williams

Paradise Lost by John Milton

Works Cited Entries

Your paper contains a roadmap. Each citation in the text is a county road that leads to the interstate highway, the Works Cited page.

The reader can, if s/he wants, actually locate each article cited in the correct newspaper or journal and read the entire source. Teachers *can and do* check the sources for accuracy.

Works Cited pages always come at the very end of your paper. If the text of your paper is six pages long, your Works Cited page will be page 7. See the example paper near the end of this chapter.

Your Works Cited page includes a complete citation for each of the sources that you used in your paper, including the primary source if you are writing about literature.

THE MECHANICS OF A WORKS CITED PAGE

Remember to give your page the title **Works Cited** and to center this title on the top line of the page. After typing each entry, highlight it and create a **hanging indention**. Hanging indention means that the first line of each entry will line up with the left margin, and each subsequent line will be indented one-half inch.

In Microsoft Word, hanging indents are easily created by highlighting the entire entry and using the shortcut "Ctrl + T." You can also set defaults so that the hanging indent will be automatic.

The authors' last names, which **must be listed in alphabetical order**, will stand apart by being separated from the rest of the citation; this makes locating any given author on the list very easy to do. If no author exists for your source, alphabetize the source according to its title. Sources with and without authors are all put in alphabetical order based on the first letter of the author's last name or the first important word of the title. Do not separate the sources on the Works Cited page by whether or not they have stated authors.

On the next pages are examples of how to construct your sources' citations. Notice that each type of source uses a different type of structure, so make sure that you understand what type of source you are using. If you are ever unsure about your source, ask your instructor.

MLA 8th edition changed the format for Works Cited entries in 2016. The citations are simplified but are different from those you may have used in previous classes or in high school. Be very careful to format your Works Cited entries properly.

ABBREVIATIONS AND SHORTCUTS

MLA allows writers to use a few shortcuts when composing the Works Cited page(s). One of them pertains to the use of "the" in titles. A newspaper entitled *The Clarion-Ledger* should be cited as *Clarion-Ledger*. The same goes for *The New York Times*; it becomes *New York Times*.

For publishers' names, the process is a bit more complex. In general, however, the titles are shortened. Here's a famous example:

> Harcourt Brace
>
> Harcourt, Brace, and World
>
> Harcourt Brace Jovanovich

All three of these companies are the same; the names changed as the company was bought and sold. Rather than worry about listing the entire, ever-changing name, just list this:

> Harcourt

Here are a few more examples:

> HarperCollins Publishers → Harper
>
> Harper and Row → Harper
>
> W. W. Norton and Company → Norton
>
> McGraw-Hill, Inc → McGraw
>
> Random House, Inc. → Random
>
> Charles Scribner's Sons → Scribner's

In addition, MLA allows writers to abbreviate the words "University Press" into "UP" whenever these words are in the title of a periodical. University Press of Mississippi becomes UP of Mississippi. This applies to all university presses across the country.

The *MLA Handbook for Writers of Research Papers*, Eighth Edition, no longer requires listing the city of publication or medium of publication in Works Cited entries in most instances.

> **NOTE:** All examples in this chapter are single spaced here to conserve paper. However, in your paper, you should double-space everything, thereby complying with MLA guidelines.

FORMULAS AND EXAMPLES OF WORKS CITED ENTRIES

Books

A book with one author·······································
Author's last name, First name. *Title of Book.* Publisher, year of publication.

Bermann, Linda S. *Academic Research and Writing.* Longman, 2010.

A book with two or three authors ·

First listed author's last name, first name, and second listed author's first and last name. *Title of Book.* Publisher, year of publication.

First listed author's last name, first name, second listed author's first and last name, and third listed author's first and last name. *Title of Book.* Publisher, year of publication.

DiYanni, Robert, and Pat C. Hoy II. *Frames of Mind.* Cengage, 2009.

A book with more than three authors ·

First listed author's last name, first name, et al. *Title of Book.* Publisher, year of publication.

NOTE: The term "et al." is Latin for "and others" and is used to indicate more than three authors.

Axelrod, Rise B., et al. *Reading Critically, Writing Well: A Reader and Guide.* 8th ed. Bedford, 2011.

A book with an editor or editors ·

First listed editor's last name, first name, and second listed editor's first and last name, eds. *Title of book.* Publisher, year of publication.

Hammons, Laura, and Beverly Fatherree, eds. *For Our Students.* Expanded Ed., Bedford, 2009.

Two books with the same author ·

Alphabetize by author's last name, then by the title of the book.

First book:

Author's last name, first name. *Title of Book.* Publisher, year of publication.

Second book:

Three unspaced hyphens instead of name. *Title of Book.* Publisher, year of publication.

Examples:

Kirszner, Laurie G., and Stephen R. Mandell. *Focus on Writing: Paragraphs and Essays.* Bedford, 2008.

---. *Patterns in College Writing: A Rhetorical Reader and Guide.* 11th ed., Bedford, 2010.

A book with an author and an editor··
Author's last name, first name. *Title of Book*, edited by editor's first and last name. Publisher, year of publication.

Woodward, Jeannette A. *Writing Research Papers*, edited by Lisa A. DeMol. NTC, 1997.

An anthology···
Editor's last name, first name, editor. *Title of Anthology*. Edition (if applicable), publisher, year of publication.

Charters, Ann, editor. *The Story and Its Writer: An Introduction to Short Fiction.* 4th ed., Bedford, 1995.

A work from an anthology··
Author's last name, first name. "Title of Work." *Title of Anthology*, edited by editor's first and last name. Edition (if applicable), publisher, year of publication, page numbers of cited work.

Faulkner, William. "A Rose for Emily." *The Story and Its Writer*, edited by Ann Charters, 4th ed., Bedford, 1995, pp. 457–63.

Two works from the same anthology··
Provide an entry for the anthology:

Charters, Ann, editor. *The Story and Its Writer: An Introduction to Short Fiction.* 4th ed., Bedford, 1995.

Then provide a shortened entry for each selection from the anthology.

Author's last name, first name. "Title of Selection." Editor's last name, page numbers.

Faulkner, William. "A Rose for Emily." Charters, pp. 457–63.

Jackson, Shirley. "The Lottery." Charters, pp. 634–40.

An article reprinted in a book
(or, a work originally from another source)·································
Author's last name, first name. "Title of Work." Original publication information for whatever type of source it is. Reprinted in *Title of Current Source*, edited by editor's first and last name. Edition or volume, publisher, year of publication, page numbers.

Smith, Eric. "Academic Honesty in a Dishonest World." *Education Quarterly*, vol. 32, 2001, pp. 356–58. Reprinted in *Readings for Writers: A Composition Reader*, edited by Christa Higgins and Jill Riley. 8th ed., UP, 2003, pp. 10–13.

Periodicals··

Periodicals include scholarly journals, magazines, and newspapers. Periodical Works Cited entries include three main pieces—author of the article, title of the article, and information about the source periodical. MLA now uses the term "container" to refer to the medium (a website or print journal, for example) in which an essay or article may be included.

Use the following format for all citations:

> Author. Title. Title of container (self contained if book), other contributors (translators or editors), version (edition), number (vol. and/or no.), publisher, publisher date, location (page, paragraph, etc.).

Periodicals—Journals

Journals: A Quick Overview

Academic and professional journals present cutting-edge research and ideas. They are generally published four times a year, which means that they have four issues. The volume number changes every year, and the 1–4 numbering system with the issues starts over with each new volume number/year.

An article from a journal ····································

> Author's last name, first name. "Title of Article." *Title of Journal*, volume #, issue #, date, page numbers.

> Henning, Kristin. "What's Wrong with Victims' Rights in Juvenile Court? Retributive versus Rehabilitative Systems of Justice." *California Law Review*, vol. 97, no. 4, 2009, pp. 1107–70.

Periodicals—Magazines and Newspapers

A magazine ···

> Author's last name, first name. "Title of Article." *Title of Magazine*, Day (if available) Month Year, pages.

> Collins, Lauren. "Troubled State." *New Yorker*, 15 Mar. 2010, pp. 21–22.

> Chappell, Kevin. "NOLA 2010." *Ebony*, Mar. 2010, pp. 68–78.

A newspaper article·······································

> Author's last name, first name. "Title of Article." *Title of Newspaper* [Name of city, if not in title], Day Month year, edition (if given), page.

> Krugman, Andrew. "Fear of Eating." *New York Times*, 21 May 2007, late ed., p. A1.

If the newspaper is local or is not well known, include the city name in brackets after the title of the newspaper.

> Franklin, Jonas. "A New Look at Juvenile Justice." *Clarion-Ledger* [Jackson, MS], 13 Apr. 2010, p. B3.

An article with no author given ·
On the Works Cited page, you alphabetize this source by the first major word in the title; that means not to alphabetize based on the articles or the words "a," "an," and "the." If articles are present, look at the next word for the alphabetical order.

"Title of Article." *Title of Source*, Necessary publication information for type of source.

"Remembering Peter Drucker." *USA Today*, 10 Nov. 2008, p. A3.

Periodicals—Government Publications

A government publication ·
Begin with the government, followed by the agency that produced the document, including any subdivisions of the agency. If there is an author, insert "By" after the title of the document, followed by the author's name. U.S. government documents are generally published by the Government Printing Office.

Formula for Example #1
Government. Name of Agency. *Title of Document*. Author's first name last name (if available). Publication information for source according to what type of document it is.

United States. U.S. Department of Homeland Security. *Domestic Aid in Wartime*. By Elaine Williams. Government Printing Office, 2005.

Formula for Example #2, online publications
Name of Government. Name of Agency. *Title of Document*. Publication information for source according to what type of document it is. Date of access.

United States. Department of Corrections. *Federal Prison Work Release Statistics: 2005*. Government Printing Office, 2005. Accessed 25 Oct. 2006.

Formula for Example #3, Congressional publications
Government. House. Committee. *Title of Document*. Publisher, year. Number of Congress, session, report number.

United States, Congress, House, Committee on Ways and Means. *American Jobs Creation Act of 2004*. Government Printing Office, 2005. 108th Congress, 2nd session, House Report 108-548.

ELECTRONIC SOURCES

MLA 8th Edition requires a URL or web address to be included from web sources, and encourages the citation of containers such as JSTOR, YouTube, Netflix, or, Spotify in order to easily access and verify sources. MLA does not require the use of http(s):// address, so eliminate all instances when citing URLs; use only the www. address.

Many scholarly journal articles found in databases include a **digital object identifier (DOI)**. If available, cite the DOI rather than the URL. Online newspapers and magazines sometimes include a shortened, stable version of a URL called a **permalink**. Look for a "share" or "cite this" button to see if a source includes a permalink. If available, use the permalink instead of a URL.

MLA also encourages the use of the phrase "Accessed" to denote the date on which the web page was accessed. It is not required, but especially encouraged when there is no copyright date listed on a website.

> Basic Format for Electronic Sources . . . .
> Author. Title. *Title of container* (self contained if book), other contributors (translators or editors), version (edition), number (vol. and/or no.), publisher, publication date, location (pages, paragraphs and/or URL, DOI or permalink). Date of access (if applicable).

Periodicals—Online

> Online journal . . . .
> Author's last name, first name. "Title of Article." *Title of Journal*, vol. #, issue #, year of publication, DOI/URL. Day Month Year of access.

> **NOTE:** If the online article is also available in print, include the page numbers before the URL.

> Author's last name, first name. "Title of Article." *Title of Journal*, vol. #, issue #, year of publication, pp. #, DOI/URL. Day Month Year of access.

> Kolowich, Steve. "On the Front Lines of a New Culture War." *The Chronicle of Higher Education*, vol. 63, no. 18, 2017, http://www.chronicle.com/article/On-the-Front-Lines-of-a-New/238770. Accessed 17 Jan. 2017.

Online magazine ·································

Author's last name, first name. "Title of Article." *Title of Magazine.* Publisher, Day Month Year, URL/DOI/Permalink, Day Month Year of access.

Grace, Sarah. "From 2026, the FIFA World Cup Will Have 48 Teams." *Time.com, Time* Magazine, 10 Jan. 2017, time.com/4629939/fifa-world-cup-teams-48-2016/?xid=homepage. Accessed 10 Jan. 2017.

Online newspaper ·······························

Author's last name, first name. "Title of the article." *Title of the newspaper,* first name last name of any other contributors, version (if applicable), numbers (if applicable), publication date, location (generally page numbers, if available). *Title of the Database,* location (such as a URL).

Pelley, Lauren. "Toronto Public Library Opens its 100th Branch." *Toronto Star,* 21 May 2015. *Newspaper Source,* search.ebscohost.com.i.ezproxy.nypl.org/login.aspx?direct=true&AuthType=cookie,ip,url,cpid&custid=nypl&db=nfh&AN=6FPTS2015052133436501&site=ehost-live.

ELECTRONIC DATABASES

These sources follow the same guidelines as the print or online sources, but you must also add the database information. Cite articles from online databases (e.g., EBSCOhost, LexisNexis, ProQuest, JSTOR, ScienceDirect, etc.) and other subscription services as containers. Provide the title of the database italicized before the DOI or URL. Providing the date of access is optional.

Basic Format for Electronic Databases·················

Author's last name, first name. "Title of Article." *Title of Journal,* vol. #. issue no., year, page numbers. *Name of Database,* DOI/URL, Day Month Year of access.

Faney, Dixie. "Correcting the Curved Spine of Scoliosis." *FDA Consumer,* vol. 28, no. 6, 1994, pp. 26–29. *Health Source Plus,* connection.ebscohost.com/c/articles/9407067515/correcting-curved-spine-scoliosis. Accessed 18 Apr. 2010.

McLendon, Joseph. "Con Artists Prey on Katrina Victims with Repair Scams." *Chicago Tribune,* 11 Oct. 2006, p. A7. *NewsBank,* www.newspapers.com/newspage/231917841/. Accessed 12 Oct. 2006.

WEBSITES

Instructors have different views on the use of general websites in an academic paper. Some instructors allow their use; others do not. Because websites have less oversight than publications, you must evaluate a website carefully to determine if it is appropriate. Web URLs that end in ".com" are commercial; they may have advertisements or may try to sell a product. Web URLs that end in ".edu" are from colleges; those ending in ".org" are from nonprofit organizations. Look for a website that gives a date when material was placed on it, as well as contact information or author names. **In general, when you are conducting research for an academic paper, you should use material from your library in the form of books, periodicals, or databases rather than random websites that you get from a Google search. See Chapters 16 and 19 on research to help you.**

Entire Website· ·

It is a good idea to list your date of access because web postings are often updated, and information available on one date may no longer be available later. When using the URL, be sure to include the complete address for the site except for the https://.

Editor, author, or compiler name (if available). *Name of Site.* Version number, Name of institution/organization affiliated with the site (sponsor or publisher), date of resource creation (if available), URL, DOI or permalink. Date of access (if applicable).

Name of author, editor, corporate author if available. *Title of Website.* Version number, Sponsor/publisher/organization affiliated with the site, Day Month Year of publication or last update, URL/DOI/ Permalink. Day Month Year of access.

Lawyershop.com. Lawyer Shop, 2015, www.lawyershop.com. Accessed 17 Jan. 2017.

Short work/Page from a website· ·

For an individual page or short work on a website, list the author (if known), followed by the information required for entire websites. If the publisher is the same as the website name, only list it once.

Last name, first name of author (if known). "Title of Article." *Title of Website.* Sponsor of website, Day Month Year of date of publication or last update. URL/DOI/Permalink. Day Month Year of access.

"Idaho Prison Officials Agree, More Humane Prison Conditions Are Necessary." *Prisonlaw.com.* Prison Law Office, 25 Nov. 2016, prisonlaw.com/news/idaho-prison-officials-agree-humane-prison-conditions-necessary/. Accessed 17 Jan. 2017.

ANNOTATED BIBLIOGRAPHY AND WORKS CITED

Some instructors may assign an Annotated Bibliography rather than a Works Cited page to serve as a documentation page. Sometimes they assign both.

An Annotated Bibliography is similar to a Works Cited page. Both alphabetically list the citations (publication information) for each of the sources in your paper. However, in the Annotated Bibliography, after each source's citation, you also write a critical summary, called an **annotation**, which overviews the source's author, its main idea, and its use in the research paper.

Keep in mind that the citation structures of your sources' publication information are the same in both the Works Cited page and Annotated Bibliography, so refer to the source citation structures mentioned earlier in this chapter.

For the sources' annotations, make sure to examine each source's information so that you can clearly overview its author, its main idea, and its use in the research paper.

In the first sentence of the annotation, mention the author's name and, if provided, his or her educational and professional background. If the author is an organization, like the American Heart Association, you need to overview the mission of the group. Citing the authorship of the source shows its credibility. However, if no author is listed for the source, you must clearly state in the first sentence of the annotation that no author is identified.

In the proceeding sentences of the annotation, overview the source's main idea and any points relevant to its thesis. Specifically, mention the source's ideas cited in your research paper. This summary reveals why this source's information is pertinent to your research paper.

In the overall annotation, use the same level of formality that you do in your research paper: no first or second person, no contractions, and no informal wording (slang).

Sample Works Cited

Smith 5

Works Cited

Clemmitt, Marcia. "Climate Change: Is Tougher Action Needed to Slow Rising Temperatures?" *CQ Researcher*, vol. 16, no. 4, 27 Jan. 2006, pp. 73–96. *CQ Researcher Online*, library.cqpress.com/cqresearcher/cqresrre2006012708. Accessed 6 Nov. 2007.

Cooper, Mary. "Global Warming." *CQ Researcher*, vol. 6, no. 41, 1 Nov. 1996, pp. 961–84. *CQ Researcher Online*, http://library.cqpress.com/cqresearcher/document.php?id=cqresrre1996110100&type=hitlist&num=1. Accessed 11 Jan. 2008.

Parks, Peggy. *Global Warming*. Lucent, 2004.

Shaw, Jane S. *Global Warming*. Greenhaven, 2002.

"Twelve Ideas for the Planet." *Chicago Tribune*, 11 Oct. 2006, pp. 1–4. *NewsBank*, www.newspapers.com/newspage/231917841/. Accessed 12 Oct. 2007.

U.N. Report. "Evidence Is Now 'Unequivocal' that Humans Are Causing Global Warming." *UN News Centre*, 2 Feb. 2007, www.un.org/apps/news/story.asp?NewsID=21429#.WH4jrpKT5Rk. Accessed 8 Nov. 2007.

United States. Environmental Protection Agency. *Climate Change*, 20 Dec. 2016, www.epa.gov/climatechange. Accessed 17 Jan. 2017.

Sample Annotated Bibliography

Annotated Bibliography

Clemmitt, Marcia. "Climate Change: Is Tougher Action Needed to Slow Rising Temperatures?" *CQ Researcher*, vol. 16, no. 4, 27 Jan. 2006, pp. 73–96. *CQ Researcher Online*, library.cqpress.com/cqresearcher/cqresrre2006012708. Accessed 6 Nov. 2007. Clemmit emphasizes that global warming is definitely caused by humans and is rapid and hard to predict. She also states that the whole world is at great risk concerning dangerous climate change. Clemmit further suggests that the United States should cap energy in order to reduce global warming.

Cooper, Mary. "Global Warming." *CQ Researcher*, vol. 6, no. 41, 1 Nov. 1996, pp. 961–84. *CQ Researcher Online*, http://library.cqpress.com/cqresearcher/document.php?id=cqresrre1996110100&type=hitlist&num=1. Accessed 11 Jan. 2008. Cooper explains that global warming has been consistently on the rise since the nineteenth century. In her article, she cites that scientists argue that human activity is responsible for global warming. She also overviews several global warming summits that have taken place since the early 1990s.

Parks, Peggy. *Global Warming*. Lucent, 2004. Parks holds a Bachelor of Science degree from Aquinas College in Grand Rapids, Michigan. She is a freelance writer and author. Parks states in her book that the earth's temperature is rising and it is affecting the earth's agriculture and its population. Parks also suggests preventative measures that humankind can take to control global warming.

Shaw, Jane S. *Global Warming*. Greenhaven, 2002. Shaw is a senior associate of PERC, the Center for Free Market Environmentalism in Bozeman, Montana, which is a nonprofit organization. Shaw discusses in her book the controversies that surround global warming such as whether or not the threat is real, the climate is changing, and the greenhouse effect can be reduced. She also explains how humans' lives will change if they do nothing to prevent global warming. She also offers readers the benefits of doing their part to resolve the environmental problem.

"Twelve Ideas for the Planet." *Chicago Tribune,* 11 Oct. 2006, pp. 1–4. *NewsBank*, www.newspapers.com/newspage/231917841/. Accessed 12 Oct. 2007. No author is cited for this article. The article cites John R. McNeill, who argues that global warming and climate change have been important environmental issues for some time. The article also refers to Laurie David, who argues that everyone can take part and do something to combat global warming.

U.N. Report. "Evidence Is Now 'Unequivocal' that Humans Are Causing Global Warming." *UN News Centre*, 2 Feb. 2007, www.un.org/apps/news/story.asp?NewsID=21429#.WH4jrpKT5Rk. Accessed 8 Nov. 2007. Web. 8 Nov. 2007. No author is cited for this article. The article explains that human impact is very probable where climate change and global warming are concerned. It also cites that gas emissions contribute greatly to the increase in the earth's temperature.

United States. Environmental Protection Agency. *Climate Change*, 20 Dec. 2016, www.epa.gov/climatechange. Accessed 17 Jan. 2017. The Environmental Protection Agency (EPA) is a United States government organization dedicated to environmental issues. This particular EPA report discusses the science behind climate change and the effects on the environment. The EPA also explains what Americans can do to prevent greenhouse gas emissions.

Please be sure to check with your instructor if you are unsure about outline form or requirements.

Sample Student Term Paper in MLA Format

Braswell 1

Ryan Braswell

English 1123 RY01

Ms. Hammons

25 April 2014

Mississippi's Veterans Are Missing Credit

After transitioning out of the military, veterans learn that college degrees have nearly become mandatory for significant employment. This emphasis on postsecondary education makes graduating from college the highest priority for Mississippi's returning veterans. Promises of academic credit for service and offers of complete scholarships are commonplace at the federal-government-sponsored Transition Assistance Programs for soldiers returning to the Magnolia State. However, as college student and a veteran of the Armed Forces, I have witnessed firsthand that in Mississippi many of these promises are empty. The most significant promise that of academic credit for military experience is completely false. Mississippi should implement legislation ensuring service members receive the maximum academic credit for their military experience.

When selecting a college, a veteran will soon realize that most schools refuse to award credit for military service (Herrmann 2). While training in the military consists of many strenuous hours in a formal classroom and in practical application settings, it is not widely accepted as a viable learning experience by postsecondary institutions (Snead 12). The reason for this denial can vary, but the fundamental cause behind this action is the institution's failure to comprehend the level of training which occurs in the military (Bradley 7). As a result of this failure, many institutions are reluctant to award any substantial amount of credit for fear of compromising accreditation standards or academic integrity (Snead 12). Reluctance on the part of the institution leads to a sporadic system of evaluating and awarding credit at college. Paul Bradley addresses this random selection process in *Community College*

Week: "Each college makes its own decision on how much credit to award. Practices, predictably vary widely, leading to frustration" in the student veteran community (Bradley 7). For example, an Army medic may be awarded credit for a basic first aid course at one university but denied that same credit at another. The need for an established system for awarding credit could not be more prevalent.

Often the varying practices are coupled with untrained and over-worked staff, making the entire process of evaluating and awarding academic credit even more unreliable. In most cases, a single staff member with many other responsibilities outside of the scope of assessing adult experiential learning is assigned to evaluate military training. The employee has limited options to develop the skills needed to award credit properly, and being that evaluating military credit is not the primary focus of the position, training is not pursued (Herrmann 2). In fact, many schools do not even offer a policy outlining the reception of military training as academic credit for the individual to consult when evaluating military transcripts. This absence of direction puts the veteran entirely at the mercy of the untrained staff member, who is neither focused nor prepared for the task at hand. Service members throughout Mississippi, where most institutions have not established a separate military student department or created a military transfer policy in their catalog, are finding that they cannot expect a fair evaluation from the inexpert, freehand staff.

In an effort to assist school official's that evaluate military training the American Council of Education developed guidelines for awarding credit to veterans who completed specific training programs in the military. It has quickly become the standard by which military programs are evaluated and translated into academic recommendations. ACE's Military Guide is the product of several evaluation teams composed of experienced college faculty and military instructors, who make credit hour recommendations for the specific military training regime completed by a veteran (Snead 13–14). These credit recommendations are often broad descriptions that allow for interpretation by different

Braswell 3

institutions. The school official can then evaluate how those credits can be applied to a veteran's program of study at their institution. Even though ACE makes these credit recommendations directly on a military transcript, school officials still refuse to apply those credit hours to a veteran's transcript from lack of guidance by the institution (Bradley 7). When the credit is denied, the service member is not allowed to dispute the decision by demonstrating proficiency in the subjects listed on his/ her military transcript. Often the service member is never made aware that no credit was awarded.

Many veterans who have found themselves in similar positions in the past have voiced their concerns to their state legislatures. Several legislatures have responded to the lack of consistency and direction for awarding military credit by implementing policies that improved the reception of military transfer credit at public colleges and universities. Often this legislation focused on the development of a uniformed process or in some cases a state department that would evaluate and award college credit for military service (Liu, "Easing" 26). In Texas, for example, Senator Van de Putte authored Texas Senate Bill 1736 to create a comprehensive military credit evaluation program that consists of a coalition of Texas public institutions of higher learning (qtd. in Ginn 32). This coalition, College Credit for Heroes, uses consistent methodology for evaluating and determining which courses to be awarded college credit at Texas' public universities and colleges (Liu, "Helping" 9). A direct policy from state legislation is the only viable way to ensure that all institutions treat military service credit in the same manner.

An efficient methodology of evaluating military service transcripts can decrease the amount of time a service member spends pursuing a degree (Ginn 32). This in turn holds several economic advantages for Mississippi, because according to White House statistics, a dramatic increase of service members leaving the military will occur over the next few years. This influx of veterans into the civilian job market coincides with economic reports that show an escalation of employment opportunities for college graduates (qtd. in Azziz 19). Many of these

Braswell 4

veterans who are discharging from the military will face challenges that prevent them from obtaining a college degree in a timely manner. With the lack of a college degree preventing new employment and the absence of income from leaving the military, veterans will be forced to seek financial relief from unemployment offices in their communities. By adjusting the education system in Mississippi to ensure veterans can take advantage of their military training to quickly obtain a degree, the state will be bolstering the work force, while at the same time reducing unemployment in the local population.

Education reform for military students has not gone unnoticed in Mississippi on the institutional level. Several local colleges and universities are beginning to implement programs to improve the military student experience. Both Hinds Community College and Jackson State University have established standalone departments for addressing student veterans' needs. In addition, Copiah-Lincoln Community College has gone as far as to create an entire degree program designed for military students ("New Military-Friendly Degree" 8). However, these efforts are limited in scope to specific institutions and serve primarily as recruiting techniques for attracting more military students. They do not create a measurable impact on the military community in Mississippi.

Veterans are finding it difficult to receive college credit for their military service, none more so than those in Mississippi. As veterans return home, their desire to begin a fruitful career is strong. The startling realization that while their service is appreciated but not accepted by the Mississippi's institutions of higher learning is enough to destroy their dreams. At the very least, it will send veterans to colleges in other states that are accommodating their needs. Instead of pushing veterans to seek refuge in other states or leaving them at the whim of various untrained educational staff, Mississippi should introduce a statewide policy that ensures veterans will receive adequate college credit for their military training.

Braswell 5

Works Cited

Azziz, Ricardo. "A Call to Arms: Academe Must Meet Demands of Downsizing Military." *DIVERSE: Issues in Higher Education*, 19, Sep. 2013, *Education Full Text (H.W. Wilson)*, greport.gru.edu/archives/4663. Accessed 1 Apr. 2014.

Bradley, Paul. "Forward, March." *Community College Week*, 11 Nov. 2013, 6–7. *Academic Search Complete*. ccweek.com/article-3645-cover-story:-forward,-march.html.

Ginn, Jennifer. "States Find Ways to Tackle New, and Old, Problems." *Capitol Ideas*, July/Aug. 2012, 32-33. *Academic Search Complete*, www.csg.org/pubs/capitolideas/jul_aug_2012/innovativelegislation.aspx. Accessed 18 Mar. 2014.

Herrmann, Douglas, Douglas Raybeck, and Roland B. Wilson. "College Is for Veterans, Too." *Chronicle of Higher Education*, Nov. 2008, *Academic Search Complete*, www.researchgate.net/publication/220034252_College_Is_for_Veterans_Too. Accessed 18 Mar. 2014.

Hoover, Eric. "Where Life Earns Credit: 'Prior Learning' Gets a Fresh Assessment." *Chronicle of Higher Education*, vol. 56, no. 27, 2010, *MasterFILE Complete*, www.chronicle.com/article/Where-Life-Earns-Credit-/64618. Accessed 18 Mar. 2014.

Liu, Michelle Camacho. "Easing The Path To College." *State Legislatures*, vol. 26, April 2012, *Academic Search Complete*, www.ncsl.org/research/military-and-veterans-affairs/easing-the-path-to-college.aspx. Accessed 18 Mar. 2014.

Liu, Michelle Camacho. "Helping Vets Hit The Books." *State Legislatures*, vol. 9, 2013, *Academic Search Complete*, www.ncsl.org/Portals/1/Documents/magazine/.../SL_1013-.pdf. Accessed 18 Mar. 2014.

"New Military-Friendly Degree Offered By Mississippi College." *Community College Week*, 5 Sept. 2011, 8. *Professional Development Collection*, npaper-wehaa.com/ccweek#2011/09/05.

Braswell 6

Snead, Kathy M. and Clifton L. Anderson. "Awarding College Credit For Military Training And Experience: Campus Strategies For Adopting ACE Guide Credit Recommendations." *Duty, Honor, Country . . . & Credit.* Council for Adult and Experiential Learning, 2010, 12-15, *ERIC*, files.eric.ed.gov/fulltext/ED524754.pdf. Accessed 20 Mar. 2014.

Chapter 21

APA: A Guide to Research and Documentation

Introduction to the APA Style

The American Psychological Association (APA) is just one of several organizations with research style formats that students and professionals can use for research papers. APA style lends itself to papers focusing on topics concerning the social sciences, natural sciences, and applied sciences. Social sciences include anthropology, economics, education, management, nursing, political science, psychology, sociology, and social work. The natural sciences and applied sciences include major areas such as biology, chemistry, computer sciences, engineering, mathematics, physics, and other related branches. The most recent publication, the 6th edition, was published in 2009 and updated in 2016.

The APA style is versatile and allows the writer to approach the paper in several ways: providing information to prove or disprove a stated hypothesis, providing working parameters that result in information for case studies and supporting inferences and conclusions from those studies, or providing support information from a research-based topic with a thesis statement.

The purpose of the APA format is to allow the writer to work from topical areas concerning the social, natural, and applied sciences using the approaches listed above. APA style is designed to focus on the most current research. Therefore, APA style prioritizes for authors first and then publication dates for both the abbreviated in-text citations and the full documentation listed at the end of the research paper, known as References.

A research paper in APA format has four distinct parts or sections: the **title page**, the **abstract**, the **body** of the research paper itself with in-text citations and figures or charts, and the **references page(s)** at the end.

APA GUIDELINES FOR FORMATTING PAPERS

- The essay should be typed, double-spaced in 12-point, easy-to-read font (such as Times New Roman) on 8 ½" × 11" paper, with 1" margins on all sides.

- Include a title page, with the title (in title case—upper- and lowercase letters) centered in the upper half of the page, with the author's name and any other relevant information centered below the title.

- Paginate the essay in the upper right header portion of the page, beginning with the title page.

- Include running headers of the essay title in all capital letters on the upper left portion of the page, beginning with the title page.

- Change underlining to italics. However, some underlining may need to be preserved, depending on the original material.

- Fix commas and periods relative to quotation marks (commas and periods go inside the quotation marks, not outside: "Chapter 1," rather than "Chapter 1", for example).

- Use em dashes (—) and ellipses (. . .) where appropriate, and make consistent.

- Replace hyphens (-) with en dashes (–) where appropriate.

- The second printing of the 6th edition of the APA style guide recommends, but does not require, using two spaces after the end punctuation of a sentence, for ease of readability.

- The reference page should begin on a new page, separate from the essay.

Following is an example of the title page.

Sample Title Page

Running Head: FAMILIES AND TEENS   1

Families and Teens:

Eliminate the Negatives and Accentuate the Positives

Eric Smith

English 1123: English Composition II

Instructor Glynda Duncan

The Abstract

The APA format is known for its use of the abstract, a brief overview of the research paper stating all major points listed in the research and a thesis statement, if applicable. Abstracts assist a person researching related materials. A researcher can review the abstract to see the major points discussed in the research paper.

According to APA format, the abstract is always dedicated to page 2 and should be between 150 and 250 words. The abbreviated title of the research paper is typed in all caps flush left on page 2 while the page number "2" is typed flush right (without quotation marks). All subsequent pages of the research paper follow the same rules: the abbreviated title in all caps is flush left and the page numbers are flush right. The writer's name is only found on the title page; the writer's name is never listed on any other pages of the research paper.

The following tips will help you create an abstract:

- Clearly and briefly state the purpose of the paper.
- Report the problem being studied and the participants included in the study.
- Briefly explain conclusions.

Do not indent as block format is used for the abstract. Do not consider the abstract as a paragraph, but rather an overview of the paper.

The following page is an example of an abstract.

Sample Abstract

FAMILIES AND TEENS 2

Abstract

In today's society, successful families are fighting for the livelihood of their children. Families are fighting for more quality family time, a balance in community ties and involvement, and control of outside influences of various electronic media and peers. Americans are seeing a vast increase in the number of weekly working hours; therefore, quality time is lost due to parents being forced to work longer hours or families splitting up and losing quality time due to divorce or abandonment. A solution to loss of family time is working fewer hours, living a simpler life, or even spending more time with children through home schooling. Community ties can be strengthened by sharing space such as day cares, gardens, workshops, or by joining a religious group or support group that provides day care or watch care programs. The negative influence of media can be controlled to a point by implementing stricter rules of viewing television programs together, installing V-chips which block certain programming from children's viewing, and closer monitoring of computer and cell phone use by children by adult family members.

The Body of the Research Paper

The body of the research paper is written to include in-text citations, tables, charts, artwork, or any auxiliary material that adds to the content of the research. Any information that you intend to include in the paper, whether it is a direct quote or not, must have the source cited as soon as you use it in the paper. This type of documentation is known as in-text citation; the full documentation is on the last page(s) under the heading "References." All information cited within the text must be represented with a full citation on the References page(s). All works fully cited on the References page(s) must correlate to an in-text citation within the paper. Using citations for print or online sources within text and not listing them on the References page(s), or citing such reference works on the References page(s) but not within the text, are direct and explicit examples of plagiarism.

Third Person and Historical Present Tense

Research papers are formal writings and need to be written in third person point of view. The writer of the research paper is expected to make personal inferences and conclusions based on the findings stated in the research. However, the writer must state inferences and conclusions in third person point of view, not as first (I, me, my) or second (you).

APA allows for present tense and historical present tense. Although research has been completed or authors of research are deceased, the writer can use historical present tense to discuss the information. The information does not die; it lives on in the research.

However, when describing or using earlier research within your own paper, APA style mandates that you use the past tense or present perfect tense in writing about the research.

> Example. ·
> Green's research (2001) found the following information . . .

> Example. ·
> Green (2001) has found or has noted the following information . . .

Appropriate Topics and Narrowing Topics

APA research formatting focuses on "research-based" and not "information-based" topics. Defining a disease and listing symptoms is information-based, not research-based. Research is not a report that is documented by sources. Research-based topics emphasize the research and conclusions that point to solutions or strategies.

When choosing and narrowing the topic, ask questions that will shape the scope of the paper. Those questions or elements should be included in the organization and content of the paper. For example, how does the topic affect a group, a country, etc., economically, educationally, environmentally, politically, psychologically, or socially? What are the repercussions of this topic to citizens, groups, countries, etc.?

Choosing the topic of Attention Deficit Disorder (ADD) is too broad. Defining it and giving the symptoms are not research-based. However, the paper's scope could focus on ADD in the elementary classroom. What policies are stated to deal with ADD students in the classroom and how are these policies determined and implemented? How are teachers, parents, the ADD student, and other students affected by these policies and procedures? Continue to narrow the topic in the ways mentioned above.

APA research papers focus on the most current information and data; therefore, new materials and information are required. Your topic must allow the most updated information, not information from 10 years ago or even further back.

Appropriate Sources

Most instructors have definite ideas on where students can find available and valuable resource materials. Instructors also have very strong opinions on inappropriate sites such as Wikipedia, encyclopedia.com, and all or some of the selections of encyclopedias, Facebook, and other social networking sites. Never proceed with collecting data until you have received permission or instructions from your instructor on what s/he considers appropriate databases, websites, etc.

Know the difference between primary and secondary sources. The References listed at the end of an article are the *primary sources* that are cited as source information for that article. Since the author of the article used those sources, those sources are *primary* and the article is a *secondary* source. You should find the cited sources from the article (be sure you only focus on the most current dates) to read and use as your sources. You also can use the article which you read that cited the primary sources. When directly citing from a source, it is better to know the *primary source* and the *secondary source* of information.

NOTE: All examples in this chapter are single spaced here to conserve paper. However, in your paper, you should double-space everything, thereby complying with APA guidelines.

APA General In-Text Citation Rules

- It is important to provide a lead-in to source quotations or paraphrases in the text, especially the first time the source is used. Lead-ins introduce the sources to the audience and provide a smooth transition to quotes and paraphrases within the text. Example: According to Lipson (2006) . . .

- You must list the in-text citation immediately after stating information that you have used from a source, whether it is a direct quote or paraphrased material.

- The in-text citation includes the author's last name and the year of publication: (Smith, 2010). Page numbers are included only if you are using a direct quote: (Smith, 2010, p. 177).

- When referencing the title of a source in text, capitalize all words that are four letters long or more within the title of a source: *Pride and Prejudice*. Short words that are verbs, nouns, pronouns, adjectives, and adverbs are exceptions to this rule: *Everything Is Illuminated, Brave New World*.

- Italicize the titles of longer works such as books, movies, anthologies, television series, or albums: *American Idol*; *Anchorman*. Put quotation marks around the titles of shorter works within the text, such as journal articles, essays in anthologies, and song titles: "Red"; "Inventing the University."

- In titles, capitalize both words in a hyphenated compound word: *The Tell-Tale Heart*. Also capitalize the first word after a colon or dash: *The World Is Flat: A Brief History of the Twenty-First Century*.

A WORK BY A SINGLE AUTHOR

For citations not directly quoted from the author, include only the author and year of publication.

> According to Lipson (2006), there are two or more methods for citing in-text citations.

> There are two very good examples of in-text citation methods that can be used (Lipson, 2006).

If quoting directly from a work, include the author, year of publication, and the page number (preceded by "p.").

> Sedaris (1994) recalls, "We rode round and round the block on our pony, who groaned beneath the collective weight of our rich and overwhelming capacity for love and understanding" (p. 9–10).

> "We rode round and round the block on our pony, who groaned beneath the collective weight of our rich and overwhelming capacity for love and understanding" (Sedaris, 1994, p. 9–10).

BLOCK QUOTATIONS

For direct quotes that are longer than forty words, you must type the quoted material in its own freestanding block, double spaced, indented five spaces or half an inch from the left margin. Even though the quotation marks are omitted, the quoted material is set apart from the research and thus easily recognized. A *signal phrase* introduces the quote in the regular text with the author's name mentioned and the date in parentheses immediately after. The quoted material starts on a new line. The parenthetical citing of the page number comes after the block quotation, with the end punctuation mark before the parentheses. Here is an example that shows how to introduce a block quotation:

> DiYanni's (2007) research found the importance of music to the time: Music was central to the flowering culture during the Harlem Renaissance. Jazz clubs such as the Harlem Casino, The Sugar Cane Club, and the Cotton Club were frequented by both black and white patrons. Prominent jazz artists played in these clubs, including Duke Ellington, Count Basie, Bessie Smith, and Louis Armstrong. Music, in fact, is a central feature of [Langston] Hughes's poetry. (p. 991)

USING ELLIPSIS

An ellipsis is used when some portion of quoted material is not necessary; therefore, the portion is omitted. The ellipsis can be used at the beginning, middle, or end of omitted quoted material to signal that not all quoted material is stated. You must use the ellipsis, a series of three dots, to indicate that material has been omitted. Use four dots to indicate that words have been omitted between two sentences.

> DiYanni's (2007) research found the influence of music of the time: "Music was central to the flowering culture during the Harlem Renaissance. Jazz clubs . . . were frequented by both black and white patrons" (p. 991).

Author and date can follow a direct quote with ellipses:

> "Music was central to the flowering culture during the Harlem Renaissance. Jazz clubs . . . were frequented by both black and white patrons" (DiYanni, 2007, p. 991).

PRINT SOURCES

Two Authors

List both authors whenever the work is cited. In the signal phrase, "and" should be used between the authors' names, while an ampersand should be used in the parentheses.

> Research by Collins and Blum (2000) outlines the way socioeconomics and politics outside the university also play a role in instigating the division between "basic" and "normal" writers (p. 14).

> Researcher scholars outline the way socioeconomics and politics outside the university also play a role in instigating the division between "basic" and "normal" writers (Collins & Blum, 2000, p. 14).

Three to Five Authors

List all the authors by last name the first time the source is cited. In subsequent citations, use the first author's last name followed by "et al." The et in et al. should not be followed by a period.

> Ward, Burns, and Baker (1996) note, "The game varied from state to state, town to town, but town ball was the most popular" (p. 4).

> (Ward et al., 1996, p. 4)

Six or More Authors

Use the first author's last name, followed by et al.

> Cincotta et al. (1994) assert that the launch of Sputnik expanded the competitive arena between the U.S. and the Soviet Union (p. 68).

Unknown Author

If the author of a source is unknown, cite using the title in the lead-in, or include an abbreviated version of the title in the parenthetical citation.

> A similar study determined that subjects lose time when switching from task to task ("Is Multitasking," 2001).

Authors with the Same Last Name

Include first initials with the last names to distinguish between the authors.

> (R. Jones, 2012; A. Jones, 2003)

Book with Multiple Editions and No Author

(American Cancer Society, 2006).

Book with Multiple Editors (e.g., anthologies)

(Canter, Duncan, Hill, & Sledge, 2007).

If More Than Six Editors

(Cook, et al., 2007).

Multivolume Work

(Sledge, 2001–2007).

One Volume in a Multivolume Work

(Duncan, 2008).

Translated Volume

(Layrock, 1990–91/2001).

Magazine and Newspaper Articles with Author

(Duncan, 2006).

Magazine and Newspaper Articles with No Author

(Complications of Autism, 1997)

Encyclopedia/Dictionary Entry

Since encyclopedias and dictionaries rarely list an author, use the term or phrase being cited in the parenthetical citation. If there is an author listed, use the name of the author rather than the term or phrase being cited.

A citation is a "quotation from or reference to a book, paper, or author." (Citation, 2002).

Presentation, Speech, or Lecture

(Reed, 2005).

Printed Interview

(Harris, 2007).

Personal Communication

Note that personal communications (emails, personal interviews, letters, etc.) are not included in the Reference section.

In-Text Signal Phrase

G. J. Duncan states . . . (personal communication, January 8, 2010).

Parenthetical Citation

(G. J. Duncan, personal interview, January 8, 2010).

Indirect Sources

It may be necessary to use a work that has been cited in another source. For such indirect or secondary sources, use "as cited in" to indicate the primary source.

According to Harvey Graff, "We do not know what we mean by literacy" (as cited in Lunsford, p. 252).

Photograph

(Simpson, 2005).

Figures, Charts, Graphs, Maps, Tables

APA style also allows tables, charts, artwork, and photos to enhance the research. These are cited within the text only; they are not listed under References. Each one is numbered chronologically (as Figure 1, Figure 2, etc.) as it appears in the body of the research paper. The caption, information explaining the figure, and the complete referencing citation are listed in the caption. Personal communications information is also only cited within in-text citations and not found on the References page(s).

Here is an example of a caption:

Figure 1. A decade of annual enrollment figures for Coahoma Community College, 1992–2002 (shown in increments of thousands and fractions of thousands). Adapted from Coahoma Community College Office of Admissions and Records (1992–2002). In *Biennial Presidential Report: Coahoma Community College, 2003–2005.*

The figure and number of the figure are italicized. The name of the photo, chart, table, etc. is cited as a title in APA format with only the first word and proper nouns capitalized. A date or dates of the artwork follow if applicable. A parenthetical citation is noted to clarify any information that might be unclear on the chart, map, etc. The word Note is italicized after the parenthetical to tell where the chart, map, or table was referenced and has a period at the end. Then the word "In" introduces the author(s) with last name and first initials. Then the name of the document or printed source of the material goes in italics. If the artwork is retrieved from an online source, the retrieval date, URL address, or DOI address follow. The DOI may be found in the abstract of the source or at the beginning of the article. You may also use the following website to try to locate the DOI: crossref.org/quest/query.

Most figures, charts, graphs, tables, and other such explanatory information are numbered chronologically as they appear in the research paper and use captions directly beneath them with complete material for identification.

In-Text Citation

Mississippi Community and Junior College enrollment figure [2006], 2008).

Caption

Figure #. Mississippi Community and Junior College Association enrollment figure (2006). *MCJCA Annual Report*. Retrieved Jan. 15, 2008, from http://www.MCJCA.edu/annualreport.com

Government Documents

(Centers for Disease Control, 2007).

Congressional Record Citations and References

(U.S. Dept. of Education, 2007).

ELECTRONIC SOURCES

Video/Film

Big Fish, directed by Tim Burton, details the extraordinary life of Edward Bloom (2003).

Television

In Criminal Minds, a suspect awakens from a coma with no memory of having committed the crimes he is accused of ("Tabula Rasa").

WEB SOURCES

When possible, cite a web document the same as any other document.

> Bianchi (2007) suggests [. . .]

If no author or date is given, cite using the title in the lead-in, or include an abbreviated version of the title in the parenthetical citation, and use the abbreviation "n.d." ("no date").

> A similar study determined that subjects lost more time when switching from a familiar task to an unfamiliar task ("Is Multitasking," n.d.).

If no page number is available, include information that will help readers find the material being cited. If paragraphs are numbered, use "para." And follow with the paragraph number.

> (Hubbard, 2014, para. 3).

Entire Website

> (Lions' Club International, 2006).

Web Page with Author

> (Caraway, M.L., 2007).

Web Page with No Author

> (Turner Movie Classics, 2003).

Online Book

> (Cooley, 2004).

Journal Article Online (single author and multiple authors)

For Single Author

> (Manchester, 1997).

For multiple authors (up to six), in the first in-text citation, use all six names and the publication date. In subsequent citations, use the first author's last name, then et al. and the publication date.

First Citation

> (Adam, Butler, Crawford, Dante, Ellis, & Franklin, 2006).

Subsequent

(Adam, et al., 2006).

Online Magazine and Online Newspaper Articles

(Jones, 1999).

Weblog (Blog) with Entry or Comment

(Davis, 2001).

APA Reference Page

The final section of the APA research paper is the full documentation of sources cited within the paper. In-text citations are brief because all source documentation is fully recognized in the references page(s). The reference list including all sources cited in the text should appear on a separate page at the end of the text. The reference page should include the title References centered at the top of the page, with no bolding, underlining, italicizing, or quotation marks.

- The page or pages are numbered as part of the research paper and are double-spaced, with no additional spaces between entries.

- Reference list entries should be alphabetized by the last name of the first author of each work. After the last name, only first and second initials are used; no complete first names are used.

- Entries should have a hanging indent. The first line of each reference is flush left and all lines after the first line of each entry should be indented one-half inch from the left margin.

- For multiple articles by the same author, or authors listed in the same order, list the entries in chronological order, from earliest to most recent.

- Include the complete journal title, maintaining the capitalization and punctuation used in the original title.

- When referring to books, chapters, articles, or web pages, capitalize only the first letter of the first word of a title and subtitle, the first word after a colon or a dash in the title, and proper nouns. Do not capitalize the first letter of the second word in a hyphenated compound word. Example: *Give me life right now.*

- Italicize titles of longer works (books, films); do not italicize, underline, or put quotes around the titles of shorter works (articles, songs).

REMEMBER: Your References pages will be double-spaced and will begin on a new page.

BOOKS

Book with One Author

Author's last name, First & Second initial. (date). *Title of the book: Only in lower case style.* City of publication (state is optional unless city is not well known): Publisher's name.

Klause, S. B. (2006). *The elf wars: An insider's guide.* North Pole: Cookie Press.

Book with Two Authors

First author's last name and initial(s), & second author's last names, initial(s). (date). *The title written in italics and in lower case.* City of publication and state if city is not well known: Publisher's name.

Black, L., & Brown, M. (1942). *The art of slap-stick comedy.* Chicago, IL: Pantomime Press.

Book with Three to Seven Authors

First author's last name, initials, second author's last name, initial(s), & third author's last name, initial(s). (date). *Title written in italics.* City of publication and state if city is not well known: Publisher's name.

Black, L., Brown, M., Green, C., White, A., Blue, J., & Fatherree, B. (1945). *The art of slap-stick comedy: Part II.* Chicago, IL: Pantomime Press.

Book with More than Seven Authors

List by last names and initials; commas separate author names. After the sixth author's name, use an ellipses in place of the subsequent author names, then list the final author name. There should be no more than seven names listed.

Black, L., Brown, M., Green, C., White, A., Blue, J., . . . Orange, K. (1948). *The art of slap-stick comedy: The past and future laughs.* Chicago, IL: Pantomime Press.

Two or More Works by the Same Author

Use the last name, initials format for all entries and list the entries by the year, earliest first.

Child, L. (2007).

Child, L. (2010).

Unknown Author

When a source does not include an author's name, use the source's title (abbreviated, if the title is long) rather than an author's name.

Beowulf. (2000). New York, NY: Farrar, Straus and Giroux.

Author with an Editor ·
Fielding, H. (1973). *Tom Jones*. S. Baker (Ed.). New York, NY: W. W.
   Norton & Company, Inc.

Editor as Author ·
Hart, J. (Ed.). (2003). *Che: The life, death, and afterlife of a revolution-
   ary*. New York, NY: Thunder's Mouth Press.

For books with more than one editor, use the same formatting guidelines as
those used for books with multiple authors.

Book with Multiple Editions ·
Last name, initial(s), & last name, initial(s) (Eds.). (Date). *Title of book.*
   (Edition in parentheses if there is one). City of publication and state if
   city is not well known: Publisher's name.

Black, L. (1948). *Those were the laughs: Comedy from the past* (3rd
   ed.). Chicago, IL: Pantomime Press.

Book with Multiple Editions and No Author · · · · · · · · · · · · · · · · · · ·
American Cancer Society directory for oncologists (9th ed.). (2006).
   Washington, D.C. American Cancer Society.

Multivolume Work ·
Sledge, B.D. (2001–2007). *The walking woes of fasciitis* (Vols. 1–7).
   Dallas: Southern Methodist University Press.

One Volume in a Multivolume Work ·
Duncan, G.J. (2008). *Electrical engineering contrasted to civil engi-
   neering in 20th century and beyond 1998–2008:* (Vol. 8). New
   York: Columbia University Press.

Translated Volume ·
Layrock, Z.I. (2001). *Happy women*. (G.J. Duncan, Trans.). New York:
   American Press. (Original work published 1990–91).

Chapter or Chapters in a Book ·
Brooke, S. (2002). When soldiers march to war. In S. Crawford (Ed.),
   Wars and other strategies (pp. 31–39). Princeton: Princeton
   University Press.

PERIODICALS

In the references list, the titles of articles do not use quotation marks. The title of the journal and the volume number of the journal are italicized. Include the complete journal title, maintaining the capitalization and punctuation used in the original title. Neither the word "volume" nor an abbreviation is used. Issue number, if used, is used in parentheses to help find the quoted material, especially if each volume or issue begins with page 1.

Article in Journal Paginated by Issue

Because journals paginated by issue begin with page one for each issue, the issue number is included in the citation. The parentheses and issue number are not italicized or underlined.

Collins. T. & Blum, M. (2000). Meanness and failure: Sanctioning basic writers. *Journal of Basic Writing*, 19(1), 13–21.

Jakes, T.J. (2007). Are we headed for World War III and IV? *Combat*, 23(47), 13–19.

Article in Journal Paginated by Volume

Journals paginated by volume begin with page one in issue one, and page numbers continue in issue two where issue one left off. Therefore, it is not necessary to include an issue number.

Sledd, A. (1998). Readin' not riotin': The politics of literacy. *College English*, 50, 495–508.

Griffin, D.V. (2002). Where have all the soldiers gone in Iraq, Afghanistan, and Pakistan? *Mercenary Soldier*, 12, 956–959.

For journal articles with multiple authors, use the same formatting guidelines as used for books with multiple authors (see p. 296).

Magazine and Newspaper Article with Author

Duncan, G.J. (2006, April 19). Boston mafia underlings indicted in Massachusetts sting. *Time* 101, 16–17.

Duncan, G.J. (2006, April 10). Harbor mafia makes big splash in federal court proceedings. *Boston Globe* [state ed.], p. A1.

Magazine Article and Newspaper Article with No Author

Newspaper references require page number designations of p. or pp.

Complications of Autism. (1997, Dec. 17). *Mental Health*, p. 16.

The trouble with Autism and Asperger Syndrome. (2007, August 4). *Chicago Tribune* [state ed.], p. D16.

Review with Author••••••••••••••••••••••••••••••••••••••
Smith, W.W. (2003, August 10). What they don't tell you about vitamins. [Review of the book *Vitamins, herbal remedies, and homeo-
pathic cures*]. *Mississippi Authors Review of Books*, 33, 16–17.

Encyclopedia Entry ••••••••••••••••••••••••••••••••••••••
Civil Rights. (1999). In *World book encyclopedia* (35th ed., Vol. 7., pp.
213–222). New York: World Book Encyclopedia.

Reference Book••
Johnson, C.L., & Johnson, J.H. (Eds.) (2001). *Reference guide to chil-
dren's health* (4th ed., 4 vols.). New York: Columbia University
Press.

Dictionary Entry•••
Fugue, *n.* (2001). *Webster's II new collegiate dictionary* (3rd ed.).
Boston, MA: Houghton Mifflin Company.

Presentation, Speech, or Lecture•••••••••••••••••••••••••••
Reed, W. (2005, October 29). Award recipient address. Mississippi
Humanities Council Outstanding Teacher of the Year at Coahoma
Community College. Annual Awards Program. Clarksdale, MS.

Printed Interview•••
Harris, M. (2007). Blues in the Delta. Interview with philanthropist and
actor Morgan Freeman. *Here's Clarksdale*. November 1, 2007.

Personal Interview or Communication ••••••••••••••••••••••••
Personal communication (Glynda J. Duncan, personal communication, January 28, 2010).

The citation within the text is complete, and personal interview and communication information is not included on the References page(s) since
there is no official publication to which readers might refer.

Abstract from Original Source•••••••••••••••••••••••••••••••
MacFayjden, A.B. (2000). Modern art forms blend with horticultural
landscaping. [Abstract]. *Modern Art Today*, 33, 99–100.

Abstract from Secondary Source••••••••••••••••••••••••••••
McFayjden, A.B. (2000). Copper sculptures with hydraulic lifts successful for mobile art forms. *Studies in Modern Art for Commercial
Use*, 31, 16–19. Abstract obtained from *Modern Sculptures and
other Art Forms*, 71, 2003, 17, Abstract No. 131789.

Photograph ·

[Photograph by L.K. Simpson]. (2005). *Single mother with three children at Super Dome after Hurricane Katrina*. Mississippi Art Museum, Jackson, MS.

Government Documents ·

Government Agency. (Date). *Title of document* (Publication name/number of document). City: Publisher.

Centers for Disease Control. (2007, July 29). *Statement on restrictions of travel within and outside of the United States for patients of tuberculosis*. Atlanta, GA: Publisher.

Congressional Record Citations and References · · · · · · · · · · · · · · · ·

U.S. Dept. of Education. (2007). *National standardized test scores for 11th graders*. Washington, D.C.: U.S. Government Printing Office.

ELECTRONIC SOURCES

Video/Film ·

Cohen, B., Zanuck, R. & Jinks, D. (Producers), & Burton, T. (Director). (2003). *Big Fish* [Motion picture]. USA: Sony Home Pictures Entertainment.

Music Recording ·

Howard, T., Lambert, M., & Monroe, A. (2009). Heart like mine [Recorded by Miranda Lambert]. On *Revolution* [CD]. Nashville, TN: Columbia Nashville.

Television Program ·

Duff, J., Robin, M.M., & Shephard, G. (2006, October 7). To protect & serve [Television series episode]. In J. Duff, M. Robin, and G. Shephard (Executive producers), *The Closer*, Los Angeles: TNT.

WEB SOURCES

Entire Website

In the references list, put (n.d.) where the year usually appears if the website does not include a date when it was created or updated.

Note that APA format does not include a period after the URL.

Format for a Website with an Author

Author, F.M. (Year, Month Date of publication). *Article title.* Retrieved from URL

Limer, E. (2013, October 1). *Heck yes! The first free wireless plan is finally here.* Retrieved from http://gizmodo.com/heck-yes-the-first-free-wireless-plan-is-finally-here-1429566597

Format for a Website with No Author

Article title. (Year, Month Date of publication). Retrieved from URL

Lions' Club International Website. (2006). R. Dickson (Ed.). Retrieved from http://www.lionsclub.org/international/index

Online Book

Cooley, R. D. (2004). *Damages and debris in the divorce world.* Retrieved from http://MELO/divorce/damagesdebdwrld/pub/books

Online Journal and Magazine Articles

If available, use the Digital Object Identifier (DOI) in the reference for a journal article. If there is no DOI available, use the "Retrieved from URL" format.

Author, A. A., & Author, B. B. (Date of publication). Title of article. *Title of Journal,* volume number, page range (if available). doi:0000000/000000000000 or http://dx.doi.org/10.0000/0000

Adam, A., Butler, B., Crawford, C., Dante, D., Ellis, E., & Franklin, F.G. (2006). Why can't we be friends? *Friends and Acquaintances,* 15(3), 22–23. Retrieved from http://friendsandacquaintances/journal/edu_text/V15/15.3adam.html

Online Newspaper Article

Author, A. A. (Year, Month Day). Title of article. *Title of Newspaper.* Retrieved from http://www.someaddress.com/full/url/

Jones, D.J. (1999, January 31). Whatever happened to truth in lending? *New York Times.* Retrieved from http:///wwwnewyorktimes.com/ny-ny/articles/C3234-1999Jan.31html

Blog Post

Lubke, D. (2016, December 30). Storing stuff for other. [Web log post]. Retrieved from http://www.davelubke.com/blog

Blog Comment

Lubke, D. (2016, December 30). Re: Storing stuff for others. [Web log comment]. Retrieved from http://www.davelubke.com/blog

Online Encyclopedia/Dictionary Entries

Encyclopedias and dictionaries often do not include author names. If no author is provided, move the entry name to the front of the citation. Provide the date if possible, or specify (n.d.) if no date is present in the entry.

With Author

Davis, C. (2003). Southern civil rights. In (Editor if available) *World book encyclopedia* (edition if available). Retrieved from http://search.eb.com/eb/entries/southernpolitics/civilrightsinsouth

No Author

Civil Rights. (2003). *World book encyclopedia* (edition if available). Retrieved from http://search.eb.com/eb/article?eu=211987

Government Documents

Centers for Disease Control. (2007, July 29). *Statement on restrictions of travel within and outside of the United States for patients of tuberculosis.* Retrieved from http://www.CDC.gov/agent/tuberculosis/travelrestrictions.asp

Congressional Record Citations and References

U.S. Dept. of Education. (2007). *National standardized test scores for 11th graders.* Retrieved from http://www.deptofeducation.doc.edu/nationaltestscores.pdf

Sample Student Research Essay

Running Head: MISSISSIPPI VETERANS   1

Mississippi Veterans Are Missing Credit

Ryan Braswell

English 1123 RY01

Abstract

After transitioning out of the military, veterans learn that college degrees have nearly become mandatory for significant employment.
Promises of academic credit for service and offers of complete scholarships are commonplace at the federal-government-sponsored Transition
Assistance Programs for soldiers returning to the Magnolia State. The
most significant promise that of academic credit for military experience
is false. Mississippi should implement legislation ensuring service members receive the maximum academic credit for their military experience. Veterans are finding it difficult to receive college credit for their
military service, none more so than those in Mississippi. As veterans
return home, their desire to begin a fruitful career is strong. The startling realization that while their service is appreciated but not accepted
by the Mississippi's institutions of higher learning is enough to destroy
their dreams. Instead of pushing veterans to seek refuge in other states
or leaving them at the whim of various untrained educational staff,
Mississippi should introduce a statewide policy that ensures veterans
will receive adequate college credit for their military training.

Mississippi Veterans Are Missing Credit

After transitioning out of the military, veterans learn that college degrees have nearly become mandatory for significant employment. This emphasis on postsecondary education makes graduating from college the highest priority for Mississippi's returning veterans. Promises of academic credit for service and offers of complete scholarships are commonplace at the federal-government-sponsored Transition Assistance Programs for soldiers returning to the Magnolia State. However, as college student and a veteran of the Armed Forces, I have witnessed firsthand that in Mississippi many of these promises are empty. The most significant promise that of academic credit for military experience is completely false. Mississippi should implement legislation ensuring service members receive the maximum academic credit for their military experience.

When selecting a college, a veteran will soon realize that most schools refuse to award credit for military service (Herrmann, 2008). While training in the military consists of many strenuous hours in a formal classroom and in practical application settings, it is not widely accepted as a viable learning experience by postsecondary institutions (Snead & Anderson, 2010). The reason for this denial can vary, but the fundamental cause behind this action is the institution's failure to comprehend the level of training which occurs in the military (Bradley, 2013). As a result of this failure, many institutions are reluctant to award any substantial amount of credit for fear of compromising accreditation standards or academic integrity (Snead & Anderson, 2010). Reluctance on the part of the institution leads to a sporadic system of evaluating and awarding credit at college. Paul Bradley addresses this random selection process in *Community College Week*: "Each college makes its own decision on how much credit to award. Practices, predictably vary widely, leading to frustration" in the student veteran community (Bradley, 2013). For example, an Army medic may be awarded credit for a basic first aid course at one university but denied that same credit at another.

MISSISSIPPI VETERANS   4

The need for an established system for awarding credit could not be more prevalent.

Often the varying practices are coupled with untrained and overworked staff, making the entire process of evaluating and awarding academic credit even more unreliable. In most cases, a single staff member with many other responsibilities outside of the scope of assessing adult experiential learning is assigned to evaluate military training. The employee has limited options to develop the skills needed to award credit properly, and being that evaluating military credit is not the primary focus of the position, training is not pursued (Herrmann, 2008). In fact, many schools do not even offer a policy outlining the reception of military training as academic credit for the individual to consult when evaluating military transcripts. This absence of direction puts the veteran entirely at the mercy of the untrained staff member, who is neither focused nor prepared for the task at hand. Service members throughout Mississippi, where most institutions have not established a separate military student department or created a military transfer policy in their catalog, are finding that they cannot expect a fair evaluation from the inexpert, freehand staff.

In an effort to assist school official's that evaluate military training the American Council of Education developed guidelines for awarding credit to veterans who completed specific training programs in the military. It has quickly become the standard by which military programs are evaluated and translated into academic recommendations. ACE's Military Guide is the product of several evaluation teams composed of experienced college faculty and military instructors, who make credit hour recommendations for the specific military training regime completed by a veteran (Snead & Anderson, 2010). These credit recommendations are often broad descriptions that allow for interpretation by different institutions. The school official can then evaluate how those credits can be applied to a veteran's program of study at their institution. Even though ACE makes these credit recommendations directly on a military transcript, school officials still refuse to apply those credit hours to a veteran's transcript from lack of guidance by the institution. (Bradley, 2008). When the credit is denied, the service member is not allowed to dispute the decision by demonstrating proficiency in the subjects listed on his/her military transcript. Often the service member is never made aware that no credit was awarded.

Many veterans who have found themselves in similar positions in the past have voiced their concerns to their state legislatures. Several legislatures have responded to the lack of consistency and direction for awarding military credit by implementing policies that improved the reception of military transfer credit at public colleges and universities. Often this legislation focused on the development of a uniformed process or in some cases a state department that would evaluate and award college credit for military service (Liu, 2012). In Texas, for example, Senator Van de Putte authored Texas Senate Bill 1736 to create a comprehensive military credit evaluation program that consists of a coalition of Texas public institutions of higher learning (as cited in Ginn, 2012). This coalition, College Credit for Heroes, uses consistent methodology for evaluating and determining which courses to be awarded college credit at Texas' public universities and colleges (Liu, 2013). A direct policy from state legislation is the only viable way to ensure that all institutions treat military service credit in the same manner.

An efficient methodology of evaluating military service transcripts can decrease the amount of time a service member spends pursuing a degree (Ginn, 2012). This in turn holds several economic advantages for Mississippi, because according to White House statistics, a dramatic increase of service members leaving the military will occur over the next few years. This influx of veterans into the civilian job market coincides with economic reports that show an escalation of employment opportunities for college graduates (as cited in Azziz, 2013). Many of these veterans who are discharging from the military will face challenges that prevent them from obtaining a college degree in a timely manner. With the lack of a college degree preventing new employment and the absence of income from leaving the military, veterans will be

forced to seek financial relief from unemployment offices in their communities. By adjusting the education system in Mississippi to ensure veterans can take advantage of their military training to quickly obtain a degree, the state will be bolstering the work force, while at the same time reducing unemployment in the local population.

Education reform for military students has not gone unnoticed in Mississippi on the institutional level. Several local colleges and universities are beginning to implement programs to improve the military student experience. Both Hinds Community College and Jackson State University have established standalone departments for addressing student veterans' needs. In addition, Copiah-Lincoln Community College has gone as far as to create an entire degree program designed for military students ("New Military-Friendly Degree," 2011). However, these efforts are limited in scope to specific institutions and serve primarily as recruiting techniques for attracting more military students. They do not create a measurable impact on the military community in Mississippi.

Veterans are finding it difficult to receive college credit for their military service, none more so than those in Mississippi. As veterans return home, their desire to begin a fruitful career is strong. The startling realization that while their service is appreciated but not accepted by the Mississippi's institutions of higher learning is enough to destroy their dreams. At the very least, it will send veterans to colleges in other states that are accommodating their needs. Instead of pushing veterans to seek refuge in other states or leaving them at the whim of various untrained educational staff, Mississippi should introduce a statewide policy that ensures veterans will receive adequate college credit for their military training.

MISSISSIPPI VETERANS   7

References

Azziz, R. (2013, September). A call to arms: Academe must meet demands of downsizing military. *DIVERSE: Issues in Higher Education*, 19. Retrieved from http://greport.gru.edu/archives/4663

Bradley, P. (2013, November 11). Forward, march. *Community College Week*. Retrieved from http://ccweek.com/article-3645-cover-story: -forward,-march.html

Ginn, J. (2012, July/August). States find ways to tackle new, and old, problems. *Capitol Ideas*. Retrieved from http://www.csg.org/pubs/ capitolideas/jul_aug_2012/innovativelegislation.aspx

Herrmann, D., Raybeck, D., & Wilson, R.B. (2008, November 21). College is for veterans, too. *Chronicle of Higher Education*. Retrieved from https://www.researchgate.net/publication/220034252_College _Is_for_Veterans_Too

Hoover, E. (2010, March 14). Where life earns credit: "Prior learning" gets a fresh assessment. *Chronicle of Higher Education*, 56(27). Retrieved from http://www.chronicle.com/article/ Where-Life-Earns-Credit-/64618

Liu, M.C. (2012, April). Easing the path to college. *State Legislatures*, 26. Retrieved from http://www.ncsl.org/research/military-and- veterans-affairs/easing-the-path-to-college.aspx

Liu, M.C. (2013, October/November). Helping vets hit the books. *State Legislatures*. Retrieved from www.ncsl.org/Portals/1/Documents/ magazine/ . . . /SL_1013-.pdf

New military-friendly degree offered by Mississippi College. (2011, September 5). *Community College Week*. Retrieved from http:// npaper-wehaa.com/ccweek#2011/09/05/

Snead, K.M. & Anderson, C.L. (2010). Awarding college credit for military training and experience: Campus strategies for adopting ACE Guide credit recommendations. *Duty, Honor, Country . . . & Credit*. Retrieved from files.eric.ed.gov/fulltext/ED524754.pdf

Timed Writing: Writing under Pressure

During your college career, you will probably be called upon at some point to write essays which are composed in a limited time frame, often with no notes or outside sources to help. These essays might be in the form of essay questions on tests in your class.

They might be part of a standardized test such as the Praxis or the Graduate Record Exam when you reach that point in your college education. Or they could be in response to an application for a job or a scholarship. If you have had experience with these types of tests on the American College Test (ACT) or the Scholastic Aptitude Test (SAT) or on standardized tests through your high school years, then you will be ahead of the game in doing well on essay tests and timed writings.

However, if you have not had previous experience, you will need to learn—and learn quickly—how to perform well on timed writing assignments.

Writing an Essay in a Set Amount of Time

Perhaps your previous experience with writing has allowed you to take as much time as you needed to complete your work, with no solid deadlines and no deductions for late papers. In a college setting, you probably will not be afforded such luxury!

Most instructors have a specific time to begin and a specific time to complete an essay; if you begin too late or turn in your paper after the completion date, your grade will suffer. Don't allow chaos to keep you from completing your work on time, as Chapter 3 in this text discusses.

Tackle the Fear

Everyone has some form of fear when it comes to writing. The most common type of fear relating to writing, especially for timed writing, is finishing the assignment in the specified time period. Whether you have to finish the paper by the end of the hour or by the end of the class, each assignment has a strict due date and/or time. Your instructor will typically let you know these details when he or she assigns the writing. Pay attention!

Once you know how long you have to complete the assignment, you can plan a strategy to start and finish it.

Another common anxiety associated with timed writing centers around the content. If you often have trouble focusing on a specific idea for a paper, brainstorm and prewrite first, even if it seems impossible to do in the time period. Write everything you associate with the given topic down. Quickly organize your ideas in a format that makes sense to you.

Once you physically see your ideas written on paper, forming sentences and even paragraphs based on those ideas will seem much less stressful.

The best way to ease timed writing anxiety is to practice. You can find an unlimited number of prompts on the Internet. Choose one and time yourself. The more you practice, the more comfortable you'll be when writing under pressure.

Taking an Essay Test

Essay tests are designed to test your critical thinking skills, your ability to "think on your feet," and your knowledge of subject matter. Luckily, if you have paid attention to the processes taught to you in your composition classes, you can easily handle the first two parts of the requirements mentioned above.

However, obtaining the knowledge necessary to back up the points in your timed essay will come from your attention to the material covered in class and your study habits; slacking off in either area will result in a bad grade that the most impressive writing skills cannot hide. Rephrasing and restating the question, throwing in some big words, and writing in circles will not fool your college instructor, who is looking for substantive facts to support an answer. Don't try to be sneaky by avoiding the prompt: your instructor *will* know if you fail to address the prompt correctly, or if you fail to address the prompt all together.

When taking an essay test, you cannot waste time thinking too long about what you are going to write; you must go with an idea and write because turning in an unfinished—or worse, blank—test is unacceptable. It is equally unacceptable to use the excuse that you do not perform well under pressure in a timed format.

Professors and employers are testing you to see exactly how well you can perform under pressure, so you must develop the skills necessary to write effectively in any situation.

Assuming that you have prepared adequately for the essay test, you must then determine what information the instructor is requesting. A question such as "Discuss the disagreement between Booker T. Washington and W.E.B. DuBois concerning what is necessary for African Americans to be adequately assimilated into white society" is asking for a specific discussion of the main points which these two early activists advocated in their works.

Since you have carefully read both Washington's *Up From Slavery* and DuBois' *The Souls of Black Folk*, as well as studied your notes from class discussion and asked questions of your American literature instructor to clarify unclear areas, you know the main areas of disagreement: voting rights, civic equality, and education. Your answer could easily be set up as a comparison/contrast essay, developing the main points by either the subject-by-subject style or the point-by-point style. Your answer might look something like this:

Booker T. Washington and W.E.B. DuBois were both instrumental in helping the cause of African Americans who were yet to be assimilated into a post-slavery America. However, their approaches to the struggle differed greatly in areas of voting rights, civic equality, and education. Booker T. Washington, born a slave in the South and educated at Hampton Normal School, realized firsthand the struggle that many former slaves and their children would have in the years after the Civil War. In his Atlanta Exposition speech, Washington recommended that African Americans "cast down [their] buckets" where they were to prepare themselves for a future place in American society. To do that, he advocated that they give up for the time being a push for universal suffrage as they developed literacy skills, as they accumulated financial stability, and as they became landowners. Furthermore, he recommended that rather than attempt to compete in white institutions of higher learning, they educate themselves in the trades and in agriculture to improve their community status, and that they establish working relationships with the white citizens who were their neighbors.

W.E.B. DuBois, on the other hand, was born in the North after slavery was abolished; he was educated at Harvard, as well as abroad, and had never experienced slavery firsthand. Though he said that he respected Washington's attempts to guide African Americans, he totally disagreed with Washington's approach. He said that Washington's influence had helped disenfranchise African Americans, had relegated them to an inferior social status, and had allowed unequal support of African-American institutions of higher learning. DuBois ends his argument with the admonition that to prosper in the world, African Americans must have three things: the right to vote, civic equality, and equal education of youth according to ability. Without these privileges, according to DuBois, the African American would have no place in American society.

Most instructors want your essay answer to exhibit all of the skills that have already been required of you in composition classes: grammar, mechanics, and spelling skills reflective of a college-level student. As noted above, using appropriate transitions also moves the essay along, making connections or pointing out differences where necessary.

A word to the wise! No amount of word-smithing can help you if you do not have the information necessary to answer the questions asked, so prepare yourself on the front end with good note-taking skills, with good attendance skills, and with good study skills. Then you'll be able to dazzle your instructor with your critical thinking and organizational skills in writing the required essay.

Developing a Response for a Specialized Assignment outside of the Classroom

At some point, you might have to develop your opinion on a certain subject for an application—for a job, for a scholarship, for a transfer to another institution or a specialized program. You might have to type in a response in an allotted amount of space on the computerized form, or you might be given a certain number of words to respond to the prompt. Pay attention to those word limits! Whoever is assigned the task of reviewing your written response will most likely delete your work or throw your paper in the trash if you go over the word count.

If you feel as if your word count is too low, do not add unnecessary words or phrases just to up the word count. Doing so can only harm the quality of your essay. Again, all of the information you have learned in your composition classes can help you perform this task. Since the thesis statements that you have written on countless essays have all been opinions, you have had lots of experience in formulating and supporting your opinion. You will do the same on this type of task, too.

Let's say that you have received an application for the nursing school you want to attend. You are asked to explain in 200 words or fewer why you want to attend that particular school. Luckily for you, you can take more time in formulating this answer and making sure that you adhere to the word limit. Just as you have done in your composition classes, develop your thesis, stating it first.

In 200 words or fewer, you don't have room for a catchy introduction, so you will have to get to the point, support your thesis, and end. Give some specifics to back up what you have said, and then proofread to make sure that you have no grammatical or spelling errors in your essay. Your essay might look something like this:

> I want to attend the Hinds Community College nursing program because it is the highest rated program in the state, it provides the best access to hospital training, it is very affordable, and it is close to my home. Hinds has the highest pass rate of any of the community college nursing programs in the state, with almost 90% of the students passing the state nursing exam on the first attempt. Furthermore, the school is located adjacent to Merit Hospital, where I will acquire hands-on training in all areas of working in a hospital setting. Because Hinds has made an effort to keep tuition rates low and to provide a variety of scholarships and grants, I can easily afford to attend school without having to take a part-time job to supplement my income. Thus, I can spend time out of class studying and preparing for my future. If those reasons were not enough to make me want to attend Hinds, the convenience of my living at home and not having to move away just further convinces me that the Hinds nursing program is the best one for me.

That answer is a concise 188 words, under the requirement but fully supported. Formulating your thesis, developing your main ideas, and supporting those main ideas will convince the individual reading your application that you should be accepted into the program.

The more confident you are of your writing skills, the easier you will find writing essays in the required time frame, taking essay tests, and filling out applications. The skills that you learn in your composition classes will provide you with the tools you will need in all areas of your college education, as well as in your career after college.

Tips for Writing Assignments Based on Due Date

LONG-TERM ESSAY (Outside of the classroom)	• If the essay is based on a book, play, movie, or any other material, analyze the material carefully. • Start on the assignment early. The earlier you start, the more time you have to edit and perfect your work. • Follow the steps for good writing: prewriting, outlining, solid thesis, good organization, and stellar proofreading.
IN-CLASS ESSAY (Over time)	• If you have any questions about the information that should be included in your writing assignment, ask your instructor. If you are still confused, ask a classmate. • Be focused on your topic and use the time allotted wisely. • Don't goof around when you have work to accomplish. • Follow the steps for good writing: prewriting, outlining, solid thesis, good organization, and stellar proofreading.
SINGLE-SITTING ESSAY	• Brainstorm loosely and quickly. Most of the allotted time must be used on actually writing the paper. • Have a sound thesis sentence. • Write out the rest of your essay and then finish the introduction. This ensures all of the necessary information is written down in case you lose track of time.

Dos and Don'ts in Timed Writing

DO . . .	DON'T . . .
If you are anxious, close your eyes and take a deep breath to relax.	Don't let the time tick by as you stare at a blank screen or out the window.
Brainstorm: Doing so organizes your ideas.	Don't write your stream of consciousness with no plan for organizing your thoughts.
Edit after you finish writing (if time allows), but at least proofread.	Don't waste leftover time by not proof-reading your work.

Business Correspondence

The ability to communicate effectively ranks among the top skills that employers are seeking, according to numerous surveys each year. Listening, writing, and speaking effectively can determine success in your career.

Many will judge your expertise in your field based on your ability to communicate effectively. Often, the first stages of a business relationship are formed solely through letters and email exchanges. If your letters contain spelling errors, the reader might conclude that since you are the sort of individual who doesn't pay attention to detail, you will likely miss the finer points of other business dealings.

Paying careful attention to the wording and content of your written correspondence will polish your professional image.

You are already using email, instant messaging, and text messaging as your primary means of written correspondence, but you will continue to use these means of communication in the workplace in a more business-like manner.

Language

Business and academic writing are more *formal* and must follow the rules and patterns of standard English. Informal language and abbreviations that you use for private communication are not acceptable in college writing, nor are they acceptable in the workplace.

EMOTICONS

You might email a friend to offer congratulations on a new job and follow that message with a smiley face emoticon. However, you should never use these images in business correspondence.

TEXT LANGUAGE

Have you ever sent a text message similar to the following: "R U kidding? LOL." Abbreviations that allow you to text a friend quickly should not be used in a college paper or any business communications, including letters, text messages, or emails.

SLANG

Everyday language that you use with friends and family is often informal and sometimes grammatically incorrect. If you are emailing a business associate in Singapore, can you be certain he or she will understand if you reply to a message with, "She's buggin"? If you like a certain movie, you might say, "The last *Avengers* movie was so sick!" But in writing, you should *never* use slang expressions of this sort.

POMPOSITY

Perhaps you've used a thesaurus while writing papers. This tool can be very beneficial to a writer, but when it is overused, communication suffers. Never use overblown language that sounds smart: "The cinematic endeavor enlightened my mind concerning the realities of viral epidemics in our execrable universe." It would be much better to write, "That movie discussed fatal viral epidemics."

CAPITALIZATION

Don't type your business correspondence in all capital letters. IF YOU USE ALL CAPS, YOU APPEAR TO SCREAM OR SHOUT AT YOUR AUDIENCE.

PUNCTUATION

With business and academic writing, you do need to pay close attention to small details. In a text message to a friend you might omit punctuation, but you don't have that option with a business message. Correct use of apostrophes and commas does matter.

Be Sure to Proofread!

Every form of written communication, whether submitted in the course of a business transaction or a college assignment, should be proofread very carefully. There are several effective methods for proofreading your work.

READ ALOUD

Slow down and read your message aloud. Listen to how the email or letter sounds. If you are uncertain about whether a particular idea is clear, read a passage aloud to someone else or record yourself reading it. It is always a good idea to get a fresh perspective. A new reader may even catch on to mistakes that are not be apparent to you.

LET THE MANUSCRIPT "COOL OFF"

Business correspondence should be completed in a very timely manner. However, if your reply doesn't need to be sent immediately, write your message, put it aside for an hour or so, and then read it again. Errors will usually be much easier to spot when looked at with fresh eyes.

READ BACKWARDS

Read from the last paragraph to the first. This method enables you to read for grammar and structure rather than content. Try this method when you must write under pressure.

Starting with the last word—not paragraph or sentence—and then reading backwards is a great way to review spelling and word choice. This works well in short emails.

Emails and Text Messaging

Much business correspondence is conducted "on the go" from a PDA portable digital device. The swiftness and ease with which these messages can be sent should not lull you into thinking that this writing can be as informal as your personal text messages.

For business and academic writing, you must hold yourself to a higher standard. Here are several important points to consider when you use email in a professional setting:

EMAIL ID

You probably have a personal email account established already. Does your account have a name that makes you sound like a serious student or a respected professional? If your ID is "sweetcheeks32" or "chillinDC," you should create a new account that identifies you as a professional. It is a good idea to keep it simple, limiting it to consist of variations of your first, middle, and last name. For example, if your name is Mark Jones, something along the lines of "mark.jones@hostname" or "mjones@hostname" would be an acceptable email ID. If you have an email account provided to you through your college, use it.

RESPOND IN A TIMELY MANNER

Get in the habit of checking your email regularly and responding promptly. If a teacher or potential employer takes the time to contact you by email, you can expect assume that he or she expects you to respond before the next class meeting!

CAREFULLY USE THE "REPLY" BUTTON

When you respond to an email, don't use the "New" message button. Instead, use "Reply." This option allows the original sender the chance to review the information s/he originally requested of you.

Be very, very careful not to use the "Reply All" button when replying to one person.

USE THE SUBJECT LINE

Teachers and other business professionals are extremely busy. Providing a brief statement of the content of the email in the subject line helps your recipient to grasp your message more quickly. In order to do so, think of the main point of the email and condense it into one sentence or phrase. If the purpose of an email is about inquiring about whether or not your teacher can reopen a homework assignment, the subject line could read "Homework assignments 4.1 and 4.2."

BEGIN AND END WITH TRADITIONAL FORMS

Resist the urge just to launch into your message/reply. Instead, identify the individual you are writing, as you would in a letter (Dear Mr. Kraus). At the end of your message, include a closing before typing your name (Regards, Sincerely, etc.).

When quickly replying to a prior email, be careful not to launch into the message with an informal tone or email format. It's easy to do, but the potential employer may be looking for someone who is steadfastly attentive to details.

KEEP IT SIMPLE

Limit the content of your email. If the message is extremely detailed, a letter might be a better choice for correspondence. Discuss only one key idea per paragraph and use numbered or bulleted lists when appropriate. Condense the information enough to get your point across without any unnecessary information.

DON'T BE TOO FAMILIAR

Avoid silly jokes or sarcasm in your messages. Often, these don't translate well into the written word. Keep it professional. Remember that no one can hear the tone of your voice in an email.

DON'T FORWARD CHAIN LETTERS.

Email at work and in college should be used for business only. Don't forward these messages to anyone or group email. People will respond more freely when addressed one-on-one.

COUNT TO 3

If you have a negative message, don't ever fire off an email in a huff. In all forms of business and academic communication, you must maintain professionalism. Consider the consequences of doing so because one angry email may create a firestorm of negative responses.

HAVE A PROFESSIONAL EMAIL SIGNATURE

Many of us use the automatic signature in our emails. Be sure that your email signature matches the professionalism you are trying to portray. Anything too informal should be changed in business correspondence.

USE COMMON SENSE

Emails are written records of business that are the legal property of that business. Emails can be subpoenaed in court cases and have been used in hiring and firing decisions. Do not ever make unkind statements about your place of business, a teacher, or a colleague in an email. Do not spread rumors and do not gossip.

TIPS TO REMEMBER:

- Remember whom you're addressing/your audience.
- Think like the employer or whomever you're addressing: What would you think if you were in their place?
- Consider the consequences of your responses or actions.

Social Networking Sites: A Warning

Being able to develop a network of friends and professionals is one of the positive benefits of a college education. More than likely, you are among the 7.5 million college students who spend time on Facebook or similar social networking sites. These are fantastic tools for keeping in touch with friends and for building a network of professionals. However, it is vital to exercise caution concerning what you decide to post to these sites.

As an adult, you already know that you shouldn't post personal information that could put you in harm's way. You should also be very judicious in the photos and comments that you post to your profile.

In fact, businesses and college scholarship committees use Facebook and similar sites to screen applicants. Research completed by Microsoft in December 2009 found that 79 percent of the 1,200 hiring managers and job recruiters surveyed had used online information for screening applicants. Seventy percent reported using an online reputation to eliminate applicants.

You might be under the impression that recruiters or future employers will not be able to gain access to your profile. However, can you be absolutely certain that every person you have "friended" is going to use the information on your site in the right manner? What if one of those individuals happens to work for a company where you recently applied? Would you want that company to know what's on your profile? Be cautious of who you choose to be able to view your social media profiles.

Employers report eliminating candidates for the following reasons:

- Inappropriate pictures
- Poor communication skills
- Apparent lies about skills/training
- Drug/alcohol use or abuse
- Criminal activity

You are enrolled in college and working hard so that you can pursue a career. Make certain that your online reputation matches the image you wish to portray to future employers. Before posting on social media, ask yourself if you'd be okay with a potential employer seeing it. Once a photo or statement is online, it cannot be completely removed. It lasts forever.

Business Letters

The business letter is still a primary means of communication in the workplace. Therefore, reviewing the parts of a standard business letter is a good idea. Remember, also, that all business letters are single-spaced, with double spaces between paragraphs and sections. This is the standard format.

HEADING

The heading consists of two parts: your return address and the date, with no spaces between. Don't include your name at the top of the letter. If you are writing a business letter, you will probably have letterhead, preprinted stationery that already has your return address included. In that case, just begin with the date. After the date, double space lines (hit the Enter key twice).

> **NOTE:** Pre-printed stationery (with the inside address) was more common before email became the primary means of communication and is still used as official correspondence in some businesses and law firms. Pre-printed stationery is becoming obsolete but has not left the workplace.

INSIDE ADDRESS

The name and complete mailing address of the individual to whom you are writing come next. Use four-digit zip code extensions if you know them. For states, use the two-letter state abbreviations. Double space.

SALUTATION

Use a title (Dr., Mrs., Ms., Mr., Miss) plus a surname (Dear Ms. Hall), or write directly to an individual (Dear Monika Hall). If you do not have a name of an individual, write: Dear Sir or Madam. If you are unsure which salutation to use for a woman, use "Ms." to avoid offending the recipient. After your salutation, type a colon and double space.

Addressing a letter "To Whom It May Concern" was popular fifty years ago. In the era of Internet searches and transparency, you are expected to be able to find a specific name to use in the salutation. However, if you are writing to an unnamed groups—a committee, for example—"To Whom It May Concern" is acceptable.

Do not leave the salutation line empty.

BODY

Type all parts of the letter, including each body paragraph, flush with the left margin and single spaced. Do not indent. Keep the paragraphs short, with one important piece of information in each. Double space between paragraphs.

COMPLEMENTARY CLOSE

The most common closing for a letter is the word "sincerely," capitalized and followed by a comma. Insert four blank lines after the closing for the hand-written signature. Fewer lines are needed if you insert a signature with a cursive font.

SIGNATURE

The signature requires two parts. First, type your name at the bottom of the letter. Then, after you print your letter, use a blue pen to write your signature in the four spaces that appear just above your typed name. A blue pen is standard and sets a contrast with the black toner/ink color.

Do not use metallic pens. If a blue pen is not available, use a black pen.

FULL BLOCK FORM

Full block form is the most common format for business letters. To use full block form, start all parts of the letter at the left margin. Do not tab or indent. Do not justify the right margin. Although full block is the most common, a hybrid of forms is also acceptable. Just be sure to include all of the necessary information and elements of a business letter.

STATE ABBREVIATIONS

Be careful. "Ms." is not the abbreviation for "Mississippi"; it is a title of address for a woman. The state abbreviations are two capital letters without periods: MS, TN, KY, and so on.

SHORT LETTERS

Position your letter so that the text is centered lengthwise your page.

Heading. . . . .
409 Rosewood Rd.
Jackson, MS 39201
February 10, 2013

Inside Address. . . . .
Ms. Lindsey McGrath
McGrath, Morgan, & Company
1513 Capital St.
Jackson, MS 39211-1513

Salutation . . . .
Dear Ms. McGrath:

Body . . . .
Thank you for this business opportunity. I would be delighted to join you and your team during the upcoming company merger.

I know how difficult it can be to accomplish a successful unification. I will send an outline of a strategy I believe will ease the process.

Please let me know of any modifications you wish to make before we meet next week.

What time should we meet Monday morning? Please send your reply by email to nvmorrison@gmail.com.

Sincerely,

Nathan Morrison

Nathan Morrison

Special Note

For many years, Killian Advertising has included a section on its website entitled "Cover Letters from Hell." Reading only a few selections from this site will convince you of the importance of creating a flawless résumé and cover letter.

Visit http://www.killianbranding.com/cover-letters-from-hell for these examples.

Résumé

A résumé lists your accomplishments, endeavors, and skills. This document can be used to secure an interview for a job and is also very important when beginning a scholarship search.

While you are still a student, you should keep an regularly updated copy of your résumé for several reasons.

- Most scholarship applications require you to send a listing of your academic accomplishments and endeavors.

- When you ask a teacher or other individual for a letter of recommendation, a copy of the résumé assists the person with completing the letter.

- If you hear of a job opening, chances are that you will be competing with many other students for the same part-time work position. With an up-to-date résumé on hand, you will be able to react quickly to opportunities as they arise.

Many companies offer their expertise in crafting résumés—for a hefty price. However, if you are just beginning your job or scholarship search, you don't need to spend a lot of money to create a pleasing product. Many online sites offer examples and suggestions for crafting your own résumé. Also, your college English writing lab, Workforce Development Center, or student work study office can assist you.

APPEARANCE

The résumé should be flawless. One spelling error could make the difference in a committee or employer decision.

- Don't use flowery fonts or colored paper. Use Arial as your font; it works best when you must send an electronic copy. Often organizations will scan résumés into their computer system, and Arial creates a more pleasing scanned copy.

- Use white space. White space enables the reader to focus on one bit of information at a time. One easy way to create a nice product is to create a table into which you will type your information. Then, you can simply hide the gridlines of the table.

- Organize in reverse chronological order or from your most recent accomplishments back to high school.

- Restrict your résumé to one single-sided page in length if possible. Fear not if you have an overwhelming list of jobs or activities. The information on your resume can be condensed based on the position you're applying for. List only information relevant to the anticipated field or position.

PARTS OF THE RÉSUMÉ

Résumés can be organized in numerous ways. If you do not have an extensive employment history, you may wish to develop a skills-based résumé, organized into sections discussing your abilities and methods by which you developed these skills.

The most common format for a résumé is the chronological format. A chronological résumé. can include the following information (in no one set order):

Heading

Center your name, address, and phone number (with area code) at the top of the page. If you are living in a dorm or apartment while in college, you might also include/add your permanent address. To guard against identity theft, do not include your Social Security number or birth date on the résumé.

Objective and/or Career Goals

Give a succinct statement of what you are trying to accomplish by sending the résumé. This can also be included in a cover letter when it is accompanied by a résumé.

> *Objective:* To obtain part-time employment while studying full time at Mississippi College.

Education

If you are completing your education, start with your current college and work backward to high school. Give dates of attendance, major, grade point average (if 3.0 or higher), degrees conferred, and date of graduation. For high school, just include the institution you graduated from and the graduation year.

If the GPA in your major is higher than your overall GPA, emphasize this positive difference in your resume. Most potential employers focus on academic qualifications that apply to a future profession.

Skills/Talents

List certifications, such as life saving or CPR, as well as expertise in software or other technical training. If you have studied more than one language, you can include that information in this section.

Volunteer Experience

Increasingly, scholarship criteria require students to show their commitment and service to their communities. Also, employers are seeking well-rounded individuals who have donated their time to important causes. Keep an accurate record of your service endeavors as well as names of contacts within each group. Do not neglect listing civic and church activities in which you had a supervisory role.

Languages

List languages in which you are fluent.

Work Experience

List jobs starting from the most recent. For each, give dates of employment, employer's name, your position, and, most importantly, your duties. If you have never been employed, you will want to consider developing a skills-based résumé. Many examples are available online. If you have held many jobs, include the most recent or the most relevant to the business or organization to which you are submitting your résumé.

Military

If you have served in the military or have been in ROTC, mention this on your résumé. Give dates, branch of service, rank, and any special training. Employers are impressed with the discipline that the military imbues into their recruits.

Scholarships/Awards

Give the names of all scholarships you have received while enrolled at your college and any honors, such as Dean's or President's List. Work your way back to high school awards and recognitions.

Activities

List membership in clubs and honor societies (such as Phi Theta Kappa or Mu Alpha Theta). Be certain to include any leadership roles that you have held in the organizations.

Felony Conviction

If you have been convicted of a felony, you should include this on your résumé. You do not need to specify what you were convicted of but you do need to mention that you were convicted to avoid future problems with the organization to which you are submitting your résumé.

> **NOTE:** The format and information within your résumé is dependent on your experiences. Each résumé is unique because no two people have the exact same skill set, education, or work experience.

LIST OF REFERENCES

Ask three people who know you well if you may include them in your list of references. Make sure these people can make positive statements about your skills and abilities. Do not choose family members or former employers. References that are professionals, especially those related to whatever job or field you are pursuing are even better to list. This list should consist of no more than four references. Then, list each person's name, title, address, and phone number, and email address at which s/he may be reached. A business email would be preferred, if the person has an email address at all. This page of references can be separate from the résumé and should be polished and available to mail on request.

This page should be full-sized, of course. The references list can be centered.

Business Etiquette for the Interview (and Afterwards?)

Some people sleep with a cell phone in their hands, but cell phones should disappear when a job interview occurs. Your cell phone should be silenced and tucked completely away so that you cannot see it. *Concentrate on the interview, not on the cell phone.* Look the interviewer in the eyes and never glance at a phone.

If you are invited to lunch or dinner, keep your cell completely put away. Do not show that you have a cell phone addiction until after you are hired. If your boss takes calls and texts, that's fine—it may be a test to see if you will do the same. Do not give in.

The Dos and Don'ts in the Workplace
(both before and after you land the job)

DO . . .	DON'T . . .
Be polite and amiable.	Let a bad attitude or chaotic day get in the way of a great opportunity.
Dress appropriately.	Ignore the dress guidelines often set by the employer.
Be punctual.	Be fewer than 5 minutes early (if you can help it).
Turn your cell phone to "silent" mode.	Text or take a phone call during an interview.
Show gratitude for the job opportunity.	Be disheartened if you're ineligible for the job.

Résumé Example

FIONA B. FORREST
113 Kashmir Cove
Ridgeland, MS 39257
Home: (662) 544-6010
Cell: (601) 867-5390
Email: fforresty@go.hindscc.edu

OBJECTIVE:
To gain experience in a prospective career field.

EDUCATION:
Hinds Community College, Raymond, MS GPA: 4.0/4.0
Currently enrolled; Major: Language Communications
Terry High School, Terry. MS ACT: 20
Diploma Received: May 2013, GPA: 3.55/4.0

ACTIVITIES:
Ultimate Frisbee Intramural Team Captain, Hinds CC Raymond
Phi Theta Kappa Vice President
President, Hinds Spanish Club
Terry High School Tennis Team Player
Terry High School Debate Team Captain
National Honor Society, 2011–2013
President, Cultural Awareness Society

HONORS/AWARDS:
Dean's List Scholar
President's List Scholar
Who's Who Among American High School Students

SPECIAL SKILLS:
Fluent in written and conversational Spanish
Fluent in written and conversational French
Proficient using Microsoft Office
Basic web page design skills

CERTIFICATIONS:
Certified in CPR and First Aid
Microsoft Office Specialist Certification

VOLUNTEER EXPERIENCE:
CARA—Jackson, MS
Volunteer Spring 2012–2014
Terry High School Terry, MS
Volunteer, Translator for foreign exchange students, 2011–2013

WORK EXPERIENCE:
FAT CAT ART CAFE—Ridgeland, MS
Assistant Manager, Fall 2012–2013

References Example

Personal References

Mr. Stephen Gust
Business Owner
Arrowhead Printers
703 Stardust Lane
Los Angeles, CA 90005
(213) 974-3211
steph.gust@arrowmail.com

Ms. Monica Tribbiani
Biology Instructor
Hinds Community College
P.O. Box 78
Raymond, MS 39153
(601) 857-3784
m.tribbiani@hindscc.edu

Dr. Jesse Tanner
Superintendent
Pandori Public School District
401 Newark Drive
Greensboro, NC 27403
(336) 373-2549
jtanner@ppsd.edu

Cover Letter

What do you do if your friend tells you about that super job where he or she works? Or, what do you do if you read of the perfect position in the classified ads of a newspaper? The first thing to do is to send your possible future employer a résumé. However, you never send the résumé only; you also need to send a cover letter, a résumé, and, after being granted an interview, a follow-up letter.

A résumé gives detailed information about you, but a cover letter tells everything else—how you heard about the job, why you want the position, and what you have to offer the company. This letter, always sent with a résumé, may very well be the most important one you'll ever write, for it may make the difference in whether or not a company considers your résumé. This is your opportunity to sell yourself to a future employer. Remember, this letter must be *flawless*, so you might want to consider having a friend or a staff member at your English lab help you to proofread. Divide your cover letter into at least three paragraphs.

1. **Background.** In this paragraph introduce yourself and tell how you heard about the position. Also, be specific about which position you are seeking.

2. **Highlights of résumé.** The next paragraph gives the brightest points found on the résumé and invites the individual to read your résumé. Sound positive about your abilities, but be wary of tone. You don't want to sound like a braggart or to sound insincere. (For example: "Your world-class company needs a bright, intelligent young entrepreneur like me heading up the Public Relations office.")

3. **Request an interview.** Request an interview at the employer's convenience. However, if you are in classes or work during certain hours of the day, give the hours that you will be available. Then, give a phone number where you can easily be reached. Finally, thank the reader for his or her time and consideration. Some companies prefer virtual interview via a phone or video call. Make sure you inquire about which type of interview the company in question prefers.

Cover Letter Example

P. O. Box 348
Raymond, MS 39154-9799
21 February 2010

Ms. Joycelyn Reeves
Personnel Director
Williams Pharmaceuticals
P. O. Box 329
Jackson, MS 39209

Dear Ms. Reeves:

Our Director of Student Placement at Hinds Community College informed me that you are looking for a part-time lab assistant. Please consider me for this position because the skills learned in this job will be invaluable in my future career.

I am presently enrolled at Hinds Community College where I have maintained a 3.8 grade point average. I am serving as President of the Hinds Biology Club and am currently enrolled in my third lab science course at the college. Also, I won the Biology Award my senior year in high school. You will see additional information about my background on the enclosed résumé.

I would appreciate an interview at your convenience. After 2:00 p.m. I have no classes and can be reached at 601-373-4572. I hope to hear from you soon.

Sincerely,

Julie Smith

Julie Smith

Follow-up Letter

After you are granted an interview, sending the interviewer a follow-up letter is always a good idea. Because numerous people usually apply for one position, you will want to remind the interviewer of your special qualifications for the job. Also, the letter is a courtesy and shows you to be very organized. Let two or three days elapse between the interview and the letter. Address the letter to the person who interviewed you; out of respect, include this person's job title in your inside address. Then, be certain to include the following:

1. **Thank you.** Begin paragraph one by thanking the person again for your interview. Give the specific date. Try to refer to one important or personal idea that you discussed on that day.

2. **Reminder or regrets.** Remind the reader of your interest in the position or let the reader know that you have accepted another position elsewhere. End with a final, brief expression of appreciation.

Follow-up Letter Example #1

P. O. Box 348
Raymond, MS 39154
3 March 2010

Mr. James Ridgeway
Administrative Assistant
Williams Pharmaceuticals
P. O. Box 329
Jackson, MS 39209

Dear Mr. Ridgeway:

Thank you again for my interview on February 26, 2010. I enjoyed our conversation about my home state of Colorado and our common love of snow boarding.

You certainly know of my interest in the opening that Williams Pharmaceuticals has for a part-time lab assistant. I hope that you will carefully consider my qualifications as you review the candidates for the position. Again, thank you for your time and consideration.

Sincerely,

Julie Smith

Julie Smith

Follow-up Letter Example #2

202 Windmill Drive
Raymond, MS 39154-9799
27 February 2017

Ms. Amanda Kazowsky
Administrative Assistant
Grant's Pharmaceuticals
P.O. Box 239
Jackson, MS 39209

Dear Ms. Kazowsky:

Thank you again for my interview on February 21, 2017. I really meeting you and discussing how much Hinds has changed in the last ten years.

You are certainly aware of my interest in the opening that Grant's Pharmaceuticals has for a part-time lab assistant. I hope you will carefully consider my qualifications as you review candidates for the position. Again, thank you so much for your time and consideration.

Sincerely,

Linda Kaur

Linda Kaur

One Last Piece of Advice about the World of Work

If the boss is a jerk, get over it. First of all, don't you think there's a good chance that your boss's boss knows what's going on? If so, just keep your head down and do the work. Usually, if you put in maximum effort and produce excellent results, someone in the company is going to take notice. Either you will get promoted or your jerky boss will get the heave-ho. It happens all the time.

—Suze Orman

Chapter 24

Literary Analysis and Approaches

You may wonder why you are being called upon to write essays that focus on analyzing a piece of literature. One reason your teacher might give is that the core classes for most community college degree programs and many college or university majors require that you take at least one semester of literature to graduate. Being adept at analyzing the literature you read in your sophomore level classes will improve your grade in the future.

Also, although a Composition II class will not satisfy that literature requirement mentioned above, it will prepare you for the task of reading and understanding the works incorporated into whichever literature class you take, thus improving your grade.

Another reason your teacher might give is that such analysis requires critical thinking skills, advancing the level of skill which you have already developed in Comp. I. Good critical thinking skills are necessary in any program in any discipline; consequently, even if you are not an English major, you will still benefit from this approach.

Though you may not realize it, you already have experience in analyzing different forms of literature. For instance, when you see a movie with a friend, you probably discuss the movie afterwards, critiquing everything from the characters' actions, to the development of the plot, to the believability of the conclusion. You may have loved the film, and your friend may have hated it, or vice versa. You will argue your points; your friend will argue his or hers.

The same type of discussion may occur with a television show or the last Harry Potter novel. In those situations, you probably feel very comfortable with your opinions, and you probably feel very safe in expressing them, even if they differ from your friend's view. Unfortunately, many students approach literary analysis with much anxiety, feeling that their skills are inadequate to assess and critique a work in a literature book. That simply is not true; you have all of the abilities and tools necessary to analyze a literary work, and to do so skillfully and accurately.

To be a confident reader and writer, you must have a good understanding of the work to be discussed. You might have seen the movie that you so enjoyed or read the novel that engaged your attention more than one time, each time seeing something different which added to your understanding. You must be prepared to do the same thing in approaching a work of literature for analysis.

The first reading introduces you to the characters and a general understanding of the plot. The second reading should take you deeper, causing you to question elements of character or plot. Why does Faith, the young wife of Goodman Brown in that story by Nathaniel Hawthorne, wear *pink* ribbons in her hair? To whom is Montresor speaking in Edgar Allan Poe's "The Cask of Amontillado"? To whom is Robert Browning's Duke of Ferrara speaking in "My Last Duchess"? Answers to these questions inform the plots of each of those works, but you won't have the answers if you don't ask the questions.

Even after a second reading, you might say to yourself, "I don't get it!" Read the work again, asking yourself why an author would have chosen that word or that phrase or that detail. Robert Frost repeats the last two lines of "Stopping by Woods on a Snowy Evening." Why does he do that? Frost knew lots of rhyming words, so probably it wasn't because he just ran out of rhymes. I doubt, too, that he was just tired of that poem and was ready to move on. In reading that poem carefully, more than one time, you will realize Frost's intent, which will help you get to the bottom of his meaning.

As you gain confidence as a reader, you will begin to trust your interpretation and assessment. As long as you stay within the work, not going far afield to pull some random ideas or interpretation out of thin air, your interpretation is as valid as anyone else's. However, be sure that you have read carefully and thoughtfully first to ensure your understanding of the work.

Hopefully, this course will increase your enjoyment of those works that you have avoided in the past, thinking yourself incapable of deciphering them. Some of the works you will surely like immediately, even without delving deeper. Others you might not like quite so much, even after having a full understanding of what is going on.

Either way, it is necessary that you realize now, before you step into a literature class, that there is often a difference between *liking* and *appreciating* a work. Even if you do not like the work from the standpoint of personal enjoyment, you should be able to *appreciate* its literary worth. That's the sign of a mature reader.

Critical Approaches to Literary Analysis

When you write a critical analysis essay—or a "critique"—about a piece of literature, whether it is prose, poetry, or drama, you are analyzing some aspect of that work. You may be analyzing a particular character, the importance of the setting, the most important theme, the imagery or figurative language, or some other area. Chapters in the literary section of this book can help you deal with specific types of analysis. Before you begin, though, it might help you to know a bit about what "criticism" actually means when applied to a piece of literature, and what some of the more popular approaches to literary criticism are.

CRITICISM: NOT ALWAYS NEGATIVE

When you are asked to write literary criticism, you are not being asked to look only for negatives in the work, as the word "criticism" often implies in other contexts. In fact, your main experience with artistic "criticism" at this point might be the comments that your instructor has written on your essays; although you might see those as negative, the instructor is actually "critiquing" your work, assessing and analyzing how it is put together. In approaching a piece of literature, you, too, might very well end up writing some negative comments in your essay about the assigned work, about the believability of a character, or about the development of theme. However, the term "criticism" as it applies to the arts means evaluation, judgment, or analysis.

Using your critical thinking skills, you will become the critic and examine the work, usually a specific aspect of the work for a freshman composition essay, to determine what it means, how it is put together, and what components are most worthwhile. Through the years, critics who study literature have developed many different approaches to help this examination. Below are some of the most common ones, though there are many others as well.

HISTORICAL APPROACH

In the historical approach, the critic looks at the historical environment in which the literary work took place and the time in which the author was writing. Taking such an approach can be very valuable when looking at a literary piece written in the distant past. For instance, Kate Chopin's "The Story of an Hour" was written in the late 1800s, a time when women had few, if any, rights. To understand fully why Louise Mallard, the main character in that story, rejoices that her kind, good husband is dead, you must look at Mrs. Mallard's life within her marriage and at what freedom from that life would mean to a woman in that time period.

If you wanted to go further with that examination, you could look at the **biographical** details of Chopin's life, which might help you further analyze the story. Chopin said that she would have never been able to become a writer if her husband had not died young. How would that biographical fact influence your understanding of the story? Twenty-first century students who do not take a work in the context of the time in which it was written often miss vital clues that would help them discover an author's meaning.

Psychological Approach

We all have some experience with this approach; we're quite comfortable analyzing the motivations of our friends and family, and we often speculate on what drives their actions. Just as we analyze our friends and family, we can also use this approach to analyze the motivations or actions of a character. Some critics extend the psychological examination to include a study of the author and his/her motivation in handling such a subject, combining psychology with the biographical approach mentioned above.

The psychological approach is used often in analyzing both the works and the life of Edgar Allan Poe. Poe's characters always have mental aberrations: strange obsessions, unrelenting thoughts of revenge, or unmanageable anger, to name a few. Examining those mental aberrations from a psychological standpoint, whether it be that of Freud or some other theorist, lends a new perspective to the work. The narrator in "The Tell-Tale Heart" obviously exhibits an obsession with the "evil eye" of the old man for whom he works. The critic/essayist can analyze that obsession from a psychological standpoint to determine whether our narrator is, in fact, mad—a condition that he denies repeatedly. Another psychological approach might be to examine Poe's own unique life and background; knowing and understanding the reasons behind his obsession with the deaths of beautiful young women might inform an interpretation of "The Raven" or "Annabel Lee."

Archetypal/Mythological Approach

The archetypal/mythological approach requires a working knowledge of mythology and of archetypes that have been identified in all centuries and all lands and all cultures, and it's an approach still used today in films and literature. One of the most popular archetypes is the journey. Popular movies such as *The Hangover*, *National Lampoon's Vacation*, and *O Brother, Where Art Thou?* all utilize the journey motif in their plots.

Throughout literary history, the journey has been a popular plot element. From Beowulf, who travels to Geatland to hunt down Grendel, to Phoenix Jackson, who travels to Natchez to get medicine for her grandson, the journey by a hero or heroine on a quest in search of something important has been a prominent feature in literature for centuries. In Eudora Welty's "A Worn Path," old Phoenix, the traveler on the journey, has obstacles to overcome before she can complete her quest and return home. These obstacles can be symbolic, magical, or literal, as they most often are in the case of Phoenix and her journey.

Many times, a standard number of obstacles appear—often three—which our hero or heroine must surmount. In some works the traveler must lose his quest, sacrificing himself or herself for the greater good. Harry Potter's willingness to die—to sacrifice himself to rid the wizarding world of Voldemort in the last of J. K. Rowling's series—is a good example of this plot element. A background in archetypes and/or mythology, as well as the standard symbols involved in each, would help you interpret a literary work using this approach.

Reader-Response Approach

This critical approach requires the reader to bring his or her own background and experiences to the table in analyzing a work. Because we all have life experiences that have an impact on our reactions to or opinions on a subject, the interpretations of students within a class will often vary in literary analysis. For instance, an older, nontraditional student who has gone through a messy divorce might be scornful of Shakespeare's "Sonnet 116" and its look at unconditional, unwavering love; he or she might argue from personal experience that "[L]ove is not love / which alters when it alteration finds" (2–3) is not a realistic picture of relationships. On the other hand, a traditional 18-year-old experiencing first love might be completely in agreement with Shakespeare's views, accepting that "[L]ove alters not with his brief hours and weeks, / But bears it out even to the edge of doom" (11–12). Both opinions are valid, but each is governed by the experiences of the critic/essayist.

Likewise, a victim of child abuse might see a darker picture in Theodore Roethke's "My Papa's Waltz," but a reader who experienced a happy childhood might focus on the narrator's memory as presented in the poem as a happy one. The persona in that poem tells us that he "hung on like death" (3); the critic/essayist must interpret that phrase to determine whether the "small boy" (2) is trying to keep the dance from ending or whether he is trying to keep from being injured. Is he desperately happy, or just desperate, as he is "clinging" (16) to his papa's shirt? The reader-response approach encourages you to use your own experiences in your critique, but you must always stay within the confines of the work in any interpretation and not read into the literary piece a meaning that can't be defended.

As mentioned in the chapter entitled "Writing about Drama, Poetry, Film, and Books" later in this book, you must always identify the work and the author early in your essay, and you must never, ever refer to the author by his/her first name! You will always use the first and last name with the first reference and the last name after that. Also, make sure that you punctuate the titles of the literary works correctly; short stories and most poems require quotation marks, and most dramas and very long poems, like *Paradise Lost*, require italics.

We all become critics when we approach a piece of art, whether we're looking for a new painting to hang in our living rooms or a movie to watch on a Saturday night. Your ability to criticize a literary work requires the same critical thinking skills that you apply in any other writing class. Follow your instructor's lead in the approach that you take in doing so. Different approaches to literary analysis require different approaches to writing your literary critique essay. You might like one approach more than another, or you might choose to explore some of the other approaches to literary criticism not mentioned here. Again, your instructor will direct you on the approach to take as part of the essay assignment. With thoughtful analysis and careful reading—more than one time, of course—you can be as astute a critic as one who gets the big bucks for writing in *The New Yorker*!

Chapter 25

Writing a Literary Analysis Essay

When you write the essay, consider that you are writing to an audience who has read the literary work you are analyzing but who hasn't thought about the specific ideas that you will discuss in your essay. In other words, you are not summarizing the literary work in your body paragraphs. You are providing unique insights about the work. Although you could briefly summarize the work in your introduction, you do have to point out specific passages from the work and explain your ideas about those passages.

Once you have read and reread the work you wish to analyze, you should use the following steps to help you write the essay:

1. mark up (annotate) the work

2. brainstorm

3. choose your topic, your thesis, and your body paragraphs' points

4. write an outline

5. write the essay

6. revise the essay

Refer to the documentation chapters and the plagiarism chapter to guide you in writing the essay. Note that the integrity/plagiarism chapter has a section of examples relating to the literary analysis.

Mark up the Work! Annotate!

Marking up or annotating the work means to make notes on the poem, short story, or play that you will analyze. Identify literary devices; make notes about the meaning of the work; make comments about your opinion of the work. Eventually, though, you should guide your thoughts to how the author gets across the work's message.

Brainstorm

Identify specific passages that you think are relevant. You also may want to brainstorm on your body paragraph points once you have chosen them. This type of brainstorming can be simply making notes about your points and listing relevant passages on scratch paper.

Choose Your Topic, Thesis, and Body Paragraphs

Choosing a topic can be a difficult task. Your instructor may give you a list of topics to choose from, or you may be free to choose your own. If so, consider any repeated concepts or patterns that you see throughout the work. You may want to build a topic around one of those concepts. Also, try to formulate a topic that is unique; *go beyond the obvious in your analysis.*

After you have narrowed your topic, write a thesis sentence, which essentially is a one-sentence summary of your essay. The thesis sentence is the controlling idea of your paper, and it should be an idea that needs to be discussed in detail.

Also, think about the thesis as an argument that you are going to prove about the literary work you are analyzing.

Of course, an argument will need to be proven, so your body paragraph topics are ideas that help prove your thesis. Hopefully, the thesis will lead you naturally to your body paragraph topics. Sometimes the thesis statement will include a listing of these, but listing the points is not required. Usually, the literary analysis will include three body paragraphs. *Follow your instructor's guidelines on both the listing of points and the number of paragraphs.*

Here are some examples of thesis statements on literary subjects:

- To depict Ralph as the leader of forces of good, William Golding, in his novel *Lord of the Flies*, describes his physical attributes and his desire to keep the boys civilized.

- In *Lord of the Flies*, William Golding portrays Piggy as an outcast because of his physical, mental, and social dissimilarities.

- By using the conflicts of man and nature, Welty illustrates Phoenix Jackson as a woman determined to complete her journey.

- Welty portrays Phoenix as a symbol of immortality by her appearance, her speech, and her actions.

- Phoenix's journey can be compared to Christ's journey through the wilderness.

Outline

To write your outline, you may find it helpful to use the following literary analysis puzzle. It incorporates the technique of outlining while also encouraging you to plan how you will analyze your essay.

Strategy: Literary Analysis Puzzle

Writing a literary analysis paper is a difficult and daunting task for most students. Students often wonder how to make a complete point, how much evidence from the primary source to add, and how to discuss the evidence that they choose to use in the paper. The simplest way to think about writing a literary analysis paper is to approach it as if it were a puzzle. If you put all the pieces in the correct order, then you will have a paper that has solid claims with strong evidence that is clearly interpreted for the audience of your paper.

THE PUZZLE PIECES

Each point that you make in a paper should be broken down into a similar structure with claim, evidence, and interpretation. A **claim** is an argument that you want your reader to accept about that piece of literature. Your **evidence** to back up that claim comes from your primary source. You can choose to quote your source directly, paraphrase your source, or summarize your source.

After you provide evidence to back up your claim, you will need to **interpret** that evidence in your own words. Tell your reader what you want him/her to get out of that evidence. Remember that your interpretation needs to relate back to your claim. In order to make this puzzle strategy effective, you must follow this pattern for each point that you make in your essay.

This pattern, demonstrated in the outline provided below, is for a student essay concerning Eudora Welty's short story "A Worn Path." The student was asked to explain why or how Phoenix Jackson, the main character of the story, is a symbol of immortality. After brainstorming on the topic, the student chose to examine Phoenix's appearance and name, her speech, and the connection of the journey to the mythological bird known as the phoenix. The following outline for this student's paper showcases how she used the puzzle approach to create a specific, detailed essay.

An Immortal Woman

Thesis: Welty portrays Phoenix Jackson, the main character in the story, as a symbol of immortality by using her name and appearance, her speech, and her actions.

I.   Topic Sentence: Phoenix's name and appearance make her a symbol of immortality.

    A.   Claim—The name Phoenix parallels the Greek myth relating to the bird called Phoenix.

        Evidence—According to the *Columbia Electronic Encyclopedia*, "When it [phoenix] reached the end of its life (500 years), it burned itself on a pyre of flames, and from the ashes a new phoenix arose."

        Interpretation—She, like the phoenix myth, has a name that represents this immortal being that rises from the ashes to create a new phoenix.

    B.   Claim—The colors Phoenix wears and the color of her skin also represent the mythological bird.

        Evidence—Welty states that Phoenix has "her head tied in a red rag" (34).

        Evidence—Welty also concurs that her skin has "a golden color [that] ran underneath" and "her cheeks were illuminated by a yellow burning under the dark" (34).

        Evidence—The *Columbia Electronic Encyclopedia* also states that "[a]ccording to Herodotus the bird was red and golden. . . . "

        Interpretation—Welty's descriptive adjectives, red and yellow, attach her character to the colors of the legendary bird.

II. Topic Sentence: Another representation of Phoenix's immortality is through her speech.

    A. Claim—Phoenix refers to herself without mentioning an actual age.

        Evidence—"My senses is gone, I too old. I the oldest people I ever know" (Welty 36).

        Interpretation—She is older than anyone with whom she comes in contact.

        Evidence—"Nobody know who made this well, for it was here when I was born" (Welty 37).

        Interpretation—The reference to the well also implies that since no one knows the age of the well, then no one can possibly know her age, not even Phoenix herself.

    B. Claim—When the hunter asks her age, Phoenix claims she does not know.

        Evidence—Phoenix encounters a hunter who asks, "How old are you, Granny?" Phoenix replies, "There is no telling, mister, . . . no telling" (Welty 38).

        Interpretation—Because she claims that she has no idea of her own age, her immortality is evident.

III. Topic Sentence: Even though Phoenix's speech and appearance give a direct symbolic embodiment of immortality, her actions also reflect her immortality to the reader.

    A. Claim—Starting her journey in the morning symbolizes the myth.

        Evidence—Welty states that it is " . . . a bright frozen day in the early morning" (34).

        Evidence—According to the legend of the phoenix, "the phoenix represented the sun, which dies each night and rises again each morning" ("Phoenix").

        Interpretation—She, as well as the sun, rises in the morning to begin the slow yet necessary journey to town.

    B. Claim—The end of her journey also coincides with the myth.

        Evidence—The reader sees the "shadows [hanging] from the oak trees" (Welty 38), which indicates the day is growing old. Once she receives the medicine she needs, Phoenix begins " . . . her slow step . . . on the stairs . . . " back home (Welty 41).

        Interpretation—The end of her journey symbolizes the myth when the phoenix "dies each night" ("Phoenix"). Therefore, the end of Phoenix's journey figuratively represents the end of the mythical creature's journey.

UNRAVELING THE PUZZLE PIECES

This outline requires quite a bit of work for a student; however, when the outline is complete, the paper is well under way. Committing this much time to an outline gives students the ability to overcome all of those questions that most students ask when they have to write a literary analysis paper.

By piecing the puzzle of your paper together in this type of outline, you will not have to worry about whether you have made a complete point, included enough evidence, or analyzed thoroughly for your reader. If you have not filled in that piece of your outline, then you know that your puzzle is not complete.

All of these pieces—claim, evidence, and interpretation—fit together to make a detailed argument that your reader can understand clearly.

> **STUDENT ALERT!** Remember that you are not summarizing the plot or telling the story! You are using the specifics from the story to support your topic sentences, which in turn support your thesis!

Structure of Your Essay

In writing your essay, follow your literary analysis puzzle outline, and use the following structure for your essay.

INTRODUCTION

Begin with an attention-getter; then introduce the literary work and author. Punctuate the title correctly, and give the full name of the author. In subsequent references, state the author's last name only. You also may give a plot summary of the literary work, and/or you may discuss the ideas that the literary work addresses. Last of all, state your thesis. Make sure that your introduction is a seamless, coherent paragraph.

Sample Introduction ·

Is immortality possible? Could a person actually live forever? (1) In actuality, immortality of the physical body is impossible. (2) However, when one reads the short story "A Worn Path" by Eudora Welty, the concept of immortality seems realistic. (2) Phoenix Jackson, an elderly woman, traverses the Natchez Trace to town in order to obtain medicine for her grandson. (3) Throughout this short story, Welty utilizes many context clues that hint at her main character's immortality. (4) Therefore, Welty portrays Phoenix Jackson, the main character in the story, as a symbol of immortality by using her name and appearance, her speech, and her actions.

Numbered sentences are explained below:

1. Asking a question pertaining to your topic is one way to begin your essay. Whichever method you choose, it is important to "grab" the reader's attention, making him or her interested in your topic.

2. These sentences give the title of the story, the author's name, and a brief plot summary that revolves mainly around the character you are writing about.

3. This sentence is an amplifying sentence. This type of sentence is used before the thesis to create a sense of transition to heighten the importance of the topic, leading your reader into the thesis sentence.

4. This sentence is the thesis. Notice that the controlling or main idea that the writer is going to prove is *Phoenix Jackson as a symbol of immortality*. The evidence the writer will use to support this idea is her name and appearance, her speech, and her actions. These are the points or divisions of support, and your topic sentences are developed from these points. These points will support *how* Phoenix Jackson is a symbol of immortality. Remember, the controlling idea is what you are trying to analyze or prove in your paper; the points restrict your idea and help you analyze how your controlling idea will be supported in the paper.

BODY PARAGRAPHS

Write each of your two to three body paragraphs using the same structure. State your topic sentence. Remember that it is on your literary analysis puzzle. Using your supporting details on your outline, create a point-of-reference sentence, where your evidence appears in the story, and a place-supporting sentence, either separately or in combination with, the point-of-reference sentence.

Next, utilize a "lead" for your quote. This informs the reader who is the speaker of the quote: a character or characters or the narrator. Then, quote a relevant passage. (Introduce quotations and document correctly). Do not combine a character's words with the narrator's words. By combining character's words and exposition (narrator's words), you distort your lead and confuse the reader as to who is actually speaking the quoted passage.

The next three to five sentences are the heart of your analysis, so focus on them. These sentences explain how the author uses the passage to prove a point. Avoid simply retelling the plot/content of the passage. (See the following examples of plot summary vs. analysis.) Continue with the body paragraph by quoting another relevant passage and analyzing it just as you did the first passage.

Add a third passage and analysis if you think the paragraph needs it. End the body paragraph with a concluding sentence that sums up the paragraph. Do not end the body paragraph with a quotation or a question. One option for the ending sentence is to reword the topic sentence. Another option is to discuss how all the quoted passages relate to one idea. Your concluding point may be more than one sentence.

Sample Body Paragraph· ·

(1) Another representation of Phoenix's immortality is by her speech. (2) During her journey to town, (3) Phoenix refers to her age ambiguously. (4) She says, (5) "My senses is gone, I too old. I the oldest people I ever know" (Welty 36). In another instance on her journey, Phoenix also says, "Nobody know who made this well, for it was here when I was born" (Welty 37). (6) These statements clearly demonstrate to the reader that her age is unknown. Through her own speech, Phoenix reiterates that she is older than anyone with whom she comes in contact; in addition, the reference to the well also implies that since no one knows the age of the well, then no one can possibly know the age of Phoenix, not even Phoenix herself. (7) Near the end of her journey, Phoenix encounters a hunter who asks, "How old are you Granny?" Phoenix replies, "There is no telling, mister . . . no telling" (Welty 37). Because she claims that she has no idea of her own age, her immortality seems evident. (8) To the reader, Phoenix appears ageless, a conclusion supported by her own words.

The numbered sentences in the sample body paragraph are identified below:

1. Topic sentence

2. Point of reference

3. Supporting detail (A on your outline)

4. Lead that introduces quoted passage

5. Quoted passage

6. Explanation of how the passage supports your main idea

7. Repetition of steps 2–6 by using supporting detail B on your outline

8. Conclusion sentence

Note that your literary analysis puzzle outline adds a C in the body paragraph. Add that information before the ending sentence.

CONCLUSION

(Except for the clincher, the order of the conclusion is flexible.) Restate your thesis. Use a different sentence but the same idea as the thesis stated in the introduction. Possibly the focus of the conclusion could be the theme of the work you just analyzed. How does the literary work relate to life? Also, discuss the connection between your body paragraphs. How do those points relate to the theme of the work? The last sentence of your conclusion, and thus your essay, should be a clincher. The clincher is a catchy phrase that sums up your paper. It should be your own wording, it should be creative, and it should give finality to your essay.

Many people consider the conclusion the inverse of the introduction. Therefore, they like to keep the order of the conclusion in the order listed above: restated thesis, general information about the literary work, and creative sentence(s).

Sample Conclusion Paragraph ·

Even though societies throughout the world have different views on mortality and immortality, the reader must draw his or her conclusions based on moral and religious beliefs. However, in Eudora Welty's short story, the character Phoenix Jackson embodies the ideals of immortality. Because of the use of color, the physical appearance, and the ambiguous speech of Phoenix, her true age is never revealed to the reader, eliciting her as a symbol of immortality. By constantly making the journey to town for her grandson's medicine, Phoenix's desire to give unconditionally to the one she loves is truly more important than her own life. Therefore, like the mythological bird, Phoenix Jackson rises from the ashes, her spirit immortal.

REVISE THE ESSAY!

Be sure to check your body paragraphs for good analysis. See the following examples that show the difference between bad analysis (plot summary) and good analysis. Remember that you are not retelling what happened in the literary work. You are analyzing how the author gets across his or her point to the reader.

Examples of Plot Summary v. Analysis

ANALYSIS OF EDGAR ALLAN POE'S "THE CASK OF AMONTILLADO"

Bad Analysis: Plot Summary—NO NO NO ·
The last example of irony is the fact that Fortunato is intoxicated and dressed as a jester. Montresor describes Fortunato when he says, "The wine sparkled in his eyes and the bells jingled" (Poe 126). Fortunato has been drinking because it's carnival time. Also, he is dressed as a jester as part of his carnival costume.

Good Analysis ·
The last example of irony is the fact that Fortunato is intoxicated and dressed as a jester. Montresor describes Fortunato when he says, "The wine sparkled in his eyes and the bells jingled" (Poe 126). Being drunk, Fortunato is easy to deceive. It is ironic that the one thing Fortunato is passionate about, wine, aids in his murder. Also,

Fortunato is compared to a jester, who normally makes other people laugh, often by making fun of someone else. However, in the story the joke is played on him. As Fortunato slowly sobers up, he begins to see more clearly that he has been tricked, and it is no laughing matter. The fun, party-like atmosphere of carnival is gone and serves as a stark contrast to the reality Fortunato faces—being buried alive.

The good analysis is an excerpt from an essay by Kaleb Robbins, ICC student.

ANALYSIS OF CHARLOTTE PERKINS GILMAN'S "THE YELLOW WALLPAPER"

Bad Analysis: Plot Summary—NO NO NO ·
Reason is somewhat backwards in the story. At first, the wife describes John as someone who uses reason; she says that "John is practical in the extreme" (Gilman 765). Such a statement exalts John as being very reasonable, but this is not what the woman truly means. She thinks that John is too practical, and he thinks she is not practical at all.

Good Analysis ·
Reason is somewhat backwards in the story. At first, the wife describes John as someone who uses reason; she says that "John is practical in the extreme" (Gilman 765). Such a statement exalts John as being very reasonable, but this is not what the woman truly means. The word "practical" is defined as "sensible and realistic in approach to a situation or problem," but she expressly says he is this way in the extreme. One way John could be extremely practical is that he sees only his own opinion as sensible and excludes any views from inferiors. John thinks that he is mentally superior to his wife when he tells her, "I am a doctor, dear, and I know" (Gilman 770). This statement exalts his ideas above hers since he is a professional. The use of his title to justify his excluding his wife's opinion is a very poor example of reason. Although taking a doctor's conclusions to be reliable may seem practical, the doctor's making light of other opinions is not logical. Instead, it is a rather biased opinion.

The good analysis is an excerpt from an essay by Greg Johnson, ICC student.

Read Chapter 26, Writing about Drama, Poetry, Film, and Books, and check your essay for any of the errors mentioned. Then, check for problems in wording, use of transitions, organization of ideas, etc. Lastly, check for grammar and punctuation errors. Remember that comma splices, fused sentences, incomplete sentences, and subject/verb agreement errors are some of the most common major errors that students make.

Chapter 26

Writing about Drama, Poetry, Film, and Books

Writing about Drama

Dramatic productions, or plays, are some of the oldest and most popular forms of literature. From the days of Greek tragedies to modern dramatists, playwriting has been around for centuries.

Since most plays or dramas—and the terms are interchangeable—are meant to be seen on a stage rather than read from a book, students often find reading them difficult.

Furthermore, if the only experience that you have had with drama is watching one that has been made into a movie, you may be even more confused because you have missed the particulars—the divisions of acts and scenes, as well as the staging—that make a drama a drama rather than a novel or a short story.

You can overcome that difficulty if you know **what to look for** and **how to approach** the play that you have been assigned to read.

THE SPECIFICS OF A DRAMA

What exactly makes a drama a drama? Like short stories, novels, and other narratives, plays have characters, setting, plot, and theme, and sometimes even a particular point of view, as in the case of Tennessee Williams' *The Glass Menagerie*, told from Tom's memory. Where they differ, though, is how they look on the page. Rather than a full page of prose with paragraph indentions and chapter numbers, or a poem with some sort of stanza form, most plays are constructed in "acts" and "scenes."

Acts are major divisions in a play, often requiring a change of set from one act to the next. **Scenes** are smaller divisions within an act which usually do not require a change of set. William Shakespeare's plays have five acts, with some sort of climax occurring in Act III. Within those acts, there can be any number of scenes, one generally flowing smoothly into the next.

However, there is more than one way to write a play. Arthur Miller and Henrik Ibsen have three acts and no separate scenes in *Death of a Salesman* and *A Doll's House*, respectively, and Tennessee Williams has seven scenes but no acts in *The Glass Menagerie*. As a reader of a play, you must pay attention to where the action takes place in those acts and scenes so that you won't be confused by the plot complications.

SETTING THE SCENE

As noted earlier, most plays are meant to be watched rather than read. In fact, your instructor may show you a version of a play made into a movie or filmed live in the theater. If you are lucky, you might get to see the play you are reading on your campus or at a local theater.

However, even if you see the play, you must also read it to appreciate the form. Because of the unique delivery of this genre, many playwrights, as the authors of plays are called, give very few descriptive notes about the appearance of either character or set. The playwright usually leaves such specifics as set design and casting to the producers and directors of the play and concentrates instead on the action on the stage and the words coming out of the mouths of the actors. Consequently, when you read a play, you must use your imagination to "cast" the characters, to "set" the stage, and to interpret meaning from the words.

Shakespeare

You are, of course, familiar with William Shakespeare, and you probably read at least one of his plays in a high school English course. Shakespeare, who was an actor as well as a writer, is an excellent example of how most traditional playwrights set up their plays. In *King Lear*, a tragedy about family betrayal, Shakespeare describes Lear, the main character of the play, simply as "Lear, King of Britain."

Because there is no physical description of Lear, a producer or director working with that drama is free to cast the part with any actor who can rise to the elegance and strength of Shakespeare's language. Two actors as different as James Earl Jones, an African American from Mississippi, and Sir Laurence Olivier, a Caucasian from England, have played Lear magnificently on both stage and screen.

In addition to having no physical descriptions for characters, Shakespeare has minimal set descriptions; the play opens in "King Lear's Palace," and other scenes are described in the same austere manner. Again, your imagination will allow you to create your own set.

Williams

Tennessee Williams, a Mississippi playwright, is an exception to this style of playwriting; he describes at great length and with poetic symbolism the settings—both figurative and literal—of his plays, as well as giving specific descriptions of the characters. In *The Glass Menagerie*, Williams provides several pages describing the lighting, the music, and the screen device he intended to be used as part of the production. He also includes eight paragraphs of detailed description of the set, both the literal and social atmosphere, before Scene I begins.

In addition, Williams' descriptions of three of the four characters in that play are quite specific, giving the reader insight into the motivations of and personalities of the characters. When you read a Williams drama, you must pay close attention to the hints and clues that he gives you in those explanatory sections. In fact, he expects you to read them. When you read that his character Amanda Wingfield is a "little woman . . . clinging frantically to another time and place," Williams is giving you a clue about what motivates Amanda's frequent references to Blue Mountain. Likewise, when he refers to Jim O'Connor simply as "a gentleman caller. A nice, ordinary young man," Williams is telling you that Jim is different from any of the Wingfields.

Whether you are reading a play by Shakespeare or Williams or some other playwright, you will be required to use both your imagination and your own experiences to move the characters through the acts and scenes that comprise the play. Just as directors and producers stage plays in different ways according to their tastes, you, too, can stage the play you read, using whatever help the playwright provides.

THE SPECIFICS OF LANGUAGE

One of the first characteristics that you notice in reading a play is that the majority of the words on the pages are in dialogue, as the speeches are called, delivered by the actors/characters. Dialogue can be long or short and can be directed to other characters; it can also be in the form of a **soliloquy**, in which a character is alone on the stage speaking to him/herself; or in an **aside**, in which the character actually speaks directly to the audience members, informing them of a plan or explaining an action.

Just like writers in other genres, playwrights give serious attention to the words they put in the mouths of their characters. They incorporate figures of speech and figurative language into their dialogues in the same ways that poets or short story writers or novelists incorporate such language into their works.

With careful reading, you can appreciate and understand the speeches and dialogues in a play as easily as you can understand them in any other work.

CHOOSING A TOPIC

Everything written about literary analysis elsewhere in this book applies to drama as well. Chapter 25, Writing a Literary Analysis Essay, covers the specific tools necessary to put your essay together. In addition, you can use the various approaches mentioned in the Literary Analysis and Approaches chapter to analyze and critique the theme, the structure, the characters, and the plot development, and you can get valuable information from each of the individual chapters on literary elements to help you develop your thesis and support your opinion. For instance, you could write a character analysis of any of the characters in *The Glass Menagerie* or you could analyze the symbols of the glass menagerie itself or the Blue Roses.

You might choose to write on what you see as the theme in *King Lear*, focusing on how Shakespeare brings that theme out. Also, you can apply most of the modes to any literary essay you write, including one that focuses on a play. For instance, you might compare and contrast two characters in the assigned drama. Likewise, you could write an argumentation paper supporting the opinion that the historical time in which the play was set informed the main action and complications of the plot.

HOW TO CITE A DRAMA

When you actually cite the play that you have chosen as your primary source, you will be using a citation form somewhat different from those used in citing poetry or short stories in a critique. Instead of referring to page numbers, you will refer to act, scene, or book, depending on the type of play you are citing.

Your instructor will guide you if you are using a play that deviates from the norm. Otherwise, your parenthetical citation should refer to the act and scene, followed by the line number(s). If you are working with only the primary source and will have only one source listed on your Works Cited page, your instructor may require only the specific act, scene, and line number without the author's name or the play title.

As always, follow your instructor's directions.

New MLA Guidelines

In the past, Roman numerals were used to identify acts and scenes in a play, and many instructors prefer that practice. However, the *MLA Handbook for Writers of Research Papers*, Eighth Edition, provides the option of using **Arabic numerals** instead. Use the format that your instructor requires. If you are splicing a quote into a sentence, you will follow the guidelines outlined elsewhere in this book, citing the quoted material by the appropriate format of act, scene, and lines if given. The act, scene, and line numbers—if line numbers are given in the play you have chosen—are separated by periods. For instance, a citation from a Shakespearean play might look like this: (II.iii.240–45) or (2.3.240–45).

If you quote several lines of dialogue from a play, you must set that dialogue off to identify that selection as dialogue, much as you would a block quote in any citation. You indent one inch from the left margin and type the character's name in all capital letters, followed by a period. Subsequent lines of a character's dialogue are indented an additional quarter of an inch.

The parenthetical citation will follow the last section of dialogue, and it is punctuated as a block quote would be, with the end punctuation following the quote and the citation after that with no further punctuation.

Below are examples from Williams' *The Glass Menagerie*, which has only scenes, and Shakespeare's *King Lear*, which has acts, scenes, and line numbers. Both begin with the necessary lead-in to set up the dialogue. Here is an example of how a quotation from Williams would appear in an essay. *It does, of course, require a lead-in:*

> The tension caused by the hasty exit of the gentleman caller after he announces that he is engaged to a woman named Betty escalates into a final confrontation between Tom and Amanda:
>
> TOM. The warehouse is where I work, not where I know things about people!
>
> AMANDA. You don't know things anywhere! You live in a dream; you manufacture illusions! . . . Where are you going?
>
> TOM. I'm going to the movies. (7)

Quoting Shakespeare, on the other hand, would require act, scene, and line numbers, as shown below. The first citation uses Roman numerals, and the second uses Arabic numbers. Follow your instructor's preference, and again, *don't forget to include a lead-in.* Here's an example of how it would appear in an essay:

> The conspiracy between Lear's daughters Goneril and Regan is revealed early in the play after Lear disowns Cordelia, the third sister, and withdraws her dowry. The two sisters discuss their father's actions:
>
> GONERIL. You see how full of changes his age is. The observation we have made of it hath not been little. He always lov'd our sister most, and with what poor judgment he hath now cast her off appears too grossly.
>
> REGAN. 'Tis the infirmity of his age; yet he hath ever but slenderly known himself. (I.i.290–95) or (1.1.290–95)

As you would do if you were writing a critique about any other literary work, you must give a careful reading—more than one time—to a drama to ensure that you understand all aspects of the work. Character interactions, plot complications, historical and social setting, and theme development are just as important in a drama as they are in other genres.

Once you adjust to the different look on the page and to your responsibility as a reader to cast the characters and set the scene, you will have no problem following your teacher's directions for writing an essay about drama.

Writing about Poetry

Although much of the language used to discuss fiction—short stories and plays, in particular—also applies to poetry, analysis of poetry requires an additional set of terms and an additional vocabulary. In addition to noting *tone*, *persona*, *theme*, *character*, *point of view*, or *setting* in a poem, you will have to look closely at the specifics of the language that the poet uses to convey meaning, as well as at the rhythmical and metrical form he or she employs.

THE SPECIFICS OF LANGUAGE

A poet, who generally has a much shorter amount of space to convey meaning or emotion than a fiction writer, must pick and choose carefully the words that will have the most impact on a reader's understanding of a work. Rather than spending two pages describing in detail a setting or a character's physical appearance, the poet must be concise. For that reason, while the terms *metaphor* (comparing two things by saying that one thing is another) and *simile* (comparing two things by using *like* or *as*) and other figures of speech certainly apply to any form of writing, they often carry more weight in poetry.

Theodore Roethke's description of "a palm caked hard by dirt" (14) in "My Papa's Waltz" informs the reader of the physical labor of the persona's father without having to go into detail about exactly which blue-collar job the father might hold. The father's hand is also described as "battered on one knuckle" (9–10). In those four words, Roethke gives a picture of the boy's father that doesn't require any more explanation.

More specific to poetry than the language, then, is the rhythm, meter, stanza form, and rhyme scheme of the poem. While you would probably not be asked to write an essay on only those parts of a poem, the rhythm, meter, and rhyme scheme are often important to the meaning of the overall poem. For that reason, you should be able to speak knowledgeably about the different types of poetic conventions that fall into those categories.

Rhythm

This refers to the beat of the poem, the pattern of stressed and unstressed syllables in each line. Sometimes the rhythm has no special connection to the poem; the author just happened to choose that particular beat. Other times, as in "My Papa's Waltz," for instance, the meaning and the rhythm are closely connected; the rhythm of the poem mimics the rhythm of a waltz—the one, two, three rhythm that a waltzing couple would follow. Rhythm patterns have names that correspond to the types and numbers of stressed and unstressed syllables in each segment; the most common patterns are trochaic (one stressed and one unstressed), iambic (one unstressed and one stressed), anapestic (two stressed and one unstressed), and dactylic (one stressed and two unstressed).

Meter

The meter of a poem refers to the number of *feet* it has; a foot is a segment or pattern of stressed and unstressed syllables repeated throughout the poem. The different types of feet are monometer (one foot), dimeter (two feet), trimeter (three feet), tetrameter (four feet), pentameter (five feet), hexameter (six feet), heptameter (seven feet), and octameter (eight feet). Edwin Arlington Robinson's poem "Richard Cory" has five feet per line: "When ev| er Rich| ard Co| ry went |down town. . . . " (1).

Stanza Form

The stanza form is the format that the poet chooses to write the poem. Some poets choose a four-line stanza, which is called a quatrain. Others use two-line stanzas, known as couplets. Perhaps the most poetic of the stanza forms is the sonnet, which consists of fourteen lines in a variety of forms within that parameter. For instance, a Shakespearean or Elizabethan sonnet is comprised of three quatrains and a couplet. The Petrarchan or Italian sonnet employs an octave, or eight-line stanza, followed by a sestet, or six-line stanza.

On the other hand, some poets choose not to use a prescribed stanza form; much of modern poetry follows this format. Walt Whitman employs no specific stanza form in "A Noiseless, Patient Spider," nor does Sylvia Plath in "Daddy."

Others use very complicated stanza forms such as a villanelle, a good example of which is Dylan Thomas's "Do Not Go Gentle into That Good Night." The poem employs five tercets, or three-line stanzas, and a quatrain, and only two rhymes are used throughout the entire nineteen-line poem. The second lines of each of the tercets and the quatrain rhyme, and all of the remaining lines rhyme.

Rhyme Scheme

The rhyme scheme refers to the type of end rhyme that the poet chooses. For instance, every other line in a quatrain might rhyme; the rhyme scheme would then be *abab*, and that rhyme might be repeated in the next quatrain, or a new rhyme following the every-other-line format might be used, which would then be *cdcd*.

On the other hand, the poet might choose to have the two internal lines of a quatrain rhyme, in which case the rhyme scheme would be *abba*, *cddc*, and so on. You should also be aware of words that do not exactly rhyme; such words constitute slant or off rhyme. Theodore Roethke uses slant rhyme when he writes in "My Papa's Waltz," "The whiskey on your breath/Could make a small boy dizzy/But I hung on like death/Such waltzing was not easy" (1–4). Although "death" and "breath" are exact rhymes, "easy" and "dizzy" are slant rhymes.

Of course, many poets—modern poets, in particular—choose not to use rhyme in their work at all. If there is also no rhythm imposed on the work, the poem could be considered free verse, poetry that has neither rhythm nor rhyme. Some poets choose not to employ rhyme but to use rhythm.

Robert Frost, who felt that writing poetry that had neither rhythm nor rhyme was akin to "playing tennis with the net down," wrote many poems that have rhythm but no rhyme; "Mending Wall" and "Out, Out—" are excellent examples of this style. Though the poems don't have end rhyme, each carefully employs an iambic pentameter rhythm—every other syllable stressed with five feet per line.

Being able to speak—and thus write—intelligently about the form that the poet employs is certainly an element in explicating—or explaining—a poem. At times, that style further informs the meaning of the poem. Other times, the style has little to do with the actual meaning of the poem but contributes to the overall mood or tone of a poem.

PREPARATION AND NOTE TAKING

As you would do with any piece of literature you were writing about, read the poem carefully—more than one time—to be sure that you understand it. Determine form first, checking to see if the poem follows a particular pattern. Is it a sonnet; is it rhymed and metered; is it free verse?

After you have determined the specifics of the meter and rhythm and rhyme, look at the literary conventions that the author uses. The section on figurative language in Chapter 27 can help you determine if there are any figures of speech or special literary conventions in the work. Determine how those figures of speech work in the context of the poem.

If the poem is a narrative poem, look at the different chapters of literary elements in this book and see how character, setting, and point of view are handled. Determine if there is a theme in the poem, and look at the author's tone.

Before attempting to write a coherent essay, make sure that you understand the poem completely, including an understanding of how the author derives his/her meaning.

CHOOSING A TOPIC

After you have analyzed the poem for meaning and for form, you must decide what you want to say. Your teacher may have given you a specific topic, thus making your decision for you. He or she might want you to write an explication which focuses strictly on the mechanics and meaning of the poem, or you might be asked to write a personal response to the poem, connecting it to you.

If you have no guidelines other than to include both form and meaning, then you'll have further to go in deciding on a topic.

If you were writing about Roethke's "My Papa's Waltz," you might argue for or against the opinion that the poem is a negative view of the persona's home life. Look for clues in the poem to help make your point.

An examination of Shakespeare's "Sonnet 116" might support the supposition that Shakespeare is seriously praising the commitment in a "true marriage." Or it could just as easily defend the idea that Shakespeare is ridiculing the idea of unwavering love.

You might choose to write a character analysis of the Duke of Ferrara in Robert Browning's "My Last Duchess"—or you might attempt to characterize the Duchess herself. Or how about an analysis of either the title character in Robinson's "Richard Cory"—or the persona?

DEVELOPING A THESIS

Once you have chosen your topic and understand the particulars of the poem, it's time to plan the essay. As you would do with any assignment, write a clean, clear thesis that will be the controlling idea of the essay.

If your thesis is that Browning allows the first person narrator of "My Last Duchess" to reveal his true character through his arrogant words, then you would look for elements in the poem to back that up. Use the Duke's own words about his Duchess to show his hidden insecurity about his wife, as well as his pomposity.

WRITING THE ESSAY

After you have chosen your thesis and noted the main points of your argument, you can develop the essay any number of ways. The various rhetorical mode chapters of this text give helpful information about the how-to. You could write an exemplification essay that shows how the Duke mentioned above reveals himself.

You could write a comparison/contrast essay that compared Richard Cory as the persona saw him and the Richard Cory who really existed. Or you could develop an essay pointing out the three parts of Robert Frost's "Birches" and how those parts correspond with the theme.

You might analyze the poetic techniques and figurative language in Frost's "Out, Out—."

Of course, you must use specific details in supporting your opinion. You must also punctuate correctly, remember that lines of poetry are punctuated differently from lines of prose. For fewer than four lines of poetry, introduce the section you are quoting with a lead-in; use quotation marks and use a slash mark (/) to indicate line breaks. Identify the line numbers in parentheses following the quote. Do not include *l.* or *lines* before the numbers, as shown in the examples at the beginning of this chapter.

For a longer quote—more than four quoted lines—you would set up a block quote as is discussed in the MLA chapter of this text.

The brass tacks:

- Remember that titles of short poems are put in quotation marks.

- You must identify your author and poem title in the first paragraph, identifying the author by first and last name in the first reference and last name only in subsequent references.

- Use historical present in writing about the poem.

- Use specific examples from the poem to back up your assertions. For instance, to analyze poetic techniques in a work, you would have to show how a metaphor or simile was used by the author to create an image.

- Follow quoted lines with the line number(s) with no addition of the word *line*.

- Depending on the specifics of the assignment, reference the form of the poem—the metrical rhythm and feet, such as iambic pentameter, as well as any specifics about the type of poem you're writing about: sonnet, lyric, dramatic monologue, etc.

- Create a title for your essay that is not the title of the poem. You might use something like this: "Two Views of Death in Emily Dickinson's 'Because I Could Not Stop for Death' and 'I Heard a Fly Buzz When I Died.'"

Writing about Film

A film is—or should be—more like music than like fiction. It should be a progression of moods and feelings. The theme, what's behind the motion, the meaning, all that comes later.

—Stanley Kubrick

In many ways, writing about film is like writing any other critical analysis essay that you would be assigned to write: in a film you have characters, plot, theme, setting, point of view, tone, and language, just as you do in poetry, fiction, or drama. You might also have music or voice-overs or other unique conventions which the producers or directors added to enhance their film. So in what way would you approach this analysis differently?

PREPARATION AND NOTE TAKING

First, of course, you need to watch the film, carefully, thoughtfully, and closely. The first viewing produces an immediate reaction: Did you like it or not? Once you've decided that, you begin to break down what you liked or didn't like about the film. That's exactly the same sort of analysis you do when you see a movie with a friend, and you might disagree with your friend about the merits—or lack of them—of the production. Using the specifics of the film helps you make your point, just as those specifics do in writing about prose or poetry.

Also, the same rule that applies to other artistic works applies to approaching a film: liking and appreciating are sometimes two different responses. Although you might have initially disliked the film, you might—on closer analysis—find much to appreciate.

Then, to write a good analytical essay about a film, you must watch it again, this time taking notes about what you see on the screen. Make sure that you know the characters' names, place names, connections between characters, complications of plot, and/or themes that emerge. The Internet and any number of film websites can help you with the spelling of names and places if necessary. In the same way that you must know specifically what happens in a short story, poem, or play to write about it, you must know specifically what happens in a film. Taking a restroom or refreshment break in a key scene in a movie can be disastrous to your understanding of what takes place.

CHOOSING A TOPIC

After you are convinced of your familiarity with the film itself, you must decide what sort of essay you are going to write. Perhaps your instructor has given you a specific assignment—to write a movie review, an analysis, or a reaction essay. If that's the case, your format has been decided for you. Regardless of whether you are writing a review, an analysis, or a reaction essay, all call for an argument or judgment—in other words, an opinion that will become your thesis. **You should never just summarize what you see on the screen! A summary offers no insight, no critical thinking, and no effort, and your grade will surely reflect that!**

Perhaps you have been given the assignment to write an analysis of the original *Jaws* movie, comparing it to later movies with more advanced technology. How does that movie, with its unrealistic-looking shark and spooky soundtrack, stand up against *Jurassic Park*, with its realistic *Tyrannosaurus rex* and computer-imaged raptors? How about either of those compared to *Avatar*, which took computer imaging to another level?

On the other hand, you could write an analysis that supports the thesis that the original *Jaws* movie, with its soundtrack, giant shark, and complex characters, set the stage for a new level of suspense films. Another essay could be written employing the classification/division mode: You could classify types of horror movies, romantic comedies, or coming-of-age movies. You could just as easily review what works or doesn't work in any movie, or you could write a reaction essay about what you liked or didn't like. Whichever topic you choose, you must use specifics and concrete details to prove your point.

With so many films being remade, you could choose to compare an original film to the most recent version. *Karate Kid*, a classic with Ralph Macchio and

Pat Morito, was remade with an African-American protagonist, Jaden Smith, as the "kid" and Jackie Chan as the teacher. What is gained or lost in the remake?

Another direction to take with a movie analysis is to compare the movie to the book on which it was based. For example, does the latest Harry Potter film benefit from the translation from the book? If so, in what way? If not, why not? How about the *Twilight* movies and books? Did the Bella and Edward of your imagination translate well onto the big screen?

What about realism in films? You could be asked to analyze a movie in terms of its historical setting. Is the fact that characters are often "cleaned up" and beautified for the times in which they lived important? Few women of the reduced circumstances of the Dashwood women in the Ang Lee version of Jane Austen's *Sense and Sensibility* (1995) would be as neatly coiffed and attired as we see in that film. What about those films that take license with the very history that they are presenting on the screen? Much of *Braveheart* is strictly fictional, despite the fact that William Wallace was a real historical figure. Perhaps you would wish to focus on the entertainment versus historical aspects of that film.

Biopics are popular among the moviegoing public today. How does the movie *Ray* portray the life of the very real Ray Charles? Do you think that the depiction is realistic? If you have seen *Walk the Line*, one director's interpretation of the life of Johnny Cash, you might examine the romanticized view of Cash's romance with June Carter, his performance in Folsom Prison, or his problems with drugs.

DEVELOPING A THESIS

Once you have decided on the type of essay that you are writing and the direction that you want to take, you are ready to get to the specifics of planning the essay. The place to start is the thesis, or the main point that you are trying to make. Your thesis will set up your argument, and the main points of the essay will develop from that.

If your thesis is that *Avatar* should have won the 2009 Academy Award for best film, then the main points of your essay might focus on the 3-D technology added to the movie, the theme of corporate greed, the contrast between the peaceful characters from Pandora and the aggressive ones from Earth, the unique experience of the viewer-as-participant, or any number of subject areas found in that film. After you have brainstormed or outlined or thought through your main ideas, you must then find specifics from the movie to support your thesis.

WRITING THE ESSAY

Most movie reviews follow the same pattern as fiction reviews. First, in the introductory paragraph, you will identify the title of the film, italicizing it. Next, you should also include the name of the director and the year that the film was released, as well as identifying the main actors. If you don't intend to do so elsewhere, you could write a brief summary of the film, being clear and concise, or you could use any of the other techniques mentioned elsewhere in this book to grab your audience's attention in your introduction. Also, the thesis is included in the introductory paragraph for short essays.

The remainder of the essay will do what any critical analysis essay or argumentation essay does: prove your thesis. You will use specific supports from the movie to make your point, analyzing what you saw on the screen to shore up your arguments. The number of supports and the length of the paragraphs will be governed by the specifics of the assignment. Make sure that the topic sentences of your body paragraphs tie back in to the thesis, and that the paragraphs use specific examples to prove your argument.

WRITING THE CONCLUSION

The conclusion of the film analysis essay follows the same format as other analysis; you will restate or reiterate your thesis and give finality to your essay. You can tie back in to what you use as an attention-grabber in the introduction. The conclusion might also include a suggestion about whether or not the audience would like the film, akin to a thumbs-up or thumbs-down opinion.

The brass tacks:

1. Italicize the title of the film: *Avatar, Twilight—the Movie, Jaws, Braveheart.*

2. Identify both the characters in the film and the actors who play those characters—Mel Gibson (William Wallace) or William Wallace (Mel Gibson) depending on whether you are speaking of the actor or the character.

3. Identify the director and the date of release of the film: Ang Lee (1995).

4. Keep the characters and actors separate. Mel Gibson played William Wallace in *Braveheart*, so references to the actions of the character should be attributed to William Wallace. However, if you think that Mel Gibson embodied the characteristics attributed to William Wallace by historical accounts, you could write about Gibson's acting ability to bring that part to life. Don't get confused and don't confuse the reader!

5. Use historical present tense in writing about the film except in special circumstances, such as summarizing an event that happened in a different time, prior to the action of the film.

6. Back up your points with specific details from the film.

7. Remember that a *critique* presents a judgment, an assessment, and/or an opinion; it is not a collection of negative comments about a work. Whether you liked the work or not, your assessment of it should be fair and balanced, backed up by evidence in the work itself. To do otherwise weakens your argument and causes your reader to question your judgment.

8. Create a title for your essay that is not the title of the film; however, you may use the title of the film as part of your title. Do not put your essay title in quotation marks or italics, but italicize the title of the film if you use it as part of your essay title. For instance, something like the following might be used in an essay on *The Hangover*:

    The Many Faces of Humor in *The Hangover*

Writing about Books

Just as you would write any other analysis of a literary work, you would start an analysis or review of a book—a novel or a nonfiction work—with a careful reading of the work itself.

Often, students think that if they have seen a movie of a particular book that they are required to review or analyze, they do not really have to read the book itself. That can be disastrous! As anyone who has seen a movie adapted from a book knows, plots of movies are often very far removed from the plots of the books on which they are based. Do not make the mistake of trying this particular shortcut!

PREPARATION AND NOTE TAKING

First, of course, you, as a responsible reviewer, must read the book—all pages, carefully and critically. If you have time, read it more than once, though sometimes that is not as easily done as it is in reviewing a short story or poem or film. If you know that you will be able to read the book only once, take notes as you read.

> **Important Note**
>
> If the book is your own, you can write margin notes, underline, and dog-ear the pages to remind you of important plot elements.
>
> However, if it's a library book, a book borrowed from a friend, or a textbook that you might want to sell back to the bookstore, use sticky notes to mark places that you might want to identify later.

If you are reading a work of fiction, make sure that you have character names, place names, plot complications, emerging themes, point of view, and author's techniques clear in your mind as you follow the work through to the conclusion. If you are reviewing a nonfiction work, pay attention to specific facts that the author gives you in relating the real event.

As you are reading, think critically about the work. The first critical assessment that you might make is whether you like the book or not. After you have done that, challenge yourself to question why you like it or do not like it. Make notes as you go.

Perhaps you did not find the resolution of the plot to be realistic; perhaps you did not agree with the underlying theme which the author had embedded in the plot; perhaps you did not think that the actions of the characters in the later sections of the book were consistent with the personalities which the author had developed for them earlier in the work. Or perhaps the book came together flawlessly for you, and you loved it all!

Either way, liking or not liking a work is not a good enough topic for a college essay without a more substantial focus to guide your assessment. Also, as is mentioned in other sections of this book that deal with literary analysis, you might dislike a work that you can fully appreciate after examining it critically.

You might also want to examine how the book is developed. *Wuthering Heights*, by Emily Brontë, is told primarily in flashbacks, as a narrative told by housekeeper Nelly Dean to entertain Mr. Lockwood, who in turn writes the story. Did that technique and point of view influence your opinion of the characters of Catherine, Heathcliff, and the other characters of the novel? If you read a nonfiction work, does it conform with other books that you have read on the subject, or is it completely opposite? These are questions that you must resolve before you move on to the next steps in developing your essay.

CHOOSING A TOPIC

After you have read the book, have taken good notes, and have familiarized yourself with the specifics of the work, you will need to find a focus for your review. As always, your thesis must be an opinion which will guide the direction of the essay you are writing, so that thesis must be carefully developed.

Remember that you must be careful not to simply summarize the content of the book. As mentioned often throughout the literary section of this book, **a summary offers no insight into the work you are analyzing; you must use your critical thinking skills to analyze what you are reading!**

To develop the focus of your essay—if your instructor has not given a specific topic on which you are to write—think about why the author might have written the book. Doing a little background work on the author might help you in finding some clues to the author's purpose. Chapter 24 of this book on types of critical approaches might help you with your background work.

Is the book a political commentary on life in another part of the world? *The Kite Runner*, written by Khaled Hosseini and published in 2003, is a novel set in Afghanistan. Though it is fiction, the story portrays life as it might have been for two young boys of entirely opposite backgrounds during the 1970s and on into their adulthood. What is Hosseini's theme in that novel? What similarities and differences are there in the characters of Amir and Hassan? What is the author telling you about the different worlds of privilege and poverty in a Third World country? If you were reviewing this book, you might want to examine what you find as the author's purpose in writing the book.

Another recent work concerning Afghanistan is Greg Mortenson's *Three Cups of Tea*, published in 2004. That book provides one man's view of Afghanistan and Pakistan in the areas of both war and education. Since that work is non-fiction, you might want to focus on what Mortenson's purpose is in building schools in the war-torn areas he describes. Mortenson provides background information that explains the how and why of his crusade to help you understand why he has chosen this effort as his life's work. As a reviewer, you have the ability to examine his motives and analyze them in the context of the book. Since his book has come under harsh criticism in recent years, you could research what is now disputed in the original work.

DEVELOPING A THESIS

After you have done your background work in examining the book and perhaps the author, then you must develop your thesis—the opinion you intend to prove in the essay. If your instructor has directed you to the type of thesis you should develop, you have only then to prove that thesis. If not, you must decide what you want your essay to say. Are you going to review and explain the author's argument primarily, focusing on what he or she did—or tried to do—in the work? If so, your thesis might include an assessment of what the author's purpose was and how it was carried out.

Or are you going to make **your own opinion** the primary focus of the argument, showing how the work does or does not stand up to careful and thoughtful scrutiny? **Either way, you can easily write this essay without having to use *I*, *me*, or *my* as part of your assessment.**

WRITING THE ESSAY

As stated earlier, writing a book review or analysis is similar to writing any other type of analysis and follows the same pattern. Your introduction should capture your reader's attention, and Chapter 7 of this book has suggestions for doing that. You will also include the title of the book, italicized, and the author, identifying him or her by the first and last name in the first reference. The date of publication can be included if it is significant, and background information that pertains to the writing of the book should be included if it is relevant. For instance, if you were reviewing Kathryn Stockett's *The Help*, including the information that the author grew up in the town in which the story is set could be considered pertinent to a careful examination of that novel. Lastly, your thesis would be included in the introduction, as well.

Depending on the assignment instructions, you might want to have a paragraph which gives a brief summary of the book, focusing on the key elements or events which make up the work. This should be short, and it should lead to the point that you have chosen to develop in your thesis. Referring to and identifying key characters—whether fictional or real—and key events might smooth the way for the analysis in the paragraphs which follow.

The rest of your essay will analyze/review the book. The topic sentences for your body paragraphs should further the support of the thesis/argument you are attempting to prove. Give specifics from the work to back up your points, making sure that you reference page numbers if you quote from the book.

If you do use quotes, remember to cite correctly, using MLA style as your guide. Remember, too, that MLA documentation requires a Works Cited page.

Refer to the author by last name only in the body paragraphs of the paper, just as you would in any other literary analysis.

WRITING THE CONCLUSION

The conclusion can sum up your points, restate your thesis, or make a final judgment on the book. You might also want to recommend the book to other readers, or you might want to add it to the list of the worst books you have ever read. However, make sure that your statements in the conclusion are a reflection of the main points of your essay. For instance, if your points have been mostly negative, do not try to persuade your audience that the book is worth reading, and if your points have been positive, do not discourage your audience from picking up the book. Also, do not go off on any tangents that bring in elements you have not covered in the essay.

The brass tacks:

1. Identify the book and author—first and last names—in your introductory paragraph.

2. Italicize the title of the book.

3. Use historical present tense in writing about the action of the book. Even if you are reviewing a book written 200 years ago, the action is taking place in the present for current readers.

4. Remember that a *critique* presents a judgment, an assessment, and/or an opinion; it is not a collection of negative comments about a work. Whether you liked the work or not, your assessment of it should be fair and balanced, backed up by evidence in the work itself. To do otherwise weakens your argument and causes your reader to question your judgment.

5. Create a title for your essay that is not the title of the book; however, you may use the title of the book as part of your essay title. Do not put the essay title in quotation marks or italics, but italicize the title of the book if you include it in your essay title. For instance, you might use the following as an essay title:

    The Question of the Narrator in *Wuthering Heights*

6. Depending on the assignment, you might need to use quotations from the book to back up your points. If you do, document any quotations from the book accurately, citing page numbers from the work. If you do use quotes, remember to include a Works Cited page as part of your final paper.

Writing Reminders and Tips

1. Use historical present tense in writing about a literary work.

    Examples ·

    As Shakespeare *writes* in "Let Me Not to the Marriage of True Minds" . . .

    Phoenix Jackson *makes* her way to Natchez, overcoming . . .

    The theme of "Where Are You Going, Where Have You Been?" *is* . . .

2. Reference the title of the work and the name of the author in the introductory paragraph. In the first reference include the author's complete name exactly as it is written: for example, T.S. Eliot, Joyce Carol Oates, or John Donne.

    Subsequent references should be to the last name only: Eliot, Oates, or Donne.

3. Put titles of short stories and most poems in quotation marks: "Musée des Beaux Arts," "The Cask of Amontillado," etc.

4. Italicize titles of books, plays, or long poems: *As I Lay Dying*, *The Waste Land*, *The Glass Menagerie*, or *Conversations with William Faulkner*.

5. If no name is given, refer to the first person speaker in a work as the *persona* or the *narrator* or the *speaker*, not as the author.

    Examples ·
    The narrator in Poe's "The Cask of Amontillado" becomes obsessed . . .

    The persona in Robert Frost's "The Road Not Taken" must choose . . .

6. Almost always place commas and periods inside quotation marks; the exception to this rule is if a parenthetical citation follows the quoted material. Then the period goes after the closing parenthesis of the citation.

7. Reference quotes from prose works parenthetically by the page number(s) on which the quote appears; if the author is not mentioned in the introduction to the quote, the author's last name should be included in the citation.

    Example ·
    Phoenix Jackson is described as wearing "a dark striped dress reaching down to her shoe tops . . . " (Welty 67).

> TIP: Reference only the page number in the citation if the author's name is included in the introduction to the quoted material.

Example. ·
Welty describes Phoenix Jackson as wearing "a dark striped dress reaching down to her shoe tops . . . " (67).

NOTE: There is no "p." or "page" in MLA style—just the number. Notice also that there is no punctuation between the author's last name and the page number.

8. The title of the essay is *not* the title of the literary work and vice versa. Use a serviceable title that reflects content, such as "An Analysis of Theme in 'The Black Veil,'" or a more provocative one, such as "The Secret Sin of Every Man: Hawthorne and Theme."

NOTE: Do not put the title of your essay in quotation marks.

9. Although you do not want your essay to be a patchwork of quotes from the work, use enough quoted material to convince your reader of your point and to accept your thesis as valid. The primary work itself is the best proof that a writer has to support a thesis; it provides specific support to back up an argument. Consequently, use as many quotes or paraphrases from the work as necessary to provide a valid argument.

10. Introduce all quotes; do not just drop them in with no attribution and no connection to the point you are making in the essay.

Examples ·
The narrator tells us, "Connie viewed herself as . . . " (Oates 98).

O'Connor describes the grandmother as wearing "a navy blue straw sailor hat with a bunch of white violets on the brim . . . " (82).

11. Reference poetry by line number(s): for example, (26–28). Also, when quoting more than one line of poetry, follow the capitalization used within the poem and use a slash mark (/) to indicate line breaks.

Example. ·
W. H. Auden begins his poem with the lines, "About suffering they were never wrong,/ The Old Masters:" (1–2).

12. Reference traditional dramas by act and scene; reference verse plays by act, scene, and line number. However, if the play is not divided into acts and scenes, refer to line numbers quoted. If lines are not numbered, refer to page number of the text used.

13. In your introduction, refer to biographical information about the author only if it directly relates to the work you are discussing or the point you are trying to make.

14. When quoting material that contains a quote—that is, a quote within a quote—use double quotation marks around the original quoted material. To indicate that there is a quotation within that first quote, use single quotation marks around the second quote. Don't forget to close both sets of quotation marks.

Example. . . . .
The townspeople telling the story in "A Rose for Emily" arouse the readers' curiosity about the poison Emily Grierson buys when they tell us, "When she opened the package at home there was written on the box, under the skull and bones: 'For rats'" (Faulkner 23).

Notes about Format

Many of the modes of development you studied in Composition I can be used in essay development in Composition II. For instance, you could write a comparison/contrast essay that focuses on the characters in Walker's "Everyday Use" or Dickinson's poems on death. You could write an argumentation essay or persuasive essay that defends your interpretation of a particular aspect of theme in a Robert Frost poem. Everything learned in both classes applies to essay writing in this class and in further pursuits.

Chapter 27

Analyzing the Components of Literary Works

Theme

When we read a piece of literature, we pay attention to its author and to the context in which it was written, and also to setting, plot, characters, point of view, and so on. Analyzing all of these significant features enables us to uncover *theme*, the main idea or the underlying meaning of the work.

For example, before examining Alice Walker's "Everyday Use," the reader should consider the context in which the work was written. First published in 1973, "Everyday Use" appeared on the heels of the American Civil Rights Movement, when many

African Americans strove to establish their identity in a nation that had all but denied it for centuries. This knowledge of context lays the foundation for the development of the story's theme through setting, point of view, characters, plot, and symbols, among other features.

The setting of "Everyday Use" is that of the modest Johnson home, which rests in a pasture and contains only three rooms with holes cut for windows. Early in the story we discover, moreover, that the home is inhabited by Ms. Johnson and her daughter Maggie and that the plot consists of a conflict between these two characters and the eldest daughter, Dee, who has moved away from her childhood home in an attempt to define herself outside of her humble beginnings. All of these elements, then, develop one of the story's major themes: the search for a new identity and the risk, in searching, of abandoning an identity that is in many respects safe and secure.

Yet the search for identity is not the only theme in Walker's short story. Like many works of literature, "Everyday Use" contains more than one theme, and oftentimes multiple themes are interrelated. Additionally, the reader should be mindful that theme may be either explicit (stated openly) or implicit (hidden), that a single work may contain both explicit and implicit themes, and, perhaps most importantly, that theme is often debatable.

Is the central theme of "Everyday Use" the search for identity, familial love, race relations, or family heritage? Is it none of these? All of these? Is one theme more noteworthy or more vital for grasping the story than another? Such questions are open to discussion, and this is what makes theme such an appealing component of a literary work. What is central to a work for one reader may be secondary to another reader.

Reading poetry requires a different approach in searching for theme. We might begin by reading aloud the words on the page and acknowledging how the words and sounds are positioned in the poem. In doing this, we also attend to meter, rhyme, tone, repetition, and metaphors, among other features, all of which contribute to our search for theme. In poetry, too, it is important to gain an understanding of context before reading.

The reader of Robert Frost, for instance, should consider that the poet lived on farms in New Hampshire and Vermont as a child and as an adult. Frost's familiarity with and respect for such natural settings are evident in much of his poetry. Indeed, the rural landscape of New England serves as a backdrop for man's struggles with himself, with other human beings, with society, and with the natural world—themes that recur throughout Frost's poetry.

Point of view also influences theme in poetry, as it does in prose fiction. The speaker of Frost's "Mending Wall," for example, seems to question why it is necessary to have a wall separating his apple orchard from the pine trees owned by his neighbor. He imagines the neighbor's response: "Good fences make good neighbors," which is repeated in the final line of the poem. The speaker's point of view, which suggests his desire to befriend his neighbor, contrasts with the frugality and conservatism of the neighbor, and the two different points of view illustrate a couple of the poem's major themes: communication and human relationships.

As you read, it is important to have a clear sense of these and other important features of literature, yet such features alone will not unveil the theme of a work. Rather, they will point the reader in the direction of the theme. The actual theme—if it exists—is for us to seek and find as readers. It is determined largely by who we are as individuals and by the personal experiences that we bring to a work when we read it. The significance, the beauty of theme, is that in finding it we discover more about not only the work itself, but also about the world upon which the work comments.

Tone

Anyone who has ever been admonished by a parent or another figure of authority with the words, "Don't take that tone with me!" understands at least in a practical way what tone means.

In literary analysis, tone indicates the attitude the author takes toward his or her subject and is a term used more with poetry than with prose. However, certainly any work with a first person narrator could demonstrate tone regardless of the genre.

That tone might be *humorous, angry, ironic, sad, pensive, poignant, indignant, argumentative, disillusioned, bitter, happy, silly, uncaring, wistful, regretful,* or any number of other attitudes the author might choose. Sometimes, identifying the tone of a work can make a tremendous difference in the reader's understanding of the theme or point of the work.

Dylan Thomas's tone in "Do Not Go Gentle into That Good Night" is not the coaxing tone you might expect of a son at his father's deathbed. Rather he is angry, stern, and insistent as he urges his father to "Rage, Rage, against the dying of the light" (3). In fact, he ends his poem with the admonition to "Curse, bless me now with your fierce tears" (17), acknowledging his father's unwillingness to fight against death.

Recognizing the poignancy of the narrative tone of Theodore Roethke's "My Papa's Waltz" turns the poem from one about a child's abuse or unhappiness to one of wistful remembrance of the described event, with the narrator clinging to the memory as certainly as he is clinging to the shirt of his father as he is waltzed off to bed. A different interpretation of tone takes the poem in an entirely different direction.

As an example of the importance of tone in a prose piece, the first person plural narrator of William Faulkner's "A Rose for Emily" reveals the tone of the gossipy townspeople relating the saga of Miss Emily; they are at times accusing, petty, critical, and judgmental before eventually becoming both pitying and sympathetic to the object of their gossip. Recognizing the different tones in that story makes the reader more attuned to Emily's obvious feelings of alienation from everyone else in the town and makes her a more sympathetic character.

The commanding tone of John Donne's "Death, Be Not Proud" is in stark contrast to the teasing, seductive tone of "The Flea." In the first, the persona is vanquishing death from existence in strong, authoritative language meant to remove all power and pride from the personified Death. In the latter, the persona attempts to seduce the subject of his desire with a seemingly logical argument about the importance of a flea to their relationship. In this case, the flea is personified as the marriage bed of the two lovers. The pseudo-serious tone of the narrator who pleads for the life of the flea adds to the ironic nature of the argument.

Like Donne, Emily Dickinson uses two very different tones to write two very powerful poems about death, "Because I Could Not Stop for Death" and "I Heard a Fly Buzz When I Died." In the former, Dickinson uses a very peaceful, relaxed, engaging tone to describe death, taking the reader on what seems to be a pleasant journey through the narrator's past to eternity. In the latter, Dickinson's tone is one of desperation, of agony and tears, of fear and dread; there is no peace, and there is no light at the end of the poem—or at the end of life.

Tone is an important element to consider in interpreting a writer's work. You might need to read the work several times to notice changes in tone or to identify exactly how the author is using tone to control your attitude toward the work.

Point of View

William Faulkner said that when he wrote *The Sound and the Fury*, he originally chose one character to tell the story from a first person point of view. Unhappy with that character's voice, he rewrote the story three more times, employing a different point of view each time and ending with an omniscient narrator. Ultimately, he said that he decided to put all four narrative voices together to create the entire story, a true masterpiece of construction.

Now, whether the book came together in just the way that Faulkner claimed isn't really the point. What is important is that point of view was an essential element in Faulkner's getting that particular story told. Knowing how important point of view is to the author writing the story should emphasize its importance to you, the reader, as well.

The point of view used in a piece of literature refers to the direction from which the author covers the narration. In other words, who is telling the story? Short stories, poetry, and drama all have points of view, and the point of view is an important element in each.

Most authors think long and hard about how they will tell their story. Will they use a first person narrator, an actor or observer to the action, giving his or her perception of the events that occurred? Will they employ a third person narrator, removed from the action of the events? If the narration is third person, will the narrator have access to the thoughts, feelings, and actions of all of the characters in the work? Will the narrative voice be limited to one or two characters, or will the story be told from the point of view of a narrator who merely observes the action? All of these questions are addressed by the author as s/he puts the work together, and your knowing the answers will help you understand the story more fully.

Point of view is generally divided into four categories:

FIRST PERSON POINT OF VIEW

In first person point of view, a character in the story, poem, or play provides the narration. The personal pronoun "I" or the plural "we" is used, and that is the signal to the reader that this is one person's or one group's perception or point of view.

The narrator might be a key figure in the action, like the Duke of Ferrara in Robert Browning's "My Last Duchess." On the other hand, the narrator might be an entire town voicing a collective opinion, like the "we" in William Faulkner's "A Rose for Emily" or Edwin Arlington Robinson's "Richard Cory."

You must be especially attentive to a first person narrator because that narrator, for one reason or another, might not be an honest purveyor of the facts of the story. The narrator of "The Cask of Amontillado," Poe's brilliant short story, is obviously not reliable. What clues does he give you of this fact as he tells the story? How do you know to be suspicious of the Duke of Ferrara's assessment of his wife's behavior in the Browning poem mentioned above, and why do you question the townspeople's criticism of Miss Emily in Faulkner's story?

While most plays are presented with an objective point of view, Tennessee Williams allows Tom, the narrator of *The Glass Menagerie*, to assume a first person narrative voice when he steps out of character and becomes the moderator of the play and presents his memories of the events. Because Tom tells you that the play is a "memory play"—his memory—you have to question his version of the events he presents just as you would question the first person narrator of a poem or short story. Since Tom isn't present for some of the events he narrates, you are required to question even more.

> **NOTE:** Although poetry is often written from a first person point of view, you should not confuse the narrator with the author. The speaker in Mathew Arnold's "Dover Beach" could be Arnold, but you should not assume that he is. The same is true for John Donne's "The Flea" or "Death, Be Not Proud"; the narrator could be the author but shouldn't be identified as such. However, the Duke of Ferrara in "My Last Duchess" is far removed from Browning in every way imaginable. Likewise, the unreliable narrator of any of Poe's poems or stories is not Edgar Allan Poe, despite Poe's personal reputation.

THIRD PERSON OMNISCIENT POINT OF VIEW

In third person omniscient point of view, an all-knowing narrator relays the action of the work. That narrator knows all, sees all, understands all regarding all of the characters within the work. S/he is privy to the thoughts, feelings, and actions of each character, even if there are dozens of characters within the work. This narrator, by virtue of not having any stake in the story being told, is generally considered to be reliable.

THIRD PERSON, LIMITED OMNISCIENT POINT OF VIEW

This point of view allows the reader into the minds and actions of a select number of "actors" in the work. Perhaps the reader is privy to the thoughts and feelings and actions of only one character.

For example, in Katherine Anne Porter's "The Jilting of Granny Weatherall," the reader sees inside the mind of Granny as she is dying and must interpret her words, her thoughts, her reminiscences to make sense of her narrative. We know what only Connie is thinking in "Where Are You Going, Where Have You Been?" by Joyce Carol Oates. Knowing what Arnold Friend is planning in that same story would certainly clarify some major questions for any reader. However, knowing the thoughts of the unkind teenagers who verbally assault "Miss Brill" wouldn't contribute to that story at all. Author Katherine Mansfield's focus is on Miss Brill and her devastation at the criticism of her and her fur piece.

The limited omniscient point of view lets you in on the irony present in "The Story of an Hour" by Kate Chopin; *you* as a reader know that what kills Louise Mallard is the knowledge that her freedom will be stripped away from her, not the joy that her husband is alive.

THIRD PERSON, OBJECTIVE POINT OF VIEW

The third person, objective narrator is merely a reporter of the words and actions of the characters in the work. In much the same way that a movie is viewed in the theater, a poem or short story presented with this point of view is shown as the characters act and interact, recording their words and actions and appearances, but not their thoughts or feelings.

Ernest Hemingway's "Hills Like White Elephants" is a good example of this type of narrative: the man and woman are at odds about "something," on their way to take care of the "something" about which they are at odds, and ultimately make decisions regarding that "something." The reader must fill in all of the blanks to understand what is going on in the story.

The suspense in "The Lottery" is built as much from the point of view as from the events leading up to the climax. Shirley Jackson builds suspense by making you wonder about the lottery and the prize and by leading you to the eventual realization that the winner does not necessarily win. Surely, if Jackson allowed you inside the mind of any of the main characters, you would realize what was going to take place long before the final black dot is drawn.

Identifying the point of view in the story will help you with your overall understanding of the author's meaning.

Setting

When Eudora Welty referred to "place" as "one of the lesser angels in the racing hand of fiction," she was emphasizing the importance of setting in a work. The when and the where of a work combine to create setting—the geographical place as well as the place in time. Although it is important for the reader to know that Welty's story "A Worn Path" takes place in a rural area outside of Natchez, Mississippi, it is equally important to know the chronological time, too, to understand better Phoenix Jackson's demeanor in dealing with the white people in the story.

For a reader to understand fully Alice Walker's "Everyday Use," it is essential that the facts of the Civil Rights Movement and the return to African heritage be included in the discussion. Time and place are often key to understanding what a writer intends the reader to take away from his or her work.

To understand a story, poem, or play fully, you need to pay close attention to the time in which the work is set, as well as the time in which it was written. That element of setting—the when—often provides insight into the work itself.

Nathaniel Hawthorne's "Young Goodman Brown" has an historical setting that contributes to the plot. For you to appreciate the events leading to the climax of the story, you must put the historical events taking place in Salem in perspective. The story itself was published in the mid-1830s, but that date really doesn't figure into an understanding of the story's plot, which deals with the Salem Witch Trials and the suspicions behind them in the late 1600s. Hawthorne even adds some real historical figures from the trials to enhance the plot.

On the other hand, Richard Wright's "The Man Who Was Almost a Man," which was published in 1960, was written much earlier than the publication date, probably around 1939. It is set in the same time frame in which it was originally written, making the historical time an essential element of understanding Dave's plight in the story.

Langston Hughes' poetry was written prior to the Civil Rights Movement, so the poignancy of his verse, which often chronicles the struggle of an African-American persona in a bigoted world, is directly related to the time in which it was written. "The Negro Speaks of Rivers" was published in 1921; the rivers catalogued in that poem represent the trail of the African Americans' journey from the past to the present.

The other element of setting to determine is place—the *where*. Sometimes the locale is an integral part of the plot or character development or theme of a work. Moving a story to a different location would often change the story completely, so you must read carefully to determine why the author chose that particular locale for that story.

The Hawthorne story mentioned earlier is set in the deep forest at night. Goodman Brown's experience is dependent on the sort of mysterious occurrences that can take place in that setting, especially during the hysteria surrounding the witch hunts in Salem. His fear and confusion are compounded by the atmosphere of the forest.

The setting of "Hills Like White Elephants" is a railway station—a public place. That might explain why the conversation between the two characters is so guarded. In addition, the story is set in a foreign country, not the United States. As you work to interpret the subject of the conversation, you will begin to understand that the locale is very important.

Susan Glaspell's *Trifles* is set in a desolate farmhouse. The rural setting, added to the bleak, unfriendly landscape, contributes to the action of the play. Thus, it is an important element to consider in your forming your opinion of the characters, their actions, and the theme of the play.

"Where Are You Going, Where Have You Been?" is set about the time that Joyce Carol Oates wrote it—1966. Both the place and the time contribute to the development of the theme in the story. The rural setting of Connie's house, the recurring references to music playing, and the social mores of the day combine to allow the story to develop as it does.

Many of Robert Frost's poems have place or setting as an important element. The woods in "Stopping by Woods on a Snowy Evening," the fork in the road in "The Road Not Taken," and the stone wall and adjoining properties of the persona and his neighbor in "Mending Wall" are critical to both the narratives and the themes in those poems.

As you read, look for clues that tell you when and where the events take place. They will help you with your overall interpretation of the work.

Character

Characters inhabit a literary work and are one of the most important elements in that work. In fact, good literature is often character-driven rather than plot-driven. Often, college freshmen react to a work with the comment, "But nothing happened!" That response is the product of looking for plot or events or action within a work. However, the inner workings of a character are generally much more telling than any conventions of plot in a literary work. Short stories, drama, and even poetry have characters who move the plot along, certainly, but the characters themselves are often the focus of the work rather than the action.

For instance, Phoenix Jackson is a character about whom much can be inferred, discussed, and analyzed, but the plot of "A Worn Path" is actually fairly brief: An old woman makes a journey to Natchez to get medicine for her sick grandchild, overcoming obstacles on the way. That's it. However, within that story a wealth of complications involve Phoenix, beginning with her symbolic name and ending with the readers' questions about her grandson. The character of Phoenix is the focus of the story.

Though we often think of character as a term used only in prose works, many poems have characters, as well. Dramatic monologues, for instance, often have fascinating characters. The Duke of Ferrara, in Robert Browning's "My Last Duchess," has been the subject of character analyses for over a hundred and fifty years. The Duke himself tells us information about his character, not intentionally, which he probably would be surprised that we know. As you read and reread the poem, you will begin to see the layers of the Duke's character peel away, and his real character emerges.

Character is often discussed in terms of *protagonists, antagonists, foils, round characters,* and *flat characters.* Each term refers to a type of character seen in literary works.

1. **Protagonists** are the main characters of a work. Though we often assume that the protagonist will be the "good guy," that is not always the case. For instance, both Montresor in "The Cask of Amontillado" and the Duke in "My Last Duchess" are the protagonists of those works, and neither would qualify as a "good guy." We know that one is a murderer, and we suspect that the other might be.

   On the other hand, Phoenix Jackson is both the protagonist in Welty's story and a good character. Young Goodman Brown, in Hawthorne's story of that title, is definitely the protagonist, but whether he is a good or bad character has been the subject of debate for many years. The same question is asked about the grandmother, the main character in Flannery O'Connor's story "A Good Man Is Hard to Find."

2. **Antagonists** are those characters in conflict with the protagonist. In "The Cask of Amontillado," Fortunato, who is the subject of Montresor's hatred, would be the antagonist, though he is not as bad as his murderer. In "Where Are You Going, Where Have You Been?" Arnold Friend is clearly the antagonist and a "bad guy" all around. The three male characters in the play *Trifles* are antagonists to the female protagonists. While they are presented as "bad" characters in a way—after all, they hope to find evidence to convict Mrs. Wright—they are actually just doing their jobs.

3. **Foils** are characters who serve to point out the qualities, good or bad, of another character in a work. The emissary from the Count in "My Last Duchess" is such a character; we know by his reactions, reflected in the Duke's words, what he thinks about the Duke's treatment of his last duchess, though he never says a word. He reacts as the reader does to the Duke's story.

4. **Round characters** are those who are fully developed and have sufficient realistic characteristics to make them believable, or true to life. Connie, in "Where Are You Going, Where Have You Been?" is a very believable fifteen-year-old girl; she obsesses about her looks, dislikes her parents and sibling, and thinks that she can control any situation. Amanda Wingfield, the mother in *The Glass Menagerie*, is not only a very believable example of a faded Southern belle, but she also behaves in a way that many mothers, faced with the same worries she has about the futures of her children, would behave.

5. **Flat characters** do not change and are not developed into real people with believable characteristics. They are often stereotypes or are present simply to help move the plot along. For instance, Connie's unnamed friend whom she leaves at the drive-in, as well as Eddie, the boy with whom Connie leaves, are both flat characters in "Where Are You Going, Where Have You Been?" It is not necessary that we know any more about either character; they merely help set up Connie's actions.

Character is probably the first element you notice when you read a piece of literature. Pay attention as you read, and don't assume that what is present on the surface is all that there is to any character.

Conflict

Of all of the possible definitions of *conflict*—fight, clash, battle, strike, collision, etc.—perhaps the best application of the term to a literary work would be "struggle." Stories, narrative poems, and plays often involve a conflict or struggle of some type, though that conflict or struggle may not be of the car chase or ax-wielding type so often seen in popular action movies or fiction. The conflicts are often more subtle but nevertheless make up an important element in a student's understanding of a work.

Conflicts are usually classified first as *internal* or *external*. In other words, is the struggle within a character or between characters or with a force outside of the character? As a careful reader, you will see that most works of fiction—whether short stories or dramas or narrative poems—have at least one conflict that contributes to the plot. Many stories are filled with much more conflict, and as a reader, you might be asked to determine which is the most important to the meaning of the story.

Internal conflicts involve a character's inner struggle; these are usually identified as human-versus-him/herself. Perhaps the character has a moral dilemma to resolve, or perhaps he or she has to overcome a fear.

Montresor, in Poe's "The Cask of Amontillado," reveals his inner conflict about the murder he committed fifty years before, but you must read carefully to see it. You must read carefully to determine the identity of Montresor's audience in that story; when you realize that the listener is, in fact, a priest, you then realize that this is a confession, a deathbed confession perhaps, meant to allow Montresor to "rest in peace" (61). At that point, you know that Montresor did not fulfill his own definition of revenge: that a "wrong is unredressed when retribution overtakes its redresser" (56).

We can safely assume that the ease with which Montresor explains the events of the narrative does not carry through to his conscience; otherwise, he wouldn't need a deathbed confession. That internal conflict, in turn, allows you to see and analyze the character of Montresor more fully.

Louise Mallard, in Kate Chopin's "The Story of an Hour," is in obvious internal conflict after she learns of the death of her husband. The conflict at first appears to be grief and sorrow, but the reader soon realizes that there is perhaps more to the story than a grieving widow. We see Louise's grief turn to joy, an internal conflict so unexpected that Louise first tries to keep it from surfacing; she has trouble acknowledging that she is actually glad that Brently is dead. By the end of the story the internal conflict about her husband's death has all but dissipated as she looks forward to her new life of independence. Ironically, the story takes an unexpected turn when yet another conflict—the realization that her husband is not dead—causes Louise's death.

External conflicts can be of several types: human-versus-human or man-versus-nature, which now includes society, technology, government bureaucracy, etc. The protagonist in Jack London's "To Build a Fire" faces a human-versus-nature conflict in the true sense of the phrase: He is trying to survive in an environment for which he is woefully unprepared. Internal conflict plays into the work as well, making for a very full story. We see the man's thought processes as he struggles with nature and comes to realize that he should have listened to the "old-timer from Sulphur Creek," that he might have to kill his dog, and that he is, indeed, going to die.

In the previously mentioned Poe story, Montresor and Fortunato have a human-versus-human conflict, though the majority of the conflict is verbal sparring, much more interesting than a fistfight would have been. Eventually, the conflict does become physical, however, as Montresor chains Fortunato to the wall of the catacombs and leaves him for dead.

Likewise, "Where Are You Going, Where Have You Been?" has both internal and external conflicts. Connie's struggle with her decision to walk out of the door of her home and get into Arnold Friend's car is the conclusion of her external struggle with him—only verbal, mind you, but a struggle between the two of them nonetheless.

Most stories will have more than one conflict; however, in literary works, the internal conflict is often the one which provides the most interest to a reader.

Figurative Language

Figurative language includes imagery, symbolism, foreshadowing, figures of speech—such as metaphors, similes, and personification—which enhance the effect of any literary work and take the reader beyond the literal meaning of the words on the page. This type of language requires interaction between reader and work, and it contributes to what can be a unique experience for each reader.

It also requires a close reading, contemplation beyond the obvious words on the page, and careful thought. Just as the experience that you bring to a work affects your understanding of theme or assessment of character, that experience will also govern your interpretation of symbols, your understanding of figures of speech, and your visualization of imagery.

Imagery refers to word pictures, or images, the writer creates through use of language to invoke your senses. This type of figurative language employs sight, sound, smell, taste, and touch to invoke memories or experiences that help you fully benefit from the author's meaning.

The imagery of the landscape through which Phoenix Jackson must travel in Eudora Welty's "A Worn Path," for instance, contributes to the reader's full understanding of the obstacles which Phoenix faces. Not only must she face the challenges caused by her failing eyesight, extreme old age, and unsympathetic white people, but she must also face the challenge of her fading memory and foggy recollections. Welty shows the reader the scarecrow/ghost, the imaginary marble cake, and the hunter's dog, for instance, describing each so that the reader can experience what Phoenix does.

A **symbol** is something that stands for something else. Some symbols—like white for purity, red for evil/sin, black for death, or green for envy—are part of our culture and therefore obvious. We recognize a cross as having a religious connotation and a swastika as having an evil one.

Many of us are familiar with Nathaniel Hawthorne's works, which are full of symbolism, much of it associated with color; for example, the letter Hester Prynne wears in *The Scarlet Letter* cannot be ignored—or missed. The pink ribbons worn by Faith in "Young Goodman Brown," as well as the staff of Goodman Brown's companion, add to the meaning of that story. If you read carefully, you will pick up on these symbols and gain more insight into the work.

Other symbols are more subtle. For example, the main character in Eudora Welty's short story "A Worn Path" is named Phoenix; to get the full impact of the symbolism of that name, the reader must know that the phoenix is a mythical bird that is consumed by flame and rises reborn from the ashes every five hundred years.

Likewise, the symbolism of the gun in Richard White's "The Man Who Was Almost a Man" is an integral part of your understanding of that short story. *The Glass Menagerie* is full of symbols which add to Tennessee Williams' themes in that play. You must ask yourself what the unicorn symbolizes to Laura. Also, how does that symbolism change when the gentleman caller breaks off the unicorn's horn? What about the Victrola, the Blue Roses, the movies, the menagerie itself?

Figures of speech enhance the meaning of regular language. When a person says, "He has a tough row to hoe," he or she is referring to two things: literally, hoeing a garden row, which can be very tough work, and figuratively, having a difficult job ahead of him or her. Poetry is full of figures of speech such as metaphors, similes, and personification which pull the reader in to the author's meaning.

For instance, when Frost writes in "Out, Out—" that "the saw,/ As if to prove saws knew what supper meant,/ Leaped out at the boy's hand . . . " (14–16), he is *personifying* a table saw or giving that inanimate object human characteristics to think and make decisions.

Sylvia Plath's confessional poem "Daddy" uses a **simile**, or a comparison between two things using "like" or "as," when she writes, "Any more, black shoe / In which I have lived like a foot / For thirty years . . . " (2–4). Through that simile, Plath is very powerfully referring to the *claustrophobic* life she has experienced as her father's daughter. She further demonizes her father with a **metaphor**, or a comparison in which one thing becomes another, when she describes him as having "A cleft in your chin instead of your foot / But no less a devil for that . . . " (53–54). The allusions to Germany, to the Jews, to the Holocaust, to Satan give a personal quality to the poem as Plath pours out her pain.

Interpreting figures of speech allows you to peel back another layer of an author's meaning to get at the real intent of the work. Writers sometimes use **onomatopoeia** in their work, a term that means that the word itself sounds like the sound associated with the word: buzz, clang, snarled, etc. Use of this technique helps the work come alive for the reader. Frost's "Out, Out—" states that the "buzz saw snarled and rattled" (1), letting us hear the sound of that saw as it cuts the wood.

Another literary element sometimes seen in literature is **foreshadowing**; the author is allowing the reader to look into what will happen later in the story. Good foreshadowing is subtly incorporated into the work so that the reader doesn't really recognize it as such until the completion of the work. If you see it coming a mile away—think of the *Jaws* music here—the author's foreshadowing was not done well.

In Poe's "The Cask of Amontillado," Montresor's constant references to Fortunato's health, to the dampness of the catacombs, to the fact that Fortunato will certainly "not die of a cold" (66) become clear in the climax of the story. Likewise, the piles of stones mentioned early in "The Lottery" foreshadow the conclusion of that story. Hawthorne uses foreshadowing to present many clues which predict the events experienced by the protagonist in "Young Goodman Brown": the staff that writhes like a snake, the admonition of Faith not to go into the forest at dusk, the references to the devil Goodman Brown makes. Flannery O'Connor, in "A Good Man Is Hard to Find," foreshadows the fate of the family with the first sentence of the story: "The grandmother didn't want to go to Florida." However, like most things that writers successfully foreshadow, the fate of the family isn't obvious to the reader until the conclusion of the story.

Authors write and rewrite their works to use the precise word or symbol, to make the most revealing comparison, to paint the most vivid picture for you, the reader. By reading closely, you are making their attention to detail pay off.

Glossary of Literary and Rhetorical Terms

Abstract—a summary that provides the important points of an article or other text.

Active voice—a sentence construction in which the subject acts. Ex. The quarterback threw the ball. (subject [quarterback] acts [threw] direct object [ball]). Often, there is a direct object to receive the action, but not always. Ex. Go! (understood subject, no receiver of the action).

Alliteration—repetition of consonant sounds. Ex. The big boy broke his brand new bicycle.

Allusion—indirect reference to a literary, mythological, historical, or religious person, event, or fact. Ex. Booker T. Washington was considered by some to be the Moses of his race.

Analogy—a comparison of two things. with the intent of clarifying the more complex one by using an association with the less complex one. Ex. A car runs in much the same way as the human body; both require fuel, tune-ups, and maintenance.

Anaphora—a rhetorical device which relies on repetition of words or phrases at the beginning of clauses or sentences for emphasis or effect. Ex. "It was the best of times, it was the worst of times; it was the age of wisdom, it was the age of foolishness . . . " is part the famous anaphora which begins Charles Dickens' *A Tale of Two Cities.*

Antecedent—the word that comes before a pronoun and for which the pronoun stands. Pronouns must agree with their antecedents in number and gender. Ex. The students (*plural, gender-neutral antecedent*) did their (*plural, gender-neutral pronoun*) homework.

Aside—a situation in a drama in which an actor speaks directly to the audience, sharing his/her plans or providing an explanation for a behavior. The rest of the cast on the stage presumably do not hear the words spoken.

Assonance—repetition of vowel sounds. Ex. The injured infant was incapable of winning the beauty contest. See *alliteration* for consonant sounds.

Antagonist—the character in conflict with the main character. Ex. Fortunato is the antagonist in "The Cask of Amontillado."

Apostrophe—an address to an inanimate object, usually used in poetry. Ex. "O Wind! / If Winter comes, can Spring be far behind?" (Percy Bysshe Shelley)

Argument—a rhetorical technique used to convince an audience of the validity of one's opinion on a subject.

Audience—the reader or readers to whom a piece of writing is directed.

Ballad—a simple, repetitive verse form originally sung or recited, usually containing a dramatic narrative theme.

Ballad stanza—the stanza pattern used in most traditional ballads. It consists of a four line stanza (quatrain) with an *abcb* rhyme scheme; the first and third lines have four metrical feet (tetrameter), and the second and fourth have three metrical feet (trimeter).

Bibliographic record—an entry in an online catalog or a database that represents a specific book, article, or other item. The entry contains all the information necessary for a complete description (author, title, date copyrighted, publishing company, place of publication, etc.) of the item and is presented in a specific bibliographic format.

Bildungsroman—a coming-of-age story. A German term, this type of novel or story usually takes a protagonist on a journey of some type, either literal or figurative, which helps him or her mature. Ex. In modern literature, the *Harry Potter* series comprises a Bildungsroman, as Harry accepts his destiny to destroy Voldemort.

Blank verse—poetry which has an iambic pentameter rhythm but no rhyme. Ex. Robert Frost's poem "Out, Out—" is written in blank verse.

Brainstorming—one of many prewriting methods used to identify areas of a topic to organize and group similar areas.

Blog—originally a "Web log" that recorded daily thoughts and responses. Blogs have grown in popularity and frequency and have created celebrities like Arianna Huffington. Blogs are often used by students in classroom assignments. See the Net-Savvy chapters in this textbook for more information.

Carpe diem—literally, seize the day. The phrase often replies to poetry which advocates living life to the fullest. Ex. Andrew Marvell's seventeenth-century poem, "To the Virgins to Make Much of Time," with its advice to "gather ye rosebuds while you may," is an excellent example of a *carpe diem* theme.

Cataloging—process of creating entries for items (books, AV, etc.) and providing the entries in a catalog (usually electronic) for ease of retrieval. Cataloging includes assigning call numbers (for location on the library shelves) and subject headings and including such descriptive information as author, title, and publication information.

Cause and effect—a rhetorical mode in which an analysis of either (or both) the reasons for or the consequences of a certain action are examined.

Character—the inhabitants of a work. Characters can be major or minor, depending on their involvement in the plot of the work. Ex. Phoenix Jackson is the main character of Eudora Welty's short story "A Worn Path." Ex. The envoy in Robert Browning's "My Last Duchess" is a minor character in that poem.

Chronological order—the order in which events unfold or take place. Often, personal narratives are written in the order in which the events occurred.

Citation—as used in research, a written reference to a specific work or portion of a work (book, periodical article, report, website, recording, etc.) either printed, digital, or online, which identifies the work and where it is located. The exact placement of the information and the punctuation in the citation vary by field, but each style includes such necessary information as author, title, and date published or copyrighted, etc.

Classification/division—a rhetorical mode in which a subject area is grouped according to shared characteristics. Ex. College students can be classified by where they sit in the classroom.

Clause—a group of words that has a subject and a verb. Independent clauses have a subject and a verb and express a complete thought. Ex. The party ended. Dependent clauses have a subject and a verb but do not express a complete thought. Ex. When the police arrived.

Cliché—an overused, overworked expression that no longer has a distinct meaning. Ex. She was there for me when she had her head on straight.

Climax—the high point of a story. The climax occurs at the peak of the action.

Clustering/mapping—a prewriting technique that groups ideas or characteristics to establish common patterns.

Coherence—work that "sticks together" or coheres. Coherent essays move seamlessly from one idea to another with clear relationships established among all the parts.

Comma splice—the error of joining two sentences/complete thoughts with a comma rather than a stronger mark of punctuation. Ex. The processional for the wedding had begun, the bride was nowhere in sight. (comma splice) Corrected: The processional for the wedding had begun; the bride was nowhere in sight.

Comparison/contrast—a rhetorical mode that analyzes likenesses (comparison) or differences (contrast) or both, usually with the intent of identifying the strengths or weaknesses in the items discussed.

Conceit—a figure of speech that compares two unlike things in an exaggerated manner. Ex. John Donne's "The Flea" compares a flea's body to the marriage bed.

Conflict—a struggle between two persons (person versus person), a person and his/her conscience or belief system (person versus self), or a person and his/her surroundings (person versus nature, environment, society). Most works have more than one conflict; however, one may be more developed than the others. Ex. Phoenix Jackson, in Eudora Welty's "A Worn Path," has conflicts with herself, with her physical environment, and with the social environment of the time.

Connotation—the inferred rather than the literal meaning of a word. Ex. The word *slender* is preferable to *skinny* when describing a woman's appearance because the first word has a positive connotation and the second, a negative one.

Copyright—the legal right of an author, artist, composer, creator, or owner of a work (book, music, audio, image, website, etc.) to the exclusive distribution, sale, or display of the protected work. It is copyright infringement to use all or part of a work without prior consent of the copyright holder.

Couplet—two consecutive lines of poetry which rhyme. Ex. "If this be error, and upon me prov'd / I never writ, nor no man ever loved" is the couplet ending Shakespeare's famous "Sonnet 116."

Dangling/misplaced modifier—a phrase that is not placed close enough to the word it describes to make its meaning clear. Ex. At the age of three, my father went to work for a Fortune 500 company. Corrected: When I was three, my father went to work for a Fortune 500 company.

Database—a collection of information on one topic or field. An example of a printed database is a telephone book which contains names and telephone numbers and organizes the information for ease of use. An electronic database is a computer-based collection of information. Library databases include collections of resource materials.

Denotation—the actual dictionary meaning of a word. Ex. The latest edition of the Fatherree-Hammons *New Word Dictionary* defines "slender" as thin or narrow in size.

Denouement—the ending of a story or the conclusion of a plot. The denouement occurs when all of the questions are answered and the problems are solved.

Dewey Decimal Classification System (DDC)—a system for categorizing and arranging books by subject. All information is divided into ten main classes, and each of these is further divided into ten divisions, etc. The name "decimal" is because of the divisions by ten. Many college libraries still use the Dewey Decimal Classification System.

Dialogue (or dialog)—the spoken words of characters in a literary work. Specifically, dialogue is used to refer to the speeches of characters in a play.

Dimeter—a rhythmic pattern that has two feet per line. Ex. The first stanza of E. A. Robinson's poem "Miniver Cheevy" ends with a two-foot line: "And he had reasons" (4).

Dramatic monologue—a poem developed with a single speaker addressing a silent audience. Ex. Robert Browning's "My Last Duchess" is a dramatic monologue.

eBook (electronic book)—an electronic version of a printed book or an original Internet publication with enough pages to be considered a book. Many companies provide ebooks online for a price. Some older books that are no longer copyrighted are available free of charge online.

e-Portfolio—Electronic portfolio. An e-portfolio is an on online or digital compilation. Typically, an e-portfolio is a collection of work by a given person and/or a collection of information about that person meant to highlight the person's abilities and accomplishments. In a classroom, an e-portfolio might simply collect work completed throughout the semester. Increasingly, e-portfolios are being used by people to market themselves for jobs and graduate schools. e-Portfolios can provide the same information as traditional résumés, yet they are normally more substantial.

EBSCOhost—a variety of databases that include magazine, journal, and newspaper articles (among other items). Access EBSCO by going to MAGNOLIA on your library's electronic resources page.

Electronic database—often periodical indexes that contain either a listing of articles, abstracts of articles, or full-text articles from magazines, journals, newspapers, etc. The information may also be available in a printed format, but an online database provides accessibility from any Internet-connected computer. The companies providing the online indexes charge libraries for their use and limit usage to the registered borrowers of the library or students of the college.

Elegy—a poem about death, generally mourning and praising the dead person. Ex. Tennyson's "Ode: Intimations on Immortality" is an elegy on the death of his friend, Arthur Henry Hallam.

Elizabethan sonnet—a 14-line poem divided into three quatrains and a couplet. Elizabethan sonnets are also called Shakespearean sonnets after William Shakespeare, the English poet and playwright who perfected the form.

Epigram—a short, pithy saying, originally used as an inscription.

Epiphany—a moment of realization of an important fact or special insight. Ex. Saul had an epiphany on the road to Damascus and changed his name to Paul.

Epitaph—an inscription or poem which memorializes a dead person.

Essay—a writing that has more than one paragraph. Often referred to as themes, essays can be developed in a variety of ways to present the author's point. They usually consist of an introductory paragraph, any number of body paragraphs, and a concluding paragraph.

Euphemism—using a more pleasing word to describe an unpleasant situation. Ex. On August 3, 1964, Flannery O'Connor passed on to her great reward. (She died.)

Expletive—beginning a clause with *there is*, *there are*, or *it is*, thus moving the subject to the predicate area of the sentence and weakening the structure. Ex. There are four students who have not finished the assignment. (*Four students have not finished the assignment* is a much stronger construction.)

Exposition—the beginning of a story. The exposition provides information about the background, characters, and setting which will be used in the plot.

Fabliau—a humorous story that originated in French literature. *Fabliaux* (plural) were conventionally comprised of eight-syllable verses that featured the foibles of humans. Many of Chaucer's *Canterbury Tales* were *fabliaux* that pretended to contain a moral about human behavior.

Falling action—the unraveling of the plot that follows the climax. In tragedies, the falling action is often precipitated by a tragic force that moves the hero into danger.

Figurative language—symbols, imagery, foreshadowing, figures of speech, etc., that enhance a work and take it beyond the literal meaning of the words on the page.

Flat character—a character within a work who is not fully developed but serves to move the plot along in some way. Ex. Brently Mallard's friend Richards is a flat character in "The Story of an Hour" because he is simply in the story to relay the news of the train wreck.

Flashback—a break in the action of a work to provide commentary on events from the past.

Foil—a character within a work who serves to contrast or complement the qualities of a major character. Ex. The white hunter in Eudora Welty's "A Worn Path" is a foil who serves to point out Phoenix Jackson's dignity and resolve as she makes her way to town.

Foot/feet—a recurring set of accented and unaccented patterns in a poem, each set representing a foot. Ex. The line "My mistress' eyes are nothing like the sun," from Shakespeare's "Sonnet 130," consists of five sets of unaccented/accented feet.

Forum—a place meant for group discussion. Forums are also known as discussion boards, message boards, and bulletin boards. There are no risqué letters involved here.

Foreshadowing—hints to the reader about an action or event occurring later in the work. Ex. The first line of "The Story of an Hour," which refers to Mrs. Mallard's heart condition, foreshadows the climax of the story.

Fragment—a group of words that either does not have a subject and verb or does not express a complete thought. Ex. "When I get to town and finish my shopping" is a fragment because it does not express a complete thought. "John, Mary, Frank, and Elizabeth, my oldest and dearest friends from childhood" is a fragment because it does not have a verb—or a complete thought.

Frame story—a story within a story. A speaker introduces a story that then sets the stage for another, sometimes shorter story. Ex. Geoffrey Chaucer's *Canterbury Tales* is a frame story in which a pilgrimage to Canterbury provides the opportunity for the individual pilgrims to tell a variety of tales.

Free verse—poetry that has neither a set rhythm nor rhyme. Carl Sandburg's poem "Chicago" is an excellent example of free verse, as are the works of Walt Whitman.

Fused/run-on sentence—two independent thoughts that are incorrectly joined together with no punctuation. Ex. The groom saw that the bride was not there he left with his mother and her friends.

Genre—the class into which a literary work is categorized: short story, poem, drama, novel, biography, nonfiction, memoir.

Heptameter—a rhythmic pattern that has seven feet per line.

Hexameter—a rhythmic pattern that has six feet per line.

Historical present tense—present tense used in writing about a piece of literature, regardless of when the work was actually published. Ex. In Shakespeare's *King Lear*, Lear disowns his youngest and favorite daughter, Cordelia. The historical present is also used in research papers to discuss information gleaned from sources.

Home page—the "front page," "main page," or "hub page" of a website. Usually it is the center of the site's organization, and the other pages link out from there. It's important to identify the home page of a site when doing research because often the information necessary for documenting your source can be found there. Checking in with the home page of a site is the equivalent of looking at the title and copyright pages of a book in order to find the title, the publisher, the date of publication, and so on. The home page is usually found by shortening the URL of your source down to the part that ends with the .com, .org, .gov, or .edu.

Homonym—words that sound alike but are spelled differently. Ex. The bow of a ship and the bough of a tree.

Hyperbole—an intentional exaggeration, usually for effect. Ex. Johnny, I have told you a million times not to jump on the bed!

Iambic—a poetic line in which every other syllable is accented. Ex. "My mistress' eyes are nothing like the sun" (Shakespeare) follows an iambic pattern of unaccented/accented syllables.

Idiom—a word or an expression that differs in meaning from the literal intent, often peculiar to a specific language or culture. Ex. I'm feeling *down in the dumps* today.

Image/imagery—a picture painted with words by an author to appeal to the senses or to create or enhance a mood. Ex. "She walks in beauty, like the night of cloudless climes and starry skies . . . " is the beginning of Byron's poem, "She Walks in Beauty," and sets the mood for a poignant, reminiscent poem of lost love.

Imperative mood—a command, directive, order, or request that an action be carried out. The imperative mood is used with present tense verbs and usually has an understood you as its subject. Ex. Give me that phone, immediately!

Index—a print or online listing of information with links, page numbers, or other ways of leading to the original source. The information indexed is normally from one type of source (as periodicals—the MAGNOLIA databases) or on one broad topic, as history. Most indexes are arranged alphabetically by subject headings to aid in locating the information. Many books contain a subject/main word index at the end. Multiple volume works often contain an index to the complete set in the end of the last volume.

Internet—a "network of networks" which connects computer networks worldwide for ease of transmission of email, data, files, etc. and to locate information on the World Wide Web (WWW or Web).

Irony—the difference between expectation and reality. Ex. Wasn't it ironic that John was convicted of robbing a bank on the day that he won the 20 million dollar lottery!

Italian sonnet—a 14-line poem divided into an octave (eight lines) and a sestet (six lines). The octave generally poses the problem or presents a question, and the sestet solves the problem or answers the question. Italian sonnets are often called Petrarchan sonnets, too, after Petrarch, an Italian poet who perfected the form.

Jargon—language that is specific to a particular group, organization, or profession. When used in a context separate from that group, the meaning is often unclear. Ex. If we can increase the gigs and free up some RAM, we may be able to use this computer.

Journal—a periodical, usually of a scholarly nature, published monthly or quarterly and of interest to a specialized group. Most journals contain few if any advertisements, have long articles, and contain original research. Some scholarly journals are peer-reviewed. Examples of journals include *Journal of the American Medical Association (JAMA)*, *Journal of Strength and Conditioning Research*, *The College Mathematics Journal*, and *The Southern Literary Journal*. Not everything with the word "journal" in the title is a journal. For example, neither *Ladies Home Journal* nor *The Wall Street Journal* is a journal.

Library of Congress Classification System (LCC)—a system for categorizing and arranging books by subject. The LCC divides all information into twenty broad areas that are subdivided using letters and numbers. It was developed by the Library of Congress and is usually used in large academic libraries.

Local color/regionalism—a work set in a particular region or area, employing the language, characteristics, manners, behaviors of that particular region. Ex. Kate Chopin set most of her stories in Louisiana and is thus considered a regional writer.

Lyric—a poem that has the expression of personal emotion as its main intention. Ex. William Wordsworth's poem "I Wandered Lonely as a Cloud" is a lyric poem that expresses the persona's joy at the beauty of nature.

Mashup—when two or more digital compositions or digital elements are combined to make something new. A map mashup might combine a map with photographs and text. A video mashup might take snippets from more than one film and mix them all together in a way that creates a whole new storyline.

Meta-search engine—a search engine that searches other search engines. Dogpile is an example of one of the more popular meta-search engines. Because various search engines use their own unique formulas for locating sources, you'll either find different information from searching two different engines, or you'll get the same information in a different order. The advantage of using a meta-search engine is that you can quickly see which information shows up first in a variety of search engines without having to conduct separate searches on each one.

Metaphor—an implied comparison of two unlike things which declares that one thing *is* another. Ex. John is a pig with no manners.

Meter—repeated patterns of stressed and unstressed syllables in a poem. Examples of these patterns, which are called *feet*, are **iamb or iambic**, consisting of one unstressed followed by one stressed syllable (Ex. today); **trochee or trochaic**, consisting of one stressed followed by one unstressed syllable (after); **anapest or anapestic**, consisting of two unstressed syllables followed by one stressed (intervene); and **dactyl or dactylic**, consisting of two stressed syllables (downtown).

Microblog—blogs in miniature or micro format to which only very short pieces are posted. Twitter is perhaps the most popular microblogging service. It allows for up to 140 characters at a time to be posted.

Mode—refers to the way or method by which an essay is developed. Types of modes include narration, comparison/contrast, cause and effect, and division/classification, among others.

Mood—in reference to literature, the atmosphere, emotional or literal, of a work. Ex. The first description of the Usher house in Poe's "The Fall of the House of Usher" sets a gloomy, depressing mood which prevails throughout the story. *Also see subjunctive mood.*

MPEG4—video file format that is the video equivalent of what MP3 is to audio. It is a smaller, more easily transferred file that still retains enough image and sound quality for acceptable viewing.

MP3—the preferred audio file format for posting online. MP3 represents a compromise between sound quality and file size. In other words, it provides a smaller, more easily transferred file without losing more sound quality than is considered acceptable.

Multigenre—the combination of multiple literary genres into one composition.

Multimedia—the combination of various forms of media, such as image, text, music, video, and so on, into one composition.

Multimodal—the combination of two or more rhetorical modes into one essay.

Narrative—a story, either in poetry or prose. Robert Browning's "My Last Duchess" is a good example of a poetic narrative, any short story represents a fictional narrative, and a first person account of an event can be a personal narrative.

Narrator—the teller of the story. Ex. Montresor, the narrator in "The Cask of Amontillado," fails to tell the reader his exact reason for murdering Fortunato.

Naturalism—a movement popularized in the latter part of the nineteenth and early part of the twentieth century in which humans are depicted as being at the mercy of their environment. Often that environment is malevolent, and in some works, the only salvation for humans is a communal effort to work together to survive.

NewsBank—a database containing articles from a large selection of newspapers.

Novella—a prose work that is longer than a short story but shorter than a novel. Most novellas contain from 60 to 120 pages.

Octameter—a rhythmic pattern which has eight feet per line. Ex. Edgar Allan Poe's "Once upon a midnight dreary while I pondered weak and weary . . . " is a good example of octameter.

Online catalog (Online Public Access Catalog, OPAC)—an electronic database containing the bibliographic records for the items (books, audiovisual, etc.) held by a specific library or library system. The online catalog is available through computers and usually may be accessed through the Internet.

Online database—*see Database*

Onomatopoeia—a word that sounds like the meaning of the word. Ex. Buzz, rattle, hiss.

Opposing viewpoints—contains many pairs of articles with differing positions on the same topic. This database is particularly useful if you've been assigned to write a persuasive paper on a social issue.

Oratory—skill in public speaking. Ex. Jonathan Edwards' oratory skills in delivering his sermon "Sinners in the Hands of an Angry God" caused his congregation to weep hysterically in fear.

Oxymoron—an apparent contradiction in terms in a phrase. Ex. A deafening silence descended over the crowd.

Parallelism—wording in the structure of a sentence in which all elements are the same. Parallel structure can refer to sentences, to phrases, and to dependent clauses. Ex. My hobbies are reading, writing, and cooking.

Paradox—a statement that appears to be untrue or in contradiction to the facts, but may actually be true. Ex. "Freedom is slavery," a quote by George Orwell, is a famous paradoxical statement.

Paraphrase—to restate the context of a work or a source, using one's own words.

Parenthetical citation—an internal reference in a documented paper, enclosed in parentheses, containing information necessary to identify the source which is being cited, whether quoted directly or paraphrased. Depending on the style manual being followed and the information given within the cited material, the information might include the author's last name, the page or paragraph number of the original source, or the date of publication.

Passive voice—a sentence construction in which the subject is acted upon. Most word-processing programs, Microsoft Word included, will flag use of passive voice. Ex. The grand prize was won by a twelve-year-old boy. *Corrected:* A twelve-year-old boy won the grand prize.

Pastoral elegy—poetry combining the elements of the pastoral—shepherds and a rural, bucolic life—with grieving and death.

PDF (Portable Document Format)—the preferred format for people who want to assure the integrity of the page layout. A PDF file will keep its graphics, margins, and other elements intact from computer to computer and operating system to operating system. PDFs require the Adobe viewer, a free download, for opening, but they cannot be edited without purchasing the appropriate Adobe software. Many of the articles found in library databases are in the PDF format. Magazine articles, for example, have been scanned so that you see the page on the computer screen as it appeared in the original print version.

Peer-reviewed journals—journals which submit their articles to scholars in the field for critical evaluation before publishing the articles.

Pentameter—a rhythmic pattern which has five feet per line. Ex. Shakespeare's "My mistress' eyes are nothing like the sun . . . " has five feet, which makes it pentameter rhythm.

Periodical—a publication issued on a regular basis and on a fixed schedule. Newspapers, magazines, and journals are examples of periodicals; the most common publication schedules include daily, weekly, monthly, and bimonthly issues.

Persona—the first person speaker or narrator in a short story or poem, not to be confused with the author. Ex. The persona in Frost's "The Road Not Taken" speaks of the choices that we face in life.

Personification—assigning human characteristics to inanimate or nonhuman things. Robert Frost uses personification in "Out, Out—" when the narrator says, "The saw, / as if to prove saws knew what supper meant. . . . "

Plagiarism—intentionally or unintentionally presenting someone else's work, ideas, or words as one's own.

Plot—the events that contribute to what happens in a work. Ex. The plot of Eudora Welty's "A Worn Path" concerns an old woman's trip to Natchez to buy medicine for her grandson; along the way, she encounters numerous obstacles but still completes her journey.

Podcast—the term literally means an online audio broadcast in a format that can be downloaded for use on an MP3 player. Podcasting is also associated with subscription-based services, such as iTunes.

Point of view—the direction from which an author chooses to tell a story. There are four different points of view: **first person**, in which a singular or plural narrator (I or we) tells the story; **third person omniscient**, in which an all-knowing, all-seeing narrator tells the story; **third person limited omniscient**, in which omniscience is limited to one or two characters who tell the story; and **third person objective**, in which the narrator merely observes and reports what is happening, what is said, and what is done in the story.

Process analysis—a rhetorical mode in which the writer either explains how to execute a particular process or how a particular process works.

Protagonist—the main character of a work. Ex. Montresor is the protagonist of Poe's "The Cask of Amontillado."

Quatrain—a stanza of poetry consisting of four lines. Ex. Elizabethan sonnets are made up of three quatrains and a couplet.

Quotation—repeating another person's words or ideas. A direct quotation repeats exactly what the person said or wrote and requires quotation marks; an indirect quotation does not repeat the exact words and does not require quotation marks. Either type of quotation requires documentation of the original source to avoid plagiarism.

Realism—literature that remains true to the language, actions, motivations, and characterizations of a particular time and place. As a movement, realism strayed from the romanticism preceding it which often had a "happily ever after" outcome.

Reference room—a special area in a library or Learning Resource Center that houses books that are intended for brief consultation rather than to be read from cover to cover. Books in this area often contain statistics, definitions, formulas, and such. These books are not checked out of the library, but pages needed for research may be photocopied.

Remix—a digital remaking of some form of media. The term usually refers to music when an original sound mix has been remixed by having some tracks or elements changed or rerecorded. It can refer to any form of media in which an original version has been recrafted into a new version.

Reserves—an area in most college libraries where items are placed by instructors so that all of their students may have access to the items. Reserves are checked out for a brief period, such as one hour, and are restricted to use in the library.

Rhetoric—the presentation of ideas and/or arguments in clear, concise, effective language.

Rhetorical modes—different types of development structures which present ideas and/or arguments in clear, concise, effective language. Ex. Narration, process analysis, and description are types of rhetorical modes.

Rhetorical question—a question which is being asked for effect but neither requires nor demands an answer. Ex. A rhetorical question such as "What did I know about love at the ripe old age of 6?" might be a good technique for an introduction of a personal narrative.

Rhyme—identical or similar sounds/words, usually at the ends of poetic lines. Poets sometimes use internal rhyme as well, having the end word of the first half of a line of poetry rhyme with the last word in the second half.

Rhythm—the beat of a poem, consisting of a repeated pattern of stressed and unstressed syllables, usually referred to as feet. Ex. "My mistress' eyes are nothing like the sun," by William Shakespeare, is an example of an iambic pentameter rhythm.

Rising action—following the exposition, the rising action often begins with some sort of force or action which precipitates the complications of the plot and ends with the climax.

Round character—a fully developed, fully realized character in a work. Ex. Phoenix Jackson is a round character in Welty's "A Worn Path."

RSS—Really Simple Syndication. RSS provides a means to subscribe to websites, podcasts, and blogs so that users can know when the content is updated without the need to visit the site on a daily basis.

RTF—Rich Text Format. This is a file format for word-processing documents that is considered universal. Most word processing programs can open it. Saving to RTF will greatly reduce the chances that your classmates or instructors have problems viewing your document.

Satire—an often humorous technique used by an author to expose the weakness in a character or the ridiculousness of a situation in an effort to encourage change. Ex. Jonathan Swift's "A Modest Proposal," one of the most famous satires ever written, really intends to make the British people recognize their barbaric attitudes about the Irish.

Search engine—a web-based program that allows Internet users to search for information online. Some of the most popular search engines are Google, Yahoo, Dogpile, Mamma, and Ask.

Setting—the time and place in which a literary work takes place.

Simile—a comparison of two unlike things using *like* or *as*. Ex. John eats like a pig at an all-you-can-eat buffet.

Slant rhyme—a technique using end rhyme that is close to being rhymed. Ex. Rhyming *war* and *wear*.

Social networking—interacting with groups of people based on shared interests. Twitter and Facebook are two of the most popular social networking services online, but the concept can be put to use for more than just making friends. Shelfari and Library Thing are social networking sites based on interests in reading. CiteULike and del.icio.us are social bookmarking sites designed for sharing online research.

Soliloquy—a dramatic situation in a play in which a character talks aloud to him/herself to inform the audience of his/her thoughts, plans, attitudes. Ex. Hamlet's famous soliloquy, "To be or not to be," in Shakespeare's play reveals that he is contemplating suicide.

Sonnet—a 14-line poem, usually written in iambic pentameter rhythm. *See Elizabethan sonnet and Italian sonnet.*

Speaker—the narrator or persona in a literary work. *See persona.*

Stacks, closed—an area in most libraries housing periodicals or other items with restricted access, closed to students. To use items from "closed stacks," students must request help from a library staff person who will retrieve the items.

Stacks, open—an area in a library where books or other materials are stored for browsing and use by students/patrons. Usually "open stacks" indicates the main book collection of the library and contains the books that may be checked out of the library.

Symbol—something that stands for something else. Ex. In Hawthorne's stories, *red* is often seen as a symbol of evil or sin.

Tetrameter—a rhythmic pattern consisting of four feet per line. Ex. The line "Miniver Cheevy, child of scorn . . . " is an example of tetrameter because there are four feet per line.

Theme—the major point or dominant idea of a work. Themes are universal and have a greater scope than just the work itself. Additionally, the word "theme" is sometimes used by instructors instead of "essay."

Thesis—the main or controlling idea of an essay, traditionally only one sentence. The thesis is a statement of opinion which will be supported by the body paragraphs.

Tone—the attitude that a writer takes about her or his subject in developing a work. Some works have a humorous, a sarcastic, a serious, or a sardonic tone.

Topic sentence—the main or controlling idea of a paragraph, traditionally only one sentence.

Tragedy—a type of dramatic work that contains a significant conflict between the protagonist of the play and other characters or forces. There are usually extreme levels of disaster, destruction, and/or death present in a tragedy.

Tragic hero—the main character of a tragedy. The tragic hero faces great trials, suffers a catastrophe generally brought on by a character flaw, or a complication which either s/he caused or that fate created. Then the tragic hero realizes the error of his or her ways, often just before dying.

Transition—connection of one idea to another within and between paragraphs. Transitional techniques include using transition words, repeating key words, and creating parallel structures.

Transitional paragraphs—paragraphs of usually long types of writing that serve to provide a connection between examination of separate topics.

Transition words or expressions—words and phrases that provide connection between ideas within and between paragraphs. These can signal a continuation of an idea, a change of direction, a comparison or contrast, etc. Ex. however, therefore, for example, etc.

Trimeter—a rhythmic pattern consisting of three feet per line.

Triplet—a poetic form that consists of three rhyming lines, each having the same number of syllables.

Unity—a quality of work indicating that everything fits together and follows logically.

URL—Uniform Resource Locator. A URL is an online address. It identifies the exact location of a particular web page or file.

Vignette—a brief scene, sketch, or word picture in a work.

Voice—the unique style an author uses to tell a story in a literary piece or to present an idea in a nonfiction work. An author's voice can display humor, satire, anger, or any number of other emotions. Ex. Jonathan Swift's voice in "A Modern Proposal" is satirical as he presents his plan for keeping Irish children from being a burden on English society. Also, voice can refer to the characteristics given to the persona in a first person narrative. Ex. The narrative voice of the persona of Robert Frost's "Out, Out—" is one of resignation and acceptance.

Web browser—the piece of software on your computer that you use to navigate or to "browse" the Internet. Some of the most common browsers are Internet Explorer, Mozilla Firefox, and Netscape. On Apple computers, the browser of choice is often Safari.

Wiki—a type of website, and like blogs, the term "wiki" refers to the software used to create the website according to a certain organizational pattern. Typically, wikis have been multipage, multiauthor sites set up in a way that is easy to edit and easy to expand. The most well-known wiki is Wikipedia, which is still considered to be a questionable source by many teachers.

WorldCat—online union catalog of materials (books, maps, magazines, etc.) owned and cataloged by libraries worldwide. Anyone may search *WorldCat* to locate items that have been published or to locate a library that holds a specific title. (worldcat.org)

Appendix A

Narrative Essays

Standard Admonition

Essays and examples contained in this edition of *For Our Students* are not all *A* work nor are they acceptable to everyone's political or societal tastes.

The content of these essays reflects students' lives and interests. Some are several years old, but they still connect well with the reader.

All of the essays in this textbook have been chosen for their thought-provoking or unique content. As such, they sometimes reflect contemporary students' ethical, religious, and societal dilemmas.

In many cases, the content is sweet and dear, just like our students, their parents and families, and teachers. Others reflect the severity of our students' personal and familial turmoil, a fact that permeates our world as educators.

We celebrate our students' courage and generosity for allowing us to publish their work.

Sample Essay: Narration

Suhail Basalama, Student

Surviving High School

In my country, Yemen, the last grade of high school is the most crucial for two reasons. It reveals the outcome of twelve years of studying, and a student's future depends mostly on it. When a student wants to apply for a governmental scholarship or enroll in a university, the most important factor is the high school score. The final exams of high school are administered directly by the Ministry of Education to assure that students from all over the country have equal opportunities. Therefore, graduating from high school in Yemen with high scores requires discipline, diligence, and patience. The last year of high school was the most challenging grade that had a huge influence on my life.

Being from a modest family, I faced some financial difficulties that had some impact on my academic progress. On the first day of the new academic year, the principal gave a speech; he announced that two students from our school had achieved the first and the second places of the top ten students in Yemen. I felt that the principal was giving that speech exclusively to put pressure on me.

Since I am an only child of educated parents, my father wanted to offer me the best education by taking me to one of the best and most expensive private schools in Yemen. However, my father had difficulties paying for my school. For example, in the beginning of the year, my father could not pay the first amount of the tuition fees. Thus I stayed for a whole month without books, and that was embarrassing and frustrating.

During the year, work and study were the main obstacles I encountered. I had to work at my father's shop for four hours per day because my father could not work at the shop alone. Although it was hard to help customers, I used to bring my textbooks and study at the shop. Accordingly, I had great benefits from work and school. For example, I became more mature since I had responsibilities at both work and school. At school, most students and teachers used to idealize the two top ten students by exaggerating about their hard work. They retold the story of Omar, the first student of Yemen, who studied the whole curriculum seven times before the final exams. That made no sense to me.

The real anxiety occurred in waiting for the results after completing the final exams. My father pressured me during the year because he wanted me to become one of the top ten students. Though being one of the top ten students was my goal, the fear of my father's frustration made me more anxious. One night at 11:00 PM, I had an argument with my father, and he was so upset about something related to work and friends that he went to bed early that night. Then, while I was about to go to sleep, I remembered that I had forgotten my phone in the car. I went out to get my phone, and there were three missed calls. The number seemed familiar to me, so I checked it in my father's phone. It was the principal's phone number. He told me that the minister of education wanted to call me. Hearing this, my father jumped out of the bed with a big smile and some tears in his eyes. My mother was very happy with tears in her eyes as well. My father eventually saw our dream coming true. The Minister of Education told me that I achieved ninth place in the top ten students of Yemen. That was the happiest moment in my life.

Though twelfth grade was problematic, I learned many lessons in that year in both academic and non-academic fields. That year prepared me to be more mature, responsible, and ambitious. In addition, the Ministry of Higher Education granted me a scholarship to pursue my studies abroad. That was the most valuable gift because it would allow me to complete my future goals. It also made my father less concerned about supporting me financially.

Sample Essay: Narration

Kassie Grusz, Student

Performance at Smith Wills Stadium

An important public moment for me occurred when I danced on the baseball field with Montage Theatre of Dance at the Smith Wills Stadium in Jackson, Mississippi, for the 4th of July Extravaganza. The Extravaganza had many activities for everyone, young and old.

Dancing at the stadium was the first time I performed as a member of Montage and away from Hinds Community College (HCC). I was very nervous; my palms were sweaty, my stomach ached, and my head felt dizzy. After taking a few deep breaths, I was ready to dance. The costumes we wore varied from one another, but we were all dressed as Prince. My costume consisted of black pants, a white long sleeve shirt with ruffles down the middle and at the end of the sleeves, a jacket with bright purple, green, and orange patterns, and black jazz shoes; it was, indeed, very hot. As we were waiting for the announcer to call us onto the field, we were helping one another go over some of the more difficult dance moves. While waiting, we gathered together in the dugout and bowed our heads to pray for our performance.

When the announcer called us onto the field, I took another deep breath and was ready to go in front of a large crowd of people in the stadium. As nervous as I was in the dugout, I was more nervous on the field standing in front of everyone. We performed various pieces to Prince's songs, but the music stopped during the fourth piece. Instead of letting that interfere with our dancing, we continued to dance as if the music was still playing. The announcer was astonished by the way we continued to dance without pausing after the music stopped, and he encouraged the crowd to give us a beat by clapping. The last song we danced to was "Purple Rain." At the end of the song, we formed Prince's symbol by lying on the ground. Afterwards, we stood in the middle of the field, held hands, bowed, and walked off.

Before I left the stadium, I walked around to watch the games and activities taking place. Bouncy houses, blow-up slides, face painting, and ring tossing were scattered over the site. The slides seemed to be the most popular among those because many children were in line for the inflatable slides. So not only was I able to enjoy the atmosphere of the festivities, but I was also able to perform with Montage.

While waking around, I could smell the aroma of the food being cooked from the other side of the stadium. It was the smell of barbeque. When I reached the food stand, they had plates filled with barbequed chicken, baked beans, potato salad, and a sweet bread roll. It was delicious. Ultimately, the Extravaganza ended with an ear-splitting firework show full of bright reds, blues, and greens.

The 4th of July Extravaganza was gratifying for me. Members of Montage got to show our talent and professionalism, even in bad circumstances, and I got to enjoy the food and atmosphere. Even though the music stopped, it was a experience filled with great memories.

Sample Essay: Narration

Dustin Moore, Student

My First Hockey Game

Usually people from Mississippi have never seen a hockey game, let alone actually been to one in person. When I was very young my family and I would go to the Jackson Bandits games in the Mississippi Coliseum. After the team moved away, I never knew about any other hockey teams. However, I finally found out about another team in north Mississippi. My dad and I took a road trip to see the Mississippi Riverkings in Southhaven, Mississippi.

In the fall of 2015, I took a three and a half hour road trip to see the team play. I didn't know a lot about the team at the time, but I didn't care because I was getting to see a hockey game that I was old enough to remember. On the way up there, the only thing in view outside of the car window were trees and cornfields, and for most of the trip we listened to the Red Hot Chili Peppers. After the seemingly unending car ride, we got to the arena about thirty minutes before the game started. Some people might think sport events with lower attendance would have more expensive tickets to make up for lost profit, but actually our tickets were only twelve dollars each. After we had gotten our tickets and went through a security checkpoint, it finally hit me that I was at a hockey game.

When I first stepped into the arena, I was hit by a breeze of crisp and frigid air that gave me goosebumps. After a few minutes of walking around, we finally found the section where we were supposed to sit. I didn't know at first, but my dad had gotten tickets for seats that were on the first row, which is right up against the glass.

Just before the game was about to start, the lights went dark and a spot light came on facing the door where the zamboni drives onto the ice. It started with the national anthem which was sung by a middle school choir group. After it was done, the opposing team, the Louisiana Icegators, entered the rink followed by loud sound of boos coming from the crowd. When they were all on the rink, the announcer introduced the starting lineup for the Riverkings. The game started a few minutes after seven. As the game progressed, I could tell that a lot of the people in the audience didn't know what was going on because when two players fought and were sent to the penalty box, they didn't know where they went. With players slamming each other into the glass right in front of us, I could feel the ground shaking. Even though the Riverkings ended up losing the game four to three, it was overall an amazing game to watch.

When the game was over, they announced over the speaker that there would be a post-game meal with some of the players at Fillin Station Grill, which was about half a mile from the arena. My dad and I were the first two people there, so we were able to get the best seats. We ended up sitting next to three of the five starting players on the team. After we ate a gigantic meal and talked with a few of the players, we finally headed back for the endless ride back home, which I mostly slept through. I'm glad I got to take this memorable trip because I got to spend time with my dad, my favorite part of any trip.

Sample Essay: Narration

Lauren Walker, Student

A Tearful Reunion

In the summer of 2008, four hurricanes wreaked havoc across the country of Haiti. Over 800 people were recorded dead over a course of thirty days. Cities were deemed uninhabitable and thousands of Haitians were left homeless and starving. Many did not know if their families and loved ones were dead or alive. My extended bus ride returning to Haiti was filled with anxiety and nervousness, as the fear for the sake of my friend Patrick and his village weighed in on top of an anticipated reunion.

It had been three years since my cousin Danielle and I had last seen the dingy little sub-village that had been the site of my first missionary project. My heart felt as if it were beating out of my chest as the bus driver announced we were only two stops away from the remote village in Haiti. I began to feel suffocated by the sweating bodies that crowded all around me. I could feel every bump and hole in the dirt as the road began to get rougher. It was all becoming too much for me to endure.

As we entered the small community before Patrick's village, the devastation from the month-long storms was immediately apparent. The huts were abandoned, trees were ripped into splinters, and fields that were once filled with crops were barren. The bus weaved back and forth trying to dodge the piles of debris that lay in the dirt road. As we passed over the next hill, my eyes were squeezed shut as I could not bear to see if the storm had destroyed Patrick's village as well. I felt Danielle grab my hand and I fought the urge to close my eyes. I could not believe what I was seeing. The village looked as if had not been touched by the hurricanes.

Tears fell onto my lap as I saw Patrick standing on the hill waiting for our arrival. The smiling faces of the children warmed my heart as they waved to us. As I stepped off the bus their fragile bodies swarmed in our direction welcoming us with loving hugs. Patrick, caught up in the excitement, squeezed me so tight that it felt as if all the air was being forced out of my lungs. I finally took in an immense breath of relief knowing that my friends were all safe.

Patrick grabbed my hand and led me roaming amongst the village. As we passed the huts the familiar smells of Haitian food overwhelmed my nostrils. I watched the basket weavers as they blended complex patterns outside of their small wooden shops. From a distance I could hear the sounds of drum beats. The cries of the elders filled my ears as they belted the anthems that had been passed down from generation to generation. Tears welled up in my eyes as I was reunited with a world that had not changed in my absence.

The anticipated reunion with my friends from Haiti was filled with anxiety and nervousness after I learned the news of the hurricanes that had hit the small country over the summer. The fear for the sake of my friends was made more uneasy as I saw the damage that had been done to the surrounding villages. However, I was blessed with an unexpected reunion as I reached my destination and saw that Patrick's village had been untouched during the storms and that all of my friends were safe.

Sample Essay: Narration

Chris Williams, Student

To Lose Myself

From the very beginning, I have always known I was different. Since the first grade, it has been painfully clear to me that there was something about me that separated me from the other children. At the time, I did not have the words to describe how I felt, nor did I know the word to describe what I was. The difference that I discovered was a kind that would cause me to lose myself. I threw myself into a masquerade, and for years to come, the need to rediscover who I was would become a testament to my strength.

I was by no means the average first grader. I played without fear of judgment for that emotion was foreign. I did and said things that I would never have to courage the do or say again. With an insatiable need to be creative and a love to draw and write, I was quickly named the artist of my class. I was called to the principal's office countless times for drawing while the teacher taught. Even though I cried almost every time I went, I never once stopped my pursuit of art. It was who I was and I did not want to change for anyone. Despite the trouble that it caused me, most students and teachers smiled at me and encouraged me as I allowed my imagination to lead me on a path of endless possibilities and in-school suspensions. But through all the smiles, there was an expression on faces that I could not describe. However, I knew the feeling clearly, even though I had no the words for it. It was as if that person had looked upon a bug. The feeling that I saw eventually in those faces was that of a person who looks upon a flea-plagued dog with no home.

By the time I reached middle school, the stares that came down from those above me never stopped, and I became accustomed to seeing past the false smiles that once gave me encouragement. While those eyes pierced my very being, it took only a single question to change who I would be for the rest of my life: "Are you gay?" It was spoken with an emotion that I immediately knew to be very bad. Instinct told me to silence myself and not to act as I once had—no more fear and innocence. More and more I heard the word, and each time the clear sound of vile emotion was a cruel knife. I salvaged a few pieces and created a boy of deafening silence.

Within the grotesque masquerade that had become my childhood, I became an actor. I molded my silence into a new personality, one where I could manage just to perform each day with a smile. I called it my "mask." At times, it felt as though the world sat upon my back, but never once did I let my mask fall. The delicate porcelain never fractured for I was determined to prove myself to be unbreakable. A battle would ensue every day that would mar and cut deeper than any words. Inside was a mixture of fear, confusion, and anger.

I completely smothered my truest personality out of fear, and it is one of the truest regrets that I now have. Because of fear, I had not a single person whom I could talk to while growing up. I felt as though no one could possibly understand me as a person because I had not even understood myself. By the end of my sophomore year in high school, I had grown deathly tired of my masquerade. Out of fear, I had created the mask, and people accepted that, but it was not what I wanted. When I finally learned not to let other people define me, I then became happy. The porcelain mask finally shattered.

While I had reached a fragile resolution for being who I was, I had not yet finished my battle. It took something from me. I had played the perfect role for so long and had donned my mask for so many years that I had totally lost who I was. Throughout my junior and senior years, I worked to become myself once more, the person I did not recognize in the drawings that once got me in trouble. I wanted so badly to reclaim the past. I know my efforts were at times in vain because I lost hope and became lost in the world I had created for myself. Today I know that I do not need to look back anymore; I have created myself anew. This is the real me.

Sample Essay: Narration

Holly Wright, Student

Hillcrest Harmony

At first, the news was exciting: *We're going to Disney World!* The whole school band, choir, and winter guard were set to compete in Orlando, Florida, in the Heritage Music Festivals in 2010. The trip was going to be tied together with two days at the place where dreams come true and one day at Wet 'N' Wild Water Park. I was a first soprano under the direction of the lovely Mrs. Brumfield, and surely we would sweep the competition. But anticipation and anxiety are like brothers; where one goes, the other closely follows, and the same was true at the award ceremony.

The trip to Orlando was fourteen hours all throughout the night. My best friends Allan and Brandon sat next to me (both in band, Brandon also in choir). The scary winter guard instructor, who sat in the row behind us, got mad at us for talking too loudly, but we were too excited to sleep, and what else was there to do? Eventually, Allan fell asleep across my lap, and I fell asleep over him. The accompanying photo is not flattering.

We arrived, safe and sound, at a massive hotel that didn't have a separate smoking section, which almost ruined my lungs. We spent a day at Epcot, strolling through the newly opened fairy gardens, littered with topiaries in the shape of Disney fairies and their houses. This setting was unfortunate for Brandon because he tried to look tough in a black leather jacket and failed. No one can look tough in a fairy garden. The second day we spent at Animal Kingdom, which was a flop because hardly any of the animals were awake. However, I did get to meet Pocahontas and Rafiki. Later on the third day, everyone went to Wet 'N' Wild Water Park, which was no fun for me because it had terrifyingly gigantic water slides. I am also pretty sure that someone vomited in the lazy river, as we had to evacuate shortly after I got in.

The fun ended. We had played, and now it was time to work. My feet ached from all the walking we had done, but slipping on my familiar old ugly choir shoes felt like walking on clouds. The actual competitions are now a blur, although I still remember the winter guard's theme that year was "Be Our Guest" from *Beauty and the Beast*.

That night all the choirs gathered at the water park for the long-awaited award ceremony. I was surprised that there were any seats left. I hardly paid attention to the other categories, but when the one for my choir came up, my focus zeroed in on the presenter, and my knees went shaky. I breathed a little easier each time our group wasn't called. Then we heard: "Ninth place, eighth, seventh . . . and then—then— first place best overall women's show choir: *Hillcrest Harmony!*"

There was an immediate roar when we were called. Everyone around me surged upward, screaming in elation and relief. In a fit of euphoria, I tackled and hugged Brandon. The trophy we received was tall enough to reach my waist. It was the largest one I'd ever seen.

The victory high didn't end until long after we'd returned home to Jackson, Mississippi. Medals were distributed at our next class, and shortly after a shiny, large plaque was sent. Many photos were taken. I preened over the accomplishment for weeks. I still do occasionally.

As the years trucked on, however, the excitement faded from memory. Mrs. Brumfield left Hillcrest for greener pastures. The choir shrank alarmingly fast, and the program was cut altogether my tenth grade year. The plaque hanging on the choir room wall is now just collecting dust, the room itself demoted to storage for the band. All our trophies and plaques are still there, and I still have my medal. But I still remember the tight knot of nerves and excitement I felt at the award ceremony. I'm still a soprano.

Descriptive Essays

Standard Admonition

Essays and examples contained in this edition of *For Our Students* are not all *A* work nor are they acceptable to everyone's political or societal tastes.

The content of these essays reflects students' lives and interests. Some are several years old, but they still connect well with the reader.

All of the essays in this textbook have been chosen for their thought-provoking or unique content. As such, they sometimes reflect contemporary students' ethical, religious, and societal dilemmas.

In many cases, the content is sweet and dear, just like our students, their parents and families, and teachers. Others reflect the severity of our students' personal and familial turmoil, a fact that permeates our world as educators.

We celebrate our students' courage and generosity for allowing us to publish their work.

Sample Essay: Description

Tyler Bass, Student

A Tour of the Lake House

One Lake House on Sea Island Drive is not quite like the rest of the houses in the area. Upon approach, the first noticeable feature is a house considerably larger than the rest. After further examination of the houses around it, other features make this house differ from the others on Sea Island Drive. The most dramatic dissimilarities are the three staircases descending to the lower level and a wraparound porch that connects to a balcony on the back. On the lower level of the house is the bar. Two grills are mounted into the bar which is covered in bottle caps, old street signs, stickers from all the random tourist spots, and even the tailgate from an old Chevy truck.

The exterior is just part of the beauty of the lake house. When someone walks through the front door, immediately noticeable are the stainless steel countertops, and the huge island in the center of the kitchen made from Pecky Cyprus planks. Noticing the gorgeous wood on the island will also draw someone's attention to the hardwood floors that are stained a dark, rich brown color. Another noticeable feature is the large windows above the counter on the front wall of the kitchen that presents a view of Eagle Lake.

Similar elements are carried over to the living room which is connected to the kitchen. The same Pecky Cyprus that was used on the island also covers the ceiling in this room. On one wall there are French doors that lead out onto a seating area on the porch. On the opposite wall are two large windows above one of the couches that show the woods and houses nearby. This room is one of the most comfortable rooms in the house. It contains two large, dark leather couches, a long wooden table that extends across the room in front of the recliner, and a fifty-inch flat screen television. Although the furnishings are wonderful, what really makes this room so comfortable is the natural light flowing through the doors and windows.

This light continues on into the bathroom which is actually three different rooms. One contains the sink which is surrounded by Pecky Cyprus just like the other counters, another contains the toilet, and the last one contains a shower and a Jacuzzi tub that are encased in tinted glass. Beside the bathroom are the two bedrooms. One bedroom contains a king size bed, flat screen television, and a walk-in closet. The other bedroom contains four full-sized beds, a flat screen television, and a slightly smaller walk-in closet.

While the inside has a beautiful design, the outside of the house has an all-natural design sense. From the porch, anyone can see the yard slope down to the edge of the water where the fire pit is located. Along the edge are several Cyprus trees, and in-between them is the lighted wood pier that extends thirty feet out into the water with a swing on the end. The water is normally calm and almost glass-like which allows for an almost perfect reflection of the surroundings across the water. The scenery is always amazing, especially during a sunset when the sun glows off the water.

The lake itself is a wonderful place, but this house makes it unique to me. It is a home away from home and always a pleasant place to be. It provides a sense of luxury in a place where that is hard to find. No other place like the house at the lake exists.

Sample Essay: Description

Abbey Broome, Student

My Baby Blanket

When I was born, my mom's best friend gave me a baby blanket that became my playmate Blankey. She used to be snow white with light pink roses and silky pink lace around the edges, but now she is a just a few scraps of tan material held together by mere threads. Her appearance has changed so much because she was constantly by my side as I grew up. She was, for a large part of my childhood, my best friend and comforter.

When school was over and it was time to play, I would tuck Blankey in the waistband of my pants, sprint outside, and go immediately into the back yard woods. Sometimes Blankey and I would go explore their mystery, and other times we would just have long, funny conversations about what we thought of the chirping birds and noisy chipmunks. Blankey and I spent so much time together, but I sometimes left her lying around and forgot where we had last played together. That was a problem because I had trouble sleeping without her.

On the nights that Blankey played hide and seek, I would frantically search everywhere for her. That included tearing all of the blankets, pillows, and sheets off of my bed, and if she wasn't hiding in there, we searched desperately outside in the darkness with a headlight. If she hid all night, as soon as the sun rose and the grass was still wet with dew, I would run outside barefoot, still in my pajamas. When I found her, she was always wet with dew and smelled like outside—like a combination of grass, sweat, and damp dirt.

The smell of Blankey was one of my favorite parts. Sometimes the smell would change a little, depending on which part of her I sniffed and what we had done that day, but she always had a certain, comforting smell. One times, Blankey smelled like baby vomit for no apparent reason. When I smelled her, I would move her towards my nose, breathe in to smell her and then move her away. Breathing on her with warm air changed the way she smelled, and I didn't like that warm smell as much as the cool smell. Though my whole family thought it was weird, smelling and cuddling with Blankey was calming and comforting to me, especially when I was away from home.

No matter where I was or what games we played, Blankey always happily played with me, and no matter how many times I lost her, she always forgave me. She kept my life interesting and was a wonderful comfort when I was upset or homesick. I will always remember Blankey when I think of my childhood.

Sample Essay: Description

Emanuella Reyes, Student

Sundayz in MIA

It was almost like a therapy session for my family. It was our way of escaping all of our problems, no matter how big or small they may have been. When we were there, everyone got along and the mood matched those of the waves, smooth. What better way to spend a Sunday than on a sandy white beach, taking in the warm, bright sun, and soaking in the clear blue waters.

As early as it was, I could feel the excitement throughout the house. The chaos of getting food, drinks, lotions, and towels seemed to engulf us and make us move with more speed. The checklist of what we needed to pack was drilled into our heads after so many years of practice that it felt like we should be penalized for leaving anything, The two eldest were assigned to double check everything. Once my mom approved, we were on our way.

The car ride always felt like my first time. All I could feel was the cool breeze blowing against my face and the only thing I could hear was the sound of Beres Hammond's voice surrounding the V8 cylinder car. When we got to the beach, my mom started up the grill as we helped set up the table. Our personal radio continued our reggae concert from the car, now playing Tarrus Riley. After snacking on some chips, cookies, and a popsicle or two, we were ready to hit the waters.

The sun and sand went hand in hand with their warmth, tickling our feet and rushing up the rest our bodies. The feeling seemed to ignite more excitement in us, making us jog and then run towards the water. All we could hear was the sound of the calm waves disrupted by our bodies being thrown against them; nothing could compare to it. The ocean's movement and coolness refreshed my skin and worked its way up to my mind. Even at a young age, the memories of bad divorce, the idea of starting over, and the reality of the separation seemed to be taken by the waves and no longer ate away at my thoughts. Although it wasn't church, the water seemed to baptize all problems within me.

After spending over two hours on the beach and playing beach volleyball and Marco Polo, it was finally time to eat. Mom already had the food set up, and I could always smell the sweet barbeque walking up from the beach. After piling up my plate with smothered barbeque chicken, thick slabs of carne asada, hot dogs, chips, and cookies, I found my favorite spot in the shade and filled up my stomach. Between the chews of good flavors, we always had a group discussion of the week's events and made good laughs. I could see the glow on our skins from the sun and the rejuvenating waters.

Being surrounded by so much positivity engulfed us physically and mentally. Of all memories I've had as a child, Sunday beach days are forever installed in my brain. I still loved nothing more than Sundays at the beach in Miami.

Sample Essay: Description

Sydnie Palmer, Student

Riverbottom Farms

I am a third generation farmer of my family, and we farm in Yokena which is on the outskirts of Vicksburg, Mississippi. My family mainly farm soybeans, but in the past there have been a few years when we could not farm because of the flooding of the Mississippi River. While growing up on a farm, I got to experience many beautiful sunrises and sunsets with my dad along with many cool mornings and hot summer days. However, my favorite part about being a farmer's daughter has been learning and watching everything that goes with farming, from planting to watching the soybeans grow to harvest season. I have learned that no matter how bad or good the season went, God had a plan, and it happened for a reason.

We normally disk and dual the ground before we plant so that when we plant, the ground will be smooth for the tractor and planter. If the river comes up, then we won't do either of those jobs, but just watch as the river slowly rises and falls from our fields. I normally have to wake up at around 5:00–6:00 AM during early to late June that so I can disk and dual the fields, if the river is not up. Waking up that early during summer time, I enjoy walking outside and feeling the slight, cool summer breeze blowing against my warm face making me open my sleepy eyes. Hearing nothing but the highway noise and my dad's employees working, I walk to the tractor ready to put in the day's work. I crank up the tractor and let it warm up before I take off. It takes me a week to disk and another week to dual the fields. Then we are ready to plant.

Harvest season is one of my favorite seasons when it comes to farming because I get to watch the beautiful sunsets and feel the fall breeze. My dad and I normally go out to the fields at around 3:00–4:00 PM because that is when the moisture level in the soybeans is as low as it will get before we take the crop to the soybean mill. If the moisture level is over 12%, the mill won't take the beans. Watching the soybeans come up is so beautiful because I go from looking at freshly planted soil with little tiny seedlings popping up to medium-height beans that can get as green as a game day football field without the yard lines. Lastly, they finally turn brown.

When my family starts to harvest, we have my dad's candy apple red Peterbilt 18-wheeler with the grain trailer sitting in the hay field and the combine slowly harvesting the soybeans. The late October breeze blows, making mini dirt tornadoes in the wide open field, and while the dust rolls off the combine from the soybeans, it takes in and spits out the stems. Then we head over to the 18-wheeler to unload the soybeans, go to the mill next, and later come back to harvest the rest of the soybeans. We make as many as five to ten trips to the mill depending on how well our harvest season goes.

Being a farmer is much more than just growing and harvesting crops. It is almost like we have a bond with nature. We wake up praying that our crops don't die or wilt and that God will watch over not only our crops but our families as we have the opportunities to be able to grow food for ourselves and for everyone else. Being a farmer comes with a ton of responsibilities that a lot of people don't understand, like our dependence on weather forecasts to predict whether it will rain because the forecast affects us greatly. Farming will always be a part of who I am because it has taught me patience and responsibility.

Sample Essay: Description

Jerrold Robinson, Student

The Sounds of Peace

Waking up in the morning brought me many gifts. I had the sounds of the trains running the tracks and blowing their horns, the dogs stating their thoughts, and the sound of joy and comfort hearing my family members preparing themselves for the day. I felt as if I was a child again waiting for my mom to say, "Breakfast is ready." I would love to have some of that time back.

Now I hear an echoed sound on Saturday morning as I wake from my sleep still not totally conscious, but some of the most relaxing sounds come from outside as the workers go on with their days. Everyone's job has its own musical to showcase. The garbage man's truck rocks to the smell of the trash as the city sweepers' mellow song matches the sweep of the streets. The children outside play and yell in joy. It gives me a feeling I have not felt in a long time, one of faith and purity in the world. As I sit down to have breakfast, my spoon and glass bowl give me a tune as I scrape and pull from one side to the other.

My alarm goes off, streaming from the top of its nuts and bolts just to tell me that it's time for work. As I leave, my dog tells me to have a nice day with a great ruff and a paw the size of Texas. I continue to my car when I realize I have a flat tire. So I have to get an air pump out of the garage; the sound resembles a woman trying to get her point across in the heat of an argument. As I arrived at the clinic where I work, there was a sweet smell of chocolate and the gargling of boiling water, so I knew there is caffeine brewing on the office coffee pot because it is so old and noisy.

We also had a cafeteria in the clinic, and it is as big as a football stadium. The sounds aren't as violent, but there is aggression in the cooking of those beans. My early riser patients are always the ones who come in ready to be rehabilitated and to put in the most effort as they grunt and moan from the pain of their injuries. I am humbled to say that I help them. It's even more rewarding when they are done, and I hear them say "thank you" for all the help that was given and the respect that I showed to them.

After I'm done with my first group of patients, I always go for a swim to relax and relieve stress. The sound of the water soothes my mind from the workout I get while helping my staff. To be perfectly honest, the sounds of silence always bring me back to the beginning as a child waking to a silent room with the wind blowing in my face.

Sample Essay: Description
Joshua Wahl, Student

Beyond the Sand

Military training exercises can take place in a variety of climates and locations. Currently, a common location for modern military training is the desert, and one such exercise is conducted in the desert near Yuma, Arizona. Despite the austere environment of the desert, military training in the harsh desert surroundings is important for soldiers.

The most apparent aspect of training in a desert climate is the dry and arid geography. With little precipitation year round, the ground becomes dry, brittle, and sandy. Without sufficient rainfall, natural vegetation is also sparse. The lack of vegetation makes the concealment of tents and equipment by camouflage more challenging. Additionally, the fine texture of the dirt allows it to be easily blown around by transient gusts of wind, causing it to permeate nearly every tiny crevice of clothing and equipment. As a result, proper preventative care of all types of equipment becomes a necessity in this environment. The buildup of dirt and sand inside of a rifle chamber can easily cause the weapon to fail at a critical moment and create disastrous results.

As if the arid geography didn't present enough of a challenge, the extreme summer heat creates an additional variable in training that must be taken into account. The thick and heavy military protective equipment used in training can exponentially increase the risk of heat-related casualties. Therefore, a regimented schedule of hydration and planned rest becomes critical to successful training exercises. Camouflage netting is also set up over tents, not only for concealment, but also to create shade to cool off. In addition to heat affecting personnel, it can also damage the equipment; vehicles can become overheated if overdriven, and essential fluids such as oil and coolant are consumed more quickly. Weapons must also be lubricated more often, as the higher heat and dry air consume the lubricant faster.

Despite these unforgiving conditions, a surprising amount of biodiversity in the desert exists. The plants and animals that inhabit the desert have developed different adaptations than their more temperate counterparts. One of the better adapted plants found in the desert, the cactus, has a fruit-like flesh capable of dense moisture retention during extended periods of drought. The cactus also grows sharp, prickly barbs over its surface to deter animals from consuming it.

Animals such as reptiles and insects are also common in the desert. Most desert animals are small and burrow into the sand during the daylight hours to avoid the heat and conserve energy. Special attention is directed to the storage of food supplies because scavenging animals such as rodents can easily chew through cardboard and infiltrate food supplies. Although many desert animals are small and don't pose an immediate threat to training, some possess dangerously poisonous venom. Certain snakes and scorpions are among some of the venomous animals of the desert. Bites or stings from these creatures can be potentially fatal if left untreated. As a result, military first aid kits often contain first-line treatment to increase the odds of surviving venomous bites or stings.

With all of these variables taken into account, training in the desert was more arduous and interesting than I had expected. Although the environment can be harsh and chaotic, desert training is a valuable experience for military members. The foreign nature of the environment teaches adaptability and resilience, which are critical skills for all military members.

Argumentation Essays

Standard Admonition

Essays and examples contained in this edition of *For Our Students* are not all *A* work nor are they acceptable to everyone's political or societal tastes.

The content of these essays reflects students' lives and interests. Some are several years old, but they still connect well with the reader.

All of the essays in this textbook have been chosen for their thought-provoking or unique content. As such, they sometimes reflect contemporary students' ethical, religious, and societal dilemmas.

In many cases, the content is sweet and dear, just like our students, their parents and families, and teachers. Others reflect the severity of our students' personal and familial turmoil, a fact that permeates our world as educators.

We celebrate our students' courage and generosity for allowing us to publish their work.

Sample Essay: Argumentation
Abigail Baker, Student

Pushing for Success

The high standard for achievement that parents hold for their children limits each child's long-term growth. Every child has a different capacity for learning and achieving, but many parents expect their children to become equal to or greater than other children of the same age. This often occurs not only in an academic setting but also in general social situations. Pressure to develop into the smartest, the fittest, the fastest, the strongest, the prettiest, and many other "-ests" suppresses children in ways that often cannot be reversed.

A child's desire to please his/her parents in school leads to memorization for tests and not learning or absorbing the material. For young children, learning is important, and *B*s or even *C*s are understandable. However, some parents later expect that their children have learned the fundamentals and will therefore succeed. The standards change. *A*s become mandatory; *B*s morph into flaws, and *C*s are utter failures. This same reasoning applies to athletics. Anything less than first place becomes disappointing; anything less than second place is disgraceful.

As a result of continual attempts to remain the best of his/her class, sport, or social group, stress can consume the child. Then as a teenager, many expect this person to ace all tests, complete projects, participate in clubs, volunteer for copious hours of community service, fill leadership roles, and meet all deadlines on time. At some point in the teen years, the burden of pressure for perfection shifts from parental dominance to self-conscious anxiety. The stress of completing each action flawlessly increases. Failure becomes intolerable to the student rather than the parents, so the student feels anxiety from many angles. This feeling of overwhelming tension is highly unhealthy for any child in both a physical and mental capacity.

Anger, bitterness, and despair negatively affect teens. For instance, I once knew a student who went from a young child who treasured school to a teenager who completed only what was necessary to remain in the top percentile of her peers. At a younger age, her parents instilled a concept that anything less than the top of the class for her was intolerable. When the child returned home with a *B*, her father said, "This grade is better than most of the class, but I expect an *A* next time." As a result, this child learned to exceed in everything she completed. Once she entered high school, she inserted herself into nearly every club and jockeyed for leadership roles. Her grades remained in the top percentile, and she dedicated virtually all of her free time to community service. Despite this drive, the student received an unexpected *C* on her report card. While her parents had relinquished their standards, the child had developed even higher ones for herself. She became extremely self-aware and filled with disappointment, anxiety, misery, and anger. Subsequently, this student viewed herself as a failure and no longer believed in her ability to achieve the highest. She became withdrawn and refused to attempt anything more than mediocre work.

The notion that only the best is satisfactory can inhibit any child's development. While not every instance leads to tragedy, children who become consumed by perfection will lose self-confidence and will eventually be hurt. Emotional stability, especially from parents, is vital to the well being of the child and can prevent destructive reasoning and actions.

Sample Essay: Argumentation

Ryan Braswell, Student

Hold the Parade: Veterans Need Jobs

Most people would say that veterans are held in high esteem. They are honored with numerous holidays and thanked for their service. They are praised as heroes and proclaimed as the defenders of freedom. They leave everything they have behind to fight for other nations and people whom they may never meet. Returning home, veterans are greeted by host of grateful citizens. On the very next day though, they will be forgotten. When the pedestal is torn down and the daily routines are picked back up, the service-member is left behind. I have been awakened to many of the injustices that veterans face as a veteran of the United States Marine Corps and a Veteran Services Coordinator in higher education. Prior service-members need more than holidays and parades. Veterans should be given better opportunities for stable employment.

Veterans returning home from military service are immediately at a distinct disadvantage compared to their civilian counterparts, and skills translation is the number one reason a veteran is overlooked by hiring managers. Their military experience does not translate well to the civilian world's hiring managers. For example, despite being familiar with the jargon from movies and video games, most hiring managers do not know what a "sergeant" really does. They do, however, know what a bachelor's degree is. They also know that without one, the sergeant won't get the job, regardless of his or her overqualifications.

Veterans are also avoided by businesses because of the negative stereotypes sounding the military. Post-Traumatic Stress Disorder (PTSD) has become synonymous with soldiers, sailors, marines, and airmen. Unqualified civilians wrongly and capriciously diagnose veterans with this complicated psychological disorder. Unfortunately, overexposure to PTSD by the media has automatically programmed civilians to assume that most combat veterans are psychologically damaged. Statistics show that only thirty percent of the veterans who have been exposed to combat have been diagnosed with a mental health disorder, leaving the majority of the military healthy—a fact that the general public has ignored.

In addition to PTSD stereotypes, veterans have another negative stereotype with which to contend. A stigma that "people only enlist in the military because they could not do well in college" is rampant across educational institutions, and it has carried into the workforce. Despite the intense military training and the real world applications, veterans are still considered by many as uneducated. It can be easy to forget that in the 21st century, military members are trained to operate GPS guided rocket systems, Unmanned Aerial Vehicles, and state-of-the-art computer systems. Instead, it's much simpler to revert to delusional assumptions leftover from Vietnam. However, based on my experience in higher education, veterans are more likely to graduate earlier and with higher grades than that of their peers.

Veterans are our nation's heroes and have also given more to their country in four years than most citizens will do in their whole lives. They leave home at a young age and return with handfuls of ribbons and lifetimes of experience. They are praised, saluted, and forgotten. For many of them, however, they find themselves having to pick up where they left off after high school graduation and are told that they do not have what it takes to enter the workforce. At the very least, they should be given a genuine opportunity at a stable career in return for their self-sacrificing service.

Sample Essay: Argumentation

Charles Cannon, Student

Fixing Youth Group Culture

The Christian church has evolved a lot since its founding. Evangelism has become one of the most important goals, as has entertainment. As a young Christian who has been raised in church, I have gathered both from experience and through others' opinions about how modern changes in church, specifically those aimed at students, have affected church environment and young Christians. Modern youth group culture needs to be changed.

Teenagers in my church were not often encouraged to think. From the time I was a child to the present day, my fellow students could speak church doctrine, but did not study actual Bible verses or the contexts surrounding them. Often, entire classes were spent attempting to disprove evolution while evangelizing and helping the poor were ignored. With the emphasis on buzzwords and interpretation of doctrine, we were completely detached from the world outside of church. This lack of action became apparent when I saw my best friend, a former atheist raised in a nonreligious home, convert to Christianity. He showed more depth of thought and genuine love for God than most people I had met, including myself, who had grown up in church.

Because of the disconnection and lack of rational thinking, youth group culture often drives other people away from God. A lot of emphasis is put on evangelism because of the Christian belief of the "Great Commission," the command to make disciples. While it is good to be zealous and even uncompromising in the core beliefs of the faith, the cliquish and uniform nature of modern evangelical churches can make people feel uncomfortable. Many of my non-Christian friends stereotyped the common Christian teenager as dogmatic and hypocritical. Friends from school who did not attend church told me that certain people from my church, with whom they had little contact, told them that they were going to Hell. When questioned, these dogmatic

Christians defended themselves as speaking the truth: they ignored how hurtful and tactless their words were. This kind of attitude makes it nearly impossible for religion to sound appealing.

Along with other friends from church, I went to three youth conferences each year. All had slightly different activities, but all three had the same basic set up. The band performed a concert, a speaker got up and exhorted the crowd, and the band performed again. "Let's get ready to worship!" was often screamed before the band played. The preacher was prone to using a manipulative tone and talking like a performer. While nothing is wrong with entertaining sermons or songs, too much focus on the entertainment and emotion, not on the core Gospel message, takes away from the true message of Christianity.

The zeal that youth groups have stimulates everyone in the congregation. However, knowledge and compassion need to be added to that zeal, as well as a certain amount of self-awareness, to make Christianity sincerely appealing. These positive changes would help to fulfill the Great Commission.

Sample Essay: Argumentation
Navdeep Kaur, Student

Clanton High School's Teachers and College Preparation

Most high school graduates aren't aware of what college really entails. Clanton High School's teachers don't have enough time to educate students about college life, financial aid, the ACT, and all that goes along with college and life after high school. The most effective solution to this problem would be offering a course that informs students what they must do to get into college and what college life is really like. Clanton High School should offer a college preparation class so that the staff and teachers can more efficiently prepare students for college.

Many students are the first generation in their families to go to college and have absolutely no idea where to begin with the whole "college-thing." Others are simply lost and don't know what they want to do or what career path they'd like to embark upon. Due to my family's educational background, I had no idea what to expect out of college and wish I had been taught more about it in high school. My father never went to college due to starting work as a young man to support his family, and my mother attended college in India, an extremely different experience. Other members of my family are out of state or in India. Therefore, I had no one to turn to for information on college and careers; my only source of information on college was my teachers at Clanton High School and so it is for a lot of high school students, regardless of family background.

The teachers at Clanton High School tend to become so engrossed in trying to squeeze every lesson in by a certain deadline that they forget to look at the bigger picture: students' lives after high school. The furthest their field of view reaches is to the final exam. They make it seem as if nothing is more important than passing the final exam. At the same time, students are expected and pressured to have their careers and colleges decided, have their FAFSA completed, have scholarships filled out, and basically have their whole life planned out by the end of their senior year, if not their junior year. Finals are important, indeed, but the focus of the teachers should also be on giving their students a taste of the bigger picture. The most effective solution would be a class designed to inform students about college and all that goes along with it such as FAFSA, financial aid, scholarships, the ACT, housing, and college majors.

All teachers should explain to the students what they can start doing in high school that will prepare them for college, based on the subjects they teach. Due to the fast-paced nature of school and the volume of material covered in a small time, core-subject teachers shouldn't be expected to teach students every last detail about college; however, they can explain the importance of getting into effective study habits in high school and college.

Additionally, Advanced Placement (AP) teachers should emphasize what AP exams actually do for a student. None of the AP teachers I had at Clanton High School ever told my peers or me what the significance of AP exams was or how they could exempt a student from a class in college. The students were more concerned about the high cost of each AP exam, and most of them decided that the cost wasn't worth it. This uninformed decision ultimately made the time and effort that they had put into AP classes pointless. Advanced Placement teachers should make sure to explain to their students about the long-term benefits of these classes and exams and how they can exempt students from certain college classes. Students should know that the upfront costs of the tests are not the point, that taking the classes and exams will help save time and money for the students' college education. Having all this information is crucial in determining the amount of effort and thought that students put into their classes and into their future.

Clanton High School's staff may argue that students are, in fact, informed about college by the school's counselors. The problem in this is that the only students who have meetings with the counselors are seniors, and they have only one ten-minute meeting with the counselors during their first week of their senior year. In this meeting, the counselors ask the future college students if they've taken the ACT and what their highest score was, what college they plan to attend, and what scholarships they can receive based on their ACT score. They then inform the students of a single website that has state aid information on it. This short session is not sufficient. A single ten-minute meeting is in no way an adequate time frame for students to be informed of what they need to know about college and financial aid because too much information needs to be discussed. Students also need to be aware of this information before their senior year, and students need more proactive help in making college and career choices.

A college preparation course would help students at Clanton High School; it should be mandatory and last an entire year. Due to the amount of information one needs before going to college, a semester would not be enough to cover all the information needed in a college prep course. Throughout the duration of this course, instructors should teach students what they will need in order to be admitted to a college as well as what college life and classes will be like. The significance of ACT scores and the scholarships available based on those scores should be emphasized. The many kinds of scholarships that are available and the resources for potential scholarships should also be explored. Of course, college courses and career options should be thoroughly researched, and trips to colleges should be either encouraged or required while in this class.

The current opportunities provided by Clanton High School and its teachers are not effective for preparing students for college. A mandatory year-long college preparation class should be offered in order to prepare students for college more effectively. So much more than the cost of an AP test is at stake.

Sample Essay: Argumentation

Victoria Pagan, Student

Fantasy Literature in Schools

Standardized testing is slowly destroying students' ability to think creatively. Every exam is now based on memorization and numbers, which comprises the bulk of the curriculum. Teachers are under pressure to create students who make high exam scores; unfortunately, the result is students who have little retainable knowledge and a lack of the ability to make creative decisions. Teachers and administrators even frown upon students who do not fit into the mold that has been created. However, by integrating creative writing and fantasy literature into the curriculum, a remedy to this trend is possible.

Writing fantasy allows students to create new worlds that can be anything they dare to dream. It gives way to free-flowing thought that can be essential for solving real world problems. Fantasy writing can also be an escape for many students struggling in their personal lives, and it opens a door to creativity that younger students are now lacking. Even reading fantasy works can have the same effect, but the curriculum doesn't make time for reading fantasy in class.

Students need a creative outlet. Often, the stress of school and outside influences can weigh heavily on students and cause them to have problems in school. Some students may be able to find an escape through fantasy writing, but this is not possible if they are never given the opportunity. Giving them the chance to pour their emotions into a fantasy world may help the students that have buried emotions express themselves in a more positive way, rather than as behavior problems or emotional outbursts. I have also seen firsthand by working with elementary age students that creativity is much less important to some teachers. Children are usually much more likely to have active imaginations, but in school, they are often told that being imaginative is a distraction and that to do well in school, they need to be able to memorize and recite.

A common problem is that teachers assign literature to be read over the summer, but the assignment often does not capture the interests of the students. Few children or teens find these works interesting, so they will procrastinate reading the work until they eventually cheat or fail. However, if the assigned work were a story about adventure and worlds unknown with creatures of all manner running about and causing havoc, more students would find them interesting.

Fortunately, some schools offer creative writing classes to students. These students are allowed to write fantasy literature, and some end up working on novels because they have created entire fantasy worlds. However, this is a very hard class to fit into a schedule when the common curriculum is so full of more structured, required classes. It is usually only high school seniors who have the option for this course because previous English classes are mandatory. Also, many students try to avoid writing essays, so they take only the minimum English classes that are required for graduation.

Fantasy literature, both as reading works and creative writing, needs to be a more prominent feature in school curriculum. Children are losing the ability to think creatively and solve problems that do not include memorization and numbers. Students with a creative outlet may be less prone to behavior problems and may be more likely to finish assigned reading work if the material catches their interests. In order to achieve the goal of bringing back creativity to schools, the curriculum needs to be more flexible so that students can take creative writing classes and can read and integrate fantasy literature. Fantasy literature and writing could improve the quality of education for many students if properly embedded into the curriculum.

Cause and Effect Essays

Standard Admonition

Essays and examples contained in this edition of *For Our Students* are not all *A* work nor are they acceptable to everyone's political or societal tastes.

The content of these essays reflects students' lives and interests. Some are several years old, but they still connect well with the reader.

All of the essays in this textbook have been chosen for their thought-provoking or unique content. As such, they sometimes reflect contemporary students' ethical, religious, and societal dilemmas.

In many cases, the content is sweet and dear, just like our students, their parents and families, and teachers. Others reflect the severity of our students' personal and familial turmoil, a fact that permeates our world as educators.

We celebrate our students' courage and generosity for allowing us to publish their work.

Sample Essay: Cause and Effect
Hayden Hunter, Student

Food Quality

What we eat today is much different than what was eaten back in the early 1900s. Food quality has changed in recent years due to new technology. New medicines and fertilizers are now used to make animals and crops grow faster with higher yield. The use of these medicines and fertilizers is affecting food quality in a negative way.

One reason that the quality of food is dissimilar today than it was in the past is that the raising and caring for the animals that are used for meat has changed dramatically. Where people used to raise herds of cattle in an open field now stand the barns that hold hundreds, if not thousands, of calves being raised for slaughter. The condition of these barns is terrible: the floor is many feet deep with manure, there are diseases among the herd, and cows are dying from suffocation due to their close quarters. The chicken coops are no better. The long warehouses are full of chickens that are born and raised in cramped spaces. These chickens never see the light of day; therefore, their eggs have much less protein in them. Growth hormones are also used to produce more eggs. This process takes more of the calcium from the hen and then uses it to make more eggs faster. But it makes the animal weak and sickly. Not only are the animals grown and raised nontraditionally, but the crops such as corn and soy are also grown inorganically.

In the late 1800s and early 1900s, GMOs (Genetically Modified Organisms) were not used. This made crops more dependent on natural recourses like the sun, water, and minerals in the soil in order to grow, and now fewer proteins are in these crops because of GMOs and fertilizers. The food industries are using these crops and animals in their recipes to further their profits when selling them to both local and commercial markets.

The food industries also process meats and crops so that they last longer on the markets' shelves. While being handy, this system has caused a problem in another way. The preservatives added to canned items, pantry items, and even refrigerated items have negated a lot of the health benefits and even added unhealthy, fattening effects. The fast food industries have also added more chemicals to help their products cook faster and last longer. As a result, unhealthy eating habits have developed with many people because it's easier and cheaper to buy these fast food products. Obesity has become more of a national problem, partially as a result of these changes in the food supply.

Food quality is changing constantly, whether for good or worse. As a result, many people limit themselves on what they eat and drink because of the health problems in processed foods. Some stores and restaurants make it their priority to serve only whole foods and no processed foods, giving people more options with ways to eat healthy. Additionally, some farmers raise their animals traditionally so they get more fresh grass and sunlight, giving these animals the proteins and vitamins they need and making them healthier and safer to eat.

Sample Essay: Cause and Effect
Victoria Mulqueen, Student

The Consequences of Academic Dishonesty

Lying comes in a multitude of forms. The consequences of these lies are entirely dependent on the degree and severity of the lie. Lying in school, however, just might impact the future of the liar. One of the most serious forms of this academic dishonesty, plagiarism, will definitely have severe penalties, especially if it is committed in an institution of higher learning like a college or a university.

Students plagiarize for numerous reasons. Often times when students are not prepared for a writing assignment, they will steal the words of others because they think that they don't have the time to come up with their own words for the topic. Another major reason for plagiarism is laziness. If someone simply does not wish to use the time or brainpower required to tackle an essay or another type of writing assignment, then he or she will plagiarize, usually from an internet source like *Wikipedia*, because doing so is fast and easy.

The most common reason for plagiarism that I've witnessed, however, is carelessness. This carelessness can be deemed such because the instructors do their part to teach students ways to avoid plagiarism. Teachers will dictate the format of the writing assignment, like MLA or APA, and those styles include how to cite sources. In addition to the information within the specific paper format, instructors will also show their students the correct way to cite sources so the students won't plagiarize in the writing assignment. Even though the students are given the tools needed so they won't plagiarize by mistake, some still fail to proofread or change their paper to avoid this form of academic dishonesty.

The least severe outcome a guilty plagiarizer must worry about is failing the paper on which he or she plagiarized. This will affect his or her grade in the class, but grades can be pulled up most of the time. A larger impact based on the previous example is class failure with the weight of the failed, plagiarized paper being too significant to allow a passing grade in the class. The most significant and grave consequence of plagiarism could be expulsion from the institution. Being expelled from any educational institution can have a severe impact. Once expelled, the plagiarizer may have trouble enrolling in another college or university, especially when the prospective student needs scholarships or financial aid to cover tuition. If an individual cannot enroll in another place of higher learning to earn a degree, he or she may not be able to live the life imagined or have the career he or she had originally hoped to pursue.

The impact of plagiarism is severe. Academic dishonesty must be avoided at all costs in order to protect certain opportunities that only a degree can provide. When considering stealing or "borrowing" the words of others, one must be willing to ask whether a moment of laziness or carelessness is worth sacrificing his or her future. The answer to this question will always be, "No."

Sample Essay: Cause and Effect
William Stribling, Student

Bullying: The Double-Edged Sword

When people think of bullying, the picture that typically comes to mind is a Neanderthal stuffing a much smaller kid wearing glasses into a locker or holding him over a nasty school toilet. Though true, the forms that bullying can now take are much more diverse. The proliferation of technology has brought an increase in people harassing others through the internet and social media. Cyberbullying is a problem so widespread that nearly every state has anti-bullying laws that ban this kind of digital harassment. Bullying can take any number of forms, but many commonalities still exist between all types, relating both to the bullied and the bully.

The effects of bullying on the person being bullied are varied, much like bullying itself, but the presence of pain is definite. The simplest of these are the ones found in physical bullying. Cuts, bruises, and scrapes are the result and they're the wounds that are typically the ones most easily healed. It's the emotional impact that takes much longer to fade. Feeling ostracized is something no one enjoys and can have an even heavier impact on young people. In junior high, three goons in my class who targeted me never tripped me or knocked my books out of my hand, but they did call me "fag" and stole my lunch frequently. Reclusiveness and anxiety resulted, which still damage anyone's emotional well-being.

Depression, self-harm, and suicide are the darkest results of the cruelty faced by bullying victims. Just a simple Google search will show hundreds of stories of people who thought this battle was just too much. On the other hand, the pain can be buried until it all eventually comes pouring out. My aforementioned bullying in junior high was something I kept to myself until the end of eighth grade when I just broke down into tears in front of my parents and it finally surfaced. I thought I was fine before then, but pain from over a year's worth of negative emotion began to overflow.

Bullies share similarities in both their self-perception and their home environments. Some people may just be plain mean, but most bullies do what they do because of their own insecurities. Those who engage in physical bullying want to make themselves seem big and menacing when in really they really feel unimportant. Similarly, those who bully others verbally do so out of jealousy or to make themselves feel better in spite of their deflated self-worth. Cowardice is also a problem, as many will go along with or ignore bullying to protect themselves. These problems are also often rooted in their home environments. If a parent is a bully, there's a good chance that his or her child might become one too.

Even uncontrollable socio-economic factors play a role in bullying. They can involve a rich student picking on a poor student about clothing or, reversely, a poorer student bullying others because of a lack of self-esteem. So for one reason or another, those choosing to bully are hurting as well, and more often than not the solution could be found with some open communication and empathy toward the victimizer, not just the victim.

Bullying has existed but has morphed with technology. Unfortunately, the nature of bullying is still the same. Everyone involved is hurt in some way and the root causes are the identical. While we'll never be able to eliminate bullying altogether, we can minimize it as adults by paying attention and acting as needed. It's important to communicate clearly and to be a supportive advocate for someone who is hurting. Even though it's easy to demonize the bullies, they need help as much as their victims do. If we all would do our part in being mindful and extending kindness, bullying is only one of the many problems that would wither away to nothing.

Appendix E

Citation Chart for MLA and APA

IN-TEXT CITATIONS

PRINT SOURCES

Author Named in a Signal Phrase

MLA	Sedaris recalls, "We rode round and round the block on our pony, who groaned beneath the collective weight of our rich and overwhelming capacity for love and understanding" (9–10).
APA	Sedaris (1994) recalls, "We rode round and round the block on our pony, who groaned beneath the collective weight of our rich and overwhelming capacity for love and understanding" (p. 9–10).

Author Not Named in a Signal Phrase

MLA	"We rode round and round the block on our pony, who groaned beneath the collective weight of our rich and overwhelming capacity for love and understanding" (Sedaris 9–10).
APA	"We rode round and round the block on our pony, who groaned beneath the collective weight of our rich and overwhelming capacity for love and understanding" (Sedaris, 1994, p. 9–10).

Two or Three Authors

MLA	Collins and Blum outline the way socioeconomics and politics outside the university also play a role in instigating the division between "basic" and "normal" writers (14). The authors outline the way socioeconomics and politics outside the university also play a role in instigating the division between "basic" and "normal" writers (Collins and Blum 14).
APA	Research by Collins and Blum (2000) outlines the way socioeconomics and politics outside the university also play a role in instigating the division between "basic" and "normal" writers (p. 14).

More Than Three Authors

MLA	Cincotta et al. assert that the launch of Sputnik expanded the competitive arena between the U.S. and the Soviet Union (68). Historians assert that the launch of Sputnik expanded the competitive arena between the U.S. and the Soviet Union (Cincotta et al. 68). Cincotta, Brown, Burant, Green, Holden, and Marshall assert that the launch of Sputnik expanded the competitive arena between the U.S. and the Soviet Union (68).
APA	For the first use in text, list all author names: Cincotta, Brown, Burant, Green, Holden, and Marshall (1994) [. . .] For subsequent entries, use et al.: Cincotta et al. (1994) assert that the launch of Sputnik expanded the competitive arena between the U.S. and the Soviet Union (p. 68).

Unknown Author

MLA	A study determined that subjects lose time when switching from task to task ("Is Multitasking" 3).
APA	A similar study determined that subjects lose time when switching from task to task ("Is Multitasking," 2001, p. 3).

IN-TEXT CITATIONS

Work in an Anthology

MLA	According to David Bartholomae, students who were less successful at this "invention" were considered basic writers; those who were more successful were not (136).
APA	According to David Bartholomae (1985), students who were less successful at this "invention" were considered basic writers; those who were more successful were not (p. 136).

Encyclopedia/Dictionary

MLA	A citation is a "quotation from or reference to a book, paper, or author." ("Citation").
APA	A citation is a "quotation from or reference to a book, paper, or author." (Citation, 2002).

ELECTRONIC SOURCES

Web Sources

MLA	For electronic sources, include the first item (author name, title, etc.) in the Work Cited entry that corresponds to the citation. Do not include URLs in the text unless absolutely necessary; if included, make the URL as brief as possible, such as npr.org rather than http://www.npr.org.
APA	When possible, cite a web document the same as any other document. If no author or date is given, cite using the title in the lead-in, or include an abbreviated version of the title in the parenthetical citation, and use the abbreviation "n.d." ("no date"). If no page number is available, include information that will help readers find the material being cited. If paragraphs are numbered, use "para." and follow with the paragraph number.

Film

MLA	*Big Fish*, directed by Tim Burton, details the extraordinary life of Edward Bloom (2003).
APA	*Big Fish*, directed by Tim Burton, details the extraordinary life of Edward Bloom (2003).

Television

MLA	In *Criminal Minds*, a suspect awakens from a coma with no memory of having committed the crimes he is accused of ("Tabula Rasa").
APA	In *Criminal Minds*, a suspect awakens from a coma with no memory of having committed the crimes he is accused of ("Tabula Rasa").

SOURCE CITATIONS

BOOKS

General Book Format

MLA	Sedaris, David. *Barrel Fever*. Little, Brown, 1994.
APA	Sedaris, D. (1994). *Barrel fever*. New York, NY: Little, Brown.

Two or Three Authors

MLA	Ward, Geoffrey, Ken Burns, and Kevin Baker. *Baseball: An Illustrated History*. Alfred A. Knopf, Inc. 1996.
APA	Ward, G., Burns, K., & Baker, K. (1996). *Baseball: An Illustrated History*. New York: Alfred A Knopf, Inc.

More Than Three Authors

MLA	Barnes, Sonya, et al. [. . .]
APA	Three to seven authors: Rubenstein, J., Meyer, D., & Evans, J. (2001). [. . .] More than seven authors: Barnes, S., Buchanan, W., Chenn, H., Elrick, H., Graham, J. A., King, D. . . . Law, K. (2008). [. . .]

Unknown Author

MLA	*Beowulf*. Farrar, Straus and Giroux, 2000.
APA	*Beowulf*. (2000). New York, NY: Farrar, Straus and Giroux.

Author with an Editor

MLA	Fielding, Henry. *Tom Jones*. Ed. Sheridan Baker. [. . .]
APA	Fielding, H. (1973). *Tom Jones*. S. Baker (Ed.). [. . .]

Editor with no Author

MLA	*Impossibly Funky: A* Cashiers du Cinemart *Collection*. Ed. M. White. [. . .]
APA	White, M. (Ed.). (2010). *Impossibly funky: A* Cashiers du Cinemart *collection*. [. . .]

Author with a Translator

MLA	Gide, André. *Lafcadio's Adventures*. Trans. D. Bussy. [. . .]
APA	Gide, A. (1953). *Lafcadio's adventures*. (D. Bussy, Trans.). [. . .]

Work in an Anthology

MLA	Bartholomae, David. "Inventing the University." *When a Writer Can't Write*, edited by Mike Rose, Guilford, 1985, pp. 134–65.
APA	Bartholomae, D. (1985). Inventing the university. In M. Rose (Ed.), *When a writer can't write* (pp. 134–165). New York: Guilford.

Encyclopedia/Dictionary Entry

MLA	"Citation." *The Shorter Oxford English Dictionary*. 5th ed., 2002.
APA	Citation. (2002). In *The shorter Oxford English dictionary*. (5th ed.).

SOURCE CITATIONS

ARTICLES IN PERIODICALS

Magazine

MLA	Miller, Jeremy. "The Tyranny of the Test: One Year as a Kaplan Coach in the Public Schools." *Harper's Magazine*, 2 Sept. 2008, pp. 35–46.
APA	Miller, J. (2008, September 2). The tyranny of the test: One year as a Kaplan coach in the public schools. *Harper's Magazine*, 35–46.

Newspaper

MLA	Timson, Judith. "Stop All That Multitasking, Study Suggests." *The Toronto Star*, 7 August 2001, p. E2.
APA	Timson, J. (2001, August 7). Stop all that multitasking, study suggests. *The Toronto Star*, p. E2.

Journal

MLA	Collins, Terence and Melissa Blum. "Meanness and Failure: Sanctioning Basic Writers." *Journal of Basic Writing*, vol. 19, no. 1, 2000, pp. 13–21.
APA	Collins, T. & Blum, M. (2000). Meanness and failure: Sanctioning basic writers. *Journal of Basic Writing*, *19*(1), 13–21.

ELECTRONIC SOURCES

Entire Website

MLA	National Public Radio. *Morning Edition*. NPR, 14 January 2014. www.npr.org/programs/morning-edition. Accessed 14 Jan. 2014.
APA	National Public Radio. (2014, January). *Morning edition*. Retrieved from NPR website http://www.npr.org/programs/morning-edition/

Page from a Website

MLA	Abdullah, Mardziah Hayati. "The Impact of Electronic Communication on Writing." *EricDigests.org*. ERIC Clearinghouse on Reading, English, and Communication, 2003. www.ericdigests.org/2004-1/impact.htm. Accessed 13 Oct. 2004.
APA	Abdullah, M. H. (2004, October). The impact of electronic communication on writing. *ERIC Clearinghouse on Reading, English, and Communication*. Retrieved from http://www.ericdigests.org/2004-1/impact.htm

Online Book

MLA	Austen, Jane. *Pride and Prejudice*. Project Gutenberg, 2013. www.gutenberg.org/catalog/world/readfile?fk_files=3381939. Accessed 14 Apr. 2014.
APA	Austen, J. (1813). *Pride and prejudice*. Project Gutenberg. Retrieved from http://www.gutenberg.org/catalog/world/readfile?fk_files=3381939

Article in an Online Magazine/Newspaper

MLA	Remnick, David. "Putin and the Exile." *New Yorker*. NewYorker.com, 28 Apr. 2014. www.newyorker.com/talk/comment/2014/04/28/140428taco_talk_remnick. Accessed 28 Apr. 2014.
APA	Remnick, D. (2014, April 28). Putin and the exile. *New Yorker*. Retrieved from http://www.newyorker.com/talk/comment/2014/04/28/140428taco_talk_remnick

SOURCE CITATIONS

Article in an Online Journal

MLA	Soliday, Mary. "From the Margins to the Mainstream: Reconceiving Remediation." *College Composition and Communication* vol. 47, no. 1, 1996, pp. 85–100. www.jstor.org/stable/358275. Accessed 14 Jan. 2014.
APA	Soliday, M. (1996). From the margins to the mainstream: Reconceiving remediation. *College Composition and Communication, 47*(1). Retrieved from http://www.jstor.org/stable/358275

Film

MLA	*Big Fish.* Directed by Tim Burton, performances by Ewan McGregor, Albert Finney, Jessica Lange, Billy Crudup, and Marion Cotillard, Columbia, 2003.
APA	Cohen, B., Zanuck, R. & Jinks, D. (Producer), & Burton, T. (Director). (2003). *Big Fish* [Motion picture]. USA: Sony Home Pictures Entertainment.

Television Program

MLA	"Tabula Rasa." *Criminal Minds: Season 3,* written by Jeff Davis, Dan Sworkin, and Jay Beattie, directed by Steve Boyum, Paramount, 2010.
APA	Davis, J., Sworkin, D., & Beattie, J. (Writers) & Boyum, S. (Director). (2008). Tabula rasa. In E.A. Bernero (Producer), *Criminal minds.* Los Angeles, CA: Paramount.

Sound Recording

MLA	Miranda Lambert. "Heart Like Mine." *Revolution.* Sony, 2009.
APA	Howard, T., Lambert, M., & Monroe, A. (2009). Heart like mine [Recorded by Miranda Lambert]. On *Revolution* [CD]. Nashville, TN: Columbia Nashville.

Funnies

These words and phrases have appeared in Ms. Hammons' essays over the last two decades. This is a small sampling.

No computer program can ever substitute for a human brain and a dictionary.

Spelling and Phrasing

accident pronged

As women, men can be very tempting and persuasive.

asses v. assess

baby in a wound

bar hoping

Calm v clam

Camed up and hitted him

English writhing

frowned apron

Give a reading book instead of a video game.

held a funeraser

I could do all things throw God.

John Smith was shaved by Pocahontas.

Phones who

pinning pennies

prices of his pricey dresses

rain dust hit the windshield

replaying back

She knew the electricity went out when the WiFi went out.

smell aroma

snake for snack

taught me from right to wrong

Television is a cause of pregnancy.

text massages

The doctor said she needed a secession.

The teen pregnancy rate has climaxed.

They try to vary down the materials.

tooks and tooken

visually see